JN096060

English

vocabulary
explained
in English

Intermediate
Level

英語を英語で理解する

英英英単語®

中級編

ジャパンタイムズ出版 英語出版編集部
&ロゴポート 編

英英
英単語
SERIES

the japan times 出版

はじめに

　本書は、『英語を英語で理解する 英英英単語 上級編／超上級編』の続編です。英語学習の中核となる、中級レベルの語彙 1,000 語を取り上げています。

　既刊の『上級編／超上級編』は、英語による見出し語の語義説明を掲載することで、英語のニュアンスを正しく捉え、かつ自分の考えを平易な言葉で伝える力をつけることを目的とした、新しい単語集でした。幸い、この 2 冊は多くの方に好意的に迎えていただくことができましたが、取り上げた語彙のレベルが高かったため、より重要度の高い中級レベルの語彙を扱った続編を求める声が多く寄せられました。そこで誕生したのが、本書『英語を英語で理解する 英英英単語 中級編』です。

　Longman Dictionary of Contemporary English や *Oxford Advanced Learner's Dictionary* といった学習者用の英英辞典は、平易な単語で語義を説明しているので、見出し語のニュアンスが捉えやすく、言いたいことをシンプルな語句で表現する際の参考にもなる、優れた英語学習ツールです。一方、辞書であるために情報が多すぎて語彙学習には使いづらく、語義説明の理解が不十分だと英和辞典を引き直す手間がかかってしまう、というデメリットもあります。

　『英英英単語』シリーズは、こうした問題をクリアすべく作られています。本書では、難関大学*や英検®準 1 級・2 級の過去問データなどを基に、大学受験生だけでなく、一般の英語学習者の役にも立つ中核レベルの語彙 1,000 語を厳選しました (iWeb コーパス**の頻度順位で平均約 6,300 位レベル)。そして、各種の英英辞典を参考に、ネイティブが書きおろしたオリジナルの英語の語義説明と、見

出し語の典型的な使い方を示した例文を付けました。学習効率の向上のため、あえて見出し語の訳語、例文の和訳も掲載しています。また語法情報を充実させ、適宜、語源情報も掲載しました。類義語、反意語、派生語などを含め、約3,300語を収録しています。

　このように、本書を学習すれば、あらゆる英語学習者に必要な中級レベルの語彙を英語で理解し、その具体的な使い方を知ることができるようになっています。

　008ページでは、本書を使った学習法をいくつかご紹介しています。それらを参考に、本書を読み込み、そして使い倒してください。少しずつ頭の中に英語回路が形成され、一般的な単語集では手に入らない単語のニュアンスの知識とパラフレージング力が身につくでしょう。
　本書が読者の皆さまの語彙力向上の一助になれば、これに過ぎる喜びはありません。

編者

---

* 東京大学、京都大学、大阪大学、東京外国語大学、早稲田大学、慶応大学、上智大学、国際基督教大学の過去問3年分を分析。

** アメリカのBrigham Young UniversityのMark Davies教授が構築した140億語のコーパス (The Intelligent Web-based Corpus) を指す。

目次

はじめに　003
本書の構成　006
本書を使った効果的な学習法　008
音声のご利用案内　010
ウォーミングアップQuiz　011

Stage 1 015

Stage 2 059

Stage 3 099

Stage 4 139

Stage 5 179

Stage 6 219

Stage 7 257

Stage 8 293

Stage 9 331

Stage 10 365

INDEX　399

ナレーション：Josh Keller（米）／ Rachel Walzer（米）
録音・編集：ELEC録音スタジオ
音声収録時間：約4時間15分

カバー・本文デザイン：竹内雄二
イラスト：矢戸優人
DTP組版：株式会社 創樹

本書の構成

　本書では、中級レベルの単語1,000語を、100語ずつ10のSTAGE
に分けて掲載しています。

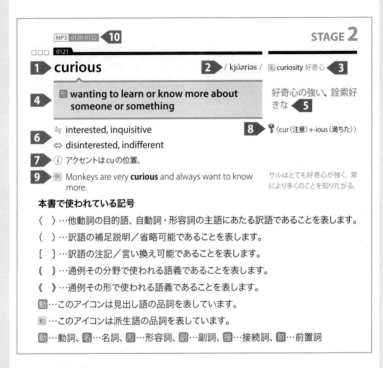

本書で使われている記号

〈　〉…他動詞の目的語、自動詞・形容詞の主語にあたる訳語であることを表します。

（　）…訳語の補足説明／省略可能であることを表します。

［　］…訳語の注記／言い換え可能であることを表します。

《　》…通例その分野で使われる語義であることを表します。

《　》…通例その形で使われる語義であることを表します。

動…このアイコンは見出し語の品詞を表しています。

動…このアイコンは派生語の品詞を表しています。

動…動詞、名…名詞、形…形容詞、副…副詞、接…接続詞、前…前置詞

1　見出し語

米つづりを採用しています。英つづりが異なる場合は注記に挙げています。

2　発音記号

米発音を採用しています。品詞によって発音が変わる語の場合、本書に
掲載した品詞の発音のみを挙げています。

3　派生語

見出し語と派生関係にある語を掲載しています。

4 品詞と英語の語義説明

見出し語の品詞を示し、語義を英語で説明しています。特によく使われる語義、学習者が覚えておくと役に立つ語義を選んで掲載しています。

> ※大きく語義の異なるものは一般の辞書では別見出しにすることがありますが、本書では適宜1つの見出しにまとめています。
> ※語義説明では英英辞典にならい、総称人称のyou（人一般を表すyou）、singular they (he or sheの代用) を使っている場合があります。

5 訳語

見出し語の訳語です。赤フィルターで隠すことができます。

6 類義語と反意語

≒の後ろに掲載されているのは見出し語の類義語、⇔の後ろに掲載されているのは見出し語の反意語です。

7 注記

①の後ろには、見出し語の語法、関連語、同語源語、発音・アクセントの注意事項など、幅広い補足情報を掲載しています。

8 語源

🔑の後ろには、語源に関する情報を掲載しています。

9 例文と訳

見出し語を使った例文とその訳です。英文中の見出し語相当語は太字になっています。訳は赤フィルターで隠すことができます。

> ※go see the movies（映画を見にいく）のような、ネイティブにとって自然な語法を使っている場合があります。

10 音声のトラック番号

付属音声には各項目の見出し語、英語の語義説明、例文（英文）が収録されています。音声はアプリまたはPCでダウンロードすることができます。ご利用方法は010ページをご覧ください。

章末ボキャブラリーチェック

各STAGEの終わりに、確認のための問題を用意しています。赤フィルターでページを隠し、本文にあった語義説明（複数ある場合は1つ目の語義）を見て、ヒントを参考に見出し語を答えましょう。間違えた場合は元のページに戻って復習しましょう。

本書を使った効果的な学習法

　本書を使った学習法をいくつかご紹介します。これらを参考に、ご自分に合ったオリジナルの学習法もぜひ考えてみてください。

◉基本的な使い方

1　訳を見ながら〈見出し語→語義説明→例文〉の順に読み進める

〈見出し語→語義説明→例文〉の順番に読んでいきましょう。音声を聞いて、自分でも発音してみるとより身につきます。この方法で一度本書を読み終えたら、2の学習法でもう1周すると、英語を英語で理解する力がしっかりとつきます。

□□□ 0347

1 ▶ **steep** / stíːp /

2 ▶ 〔形〕**rising or falling very sharply** 険しい、急な

3 ▶ 〔例〕The mountain road is very **steep**, so cars cannot get up the mountain in the winter. その山道はとても急なので、冬になると車は山を登れない。

2　赤フィルターを使って英語だけで読み進める

最初から赤フィルターで日本語部分を隠して〈見出し語→語義説明→例文〉の順に読み進める方法もあります。訳は確認に使います。やはり音声を聞いて、自分でも発音してみると、より内容が身につきます。

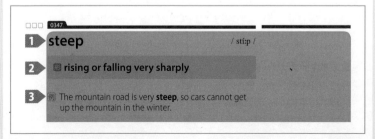

□□□ 0347

1 ▶ **steep** / stíːp /

2 ▶ 〔形〕**rising or falling very sharply** 、

3 ▶ 〔例〕The mountain road is very **steep**, so cars cannot get up the mountain in the winter.

3 テキストを見ずに耳で読む

テキストを見ずに、〈見出し語→語義説明→例文〉が収録された音声を聞く学習法です。前述の1あるいは2で学習した後に、この方法を試すと、さらに内容が頭に入り、リスニング力の強化にもつながります。

4 章末ボキャブラリーチェックを繰り返し解く

完ぺきに正解できるようになるまで、章末ボキャブラリーチェックを繰り返し解きましょう。語義説明を何度も読むことは、パラフレージング力の強化につながります。

●応用的な使い方

5 英語の語義説明の自分なりの訳語を考える

本書の英語の語義説明をもとに、辞典編集者になったつもりで、自分ならどんな訳語をあてるか考えてみましょう。この作業は英語のニュアンスを深く掘り下げることにつながります。

●本書を使った後の学習法

6 英英辞典の利用を習慣化する

本書で英語の語義を読むことに慣れたら、普段の学習でも英英辞典を使ってみましょう。オンライン辞書でも紙の辞書でもかまいません。これができるようになれば、「英英英単語」は卒業です。

音声のご利用案内

本書の音声は、スマートフォン（アプリ）やパソコンを通じてMP3形式でダウンロードし、ご利用いただくことができます。

スマートフォン

1. ジャパンタイムズ出版の音声アプリ「OTO Navi」をインストール

2. OTO Naviで本書を検索

3. OTO Naviで音声をダウンロードし、再生

   3秒早送り・早戻し、繰り返し再生などの便利機能つき。学習にお役立てください。

パソコン

1. ブラウザからジャパンタイムズ出版のサイト
   「BOOK CLUB」にアクセス
   https://bookclub.japantimes.co.jp/book/b525047.html

2. 「ダウンロード」ボタンをクリック

3. 音声をダウンロードし、iTunesなどに取り込んで再生

   ※音声はzipファイルを展開（解凍）してご利用ください。

ウォーミングアップQuiz

本文を読み始める前に、まずはウォーミングアップ Quiz を解いてみましょう。
次の単語のかけ算とイラストをヒントに、右の頭文字で始まる英単語を考えてみてください。
クイズなので気楽に挑戦してみましょう。

(1)   **ship**   ×   **underwater**   =   **s_____**

(2)   **bread**   ×   **store**   =   **b_____**

(3)   **wrist**   ×   **jewelry**   =   **b_____**

(4)   **space**   ×   **traveler**   =   **a_____**

どうでしたか？ 解けましたか？ それでは解答です。

(1) **ship** × **underwater** = **submarine**

(2) **bread** × **store** = **bakery**

(3) **wrist** × **jewelry** = **bracelet**

(4) **space** × **traveler** = **astronaut**

では、一つずつ確認していきましょう。
英英辞典を引いているつもりで、読んでみてください。

(1)

ship（船）とunderwater（水中の）をかけ合わせたら？ という問題。正解は
submarine（潜水艦）です。submarineを英語で説明すると、a ship that can
go underwater（水中を進むことのできる船）のような感じになります。
sub-は「下の」を意味する接頭辞で、subzero（氷点下の）、subconscious（潜
在意識の）、subterranean（地下の）などにも含まれています。一方、marineは
「海の；海兵」という意味です。

(2)

bread（パン）とstore（店）をかけ合わせたら？ という問題。正解はbakery（製
パン店）です。日本語だとほぼ2語をつなげただけですが、英語ではまったく別の
単語になります。bakeryを英語で説明すると、a store where bread, cakes,
and so on are made or sold（パンやケーキなどを作って売っている店）のよう
な感じです。
bakeは「〈パン・ケーキなど〉を焼く」という意味の動詞。-(e)ryは「場所」を表す
接尾辞で、brewery（醸造所）、confectionery（菓子店）、pottery（製陶所）、
refinery（精錬所）などにも含まれています。ちなみに、「パン職人」はbakerと言
います。

(3)

wrist（手首）とjewelry（宝石類）をかけ合わせたら？ という問題。正解は
bracelet（ブレスレット）です。そのままカタカナ語にもなっていますね。bracelet
を英語で説明すると、a piece of jewelry worn around the wrist（手首の周り
につける宝飾品）のような感じになります。

braceは「腕」を意味する語根で、embrace（〜を抱きしめる）という語にも含ま
れています。一方-letは「小さい」を意味する指小辞で、booklet（小冊子）、islet
（小島）などにも含まれています。ちなみに「足首」はankleと言い、足首につける
宝飾品はanklet（アンクレット）と言います。

(4)

space（宇宙）とtraveler（旅行者）をかけ合わせたら？ という問題。正解は
astronaut（宇宙飛行士）です。astronautを英語で説明すると、a person who
travels into space and works in a spacecraft（宇宙に行き、宇宙船で作業を
行う人）のような感じになります。

astroは「星」を意味する語根で、astronomy（天文学）、astronomer（天文学
者）などにも含まれています。一方naut/nausは「水夫」を意味する語根で、nausea
（船酔い）、nautical（航海の）などにも含まれています。ちなみに、ロシアの「宇
宙飛行士」はcosmonautと言います。

このように、英単語はやさしい英語で説明することができます。
こうした説明を読むことで、英単語のニュアンスがわかり、
パラフレージング力も身につきます。
それでは、次のページから、1,000語の中級レベルの単語を、
英語の語義説明と例文とともに学習していきましょう！

Stage 1

There's no time like the present.
思い立ったが吉日。

□□□ **0001**

claim / kléɪm /

動 to say that something is true (although others might not agree) 　〜を主張する

≒ insist

⇔ deny

ⓘ カタカナ語の「クレーム」（苦情）は英語ではcomplaintと言う。

例 The company **claims** that their drug makes you smarter.　その会社は、自社の薬を飲むと頭がよくなると主張している。

□□□ **0002**

facility / fəsíləti /

名 a building or equipment that is made for a specific use　設備、施設

例 The new sports **facility** will have two swimming pools.　新しいスポーツ施設には水泳プールが2つ設置される。

□□□ **0003**

specific / spəsífɪk /

動 specifically 特に
動 specify 〜を特定する

形 ① clearly said or shown (in detail)　具体的な、明確な

≒ defined

⇔ vague, unclear, ambiguous

🔑〈spec（見る）+(i)fic（〜にされた）〉

例 The teacher gave **specific** instructions on how to finish the project.　教師は課題をどのように仕上げたらよいか具体的に指示した。

② special or connected to one thing　特定の

≒ particular

⇔ general

例 Doctors give medicine to patients based on their **specific** situation.　医者は患者の個々の状況に基づいて薬を処方する。

□□□ 0004

resource

/ ríːsɔːrs /

形 **resourceful** 資源［資金］が豊富な

名 **something valuable a country has, such as oil or minerals**

資源

ⓘ ふつう複数形で使う。

例 Japan doesn't have many natural **resources**, so they have to buy oil from other countries.

日本には天然資源があまりないので、他国から石油を買わなければならない。

□□□ 0005

credit

/ krédɪt /

名 ① **a good thing that people think about someone or something**

（功績に対する）称賛

≒ praise

例 She got all the **credit** for doing the project.

彼女はそのプロジェクトを行った功績を独り占めした。

② **money you can spend now and pay back later, or a record showing how much you can be trusted to do so**

貸付金；（支払いの）信用

≒ rating

例 She has good **credit**, so the bank agreed to give her a loan to purchase the house.

彼女には十分な支払い能力があるので、銀行は彼女に家を購入する融資を行うことに同意した。

③ **something that measures how much of a school program a student has finished**

（履修）単位

例 He will only need six more **credits** to graduate.

彼は卒業するのにあと6単位必要なだけだ。

0005語

□□□ 0006

explore
/ ıksplɔ́ːr /

名 exploration 探検、探索

動 ① to travel to or in a place to learn about it or find something

～を探検する

🔑 〈ex-（外に）+plore（叫ぶ）〉

例 The boy wanted to **explore** the ocean and find new sea creatures.

その男の子は、海を探検して、新しい海洋生物を発見したかった。

② to study something to try to learn more about it

～を調べる、検討する

≒ examine, research

例 The students were told that they would **explore** more new ideas in the next class.

生徒たちは、次の授業ではさらに多くの新思想を探究する、と言われた。

□□□ 0007

thread
/ θréd /

名 a long, thin piece of material used for sewing

糸、縫い糸

≒ string

ⓘ コンピュータ用語の「スレッド」（一連のメッセージ）もこの thread。

例 You will need a lot of **thread** to sew a quilt.

キルトを縫うにはたくさんの糸が必要だ。

□□□ 0008

conference
/ kάːnfərəns /

名 a meeting where many people talk about ideas or problems, usually for several days

会議、大会

≒ convention, forum

例 She went to a **conference** on women's health.

彼女は女性の健康に関する会議に行った。

□□□ 0009

grant / grǽnt /

動 to say someone is allowed to do or have something

〈許可など〉を与える、認める

⇔ refuse, reject

ⓘ take it for granted (that)... は「…ということを許されたものと考える」→「…ということを当然のことと考える」。

例 The mayor would not **grant** me an interview.

市長は私にインタビューを許可しようとしなかった。

名 money that is given to someone by an organization to be used for something

補助金、助成金

例 The scientists were given a **grant** by the government to study cancer cures.

その科学者たちは、がんの治療法を研究するための補助金を政府から交付された。

□□□ 0010

appropriate / əpróupriət / 副 appropriately 適切に

形 right for the situation

適切な、ふさわしい

≒ suitable

⇔ inappropriate, improper

例 That book is **appropriate** for children over 12 years old.

その本は13歳以上の子どもに適している。

□□□ 0011

entirely / ıntáıərli / 形 entire 全体の

副 completely and with nothing left unfinished

まったく、完全に

≒ totally

⇔ partially

例 The artwork is made **entirely** of old tires.

その芸術作品はすべて古タイヤでできている。

□□□ 0012

sentence
/ séntns /

名 ① a group of words that shows an idea　　文

ⓘ paragraph（段落）、clause（節）、phrase（句）もあわせて覚えておこう。

例 Please answer the questions using a complete **sentence**.

完全な文で質問に答えてください。

② a punishment given in the court of law　　判決、刑罰

≒ decision, verdict, ruling

例 They are serving a 15-year **sentence** in prison for murder.

彼らは殺人罪で15年の刑に服している。

動 to officially state the punishment of someone in court　　〜に判決を下す

≒ convict

例 The man was **sentenced** to three years in prison.

その男は懲役3年を言い渡された。

□□□ 0013

overcome
/ òʊvərkʌ́m /

動 to succeed at doing, managing, or controlling something difficult　　〈困難など〉を乗り越える、克服する

≒ win, surmount

⇔ lose, give up, yield

🔑 〈over-(越えて)+come(来る)〉

ⓘ overcome-overcame-overcomeと活用する。

例 The soccer player was able to **overcome** his injury and return to playing.

そのサッカー選手はけがを克服して、競技に復帰することができた。

□□□ 0014

adopt

/ ədá:pt / 图 adoption 採用

動 ① to start using a different manner or method

～を採用する、採択する

ⓘ adaptは「順応する」。

🔑〈ad- (～に) +opt (選ぶ)〉

例 Mr. Leonard **adopted** a new way of speaking when he became a teacher.

レナード氏は教師になったときに新しい話し方を取り入れた。

② to make a child with different parents your child by law

～を養子にする

≒ foster, take in

例 The kind couple wanted to **adopt** a baby girl from Africa.

その心優しい夫婦はアフリカの女の赤ちゃんを養子にすることを望んだ。

□□□ 0015

launch

/ lɔ́:ntʃ /

動 ① to start or release something big or important

～を始める

≒ introduce

⇔ end, finish, stop

ⓘ au の発音に注意。

例 The nonprofit organization has **launched** a new program to help the poor.

そのNPOは貧しい人々を援助する新制度を始めた。

② to shoot an object into the air, water, or outer space (e.g. a rocket)

～を発射する

≒ fire

例 Only a few countries have **launched** a rocket into outer space.

ロケットを宇宙に発射したことのある国は数少ない。

□□□ 0016

landscape

/ lǽndskèɪp /

名 a piece of land that looks special

景観、景色

≒ panorama

ⓘ -scapeは「風景、景観」を意味する接尾辞。例：townscape（都会の風景）

例 The beautiful **landscape** made her forget her problems completely.

その美しい景色を見て、彼女は自分の問題をすっかり忘れた。

□□□ 0017

favor

/ féɪvər /

形 favorable 好意的な
形 favorite 気に入りの

動 ① to like or support something

～を好む、支持する

⇔ dislike

ⓘ イギリス英語ではfavourとつづる。

例 Most voters **favor** improving health care.

ほとんどの有権者は医療の改善を支持している。

② to (show that you) like someone more than others (sometimes unfairly)

～を優遇する

≒ side with, prefer, support

⇔ dislike, disapprove

例 Teachers should not **favor** certain students over others.

教師は特定の生徒たちをほかの生徒たちより優遇すべきでない。

名 something nice or helpful you do for someone

親切な行為

例 Her boyfriend did her a **favor** by driving her to the airport.

彼女のボーイフレンドは親切にも彼女を空港まで車で送ってあげた。

□□□ 0018

command / kəmǽnd /

動 ① to order someone to do something (in a forceful way)

～を命じる

≒ demand

例 The soldiers were **commanded** to guard the base.

兵士たちは基地を守るよう命じられた。

② to get or receive something (good)

〈評価など〉を受ける

≒ deserve

例 She **commands** a high salary for all her hard work.

彼女は非常に熱心に働くので高給を得ている。

名 a skill or knowledge that allows you to do something well

運用能力

≒ control

例 His students have a good **command** of English.

彼の生徒たちは英語をよく使いこなせる。

□□□ 0019

encourage / ɪnkə́ːrɪʤ /

名 encouragement 激励
形 encouraging 励みになる

動 to try to make something happen or change

～を勧める、促す

≒ inspire

⇔ discourage, dissuade

🔑 〈en-(～にする)+cour(心)+-age(動詞)〉

ⓘ 〈encourage A to *do*〉(Aに～するよう促す) の形で押さえておこう。

例 Our recycling program should **encourage** people to recycle their bottles.

私たちのリサイクル計画は、人々がビンのリサイクルをするよう促すはずだ。

0019語

☐☐☐ 0020

absolute
/ ǽbsəlùːt /

副 absolutely まったく；絶対に

形 ① complete or total
まったくの、完全な

≒ entire, full, pure

⇔ incomplete, partial

🔑〈ab-（離れて）+solute（ゆるめられた）〉

例 The introductory course is designed for **absolute** beginners.

その入門コースはまったくの初心者用だ。

② not limited or able to be changed
絶対的な

≒ definitive

例 The decisions of a king are **absolute** and cannot be changed.

王の決定は絶対的で、変更できない。

☐☐☐ 0021

conflict
/ 名 káːnflɪkt 動 kənflíkt /

形 conflicting 相反する、矛盾する

名 a strong and often angry fight or disagreement between people
対立、衝突、紛争

≒ argument, rivalry, clash

⇔ peace, agreement

🔑〈con-（共に）+flict（ぶつかる）〉

例 It's impossible for me to avoid **conflict** when I visit my family because we always argue.

私が家族のもとを訪れたら、衝突を避けるのは不可能だ。いつも言い争いになるので。

動 to be different enough that you cannot agree, or to say opposite things
対立する、矛盾する

≒ contradict

例 Your lawyer's statement **conflicts** with the facts presented by the police.

あなたの弁護士の陳述は警察が提示した事実と矛盾している。

□□□ 0022

cast / kǽst /

動 to direct something toward someone or something

〈光・影・影響など〉を投げかける

ⓘ cast-cast-castと活用する。

例 The book **cast** a shadow across the girl's face.

その本は女の子の顔に影を作っていた。

名 the people who act in a play, film, or TV show

出演者全員、キャスト

例 The supporting **cast** for the movie were all highly skilled.

その映画の脇役は全員非常に演技力があった。

□□□ 0023

expand / ɪkspǽnd /

名 expansion 拡張、拡大
形 expansive 広範囲な
副 expansively 広範囲に

動 to get or make something bigger (in size, range, or amount)

（〜を）拡張する、拡大する

≒ enlarge, increase

⇔ decrease, contract

🔑 〈ex-（外に）+pand（広げる）〉

例 Water **expands** when it freezes.

水は凍ると膨張する。

□□□ 0024

incident / ínsədənt /

形 incidental 偶発的な
名 incidence（病気などの）発生

名 something unexpected (and usually bad) that has happened

出来事

≒ episode, occurrence

🔑 〈in-（上に）+cid（落ちる）+ent（名詞）〉

例 Three people were attacked in two separate **incidents** yesterday.

昨日、2つの別々の事件で3人が襲われた。

0024語

□□□ **0025**

confirm

/ kənfɔ́ːrm /

名 confirmation 確認

動 ① to show that something is right or correct, usually with evidence

〜を確認する、裏づける

≒ certify, verify

⇔ reject, deny

🔑 〈con- (共に) +firm (固い)〉

例 An x-ray of the arm **confirmed** that the bone was broken.

腕のレントゲン写真によって骨が折れていることが確認された。

② to say or announce that something definitely has happened or will happen

〜を (事実だと) 認める

≒ affirm

ⓘ confirm a hotel reservation (ホテルの予約を確認する) のようにも使う。

例 The police **confirmed** that the missing girl had been found.

警察は、行方不明の女の子が確かに発見されたと発表した。

□□□ **0026**

define

/ dɪfáɪn /

名 definition 定義
形 definite 明確な

動 ① to clearly show the outline or edge of something

〜の輪郭をはっきりさせる

≒ illustrate

⇔ obscure, distort

🔑 〈de- (下に) +fine (限界)〉

例 The edge of the schoolyard is clearly **defined** by a tall fence.

校庭の境界は高いフェンスではっきりと区切られている。

② to state the meaning of a word or phrase

〜を定義する

≒ explain, detail

例 For homework, the students have to **define** 10 new vocabulary words.

宿題として、生徒たちは10個の新しい語彙を定義しなければならない。

□□□ 0027

sensitive

/ sénsətɪv /

副 sensitively 敏感に、慎重に
名 sensitivity 感受性

形 ① **likely to cause people to feel an emotion, especially a negative one**

微妙な、慎重を要する

≒ delicate

🔑 〈sens (感じる) +-itive (形容詞)〉

例 Politics is a **sensitive** topic for some people.

政治はある人々にとっては微妙な話題だ。

② **easily affected by the things around you (usually in a bad way)**

敏感な

例 My skin is very **sensitive** and gets dry easily.

私の肌はとても敏感で、すぐに乾燥してしまう。

□□□ 0028

output

/ áʊtpʊ̀t /

名 **an amount of something that is made by a person or thing**

生産高、産出量

≒ production, yield

例 The profit of the company depends on the daily **output** of each employee.

会社の利益は社員一人ひとりの日々の生産高にかかっている。

□□□ 0029

reveal

/ rɪvíːl /

名 revelation 暴露

動 **to make something known to someone for the first time**

〜を明らかにする

≒ disclose, unveil

🔑 〈re- (元に) +veal (覆い)〉

⇔ conceal

例 He never **revealed** the secret of his magic trick to anyone.

彼は手品のタネを誰にも決して明かさなかった。

□□□ **0030**

efficient
/ ɪfíʃənt /

图 efficiency 効率
剾 efficiently 効率的に

形 working without wasting time, money, or energy

効率のよい

≒ effective

⇔ inefficient

♥〈ef-(外に)+fici(作る)+-ent (形容詞)〉

例 An **efficient** worker should not have to do overtime.

効率のよい労働者は残業する必要がないはずだ。

□□□ **0031**

engage
/ ɪngéɪʤ /

图 engagement 婚約；約束

動 to do or be involved in something

従事する

ⓘ「婚約指輪」は engagement ring。be engaged in（～に従事している）という表現も覚えておこう。

例 Many university students **engage** in volunteer work in disaster hit areas.

多くの大学生が被災地でボランティア活動に従事している。

□□□ **0032**

arrest
/ ərést /

動 to hold someone (often a criminal) using the power of law

～を逮捕する

≒ catch, capture　⇔ release, let go

例 The couple was **arrested** for stealing their neighbor's diamond ring.

その夫婦は隣人のダイヤの指輪を盗んで逮捕された。

□□□ **0033**

threaten
/ θrétn /

图 threat 脅威

動 to tell someone that you will do something harmful to them or others

～を脅す

≒ intimidate, scare

例 The teacher **threatened** the students, saying she would fail anyone who cheated.

その教師は、カンニングした者は誰であっても落第させると言って生徒を脅した。

□□□ **0034**

capture

/ kǽptʃər /　形 captive 捕らわれた

動 ① to catch someone or something and hold them against their will

～を捕まえる

≒ apprehend, seize

🔑〈capt (つかむ) +ure (行為)〉

⇔ release, free

例 You can **capture** animals using traps.

わなを使って動物を捕まえることができる。

② to use writing, painting, or film to show someone or something accurately

（映像・言葉などで）
～をうまく捉える

例 The painting **captured** her beauty perfectly.

その絵は彼女の美しさを完ぺきに捉えていた。

名 the act of catching or controlling someone or something

捕獲

例 The spy avoided **capture** by hiding in a large freezer.

そのスパイは大きな冷凍庫の中に隠れることで捕まらずに済んだ。

□□□ **0035**

register

/ rédʒistər /　名 registration 登録

動 to record information in a book or system so you can do something

（～を）登録する

≒ sign up, join, log in

⇔ leave, log out

ⓘ スーパーなどの「レジ」は cash register と言う。

例 It's free to **register** for a library card at most libraries.

ほとんどの図書館では、図書館カードを登録するのは無料だ。

0035語

□□□ 0036

ensure
/ ɪnʃʊ́ər /

動 to make sure that something will be a certain way

〜を確実にする、保証する

≒ guarantee, confirm

🔑 〈en-(〜にする)+sure(確実な)〉

ⓘ 直後に人を目的語にとらないことを押さえておこう。

例 The local community worked together to **ensure** the safety of all the children.

すべての子どもたちの安全を確保するために、地域社会が協力し合った。

□□□ 0037

submit
/ səbmít /

图 submission 提出

動 to give something (especially a document) to someone to be approved or considered

〜を提出する

≒ hand in, give in

🔑 〈sub-(下に)+mit(置く)〉

例 If you **submit** your university application late, it might not be accepted.

大学の願書を遅れて提出すると、受理されないかもしれない。

□□□ 0038

appreciate
/ əpríːʃièɪt /

图 appreciation 感謝；評価

動 ① to be thankful for something or someone

〜をありがたく思う

例 I **appreciate** all the support you have given me in finding a new job.

新しい仕事を探すときにあなたが私にしてくれたすべての支援をありがたく思っています。

② to understand and value something or someone

〜を高く評価する

例 Starting her own company taught her to **appreciate** the value of hard work.

自分の会社を始めてみて、彼女は努力の価値がわかるようになった。

□□□ 0039

characteristic

/ kèrəktərístɪk /

名 character 特徴
動 characterize ～を特徴づける

名 a special part of something that makes it different from something else

特徴、特性

≒ feature, attribute

例 A **characteristic** of purebred dogs is that they have many health problems.

純血種の犬の特徴は、健康問題が多いことだ。

形 having a typical behavior that shows a special quality

特有の、特徴的な

ⓘ characteristic of（～に特有の）の形で押さえておこう。

例 Stealing mail is not **characteristic** of a good neighbor.

郵便物を盗むというのはよい隣人らしからぬことだ。

□□□ 0040

justice

/ ʤʎstɪs /

形 just 公正な
動 justify ～を正当化する

名 the condition of being fair in a situation

正義、公正

⇔ injustice, unfairness

🔑 〈just（正しい）+-ice（名詞）〉

例 The law is designed to provide **justice** for all citizens.

法律はすべての国民に公正を提供するよう設計されている。

□□□ 0041

compete

/ kəmpíːt /

名 competition 競争、競技
形 competitive 競争力のある

動 to try to get or win something that another person is also trying to get, or to try to be better than someone else

競争する、争う

≒ challenge, contend
⇔ give up, surrender

🔑 〈com-(共に)+pete(求める)〉

例 The two friends are **competing** to win the heart of the same girl.

友達同士の2人は同じ女の子の心をつかもうと争っている。

0041語

☐☐☐ **0042**

faith

/ féɪθ / 形 faithful 信心深い

名 ① **a strong belief or trust in a person or thing**

信頼、信用

≒ confidence, conviction

⇔ distrust

例 Many young people no longer have **faith** in the government.

多くの若者はもう政府を信頼していない。

② **belief that God or another religious being exists; belief in the teachings of a religion**

宗教、信仰

例 Having **faith** in God is an important part of being a Christian.

神への信仰心はキリスト教徒としての重要な要素だ。

☐☐☐ **0043**

preserve

/ prɪzə́ːrv / 名 preservation 保存

動 **to keep something how it originally was or keep it in good condition**

〜を保存する

≒ protect, conserve

⇔ neglect

🔑 〈pre-（前もって）+serve（保つ）〉

例 It is the job of the committee to **preserve** the city's historical buildings.

市の歴史的建築物を保存することがその委員会の仕事だ。

名 **a place where things such as plants or animals are protected**

自然保護地域

≒ reserve, sanctuary

例 There are many nature **preserves** in Canada to keep wildlife safe.

野生生物を守るため、カナダには多くの自然保護地域がある。

☐☐☐ 0044

administration

/ ədmìnəstréɪʃən /

動 administer ～を管理する
形 administrative 管理の

名 ① a government or a part of government that people connect with its leader (such as a president or prime minister)

政権、行政機関

例 The Abe **administration** is well known for its policy Abenomics.

安倍政権はその政策であるアベノミクスで有名だ。

② the activities needed to run a company, school, or other organizations

管理、経営

≒ management

例 **Administration** costs for the program will be passed on to customers.

そのプログラムの管理コストは顧客に転嫁されるだろう。

☐☐☐ 0045

commission

/ kəmíʃən /

動 commit 〈犯罪など〉を犯す；～を託す

名 ① a group that has been organized and given an official job to find information or manage something

委員会

≒ committee, board

例 The government has set up a **commission** to study the public school system.

政府は公立学校制度を研究する委員会を設置した。

② a payment made to an employee by their employer for selling something

（販売員などが受け取る）
手数料、歩合

例 Car salespeople who sell more cars make more money in **commission**.

より多くの車を売る販売員の方が手数料としてより多くの稼ぎを得る。

0045語

□□□ 0046

extreme

/ ɪkstríːm / 副 **extremely** 非常に、極度に

形 very great in degree or intensity

極度の、極端な

≒ strong, high

⇔ weak, low, mild

例 Many plants are sensitive to **extreme** heat and cold.

多くの植物は極端な暑さや寒さに弱い。

□□□ 0047

contribute

/ kəntríbjuːt / 名 **contribution** 貢献

動 to give something, such as money or time, to help others

〜を与える、寄付する

≒ donate

例 The family **contributed** 10,000 yen to charity after the tsunami.

津波が起きた後、その家族は1万円を慈善団体に寄付した。

□□□ 0048

secure

/ sɪkjúər / 名 **security** 安全
副 **securely** 安全に；確実に

形 safe and protected from something dangerous

安全な

⇔ unsecure, unsafe

💡 〈se-（離れて）+cure（心配）〉

例 Having a dog helps many people feel **secure** in dangerous situations.

犬を飼っていると、多くの人は危険な状況でも安心感を得られる。

動 to protect or guard something to make sure it is safe

〜の安全を確保する

≒ defend

例 The government worked hard to **secure** its borders to stop drugs from entering the country.

政府は薬物が国内に入ってくるのを防ぐため、国境の警備に懸命に取り組んだ。

□□□ 0049

guarantee
/ gèrəntíː /

動 to promise that something is or will be a certain way

～を保証する

ⓘ アクセントは ee の位置。

例 The store **guarantees** that their tea is of the highest quality available.

その店は、店の紅茶が購入できる紅茶の中で最高品質のものだと保証している。

名 a promise (usually written) that something is true or will happen

保証（書）

≒ warranty

例 They sent a written **guarantee** that the sword was authentic.

彼らはその刀が本物であるという保証書を送った。

□□□ 0050

acquire
/ əkwáiər /

名 acquisition 取得、習得
形 acquired 後天的な

動 ① to gain something

～を入手する、取得する

≒ achieve, collect

⇔ lose, give up

🔑 〈ac-（～に）+quire（求める）〉

例 Mrs. Anderson was lucky enough to **acquire** a rare original copy of *Alice in Wonderland*.

アンダーソンさんは幸運にも『不思議の国のアリス』の希少な初版本を手に入れることができた。

② to gain a new skill using your own time and energy

～を習得する、身につける

≒ pick up

⇔ lose

例 The professor was researching how children **acquired** language skills.

その教授は子どもたちがどのように言語能力を身につけるのかを研究していた。

0050語

□□□ **0051**

bond
/ bάːnd /

名 something that connects people or groups to each other

きずな

≒ connection, affiliation, attachment

ⓘ 接着剤の「ボンド」もこのbond。

例 A daughter's **bond** with her mother is not always strong.

娘と母親のきずながいつも強いとは限らない。

□□□ **0052**

investigate
/ ɪnvéstəgèɪt /

名 investigation 調査

動 to look for information about someone or something

～を調査する、捜査する

≒ search, probe

⇔ ignore

例 The police have been **investigating** the girls' disappearance for 10 years.

警察はその少女たちの失そうを10年間調査している。

□□□ **0053**

associate
/ 動 əsóʊʃièɪt 形 əsóʊʃiət /

名 association 協会
形 associated 関連する

動 to connect one person or thing to another when you think of it

～を関連づける、結びつける

≒ relate, link

⇔ disconnect, separate

🔑 〈as-（～に）+soci（仲間）+ -ate（動詞）〉

例 I **associate** cherry blossoms with the arrival of spring.

私は桜から春の訪れを連想する。

形 being in a lower rank or position in a group or organization

補助の、副～

例 The man was promoted from **associate** recruiter to senior recruiter.

その男性は人事採用の副担当者から上級担当者に昇進した。

☐☐☐ 0054

alternative
/ ɔːltə́ːrnətɪv /

副 alternatively 代わりに

形 offering a different choice or option

代わりの

≒ substitute

⇔ same, identical

例 There was heavy traffic, so we took an **alternative** route to the store.

交通が渋滞していたので、私たちはその店まで代わりの道を通って行った。

名 a different choice or option

代わりの手段

例 There were no vegetarian **alternatives** at the restaurant.

そのレストランには菜食主義者のための別メニューがなかった。

☐☐☐ 0055

remote
/ rɪmóʊt /

形 far from other people or things

遠い、人里離れた

≒ distant, inaccessible, isolated

⇔ close, near, accessible

ⓘ 「在宅勤務」は remote working と言う。

例 He liked to read about **remote** places that were hard to get to.

彼は行くのが難しい遠い場所について読むのが好きだった。

☐☐☐ 0056

bury
/ béri /

動 to put something in the ground or under many things, often to hide it

～を埋める

⇔ uncover, find

ⓘ 発音に注意。

例 Pirates usually **bury** their treasure so that no one can steal it.

海賊はたいてい、誰にも盗まれないように自分の宝を埋める。

0056語

commit

/ kəmít /

图 commitment 約束

動 ① to do something that is against the law or hurts others

〈罪・過失など〉を犯す

例 She was punished for the crime she **committed**.

彼女は犯した罪に対する罰を受けた。

② to say or promise that you will do something

（〜すると）約束する

例 By signing the contract, the company **committed** to finishing the building before the end of the year.

契約書にサインすることによって、その会社は年末までに建設を終える約束を負った。

③ to decide to give long-term love or support to someone or something

取り組む（ことにする）

ⓘ be committed to/commit *oneself*（〜に取り組む）の形も押さえておこう。

例 The football coach has **committed** to making sure that all of his players go to college.

そのアメフトのコーチは選手全員が確実に大学に進学できるよう取り組んでいる。

convince

/ kənvíns /

图 conviction 確信
形 convincing 説得力のある

動 to get someone to believe something or agree to do something

〜を納得させる、確信させる

≒ persuade

⇔ dissuade, discourage

ⓘ 〈convince ＋人＋ (that).../of A〉（人に…ということ／Aを納得させる）の形も重要。

例 The girl was able to **convince** her boyfriend to go see the movie.

女の子は映画を見に行くよう彼氏を説得することができた。

□□□ 0059

accompany / əkʌ́mpəni / 名 accompaniment 随伴

動 ① to happen with or at the same time as another thing

～に付随して起こる

≒ connect to, coincide with

🔑 〈ac-(～に)+company(仲間)〉

ⓘ 他動詞である点に注意。

例 The thunderstorm was **accompanied** by strong rain and winds.

その雷鳴とどろく嵐は強い雨と風を伴っていた。

② to go somewhere or do something with another person

〈人〉についていく、同行する

≒ escort

例 The old man couldn't walk by himself, so his daughter **accompanied** him to the hospital.

その高齢の男性は一人で歩けなかったので、娘が病院まで付き添った。

□□□ 0060

accurate / ǽkjərət / 名 accuracy 正確さ
副 accurately 正確に

形 correct and without mistakes

正確な、精密な

≒ true, right

🔑 〈ac-(～に) +cur (注意する) +-ate (形容詞)〉

⇔ inaccurate, false

例 The information in old guidebooks is usually not **accurate**.

古いガイドブックの情報はたいてい正確ではない。

□□□ 0061

invest / ɪnvést / 名 investment 投資

動 to use your money to make more money (e.g. by buying stocks or rental properties)

(～を)投資する

例 **Investing** in property is not always a good way to make money.

不動産に投資することは必ずしもよいお金の稼ぎ方とは限らない。

0061語

□□□ **0062**

swallow

/ swá:loʊ /

動 ① to move something from your mouth down to your throat and stomach

～を飲み込む

≒ consume, ingest

⇔ vomit, throw up

ⓘ 「ツバメ」もswallow。

例 My sister couldn't **swallow** pills until she was 15 years old.

私の妹は15歳になるまで錠剤を飲み込めなかった。

② to accept that something is true

〈話など〉を信じる

≒ believe

例 His story about fighting a lion in Africa is pretty hard to **swallow**.

アフリカでライオンと格闘したという彼の話はちょっと信じがたい。

□□□ **0063**

brilliant

/ bríljənt /

形 ① great or very good

素晴らしい、見事な

≒ fantastic, amazing, wonderful

⇔ awful, terrible, bad

例 The actor was well known for his **brilliant** stage performances.

その俳優は素晴らしい舞台演技で有名だった。

② very smart (usually much smarter than others)

優秀な、才能のある

≒ bright, clever, gifted

⇔ dull, stupid

例 She was a **brilliant** scientist who found cures for many diseases.

彼女は優秀な科学者で、多くの病気の治療法を発見した。

☐☐☐ 0064

pursue

/ pərs(j)úː /

名 pursuit 追跡

動 ① **to try to do or get something over a period of time**

〜を追求する

≒ seek, attempt, work toward, strive for

🍳 〈pur- (前に) +sue (追う)〉

例 The boy decided to **pursue** a law degree and become a lawyer.

その男の子は法律の学位を目指して勉強し、弁護士になろうと決意した。

② **to follow and try to catch someone or something (usually over a long time or distance)**

〜を追跡する

≒ chase, go after

例 The dogs **pursued** the criminal for hours until they finally caught him.

犬たちは犯人を何時間も追跡し、とうとう捕まえた。

☐☐☐ 0065

council

/ káʊnsl /

名 **a group of people who make rules or decisions about things**

（地方自治体の）議会

≒ assembly, committee, commission, panel

例 The city **council** has banned smoking in restaurants.

市議会はレストランでの喫煙を禁じた。

☐☐☐ 0066

emergency

/ ɪmə́ːrdʒənsi /

形 emergent 緊急の

名 **an unexpected situation that requires fast action (and is usually dangerous)**

緊急事態

例 The airplane had to make an **emergency** landing when its engine caught on fire.

その飛行機はエンジンが発火したときに緊急着陸をしなければならなかった。

☐☐☐ **0067**

internal / ɪntə́ːrnl /

形 being inside something 内部の

≒ interior, inner ⇔ external, exterior, outer

例 No one can completely understand the **internal** structure of Earth.

誰も地球の内部構造を完全に理解することはできない。

☐☐☐ **0068**

portion / pɔ́ːrʃən /

名 one part of a bigger thing 部分

≒ section

ⓘ part（部分）と同語源語。

例 They aren't selling their whole property, just a **portion** of it.

彼らは所有地をすべて売ろうとしているのではない。ほんの一部を売ろうとしているだけだ。

☐☐☐ **0069**

apparently / əpérəntli /

形 apparent 明らかな；外見上の

副 used when describing something that looks like it is true based on current information

どうやら（…らしい）

≒ supposedly, seemingly

ⓘ「明らかに」の意味で使うことはまれ。

例 **Apparently**, the winner of the contest will be given a free trip to Singapore.

どうやらコンテストの優勝者にはシンガポールへの無料旅行が進呈されるようだ。

☐☐☐ **0070**

restore / rɪstɔ́ːr /

名 restoration 修復

動 to return something to its original condition (e.g. by fixing or cleaning it)

〜を修復する

例 It will cost 500 dollars to **restore** this antique clock to its original condition.

この年代物の時計を元の状態に修復するには500ドルかかる。

□□□ 0071

candidate / kǽndədèɪt /

名 a person who is being considered for a position

候補者

≒ applicant, contender, hopeful

⇔ reject

例 Even if there are no good **candidates**, it is still important to vote in the election.

たとえよい候補者がいなくても、やはり選挙で投票することは大事だ。

□□□ 0072

consequence / kάːnsəkwèns /

名 consequential その結果
生じる
副 consequently その結果

名 a result of an action or actions, especially one that is undesirable

結果、影響

≒ fallout, effect, reaction

ⓘ as a consequence（その結果）という表現も覚えておこう。

例 Death is sometimes the **consequence** of careless driving.

不注意な運転は時に死という結果になる。

□□□ 0073

extend / ɪksténd /

名 extension 延長、拡張
形 extensive 広範囲にわたる

動 ① to continue across a certain area, distance, or time

広がる、及ぶ

≒ stretch

🔑 〈ex-（外に）+tend（伸ばす）〉

例 The singer's influence **extends** to millions of people across the country.

その歌手の影響力は国中の何百万人もの人々に広がっている。

② to increase or lengthen something

～を拡大する、延長する

≒ enlarge, broaden

例 They enjoyed Italy so much that they **extended** their trip for another week.

彼らはイタリアがとても気に入り、旅行を1週間延長した。

0073語

□□□ 0074

praise / préɪz /

動 to say or write nice things about someone or something

〜を褒める、称賛する

≒ compliment, appreciate

例 Students should be **praised** by their teachers when they do a good job.

生徒が頑張ったら先生は生徒を褒めてやるべきだ。

名 speech or writing stating that someone or something is good

褒めること、称賛

≒ acclaim

⇔ criticism

例 Her latest film was not only popular with fans but also received **praise** from critics.

彼女の最新映画は、ファンに好評だったばかりでなく批評家たちからも称賛を受けた。

□□□ 0075

predict / prɪdíkt /

名 prediction 予測
形 predictable 予測できる

動 to say that something will or might happen in the future

〜を予測する、予言する

≒ forecast, project, estimate, guess

🔑 〈pre-（前に）+dict（言う）〉

例 Many scientists are **predicting** that it is already too late to fix climate change.

多くの科学者は、気候変動を元に戻すにはもう遅すぎると予測している。

□□□ 0076

rural / rúərəl /

形 of or relating to a place where people live in the countryside

田舎の

≒ agricultural, provincial

⇔ urban, suburban

例 She grew up in a **rural** area before moving to the city to go to university.

彼女は大学に通うために街に引っ越すまで田舎で育った。

□□□ 0077

crisis
/ kráisis /

名 a situation that needs serious attention, especially because it is dangerous

危機

≒ disaster, catastrophe, emergency

(i) 複数形は crises[kráisi:z]。

例 During the 1980s, the country faced a severe economic **crisis**.

1980年代、その国は深刻な経済危機に直面した。

□□□ 0078

outcome
/ áutkλm /

名 the result of an activity or process

結果、成果

⇔ source

🔑〈out-（外に）+come（出てきたもの）〉

例 The **outcome** of the experiment was not as good as the scientists had hoped.

その実験結果は科学者たちが期待していたほどよいものではなかった。

□□□ 0079

pose
/ póuz /

動 ① to ask or present a question

〈問題・疑問など〉を提起する

≒ suggest

(i)「（写真・絵のためにとる）ポーズ」も pose。

例 My mother always **poses** difficult questions that I cannot understand.

私の母はいつも私が理解できない難しい質問をする。

② to be or create danger or problems

〜を引き起こす

例 His poor driving skills **pose** a risk to the safety of others.

彼は運転技術が劣っているので、ほかの人々の安全に対するリスクになっている。

0079語

□□□ 0080

reputation

/ rèpjətéɪʃən / 形 reputable 評判のよい

名 a common opinion or knowledge that people share about someone or something

評判、名声

≒ prominence

例 The man had a **reputation** for liking alcohol too much.

その男は大の酒好きで評判だった。

□□□ 0081

deposit

/ dɪpάːzət /

名 ① an amount of money that is put in a bank account

預金

🔑 〈de- (下に) +posit (置く)〉

例 Anyone can make a **deposit**, but only the owner of the account can make a withdrawal.

預金は誰でもできるが、引き出しは口座の持ち主しかできない。

② money you give someone when you buy or rent something that you can get back if you return the thing in good condition

保証金、手付金

例 The **deposit** for my Tokyo apartment cost me three months' rent.

私は東京のアパートの敷金として3か月分の家賃を支払った。

動 to put or leave something somewhere over a period of time

〜を堆積させる

例 Tomorrow's storm will **deposit** around 30 centimeters of snow.

明日の嵐で雪が30センチくらい積もるだろう。

☐☐☐ 0082

disaster

/ dɪzǽstər /

形 disastrous 壊滅的な

名 an event that happens suddenly and causes harm to many people, such as an earthquake or flood

災害

≒ catastrophe, emergency

💡⟨dis-(不吉な)+aster(星)⟩

例 The events of March 11, 2011 were one of the worst natural **disasters** of the decade.

2011年3月11日の出来事は、その10年で最悪の自然災害の一つだった。

☐☐☐ 0083

decline

/ dɪkláɪn /

動 ① to decrease in amount or grow smaller in number

減少する、低下する

≒ fall, drop

💡⟨de-(下に)+cline(曲げる)⟩

⇔ increase, rise, hike

例 The users of the language steadily **declined** until no one was left.

その言語を使う人は着実に減り、ついに一人もいなくなった。

② to refuse to do something

(〜を)断る

≒ reject, turn down

⇔ accept, welcome

例 The company **declined** to comment on the death of their employee.

その会社は社員の死についてコメントするのを拒んだ。

名 a change to a lower number or amount

減少

≒ decrease, fall, drop

⇔ increase, rise, hike

例 The **decline** in kimono as everyday clothing is sad.

着物が普段着として着られなくなっていることは残念だ。

0083語

□□□ 0084

fortune

/ fɔ́ːrtʃən / 形 fortunate 幸運な

名 ① a large amount of money or things that are owned

財産、資産

≒ wealth, capital

ⓘ large [vast] fortune は「莫大な財産」、small fortune は「ひと財産、大金」の意。

例 It cost a small **fortune** to renovate their house.

彼らの家を改修するのにかなりの金額がかかった。

② something that happens based on luck or chance

運、運命

≒ destiny, fate

例 The couple had the good **fortune** of getting their flight upgraded to first class for free.

その夫婦は幸運にも、ただでフライトをファーストクラスにアップグレードしてもらえた。

□□□ 0085

scheme

/ skíːm /

名 ① an official plan or program that is used to change something

（大規模な）計画

≒ policy

ⓘ sche の発音に注意。

例 The government introduced a new **scheme** to improve communication between research institutes.

政府は研究組織間の連絡を改善するための新計画を導入した。

② the way something is set up or organized

配置、組織

≒ arrangement

例 The color **scheme** of the kitchen reminded the woman of a hospital.

そのキッチンの配色は女性に病院を思い出させた。

□□□ 0086

admire / ədmáɪər /

形 admirable 称賛に値する
名 admiration 称賛

動 to feel respect and approve of someone or something because of something they have done

～を称賛する

≒ appreciate, cherish, treasure

🔑 〈ad- (～を) +mire (驚く)〉

例 His mother **admired** his ability to keep calm in all situations.

母親はあらゆる状況で冷静でいられる彼の能力を褒めた。

□□□ 0087

bet / bét /

動 ① to make a guess and offer to give something (usually money,) if your guess is wrong

〈金〉を賭ける

≒ gamble, stake

ⓘ bet-bet(ted)-bet(ted)と活用する。

例 My grandfather **bet** all his savings on a horse race.

私の祖父は貯金すべてを競馬に賭けた。

② to be confident that something will probably happen

～と断言する

例 I **bet** that we're going to be late for school.

私たち、きっと学校に遅刻するよ。

名 an agreement where people try to guess a result and the loser has to give something (e.g. money) to the winner

賭け

例 They have a **bet** on the game.

彼らはその試合で賭けをしている。

0087語

☐☐☐ 0088

moreover

/ mɔːróuvər /

副 **in addition to something that has already been said**

そのうえ

≒ furthermore, additionally

例 I don't think his plan would work. **Moreover**, it would cost too much money to try it.

彼の計画はうまくいかないと思う。それに、やってみるのにお金がかかりすぎるだろう。

☐☐☐ 0089

appoint

/ əpɔ́int /

名 appointment 任命；約束

動 **to choose someone for a specific job or duty**

〈人〉を〜（の役職）に指名する、任命する

≒ assign

⇔ dismiss

例 She was the first woman **appointed** to the position.

彼女はその職に任命された最初の女性だった。

☐☐☐ 0090

possess

/ pəzés /

名 possession 所有

動 **to have or own something**

〜を所有する

≒ retain, keep

⇔ lose, let go, surrender

例 The church **possessed** many beautiful paintings.

その教会はたくさんの美しい絵を所有していた。

☐☐☐ 0091

conclude

/ kənklúːd /

名 conclusion 結論
形 conclusive 決定的な

動 **to form or say an opinion, or to decide to do something after thinking about it**

…と結論を下す

≒ determine

ⓘ 〈conclude (that)...〉（…だと結論を下す）の形で押さえておこう。

例 Many studies have **concluded** that smoking is bad for your health.

多くの研究が、喫煙は健康に悪いと結論を下している。

☐☐☐ 0092

emerge

/ ɪmə́ːrdʒ /

形 emerging 台頭してきた

🔊 **to come from a hidden or unknown place or condition**

出現する、発生する

≒ appear, materialize

⇔ disappear, vanish

🔑〈e-(外に)+merge(沈む)〉

例 The panther **emerged** from the shadows, running toward its prey.

そのヒョウは物陰から現れ、獲物に向かって走った。

☐☐☐ 0093

approximately

/ əprɑ́ːksəmətli /

形 approximate おおよその
名 approximation 概算

🔊 **used to show that something is close in amount but not exact**

およそ

≒ roughly, around

⇔ exactly, precisely

ⓘ approach(近づく)と同語源語。

例 Your interview will take **approximately** three hours.

面接はおよそ3時間かかります。

☐☐☐ 0094

encounter

/ ɪnkáʊntər /

🔊 **to meet someone or something without intending to**

～に遭遇する

≒ bump into, come across

例 She **encountered** a bear while hiking in the woods.

彼女は森でハイキングをしていてクマに出くわした。

🔊 **a meeting with someone that you did not plan or expect**

遭遇

0094語

例 The woman was lucky enough to have a chance **encounter** with her favorite band.

その女性は幸運にも大好きなバンドに偶然出くわした。

☐☐☐ **0095**

chase / tʃéɪs /

動 to follow and try to catch someone or something

〜を追いかける

≒ go after, hunt, pursue

例 The hiker was **chased** by a bear because she went close to its babies.

そのハイカーは子グマに近づいたためにクマに追いかけられた。

☐☐☐ **0096**

occasionally / əkéɪʒənəli /

副 sometimes but not often

時折、たまに

≒ infrequently, periodically

例 Claire **occasionally** goes to the spa to relax.

クレアはリラックスするために時折温泉に行く。

☐☐☐ **0097**

convert / kənvə́ːrt /

名 conversion 変換
形 convertible 変換[転換]できる

動 to change something so you can use it in a different way

〜を変える、変換する

≒ transform, alter

ⓘ 〈convert A into [to] B〉(AをBに変換する) の形を覚えておこう。

例 Many people have started **converting** shipping containers into homes.

多くの人々が輸送用コンテナを家に転換し始めている。

☐☐☐ **0098**

generate / dʒénərèɪt /

名 generation 作り出すこと；世代

動 to make something or cause it to be made

〜を生み出す、発生させる

≒ produce, develop

⇔ destroy

🔑 〈gen (生み出す) +-erate (動詞)〉

例 Television ads **generate** a lot of money for the company.

テレビ広告はその企業に大金を生み出す。

□□□ **0099**

institute

/ ínstət(j)ù:t /

名 institution 社会制度、機関
形 institutional 組織の;制度の

名 an organization made to do a specific thing (e.g. research)

協会、学会、機関

💡〈in-(上に)+stit(立つ)+-ute (～されたもの)〉

例 She is a member of the largest cancer research **institute** in the world.

彼女は世界最大のがん研究協会の一員だ。

動 to start or create something new (such as a law, rule, or system)

〈制度など〉を設ける

≒ introduce

例 The government has **instituted** many law changes to support the education system.

政府は教育制度を支えるために多くの法改正を行った。

□□□ **0100**

principal

/ prínsəpl /

副 principally 主に

形 most important

主要な

≒ main, prominent

⇔ minor

💡〈prin(第一の)+cip(取る)+ -al(形容詞)〉

例 My **principal** reason for moving to Australia was to learn English.

私がオーストラリアに移り住んだ主な理由は英語学習だった。

名 the person who leads a school and is in charge

校長

≒ headmaster

例 The **principal** was known to be very strict about the school rules.

その校長は校則にとても厳格なことで知られていた。

0100語

章末ボキャブラリーチェック

次の語義が表す英単語を答えてください。

語義	解答	連番
❶ to gain something	a c q u i r e	0050
❷ to show that something is right or correct, usually with evidence	c o n f i r m	0025
❸ a large amount of money or things that are owned	f o r t u n e	0084
❹ to use your money to make more money (e.g. by buying stocks or rental properties)	i n v e s t	0061
❺ to give something (especially a document) to someone to be approved or considered	s u b m i t	0037
❻ to make sure that something will be a certain way	e n s u r e	0036
❼ something that connects people or groups to each other	b o n d	0051
❽ a situation that needs serious attention, especially because it is dangerous	c r i s i s	0077
❾ to clearly show the outline or edge of something	d e f i n e	0026
❿ to decrease in amount or grow smaller in number	d e c l i n e	0083
⓫ most important	p r i n c i p a l	0100
⓬ a person who is being considered for a position	c a n d i d a t e	0071
⓭ to meet someone or something without intending to	e n c o u n t e r	0094
⓮ a group of people who make rules or decisions about things	c o u n c i l	0065
⓯ offering a different choice or option	a l t e r n a t i v e	0054
⓰ an organization made to do a specific thing (e.g. research)	i n s t i t u t e	0099
⓱ to get or make something bigger (in size, range, or amount)	e x p a n d	0023
⓲ working without wasting time, money, or energy	e f f i c i e n t	0030
⓳ clearly said or shown (in detail)	s p e c i f i c	0003
⓴ to put something in the ground or under many things, often to hide it	b u r y	0056

語義	解答	連番
㉑ to hold someone (often a criminal) using the power of law	<u>a</u> <u>r</u> <u>r</u> <u>e</u> <u>s</u> <u>t</u>	0032
㉒ the condition of being fair in a situation	<u>j</u> <u>u</u> <u>s</u> <u>t</u> <u>i</u> <u>c</u> <u>e</u>	0040
㉓ an official plan or program that is used to change something	<u>s</u> <u>c</u> <u>h</u> <u>e</u> <u>m</u> <u>e</u>	0085
㉔ the result of an activity or process	<u>o</u> <u>u</u> <u>t</u> <u>c</u> <u>o</u> <u>m</u> <u>e</u>	0078
㉕ far from other people or things	<u>r</u> <u>e</u> <u>m</u> <u>o</u> <u>t</u> <u>e</u>	0055
㉖ an unexpected situation that requires fast action (and is usually dangerous)	<u>e</u> <u>m</u> <u>e</u> <u>r</u> <u>g</u> <u>e</u> <u>n</u> <u>c</u> <u>y</u>	0066
㉗ a piece of land that looks special	<u>l</u> <u>a</u> <u>n</u> <u>d</u> <u>s</u> <u>c</u> <u>a</u> <u>p</u> <u>e</u>	0016
㉘ to try to get or win something that another person is also trying to get, or to try to be better than someone else	<u>c</u> <u>o</u> <u>m</u> <u>p</u> <u>e</u> <u>t</u> <u>e</u>	0041
㉙ to get someone to believe something or agree to do something	<u>c</u> <u>o</u> <u>n</u> <u>v</u> <u>i</u> <u>n</u> <u>c</u> <u>e</u>	0058
㉚ great or very good	<u>b</u> <u>r</u> <u>i</u> <u>l</u> <u>l</u> <u>i</u> <u>a</u> <u>n</u> <u>t</u>	0063
㉛ to like or support something	<u>f</u> <u>a</u> <u>v</u> <u>o</u> <u>r</u>	0017
㉜ a group that has been organized and given an official job to find information or manage something	<u>c</u> <u>o</u> <u>m</u> <u>m</u> <u>i</u> <u>s</u> <u>s</u> <u>i</u> <u>o</u> <u>n</u>	0045
㉝ to change something so you can use it in a different way	<u>c</u> <u>o</u> <u>n</u> <u>v</u> <u>e</u> <u>r</u> <u>t</u>	0097
㉞ used when describing something that looks like it is true based on current information	<u>a</u> <u>p</u> <u>p</u> <u>a</u> <u>r</u> <u>e</u> <u>n</u> <u>t</u> <u>l</u> <u>y</u>	0069
㉟ in addition to something that has already been said	<u>m</u> <u>o</u> <u>r</u> <u>e</u> <u>o</u> <u>v</u> <u>e</u> <u>r</u>	0088
㊱ to try to do or get something over a period of time	<u>p</u> <u>u</u> <u>r</u> <u>s</u> <u>u</u> <u>e</u>	0064
㊲ to make something or cause it to be made	<u>g</u> <u>e</u> <u>n</u> <u>e</u> <u>r</u> <u>a</u> <u>t</u> <u>e</u>	0098
㊳ to form or say an opinion, or to decide to do something after thinking about it	<u>c</u> <u>o</u> <u>n</u> <u>c</u> <u>l</u> <u>u</u> <u>d</u> <u>e</u>	0091
㊴ very great in degree or intensity	<u>e</u> <u>x</u> <u>t</u> <u>r</u> <u>e</u> <u>m</u> <u>e</u>	0046
㊵ a result of an action or actions, especially one that is undesirable	<u>c</u> <u>o</u> <u>n</u> <u>s</u> <u>e</u> <u>q</u> <u>u</u> <u>e</u> <u>n</u> <u>c</u> <u>e</u>	0072

語義	解答	連番
㊶ a government or a part of government that people connect with its leader (such as a president or prime minister)	administration	0044
㊷ a special part of something that makes it different from something else	characteristic	0039
㊸ to be thankful for something or someone	appreciate	0038
㊹ to continue across a certain area, distance, or time	extend	0073
㊺ safe and protected from something dangerous	secure	0048
㊻ to start or release something big or important	launch	0015
㊼ a strong and often angry fight or disagreement between people	conflict	0021
㊽ to follow and try to catch someone or something	chase	0095
㊾ to order someone to do something (in a forceful way)	command	0018
㊿ to say someone is allowed to do or have something	grant	0009
(51) to give something, such as money or time, to help others	contribute	0047
(52) a strong belief or trust in a person or thing	faith	0042
(53) to say that something will or might happen in the future	predict	0075
(54) to happen with or at the same time as another thing	accompany	0059
(55) an event that happens suddenly and causes harm to many people, such as an earthquake or flood	disaster	0082
(56) to tell someone that you will do something harmful to them or others	threaten	0033
(57) to return something to its original condition (e.g. by fixing or cleaning it)	restore	0070
(58) completely and with nothing left unfinished	entirely	0011
(59) to travel to or in a place to learn about it or find something	explore	0006
(60) to have or own something	possess	0090
(61) something unexpected (and usually bad) that has happened	incident	0024

語義	解答	連番
❻❷ to choose someone for a specific job or duty	a p p o i n t	0089
❻❸ to record information in a book or system so you can do something	r e g i s t e r	0035
❻❹ to ask or present a question	p o s e	0079
❻❺ right for the situation	a p p r o p r i a t e	0010
❻❻ a meeting where many people talk about ideas or problems, usually for several days	c o n f e r e n c e	0008
❻❼ correct and without mistakes	a c c u r a t e	0060
❻❽ sometimes but not often	o c c a s i o n a l l y	0096
❻❾ a long, thin piece of material used for sewing	t h r e a d	0007
❼⓪ something valuable a country has, such as oil or minerals	r e s o u r c e	0004
❼❶ to catch someone or something and hold them against their will	c a p t u r e	0034
❼❷ to keep something how it originally was or keep it in good condition	p r e s e r v e	0043
❼❸ to say that something is true (although others might not agree)	c l a i m	0001
❼❹ to promise that something is or will be a certain way	g u a r a n t e e	0049
❼❺ being inside something	i n t e r n a l	0067
❼❻ likely to cause people to feel an emotion, especially a negative one	s e n s i t i v e	0027
❼❼ to succeed at doing, managing, or controlling something difficult	o v e r c o m e	0013
❼❽ to come from a hidden or unknown place or condition	e m e r g e	0092
❼❾ of or relating to a place where people live in the countryside	r u r a l	0076
❽⓪ to look for information about someone or something	i n v e s t i g a t e	0052
❽❶ a common opinion or knowledge that people share about someone or something	r e p u t a t i o n	0080
❽❷ to try to make something happen or change	e n c o u r a g e	0019

❽ a good thing that people think about someone or something — c r e d i t — 0005

❽ to direct something toward someone or something — c a s t — 0022

❽ an amount of something that is made by a person or thing — o u t p u t — 0028

❽ complete or total — a b s o l u t e — 0020

❽ to start using a different manner or method — a d o p t — 0014

❽ to say or write nice things about someone or something — p r a i s e — 0074

❽ to move something from your mouth down to your throat and stomach — s w a l l o w — 0062

❾ to make a guess and offer to give something (usually money,) if your guess is wrong — b e t — 0087

❾ an amount of money that is put in a bank account — d e p o s i t — 0081

❾ a building or equipment that is made for a specific use — f a c i l i t y — 0002

❾ a group of words that shows an idea — s e n t e n c e — 0012

❾ to feel respect and approve of someone or something because of something they have done — a d m i r e — 0086

❾ to make something known to someone for the first time — r e v e a l — 0029

❾ used to show that something is close in amount but not exact — a p p r o x i m a t e l y — 0093

❾ to connect one person or thing to another when you think of it — a s s o c i a t e — 0053

❾ to do or be involved in something — e n g a g e — 0031

❾ one part of a bigger thing — p o r t i o n — 0068

❿ to do something that is against the law or hurts others — c o m m i t — 0057

Stage 2

A journey of a thousand miles begins with a single step.
千里の道も一歩から。

☐☐☐ 0101

external / ɪkstɔ́ːrnl /

形 outside somewhere or something

外部の、外的な

≒ exterior, outer

⇔ interior, inner

例 The **external** features of the building made it famous.

その建物は外面の特徴で有名になった。

☐☐☐ 0102

grateful / gréɪtfl /

形 feeling or showing thanks

感謝している

≒ thankful, appreciative

⇔ ungrateful, unappreciative

例 She is very **grateful** for all the support her teachers gave her.

先生たちがくれたあらゆる援助に彼女はとても感謝している。

☐☐☐ 0103

substance / sʌ́bstəns /

名 a specific material of some kind

物質

🔑 〈sub-（下に）+stance（立つもの）〉

例 The white **substance** on the floor turned out to be spilled milk.

床の白い物質はこぼれた牛乳であることがわかった。

☐☐☐ 0104

numerous / n(j)úːmərəs /

名 numeral 数字

形 existing in large numbers

多数の

≒ many, plentiful

ⓘ number（数）と同語源語。

🔑 〈numer（数）+-ous（満ちた）〉

例 There are **numerous** reasons not to put your information online.

ネットに自分の情報を掲載しない理由はたくさんある。

□□□ 0105

ingredient
/ ɪngríːdiənt /

名 one of the parts that are used to make something

材料、食材

≒ factor, piece

例 The main **ingredient** of cake is flour.

ケーキの主材料は小麦粉だ。

□□□ 0106

estimate
/ éstəmèɪt /

形 estimated 推定の、概算の
名 estimation 概算

動 to guess what something will be like

～と見積もる

≒ predict

ⓘ esteem（～を尊重する、評価する）と同語源語。

例 Based on our research, we **estimate** that building this stadium will cost three billion dollars.

私たちは、調査に基づいて、この競技場を建設するのに30億ドルかかると見積もっている。

□□□ 0107

discipline
/ dísəplən /

名 ① a subject that is studied or taught

学科、学問分野

≒ field, area, specialty

ⓘ アクセントはdiの位置。

例 Asian Studies includes many different academic **disciplines**.

アジア研究にはさまざまな学問分野が含まれている。

② the requirement that certain rules be followed, or the act of following such rules

規律、自制

例 It has taken me a lot of **discipline** to stop eating snacks at midnight.

私が夜中におやつを食べるのをやめるには、大変な自制心が必要だった。

0107語

☐☐☐ **0108**

stupid
/ st(j)úːpəd /

| 形 not intelligent; having difficulty understanding or learning simple things | ばかな、愚かな |

≒ unintelligent, foolish, simple, dumb

⇔ smart, clever

例 She made a **stupid** mistake on her test and failed the class.
彼女はテストで愚かな間違いをして、その科目を落とした。

☐☐☐ **0109**

assign
/ əsáin /

名 **assignment** 割り当てられた任務

| 動 to give someone a job to do | (〈人〉に)〈仕事など〉を割り当てる |

♟ 〈as-(〜に)+sign(印をつける)〉

例 The teacher **assigned** the students extra homework for the long weekend.
教師は長い週末用に生徒たちに追加の宿題を出した。

☐☐☐ **0110**

reform
/ rɪfɔ́ːrm /

| 名 something that makes another thing better by fixing problems | (組織・制度などの)改革 |

≒ change, action

例 The people of the country want political **reform**.
その国の人々は政治改革を求めている。

| 動 to make something better by fixing problems | 〜を改革する、改正する |

≒ revise

ⓘ 「(建物を)リフォームする」は remodel や renovate と言う。

例 People will continue to die if we don't **reform** the health care system.
医療制度を改革しなければ、人々は死に続けるだろう。

☐☐☐ 0111

distribute / dɪstríbjuːt /

名 distribution 配布、流通

動 to give or hand out something to people

～を分配 [配布] する

≒ share

⇔ collect, receive, gather

🔑〈dis-(離れて)+tribute(与える)〉

ⓘ 〈distribute A to B〉(AをBに配る) の形で押さえておこう。

例 The teacher **distributed** the tests to her students without speaking.

その教師は何も言わずに生徒たちにテストを配った。

☐☐☐ 0112

enterprise / éntərpràɪz /

形 enterprising 冒険心にあふれた

名 a large project or activity that people do together

(困難な)事業、企て

≒ program, operation

例 Setting up offices in Europe was an expensive **enterprise** for the company.

ヨーロッパにオフィスを設立するのは、その会社にとって高くつく企てだった。

☐☐☐ 0113

grain / gréin /

名 the seeds of plants, such as wheat and rice, that are used for food

穀物

例 **Grains** are an important part of a healthy diet.

穀物は健康的な食事の重要な一部だ。

☐☐☐ 0114

drag / drǽg /

動 to pull someone or something (along the ground)

～を引きずる

ⓘ パソコンのマウスを「ドラッグする」もこのdrag。drug (麻薬) と混同しないように注意。

例 My grandmother **dragged** her old chest out of the closet with difficulty.

祖母はクローゼットから古い収納箱を苦労して引きずり出した。

0114語

☐☐☐ 0115

outstanding /àʊtstǽndɪŋ/

形 (easy to notice because it is) very good or excellent

顕著な、目立った

≒ remarkable, exceptional

⇔ poor, unremarkable

ⓘ stand out（目立つ、傑出する）という表現も覚えておこう。

例 Her book was **outstanding**, and she got many awards for it.

彼女の本は傑出していて、彼女はその本で多くの賞を獲得した。

☐☐☐ 0116

spare /spéər/

動 ① to not do or provide something

〜を取っておく、惜しんで使わない

≒ hold back, refrain from

例 No expense would be **spared** in planning the party.

そのパーティーを計画する際にはどんな費用も惜しまないだろう。

② to give a part of something you have, such as time or money, to a person

〈時間など〉を割く

≒ share

例 Could you **spare** a few minutes of your time?

2, 3分お時間を割いていただけますか。

形 unneeded but kept in case it is needed by someone

予備の、スペアの

≒ extra, reserve

例 She always keeps a **spare** pair of gloves in the car.

彼女はいつも車に予備の手袋を置いてある。

□□□ 0117

era
/ íərə /

名 a specific period of time (especially a long one) that is connected to something

時代

≒ generation, age

例 The breakup of the Beatles marked the end of an **era** for music.

ビートルズの解散は音楽の一時代の終わりを告げた。

□□□ 0118

intention
/ ɪnténʃən /

動 intend ～を意図する
形 intentional 意図的な

名 a thing that you plan on doing or causing

意図

≒ aim, goal, objective

💡〈in-(中に) +tent (伸ばす) + -ion (名詞)〉

例 They are always causing problems but it's probably not their **intention**.

彼らはいつも問題を起こしているが、それはおそらく彼らの意図ではないのだろう。

□□□ 0119

consume
/ kəns(j)úːm /

名 consumption 消費
名 consumer 消費者

動 ① to use something of which there is a limited supply

～を消費する

⇔ conserve, collect, save

💡〈com-(完全に)+sume(取る)〉

例 Making plastic **consumes** a lot of resources that we cannot get back.

プラスチック製造は私たちが取り戻せない多くの資源を消費する。

② to eat or drink something

～を食べる、摂取する

≒ ingest

例 She **consumed** all of the food on the table, but she was still hungry.

彼女はテーブルにあった食べ物を全部食べたが、それでも空腹だった。

0119語

□□□ 0120

proceed

/ prəsíːd /

名 **process** 過程、進行
名 **procession** 行列、行進

動 ① **to go or move in a particular direction**

前進する、進む

≒ go on, advance

⇔ stop, halt

例 He was warned to **proceed** with caution as he entered the haunted house.

お化け屋敷に入ったとき、彼は注意して進むように警告された。

② **to come from somewhere**

生じる、起因する

例 Strange sounds **proceeded** from the bathroom, and the girl shook in fear.

浴室から奇妙な音が聞こえてきて、女の子は恐怖で震えた。

□□□ 0121

curious

/ kjúəriəs /

名 **curiosity** 好奇心

形 **wanting to learn or know more about someone or something**

好奇心の強い、詮索好きな

≒ interested, inquisitive

⇔ disinterested, indifferent

🔑 〈cur (注意) +-ious (満ちた)〉

ⓘ アクセントは cu の位置。

例 Monkeys are very **curious** and always want to know more.

サルはとても好奇心が強く、常により多くのことを知りたがる。

□□□ 0122

grab

/ grǽb /

動 **to quickly take something or someone and hold them with your arms or hand(s)**

〜を不意につかむ、ひったくる

≒ grasp, clutch, snatch

⇔ let go, release

例 He **grabbed** my arm as I tried to run away.

私が逃げようとすると、彼は私の腕をつかんだ。

□□□ 0123

profession

/ prəféʃən / 形 professional 職業の；プロの

名 a job that requires special training or skills

職業

≒ occupation, line of work, vocation

ⓘ 主に医師、法律家などの専門職を指す。

例 Translation is a **profession** that requires you to have good writing skills.

翻訳は優れた文章力を必要とする職業だ。

□□□ 0124

shelter

/ ʃéltər /

名 ① a place where people or animals can be protected or get help

避難所、保護施設

≒ sanctuary, refuge

ⓘ カタカナ語の「シェルター」はこの shelter から。

例 Going to a homeless **shelter** helped the girl get off the streets.

ホームレスの保護施設に行くことで、その女の子は路上生活から抜け出すことができた。

② a place where you can live

住まい、住居

≒ housing

例 Your parents give you food and **shelter** until you are an adult.

あなたが大人になるまで、あなたの両親が食べ物と住まいをあなたに与える。

動 to protect someone or something from things such as bad weather or dangerous people

〜を守る、かくまう

≒ guard, shield

例 They **sheltered** themselves from the sudden rain inside a cave.

彼らは洞窟に入って突然の雨から避難した。

0124語

☐☐☐ 0125

flexible / fléksəbl /

副 flexibly 柔軟に
名 flexibility 柔軟性

形 ① able to bend or change easily

柔らかい、しなやかな

≒ elastic, pliable

⇔ stiff, firm, rigid

💡 〈flex (折り曲げる) +-ible (できる)〉

例 If a tree is not **flexible**, it'll break in windy conditions.

木がしなやかでなければ、風が強い状況で折れてしまう。

② able to change or do something differently

柔軟な、適応力のある

≒ adaptable

⇔ rigid

例 You must be a **flexible** thinker if you want to do well at this job.

この仕事をうまくやりこなしたいなら、柔軟に考えなければならない。

☐☐☐ 0126

poverty / pá:vərti /

形 poor 貧しい

名 the state of having little or no money

貧困

⇔ abundance, surplus, wealth

例 He was born into **poverty**, so he had to work hard for everything he has.

彼は貧しい家に生まれたので、今持っているすべてを手に入れるために懸命に働かなければならなかった。

☐☐☐ 0127

objective / əbdʒéktɪv /

名 object 物体、対象
副 objectively 客観的に

形 based on facts and not on feelings or opinions

客観的な

≒ factual, unbiased, fair

⇔ subjective, prejudiced

例 A judge must be **objective** in the courtroom.

裁判官は法廷で客観的でなければならない。

□□□ 0128

incredible / ɪnkrédəbl /

副 **incredibly** 信じられないほど、素晴らしく

形 **hard to believe**

信じられない

≒ unbelievable

⇔ believable, plausible, reasonable

🔑 〈in-(否定)+cred(信じる)+ -ible(できる)〉

例 It's **incredible** that someone with no training could become a famous filmmaker.

何の訓練も受けていない人が有名な映画制作者になれるなんて信じられない。

□□□ 0129

accomplish / əká:mplɪʃ /

名 **accomplishment** 達成；業績

動 **to succeed in doing or completing something**

〜を成し遂げる、達成する

≒ achieve, attain, reach

例 She was very proud of all that she had **accomplished** in her life.

彼女は人生で成し遂げたすべてのことをとても誇りに思っていた。

□□□ 0130

odd / á:d /

形 **not normal and considered strange**

奇妙な

≒ unusual, weird, peculiar

⇔ typical

例 That man has an **odd** way of chewing his food.

あの男は食べ物のかみ方が奇妙だ。

□□□ 0131

edit / édət /

名 **editor** 編集者
名 **edition** (書籍などの)版
形 **editorial** 編集の

動 **to fix mistakes or change parts of something (before it is used or sold publicly)**

〜を編集する

0131語

≒ arrange, assemble

例 A book that has not been **edited** well will have many mistakes.

しっかりと編集されていない本には多くの間違いがある。

□□□ 0132

routine / ruːtíːn /

副 **routinely** いつものように、規定通りに

名 a way of doing things that (usually) does not change

決まった手順、日課

≒ habit

ⓘ 語源は「いつも通る決まった道（route）」。

例 Children learn better when there is a **routine** to follow.

手本にする手順があると、子どもの学習効率が上がる。

形 done or happening as a usual part of something

決まりきった、いつも通りの

≒ common, normal, typical

⇔ uncommon, rare

例 Security checks are a **routine** part of flying.

セキュリティチェックは飛行機に乗るときに決まって行うことだ。

□□□ 0133

greet / gríːt /

動 to meet someone and welcome them, usually using friendly words or actions

～にあいさつをする

例 **Greeting** people is a very important part of Japanese work culture.

人にあいさつすることは、日本の労働文化のとても重要な部分だ。

□□□ 0134

transition / trænzíʃən /

形 **transitional** 移行期の

名 a change from one way of being to another

移り変わり、移行

≒ conversion, transformation, progression

🔑 〈trans（越えて）+it（行く）+ -ion（名詞）〉

例 The **transition** to the new operating system caused many problems for the bank.

新しい運営システムへの移行はその銀行に多くの問題を引き起こした。

□□□ 0135

merit / mérət /

名 ① a good quality that should be praised by others

長所

≒ benefit, advantage

⇔ fault, problem, shortcoming

ⓘ カタカナ語の「メリット」（利点）は英語では advantage と言う。

例 The greatest **merit** of her plan is that it will be easy to complete.

彼女の案の最大の長所は、達成しやすいことだ。

② the quality of being useful or valuable

価値

≒ value, worth

例 His idea has **merit**, but it requires further consideration.

彼の考えには価値があるが、さらに検討する必要がある。

□□□ 0136

heal / híːl / 名 healing 癒やし

動 ① to get better after sickness or an injury

治る、癒える

≒ recover

⇔ worsen

ⓘ heel（かかと）と同音。

例 Sally's broken foot finally **healed** after three months.

サリーの骨折した足は3か月後にようやく治った。

② to help someone or something get better after sickness or an injury

～を治す、癒やす

0136語

≒ treat

例 The woman was known for her skill in **healing** broken hearts.

その女性は失恋を癒やす能力で知られていた。

□□□ 0137

plot

/ plάːt /

名 ① a group of events that make the story in a novel, movie, etc.

（物語などの）筋、構想

≒ narrative

例 The **plots** of Thomas Pynchon's novels are always hard to understand.

トマス・ピンチョンの小説の筋はいつもわかりにくい。

② a secret (often illegal) plan to do something

企み

≒ scheme, conspiracy

例 The two men took part in a **plot** to take down the government.

その2人の男は政府を倒す企みに加わった。

動 to make secret plans to do something (usually illegal)

～を企む

≒ conspire, scheme

例 They had been **plotting** for weeks to rob the bank.

彼らは銀行強盗をしようと何週間も企んでいた。

□□□ 0138

resist

/ rɪzíst /

名 resistance 抵抗
形 resistant 耐久性のある

動 to try not to do something or prevent something from happening

～に抵抗する

≒ defy, refuse, refrain

⇔ accept, agree, conform

🔑 〈re-（後ろに）+sist（立つ）〉

ⓘ 他動詞である点に注意。

例 He couldn't **resist** the charm of the woman in front of him.

彼は目の前にいる女性の魅力に抵抗することができなかった。

□□□ 0139

consistent
/ kənsístənt /

副 consistently 一貫して
名 consistency 一貫性

形 acting the same way all the time

一貫した、堅実な

≒ steady

⇔ inconsistent, unreliable

🔑 〈con- (共に) +sist (立つ) +
-ent (形容詞)〉

例 It is important to be **consistent** when telling children how they should behave.

子どもをしつけるときには一貫していることが重要だ。

□□□ 0140

evaluate
/ ɪvǽljuèɪt /

名 evaluation 評価

動 to judge the value of something or someone with care

〜を評価する

≒ grade, classify, assess

🔑 〈e- (外に) +valu (価値がある) +-ate (動詞)〉

例 You should **evaluate** each university program before choosing where to go.

どこに進学するかを決める前に各大学の課程を評価するべきだ。

□□□ 0141

defeat
/ dɪfíːt /

動 to beat someone in a contest, war, or game

(戦い・ゲームなどで)
〈相手〉を負かす

例 Thankfully, the army was **defeated**, and the war ended.

幸いなことに、その軍は敗れ、戦争は終わった。

名 failure to win or succeed against someone or something

敗北

≒ loss

⇔ victory, success, triumph

0141語

例 That was the team's first **defeat** since entering the league.

それはそのチームがリーグに参加して初めての敗北だった。

☐☐☐ **0142**

confuse

/ kənfjúːz /

名 confusion 混乱；混同

動 ① to make someone unable to understand something easily

〈人〉を困惑させる、混乱させる

≒ puzzle, perplex

例 The twins **confused** their teacher by always dressing in the same clothes.

その双子はいつも同じ服を着ていて先生を混乱させた。

② to mix up people or things

～を（…と）取り違える

≒ confound, mistake

例 My son always **confuses** his shoes and mine because they look the same.

息子の靴と私の靴は同じに見えるので、彼はいつも取り違える。

☐☐☐ **0143**

prospect

/ prάːspekt /

形 prospective 将来の、見込まれる

名 the possibility of something happening sometime in the future

見込み

≒ expectation, forecast, probability

⇔ unlikelihood, improbability

🔑〈pro-（前を）+spect（見る）〉

例 She is worried about the **prospect** of having no job from April.

彼女は4月から仕事がない見込みで心配している。

☐☐☐ **0144**

conventional

/ kənvénʃənl /

副 conventionally 慣習的に
名 convention（社会的）慣習

形 of a style that has been around for a long time and is thought to be normal

従来の

≒ typical, common, regular

⇔ irregular, atypical, uncommon, unusual

🔑〈con-（共に）+vent（来る）+-ional（形容詞）〉

例 Microwaves are faster, but a **conventional** oven always makes better food.

電子レンジの方が速いが、従来のオーブンで作った料理の方が常においしい。

□□□ 0145

breed

/ bríːd /

動 ① to keep plants or animals and use them to make more plants or animals of a certain kind

〈動植物〉を飼育する、繁殖させる

ⓘ breed-bred-bredと活用する。カタカナ語の「ブリーダー」は breederから。

例 Plants can be **bred** to grow in different climates.

植物は異なる気候でも生育するように栽培することができる。

② to produce young animals by mating

繁殖する

≒ reproduce, mate

例 The birds return to the island once a year to **breed**.

その鳥は1年に一度、繁殖のためにその島に帰ってくる。

名 a type of dog, cat, horse, etc. that is made through breeding

品種、血統

≒ pedigree

例 There are many different **breeds** of dogs.

犬にはさまざまな品種がある。

□□□ 0146

emphasize

/ émfəsàɪz /

名 emphasis 強調
形 emphatic 強調された

動 to place extra meaning and strength on something

～を強調する

≒ stress, highlight, accentuate

⇔ understate, ignore, gloss over

ⓘ イギリス英語ではemphasiseともつづる。

例 As a teacher, you must **emphasize** that not everything can be learned at school.

教師として、あなたは何でも学校で学べるわけではないと強調しなければならない。

0146語

□□□ 0147

relevant

/ réləvənt / 名 relevance 関連性

形 ① connected or related to the subject you are talking or thinking about

関連する

⇔ irrelevant

ⓘ relevant to（～に関する）の形で押さえておこう。

例 Please avoid talking about things that are not **relevant** to your job while at work.

仕事中に仕事と関連のない話をするのは避けてください。

② having an idea that means something to people and their lives

有意義な

≒ valuable

⇔ irrelevant

例 The ideas the author talked about in his book are still **relevant**.

著者がその本の中で語った考えは今でも意義がある。

□□□ 0148

manufacture

/ mǽnjəfǽktʃər /

名 manufacturing 製造業
名 manufacturer 製造業者、メーカー

動 to make something, usually in large amounts and with machines

～を製造する

≒ create, produce, fabricate

⇔ destroy, demolish

🔑〈manu（手）+fact（作る）+ -ure（動詞）〉

例 Electronics have been **manufactured** in this community for 30 years.

この地域社会では30年間電子機器が製造されている。

名 the process of making products, usually with machines in factories

製造

≒ production

例 The metal, which is both light and strong, is used in the **manufacture** of cars.

その金属は軽くて丈夫で、車の製造に使われる。

□□□ 0149

considerable

/ kənsídərəbl /

動 consider ～を考慮する
副 considerably かなり、大幅に

形 large in size, amount, or quantity

かなりの

≒ substantial, significant

⇔ unsubstantial, insignificant, unimportant

例 The hotel received a **considerable** amount of complaints and decided to fire the staff member.

そのホテルはかなりの数の苦情を受け、該当の従業員を解雇することにした。

□□□ 0150

elementary

/ èləméntəri /

形 basic or simple

初歩的な

≒ rudimentary ⇔ complex, complicated

ⓘ「元素の」という意味もあり、elementary particle（素粒子）などの表現で使われる。

例 Getting to an **elementary** speaking level of a language is not that difficult.

ある言語の初歩的なスピーキングレベルに達することはそれほど難しくない。

□□□ 0151

alter

/ ɔ́:ltər /

名 alteration 変更

動 to change something in some way

～を変える

≒ modify, adjust

⇔ leave, keep

例 Her dress was too long, so she had it **altered** to make it shorter.

ワンピースが長すぎたので、彼女は手を加えて短くしてもらった。

□□□ 0152

draft

/ drǽft /

名 a version of something that you make before making the final version

草稿

ⓘ スポーツの「ドラフト（制度）」もこのdraft。

例 Most novels have several **drafts** before they are finished.

ほとんどの小説には完成前のいくつかの草稿がある。

0152語

□□□ 0153

enormous

/ ɪnɔ́ːrməs /

形 very great in size or amount

巨大な、莫大な

≒ huge, massive

⇔ tiny, small

🔑 〈e- (外に) +norm (尺度) +
-ous (満ちた)〉

例 There was an **enormous** elephant next to the road.

道の脇に巨大なゾウがいた。

□□□ 0154

phase

/ féɪz /

名 a step of a process or one part in a series

（発達・変化の）段階、
局面

≒ stage

例 There are three **phases** of treatment to cure this type
of sickness.

この種の病気を治す療法には
3つの段階がある。

□□□ 0155

slave

/ sléɪv /

名 slavery 奴隷状態；奴隷制度

名 a person who is owned by another person and is forced to do things without being paid

奴隷

≒ captive, servant

⇔ master

例 The large plantations in the U.S. used to be run using
only the power of **slaves**.

アメリカの大農園はかつて奴
隷の力だけを使って経営され
ていた。

□□□ 0156

inevitable

/ ɪnévətəbl /

副 inevitably 避けがたく、
必然的に

形 certain to happen in the future

避けられない、必然の

≒ imminent, impending

⇔ uncertain, doubtful

例 Trouble is **inevitable** when you tell lies to people.

人にうそをつくと、トラブルは
避けられない。

□□□ 0157

primarily

/ praɪmérəli / 形 primary 主要な

副 used to show that something is the main purpose or reason for something else

主として、第一に

≒ mainly, chiefly

⇔ secondarily, partly

🔑〈prim(第一の)+-ary(形容詞)〉

例 His book was meant **primarily** for an adult audience.

彼の本は主に成人の読者を対象としていた。

□□□ 0158

remarkable

/ rɪmάːrkəbl / 副 remarkably 極めて
名 remark 所見

形 not usual; surprising or impressive

際立った

≒ exceptional, noteworthy, outstanding

⇔ average, unexceptional, typical

例 The lady had a **remarkable** talent for clipping the nails of dogs.

その女性には犬の爪を切る際立った才能があった。

□□□ 0159

casual

/ kǽʒuəl / 副 casually 気軽に

形 ① done without much concern, effort, or thought

何気ない、思いつきの

⇔ serious

例 It was just a **casual** game of basketball, so they didn't care who won.

気軽なバスケの試合だったので、彼らは誰が勝とうと気にしていなかった。

② not formal; featuring or allowing ordinary behavior, clothing, etc.

〈服装などが〉形式ばらない、カジュアルな

0159語

≒ relaxed, informal

例 She was allowed to wear **casual** clothes to the interview instead of a suit.

彼女はスーツの代わりにカジュアルな服装で面接に行くのを許された。

☐☐☐ **0160**

abuse

/ 動 əbjúːz 名 əbjúːs /

形 abusive 乱暴な、虐待する

動 ① to treat someone or something in a way that is not nice or can cause harm

～を虐待する

≒ mistreat

🔑 〈ab-（離れて）+use（使う）〉

⇔ take care of, aid

例 She **abused** her husband, always hitting him and yelling when she was angry.

彼女は腹を立てるといつも夫をたたいたりどなったりして虐待した。

② to use too much of something (usually something that is not good for you)

～を乱用する

≒ misuse, overuse

例 Everyone knows that the man **abuses** alcohol and is usually drunk.

その男が酒浸りで、いつも酔っぱらっていることは誰もが知っている。

名 treatment that causes harm to a person or animal

虐待

≒ mistreatment

例 She couldn't handle the **abuse** from her husband any longer, so she called the police.

彼女は夫の虐待にもはや対処できず、警察に電話した。

☐☐☐ **0161**

extensive

/ ɪksténsɪv /

動 extend ～を拡張する
名 extension 延長、拡張
名 extent 広さ、範囲

形 large in size or amount, or highly detailed or lengthy

広範囲にわたる、大規模な

≒ comprehensive

🔑 〈ex-（外に）+tens（伸ばす）+ -ive（形容詞）〉

⇔ limited

ⓘ extensionには「（電話の）内線」という意味もある。

例 She made an **extensive** reading list for her book club.

彼女は読書クラブのために多岐にわたる読書リストを作った。

□□□ 0162

pile

/ páɪl /

動 to put things on top of one another

～を積み上げる

≒ stack, heap

例 She **piled** the blankets on top of herself to keep warm.

彼女は暖かくしていようと自分の体に毛布を積み上げた。

名 a group of things that have been put on top of each other

積み重ね、山

≒ heap, mass, mound

例 There always seems to be a **pile** of dirty clothes in a teenager's bedroom.

ティーンエージャーの寝室には必ず汚れた衣類の山があるようだ。

□□□ 0163

ban

/ bǽn /

動 to not allow people to use or do something

～を禁止する

≒ prohibit, prevent, outlaw

⇔ legalize

ⓘ〈ban A from *do*ing〉(Aが～することを禁じる) の形で押さえておこう。

例 They were **banned** from leaving the country after the virus was discovered.

ウイルスが発見されると、彼らはその国から出ることを禁じられた。

名 a rule that says people may not use or do something

禁止

≒ prohibition, embargo

例 Even after the alcohol **ban**, people in the United States still drank.

禁酒になってもなお、アメリカの人々は飲酒した。

0163語

☐☐☐ 0164

scratch

/ skrǽtʃ /

動 to make a mark on the surface of something by rubbing or cutting it

～を引っかく

≒ scrape

ⓘ from scratch（ゼロから、最初から）という表現も覚えておこう。

例 She was angry with her ex-boyfriend, so she **scratched** his car with a key.

彼女は元カレに腹を立てていたので、彼の車を鍵で引っかいた。

名 a mark on the surface of something caused by rubbing or cutting

引っかき傷、すり傷

例 He often drops his glasses, so there are many **scratches** on the lenses.

彼はよく眼鏡を落とすので、レンズに多くの傷がついている。

☐☐☐ 0165

sponsor

/ spάːnsər /　名 sponsorship 後援

動 to use your own money to support someone or something (often seen in sports and other large events)

～のスポンサーになる

🔑〈spons（約束する）+-or（人）〉

例 The Olympics are **sponsored** by many large companies.

オリンピックは多くの大企業がスポンサーになっている。

名 a person or organization that provides the money needed for an activity or event to be held

番組提供者、スポンサー

例 Our company is a **sponsor** of the music festival.

当社はその音楽祭のスポンサーです。

□□□ 0166

eliminate

/ ɪlímənèɪt /

名 elimination 削除、撲滅

動 **to get rid of something that you no longer need and/or want**

～を取り除く

≒ remove, dispose of

🔑 〈e-（外に）+limin（境界）+ -ate（動詞）〉

例 **Eliminating** unnecessary waste is a great way to help the environment.

不要な廃棄物を取り除くことは環境を守る素晴らしい方法だ。

□□□ 0167

logic

/ láːʤɪk /

形 logical 論理的な

名 **a way of thinking and understanding that is reasonable**

論理、理屈

≒ sense, rationale

🔑 〈log（言葉）+-ic（形容詞）〉

例 Against all **logic**, the girl decided to keep the kitten, even though she was allergic to cats.

あらゆる論理に反して、その女の子は猫アレルギーがあるにもかかわらず、子猫を飼うことにした。

□□□ 0168

rear

/ ríər /

名 **the part of an object that is opposite the front or in the back**

後ろ、後部

例 A motorcycle smashed into the **rear** of his car.

バイクが彼の車の後部に衝突した。

動 **to take care of a young person or animal until it is fully grown**

～を育てる

0168語

≒ bring up, raise

例 She **reared** her three children all by herself.

彼女は女手一つで3人の子どもを育てた。

□□□ **0169**

artificial

/ ὰːrtəfíʃəl /　　　副 artificially 人工的に

形 **not natural or real, usually used to describe something man-made**

人工の、模造の

≒ fake, counterfeit, manufactured

⇔ genuine

ⓘ AIは artificial intelligence（人工知能）の略。

例 His mother is allergic to most **artificial** sweeteners.

彼の母親はほとんどの人工甘味料にアレルギーがある。

□□□ **0170**

bow

/ 動 báʊ　名 bóʊ /

動 ① **to bend forward at the neck or waist to greet someone or show them respect**

おじぎする

ⓘ ow の発音に注意。

例 The woman **bowed** before the king, then explained her business.

その女性は王の前でおじぎをし、それから用件を説明した。

② **to stop resisting or opposing something**

屈服する

≒ give up, concede, surrender, yield

⇔ fight, struggle

例 The queen **bowed** to public pressure and gave up her title.

女王は民衆の圧力に屈して王位を放棄した。

名 **a weapon used to shoot arrows that is usually made out of wood and connected by thin string**

弓

ⓘ 「矢」は arrow と言う。

例 **Bows** were a common way to hunt for food before guns were invented.

銃が発明される前は、弓が食料を求めて狩りをする一般的な方法だった。

□□□ 0171

transform

/ trænsfɔ́ːrm /

名 transformation 変化、変形

🔵 to change something so that it is completely different, usually in a good way

～を変化させる

⇔ retain

🔑 〈trans-(向こうに)+form(形)〉

例 The couple **transformed** their old shed into a guest house for when their daughter visited.

夫婦は娘が訪ねてくるときのために、古い小屋を離れに改装した。

□□□ 0172

vital

/ váɪtl /

副 vitally 極めて、絶対に
名 vitality 生命力

形 very important to something

極めて重要な

≒ crucial, essential

🔑 〈vit(生命)+-al(形容詞)〉

⇔ unimportant, inessential

例 It is **vital** that everyone follows all safety procedures so that no one gets hurt.

けがをする人がいないように、全員がすべての安全手順を守ることが極めて重要だ。

□□□ 0173

intense

/ ɪnténs /

形 intensive 集中的な
動 intensify ～を強くする
名 intensity 強烈さ

形 ① very strong

激しい、強烈な

≒ extreme, powerful

⇔ weak, moderate

例 There was an **intense** flash of light before the whole room went dark.

部屋全体が暗くなる前に強烈な閃光があった。

② showing or involving great effort, energy, or seriousness

〈努力などが〉熱心な、猛烈な

0173語

≒ hard, strong

例 After years of **intense** study, he finally became a lawyer.

長年にわたる猛勉強の末、彼はついに弁護士になった。

□□□ 0174

reverse / rɪvə́ːrs /

名 **reversal** 逆転、反転

動 ① to put something into an opposite state or condition

〈決定・方向など〉を覆す、逆転させる

≒ undo, revert

🔑 〈re-(後ろに)+verse(曲がる)〉

⇔ maintain

例 The prime minister decided to **reverse** her decision on corporate tax cuts.

首相は法人減税に関する決定を覆すことに決めた。

② to change the order or position of some things

〈順序など〉を逆にする

≒ overturn, turn around

例 When your parents become old, you **reverse** roles and you become like their parent.

親が年を取ると、役割が逆になり、あなたが親のようになる。

名 something that is the opposite of another thing

反対、逆

例 He was certain his girlfriend would love the movie, but the **reverse** was true.

彼は自分の彼女がその映画をきっと気に入るだろうと思っていたが、実際は逆だった。

□□□ 0175

fundamental / fʌ̀ndəméntl /

形 relating to the basic form or function of something

基本的な、根本的な

≒ integral

⇔ insignificant, unnecessary, inessential

ⓘ fundは「基礎、基盤」を意味する語根で、found(〜を創設する)なども同語源語。

例 The invention of the Internet brought **fundamental** changes to the world.

インターネットの発明は世界に根本的な変革をもたらした。

□□□ 0176

proportion

/ prəpɔ́ːrʃən /

形 proportional 比例した

名 the relationship between the size or amount of two things, often represented using two numbers

割合、比率

≒ percentage, ratio

例 The **proportion** of men to women in the country's government is nine to one.

その国の政府における男女比率は9対1だ。

□□□ 0177

impose

/ ɪmpóʊz /

名 imposition 課すこと

動 to force something on someone using your authority

～を課す

≒ demand

💡 〈im- (上に) +pose (置く)〉

例 The government **imposed** a curfew on the city after the riot started to spread.

暴動が広がり始めると、政府はその都市に外出禁止令を出した。

□□□ 0178

admission

/ ədmíʃən /

動 admit ～の入場 [入会] を認める

名 the right or permission to go into a place

入場許可、入会許可、入学許可

≒ access

💡 〈ad- (～に) +miss (送る) + -ion (名詞)〉

例 In order to gain **admission** to this library, you must show your ID.

この図書館への入館許可を得るには、身分証明書を提示しなければならない。

□□□ 0179

frequently

/ fríːkwəntli /

形 frequent 頻繁な
名 frequency 頻度；周波数

0179語

副 happening a lot or regularly

頻繁に

≒ often, commonly, typically

⇔ infrequently, irregularly

例 Modern websites need to be updated **frequently**.

現在のウェブサイトは頻繁にアップデートする必要がある。

□□□ 0180

contemporary

/ kəntémpərèri /

形 ① happening currently or recently

現代の

≒ modern, present

🔑 〈con- (共に) +tempor (時間) +-ary (形容詞)〉

例 **Contemporary** furniture doesn't have as much personality as antiques do.

現代の家具にはアンティークほどの個性がない。

② existing during the same time period

同時代の

例 Her book is based on **contemporary** stories that were collected during the war.

彼女の本は戦時中に集められた当時の話に基づいている。

□□□ 0181

qualify

/ kwάːləfàɪ /

名 qualification 資格
形 qualified 資格のある、適任の

動 to give someone skills or knowledge that are needed to do a job

〜に資格を与える

≒ certify, entitle

⇔ disqualify

例 His many years of experience as a server **qualified** him to become a restaurant manager.

彼には長年にわたる接客係の経験があったので、レストランの支配人になる資格があった。

□□□ 0182

assure

/ əʃúər /

名 assurance 保証
形 assured 確信のある

動 to (strongly) tell someone that something is true or will happen

〜を〈人〉に保証する、請け合う

≒ reassure, promise

🔑 〈as- (〜に) +sure (確実な)〉

ⓘ 〈assure ＋人＋ (that).../of A〉(…だと／Aを人に保証する) の形で押さえておこう。

例 The president **assured** the people that the army would keep them safe.

大統領は、軍があなたたちを守る、と人々に請け合った。

□□□ **0183**

rescue / réskju: /

動 to save someone or something from being hurt or from danger

～を救出する

⇔ abandon

💡〈re-（元に）+scue（振り払う）〉

例 Sometimes firefighters have to **rescue** cats that are stuck in trees.

時に消防士は木から下りられなくなった猫を救出しなければならない。

名 the act of saving someone or something from being hurt or from danger

救助、救出

例 The **rescue** mission to the island was too risky to do during the storm.

その島へ救出に行く任務は、嵐の中で遂行するにはあまりも危険だった。

□□□ **0184**

congress / ká:ŋgrəs /

形 congressional 会議の、国会の

名 a formal meeting where people talk about important things and make big decisions

会議、大会

≒ committee, assembly

💡〈con-（共に）+gress（行く）〉

ⓘ Congress で「米国議会」も意味する。

例 Researchers from all across the world come to Florida for the annual academic **congress**.

世界中の研究者が年に一度の学術会議のためにフロリダにやってくる。

□□□ **0185**

quit / kwít /

0185語

動 to stop doing something

～をやめる

≒ give up, surrender, withdraw

ⓘ quit-quit-quit と活用する。

例 She **quit** her job after her boss started to harass her.

彼女は上司が彼女に嫌がらせをし始めると仕事をやめた。

☐☐☐ 0186

revenue

/ révən(j)ù: /

名 money that is made in an organization or paid to it

収入、歳入

≒ income, earnings

⇔ expenditure, expense

🔑 〈re- (元に) +venue (来る)〉

例 The hotel lost **revenue** because of a lack of visitors.

そのホテルは客がいなくなり、収入が途絶えた。

☐☐☐ 0187

modify

/ má:dəfàɪ /

名 modification（部分的な）修正

動 to only change a part or some parts of something

〜を（部分的に）修正する

≒ alter, adjust

例 The bicycle was **modified** for people without strong legs.

その自転車は脚が強くない人向けに改造された。

☐☐☐ 0188

differ

/ dífər /

形 different 異なる
名 difference 相違
動 differentiate 〜を差別化する

動 to be different from something else

〈もの・事が〉異なる、違う

≒ contradict, distinguish

例 Our opinions **differ** in many ways.

私たちの意見は多くの点で異なる。

☐☐☐ 0189

vice

/ váɪs /

名 a bad or immoral habit or behavior

悪

≒ weakness, shortcoming

ⓘ vice-president（副大統領）のように「副、代理」を意味する接頭辞としても使われる。

例 His main **vice** was gambling, and he lost all of his family's money because of it.

彼の一番の欠点はギャンブルで、そのために家族の全財産を失った。

□□□ 0190

interpret

/ ɪntə́ːrprət /

名 interpretation 解釈
名 interpreter 通訳 (者)

動 **to understand something in your own way**

〜を (…と) 解釈する

⇔ misinterpret, misunderstand

ⓘ アクセントは ter の位置。

例 There are many different ways to **interpret** the meaning of a poem.

詩の意味にはさまざまな解釈方法がある。

□□□ 0191

ray

/ réɪ /

名 **a line of light that you can see coming from something**

光線

ⓘ radiate (放射する)、radioactive (放射能の) なども同語源語。

例 **Rays** of sunlight shone through the window, warming her bedroom.

窓越しに日光が輝き、彼女の寝室を暖めた。

□□□ 0192

crucial

/ krúːʃəl /

副 crucially 非常に

形 **very important to something**

非常に重大な、決定的な

≒ critical, essential, pivotal, vital

⇔ inessential, minor, optional, trivial

例 It is **crucial** to start saving for retirement when you're still young.

若いうちから定年に備えて貯蓄を始めるのは非常に重要なことだ。

□□□ 0193

transaction

/ trænzǽkʃən /

動 transact 〈取引など〉を行う

名 **a business deal where something is passed between people or groups**

取引、売買

≒ agreement, contract, negotiation

🔑 〈trans- (貫いて) +act (行う)〉

例 You can view all of your banking **transactions** online.

あなたはすべての銀行取引をネットで見ることができる。

☐☐☐ 0194

barely / béərli /

副 ① **in a way that is almost impossible or almost does not happen**

かろうじて

≒ hardly

ⓘ 形容詞のbareは「裸の、むき出しの」「かろうじての」の意。

例 The bus was late, and they **barely** made it to the airport in time.

バスが遅れたが、彼らはかろうじて間に合う時間に空港に到着した。

② **almost not at all**

ほとんど〜ない

≒ hardly, scarcely

例 The woman had **barely** any money in her wallet.

その女性の財布にはほとんど一銭もなかった。

☐☐☐ 0195

exceed / ɪksíːd /

動 to go past the limit of something

〜を超える

名 excess 超過
形 excessive 過度の
副 excessively 過度に

≒ surpass

⇔ fall short

🔑 〈ex- (外に) +ceed (行く)〉

例 The student handed in an excellent essay, **exceeding** the expectations of his teacher.

その生徒は先生の予想を超える素晴らしい小論文を提出した。

☐☐☐ 0196

illustrate / íləstrèɪt /

動 to give examples so that something is easier to understand

(図・例などで) 〜を説明する

名 illustration 説明、挿絵

≒ show, depict

⇔ conceal, obscure, hide

例 His professor asked him to **illustrate** his point with a few examples.

教授は彼にいくつかの例を使って要点を説明するよう求めた。

□□□ **0197**

summary
/ sʌ́məri / 動 summarize 〜を要約する

名 **a brief statement that provides the most important information about something**

概要、要約

≒ outline, abstract

例 The students were told to write a **summary** of their favorite book for homework.

生徒たちは宿題として好きな本の要約を書くように言われた。

□□□ **0198**

nevertheless
/ nèvərðəlés /

副 **despite something that was just said**

それにもかかわらず

≒ even though, regardless, nonetheless

ⓘ アクセントは less の位置。

例 Her husband enjoyed the movie a lot, but it bored her **nevertheless**.

彼女の夫はその映画を大いに楽しんだが、それにもかかわらず彼女には退屈だった。

□□□ **0199**

distinguish
/ dɪstíŋgwɪʃ /

形 distinct 別個の；明確な
形 distinctive 違いを示す
名 distinction 区別

動 **to notice or recognize a difference between people or things**

〜を見分ける、区別する

≒ identify, separate

例 Even small children can **distinguish** between right and wrong.

小さな子どもでも善悪の区別はつけられる。

□□□ **0200**

complicated
/ ká:mpləkèɪtɪd / 動 complicate 〜を複雑にする

0200語

形 **not easy to understand, explain, or manage**

複雑な

≒ complex

⇔ simple

例 Hegel's philosophy is too **complicated** for many people to understand.

ヘーゲルの哲学は複雑すぎて多くの人は理解できない。

章末ボキャブラリーチェック

次の語義が表す英単語を答えてください。

語義	解答	連番
❶ to notice or recognize a difference between people or things	d i s t i n g u i s h	0199
❷ not intelligent; having difficulty understanding or learning simple things	s t u p i d	0108
❸ to judge the value of something or someone with care	e v a l u a t e	0140
❹ to save someone or something from being hurt or from danger	r e s c u e	0183
❺ to beat someone in a contest, war, or game	d e f e a t	0141
❻ to use your own money to support someone or something (often seen in sports and other large events)	s p o n s o r	0165
❼ a business deal where something is passed between people or groups	t r a n s a c t i o n	0193
❽ the state of having little or no money	p o v e r t y	0126
❾ the possibility of something happening sometime in the future	p r o s p e c t	0143
❿ money that is made in an organization or paid to it	r e v e n u e	0186
⓫ to not allow people to use or do something	b a n	0163
⓬ large in size, amount, or quantity	c o n s i d e r a b l e	0149
⓭ to understand something in your own way	i n t e r p r e t	0190
⓮ based on facts and not on feelings or opinions	o b j e c t i v e	0127
⓯ able to bend or change easily	f l e x i b l e	0125
⓰ to try not to do something or prevent something from happening	r e s i s t	0138
⓱ a specific material of some kind	s u b s t a n c e	0103
⓲ to change something in some way	a l t e r	0151
⓳ a brief statement that provides the most important information about something	s u m m a r y	0197
⓴ (easy to notice because it is) very good or excellent	o u t s t a n d i n g	0115

語義	解答	連番
㉑ a version of something that you make before making the final version	d r a f t	0152
㉒ to force something on someone using your authority	i m p o s e	0177
㉓ the seeds of plants, such as wheat and rice, that are used for food	g r a i n	0113
㉔ something that makes another thing better by fixing problems	r e f o r m	0110
㉕ hard to believe	i n c r e d i b l e	0128
㉖ to give someone skills or knowledge that are needed to do a job	q u a l i f y	0181
㉗ to succeed in doing or completing something	a c c o m p l i s h	0129
㉘ to be different from something else	d i f f e r	0188
㉙ basic or simple	e l e m e n t a r y	0150
㉚ a good quality that should be praised by others	m e r i t	0135
㉛ to place extra meaning and strength on something	e m p h a s i z e	0146
㉜ very important to something	c r u c i a l	0192
㉝ a formal meeting where people talk about important things and make big decisions	c o n g r e s s	0184
㉞ to stop doing something	q u i t	0185
㉟ to give or hand out something to people	d i s t r i b u t e	0111
㊱ a job that requires special training or skills	p r o f e s s i o n	0123
㊲ to use something of which there is a limited supply	c o n s u m e	0119
㊳ a step of a process or one part in a series	p h a s e	0154
㊴ very strong	i n t e n s e	0173
㊵ to go or move in a particular direction	p r o c e e d	0120
㊶ done without much concern, effort, or thought	c a s u a l	0159
㊷ very great in size or amount	e n o r m o u s	0153
㊸ to bend forward at the neck or waist to greet someone or show them respect	b o w	0170
㊹ to pull someone or something (along the ground)	d r a g	0114

語義	解答	連番
㊺ to quickly take something or someone and hold them with your arms or hand(s)	g r a b	0122
㊻ connected or related to the subject you are talking or thinking about	r e l e v a n t	0147
㊼ happening currently or recently	c o n t e m p o r a r y	0180
㊽ a group of events that make the story in a novel, movie, etc.	p l o t	0137
㊾ the relationship between the size or amount of two things, often represented using two numbers	p r o p o r t i o n	0176
㊿ the right or permission to go into a place	a d m i s s i o n	0178
51 wanting to learn or know more about someone or something	c u r i o u s	0121
52 to only change a part or some parts of something	m o d i f y	0187
53 in a way that is almost impossible or almost does not happen	b a r e l y	0194
54 to get rid of something that you no longer need and/or want	e l i m i n a t e	0166
55 to get better after sickness or an injury	h e a l	0136
56 a line of light that you can see coming from something	r a y	0191
57 feeling or showing thanks	g r a t e f u l	0102
58 a specific period of time (especially a long one) that is connected to something	e r a	0117
59 not easy to understand, explain, or manage	c o m p l i c a t e d	0200
60 acting the same way all the time	c o n s i s t e n t	0139
61 to (strongly) tell someone that something is true or will happen	a s s u r e	0182
62 a way of thinking and understanding that is reasonable	l o g i c	0167
63 to not do or provide something	s p a r e	0116
64 a person who is owned by another person and is forced to do things without being paid	s l a v e	0155
65 to give examples so that something is easier to understand	i l l u s t r a t e	0196

語義	解答	連番
⑯ to make something, usually in large amounts and with machines	m a n u f a c t u r e	0148
⑰ very important to something	v i t a l	0172
⑱ the part of an object that is opposite the front or in the back	r e a r	0168
⑲ to keep plants or animals and use them to make more plants or animals of a certain kind	b r e e d	0145
⑳ to put things on top of one another	p i l e	0162
㉑ to fix mistakes or change parts of something (before it is used or sold publicly)	e d i t	0131
㉒ used to show that something is the main purpose or reason for something else	p r i m a r i l y	0157
㉓ to meet someone and welcome them, usually using friendly words or actions	g r e e t	0133
㉔ a change from one way of being to another	t r a n s i t i o n	0134
㉕ a way of doing things that (usually) does not change	r o u t i n e	0132
㉖ to make someone unable to understand something easily	c o n f u s e	0142
㉗ not natural or real, usually used to describe something man-made	a r t i f i c i a l	0169
㉘ relating to the basic form or function of something	f u n d a m e n t a l	0175
㉙ one of the parts that are used to make something	i n g r e d i e n t	0105
㉚ certain to happen in the future	i n e v i t a b l e	0156
㉛ to treat someone or something in a way that is not nice or can cause harm	a b u s e	0160
㉜ not normal and considered strange	o d d	0130
㉝ not usual; surprising or impressive	r e m a r k a b l e	0158
㉞ of a style that has been around for a long time and is thought to be normal	c o n v e n t i o n a l	0144
㉟ a subject that is studied or taught	d i s c i p l i n e	0107
㊱ outside somewhere or something	e x t e r n a l	0101
㊲ despite something that was just said	n e v e r t h e l e s s	0198

語義	解答	連番
(88) to put something into an opposite state or condition	reverse	0174
(89) a place where people or animals can be protected or get help	shelter	0124
(90) happening a lot or regularly	frequently	0179
(91) a large project or activity that people do together	enterprise	0112
(92) to go past the limit of something	exceed	0195
(93) a thing that you plan on doing or causing	intention	0118
(94) large in size or amount, or highly detailed or lengthy	extensive	0161
(95) to give someone a job to do	assign	0109
(96) existing in large numbers	numerous	0104
(97) to change something so that it is completely different, usually in a good way	transform	0171
(98) to guess what something will be like	estimate	0106
(99) a bad or immoral habit or behavior	vice	0189
(100) to make a mark on the surface of something by rubbing or cutting it	scratch	0164

Stage 3

Practice makes perfect.
継続は力なり。

□□□ 0201

prime
/ práim /

形 ① main, or most important
主要な

≒ chief

⇔ secondary

ⓘ prime minister（首相、総理大臣）という表現も覚えておこう。

例 The police haven't found the **prime** suspect of the crime yet.
警察はその犯罪の主要な容疑者をまだ見つけていない。

② the best
最高の、最上の

例 **Prime** beef, which is more expensive, usually comes from young, healthy cows.
最高級の牛肉は値段が高めで、ふつう若く健康な雌牛から得られる。

□□□ 0202

limitation
/ lìmətéiʃən /

動 limit ～を制限する

名 something that controls how much of something is possible or allowed
限界

≒ constraint, restriction

ⓘ ふつう複数形で使う。

例 There are **limitations** to what translation software can do.
翻訳ソフトができることには限界がある。

□□□ 0203

reliable
/ rɪláɪəbl /

動 rely 頼る
名 reliance 信頼

形 able to be trusted to help or do things that are needed
信頼できる

≒ trustworthy, dependable, steady

⇔ unreliable, untrustworthy

例 The old man was lucky to have **reliable** friends to help him out.
自分を助けてくれる信頼できる友達がいて、その老人は幸運だった。

□□□ 0204

urge / ə́ːrʤ /

形 urgent 緊急の
名 urgency 緊急

動 to (strongly) try to convince someone to do something

～に強く勧める

≒ persuade, recommend, encourage

⇔ dissuade

ⓘ 〈urge A to *do*〉で「Aに～するように強く勧める」という意味。

例 Many international groups are **urging** countries to stop using nuclear power.

多くの国際団体が国々に原子力を使うのをやめるよう強く求めている。

名 a need or desire for something that is felt strongly

衝動、本能

≒ compulsion

例 Her **urge** to eat sweets when stressed is unbearable.

彼女はストレスを感じると、甘いものを食べたい衝動を抑えられない。

□□□ 0205

extraordinary / ɪkstrɔ́ːrdənèri /

副 extraordinarily 異常に

形 ① very different from something that is seen to be normal

異常な、驚くべき

≒ remarkable, unusual

⇔ ordinary

🔑 〈extra- (外に) +ordinary (正常な)〉

例 The race was **extraordinary**; three people tied for first place.

そのレースは驚くべきものだった。3人が同着1位になったのだ。

0205 語

② extremely good or impressive

非凡な、素晴らしい

≒ fantastic, amazing, wonderful

⇔ terrible, awful

例 The service at the restaurant was just average, but the food was **extraordinary**.

そのレストランのサービスはごく平均的なものだったが、料理は素晴らしかった。

□□□ **0206**

innovation / ìnəvéɪʃən /

動 innovate ～を革新する、導入する
形 innovative 革新的な

名 ① the act of introducing new ideas or methods

革新、(新しい事物の)導入

≒ advancement

🔑 〈in- (中に) +nov (新しい) + -ation (名詞)〉

例 The fast pace of technological **innovation** is hard to keep up with.

技術革新の速いペースにはついていくのが難しい。

---

② a new thing that people come up with

新機軸、新しい工夫

例 Driverless cars are the latest **innovation** in the car industry.

無人自動車は自動車産業における最新の画期的発明だ。

□□□ **0207**

disorder / dɪsɔ́ːrdər /

形 disordered 無秩序な

名 ① something wrong with your body or mind that is not normal or healthy

(心身の) 障害

≒ ailment, affliction

例 The girl developed an eating **disorder** when she was in high school and became very skinny.

その女の子は高校生のときに摂食障害になり、痩せこけてしまった。

---

② a lack of organization in a situation or environment

無秩序

≒ chaos

⇔ order

例 Her tax papers were in a state of **disorder**, so she couldn't find anything.

彼女の納税用の書類はごちゃごちゃになっていて、彼女は何も見つけられなかった。

□□□ 0208

fare
/ féər /

名 the money a person needs to pay to travel on buses, boats, etc.

乗車料金、運賃

≒ cost, price

ⓘ charge（サービス料金）、fee（手数料、謝礼）もあわせて覚えておこう。

例 Bus **fares** were increased so that drivers' salaries could be raised.

運転手の給料を上げられるようにバス料金が値上げされた。

□□□ 0209

rub
/ ráb /

動 to press two things together and move them back and forth

～をこする

ⓘ rubber（ゴム）の元の意味は「こするもの」。

例 She **rubbed** her hands together to try to warm them up.

彼女は両手を暖めようとこすり合わせた。

□□□ 0210

storage
/ stɔ́ːrɪʤ /　動 store ～を貯蔵する

名 ① space where you put things that are not currently being used

貯蔵庫、保管場所

例 Apartments in Tokyo usually don't have a lot of **storage** because they are small.

東京のアパートは狭いので、たいてい収納スペースがあまりない。

0210語

② the act of putting something that is not being used in a place where it can be kept safe for later use

貯蔵、保管

例 The basement of the house is used mostly for **storage**.

その家の地下室は主に保管用に使われている。

□□□ **0211**

specialize

/ spéʃəlàɪz /

形 special 特別な
名 specialization 専門化
名 specialty 得意分野

動 to limit your business or what you study to a specific thing

専門に扱う、専門に研究する

≒ focus

ⓘ イギリス英語では specialise ともつづる。

例 After entering graduate school, the woman decided to **specialize** in German linguistics.

その女性は大学院に入るとドイツ言語学を専門に研究することにした。

□□□ **0212**

venture

/ véntʃər /

名 a new thing you start that is usually risky, such as a project or business

冒険的事業、投機

≒ endeavor

ⓘ adventure（冒険）の ad が消えてできた語。

例 The man decided to pursue a new joint business **venture** with his best friend.

その男性は親友と新しい共同ベンチャービジネスを推し進めることにした。

□□□ **0213**

grocery

/ gróʊsəri /

名 ① a shop that sells food and household supplies

スーパーマーケット、食料雑貨店

≒ supermarket

ⓘ 米語では grocery store とするのが一般的。

例 Buying food at a **grocery** store is much cheaper than going to restaurants.

食料雑貨店で食品を買う方がレストランに行くよりずっと安い。

② food bought at a store (to take home)

食料品

例 He loves cooking gourmet meals, so he spends a lot of money on **groceries**.

彼は豪華な料理を作るのが大好きで、食料品に大金を費やしている。

□□□ 0214

depart

/ dɪpáːrt / 名 departure 出発

動 to leave somewhere 出発する

⇔ arrive

例 The train to Hakone will **depart** at 10:15 a.m.

箱根行きの列車は午前10時15分に出る。

□□□ 0215

initially

/ ɪníʃəli / 形 initial 最初の
動 initiate 〜を始める
名 initiation 加入；開始

副 happening at the start of something 初めに、初めのうちは

≒ originally, at the beginning

⇔ finally, at the end

例 There were **initially** four cats in the garden, and now there are seven.

初めは庭に4匹の猫がいたが、今は7匹になっている。

□□□ 0216

bold

/ bóʊld /

形 not afraid of danger or difficult situations 大胆な、勇気のある

≒ daring, brave

⇔ timid, cowardly

例 North America was settled by many **bold** Europeans.

多くの勇気あるヨーロッパ人が北米に移住した。

□□□ 0217

script

/ skrípt /

名 the written part of things such as movies and plays 台本

0217語

≒ story, plot, narrative

ⓘ scribe は「書く」を意味する語根で、script は「書かれたもの」。

例 The actor agreed to appear in the movie without even reading the **script**.

その俳優は台本すら読まずにその映画に出ることに同意した。

☐☐☐ **0218**

trace

/ tréɪs /

形 traceable 追跡できる
名 traceability 追跡可能性、
トレーサビリティ

動 **to follow something back to where it came from**

〜の跡をたどる

ⓘ track（跡、足跡）と同語源語。

例 She **traced** her footsteps and found where she had dropped the key.

彼女は自分の足跡をたどり、鍵を落とした場所を見つけた。

名 **a mark or sign that someone or something was in a particular place**

跡、形跡

例 The thieves left no **trace** behind and were never found by the police.

その窃盗犯たちは何の痕跡も残さず、決して警察に見つからなかった。

☐☐☐ **0219**

imply

/ ɪmplái /

名 implication 言外の意味
形 implicit 暗黙の

動 **to say something without directly saying it**

〜をほのめかす、暗に言う

≒ suggest, hint

🔑 ⟨im-（中に）+ply（折る）⟩

例 Early reports in the newspaper **implied** that the man's death was a suicide.

新聞の第一報は、その男性の死が自殺であることを示唆していた。

☐☐☐ **0220**

continuous

/ kəntínjuəs /

動 continue 続く
副 continuously 連続的に

形 **happening or existing without stopping**

続いている

≒ uninterrupted, steady

⇔ intermittent, unsteady

ⓘ continuousは「ずっと続いている」、continualは「途切れ途切れに続く」というニュアンス。

例 The battery in the cell phone can stay charged for up to five **continuous** hours of use.

その携帯電話のバッテリーは、最長で連続して5時間使っても持つ。

□□□ 0221

awful

/ ɔ́ːfl /　副 awfully ひどく

形 very bad and not pleasant

ひどい、嫌な

≒ nasty, terrible

⇔ lovely, wonderful

例 Andrew gets **awful** headaches whenever it rains.

アンドリューは雨が降るといつもひどい頭痛を起こす。

□□□ 0222

literally

/ lítərəli /　形 literal 文字通りの

副 used to stress that something said is true (even if it is hard to believe)

文字通り（に）

≒ actually, truthfully, really

⇔ figuratively, metaphorically

💡〈liter（文字）+-al（形容詞）+ -ly（副詞）〉

例 Her birthday party was attended by **literally** hundreds of people.

彼女の誕生日パーティーには文字通り何百人もの人が参加した。

□□□ 0223

generous

/ dʒénərəs /　副 generously 気前よく 名 generosity 気前のよさ

形 giving and sharing things with others even though you do not have to

物惜しみしない、気前のよい

≒ benevolent, considerate

⇔ greedy, mean

例 Even though they had little money, the couple was always very **generous** to charities.

その夫婦にはほとんどお金がなかったが、慈善活動には常に物惜しみしなかった。

□□□ 0224

notion

/ nóʊʃən /

名 an idea or opinion

考え

≒ concept

例 The husband and wife have different **notions** of what it means to be a parent.

その夫婦は親とはどういうものかについての考えが違う。

0224語

107

□□□ 0225

abandon
/ əbǽndən /

形 abandoned 見捨てられた
名 abandonment 放棄

動 ① to give up on doing or having something

〜を断念する、あきらめる

≒ quit

⇔ start, take up

ⓘ with abandon（気ままに）という表現も覚えておこう。

例 After many years of hard work, he **abandoned** the idea of becoming an author.

彼は長年努力した末、作家になる夢をあきらめた。

② to leave something behind and not return for it

〜を捨てる、放棄する

≒ desert, dump

例 Three kittens were **abandoned** outside of the convenience store.

3匹の子猫がそのコンビニエンスストアの外に捨てられていた。

□□□ 0226

keen
/ kíːn /

副 keenly 熱心に；鋭敏に

形 ① very excited and having a lot of interest in something

熱心な、熱中した

≒ curious, eager

⇔ indifferent

例 Sydney was very **keen** to read the next book in her favorite series.

シドニーはお気に入りのシリーズの次作を読みたくて仕方がなかった。

② showing the ability to think clearly and understand difficult things

頭の切れる、鋭敏な

≒ shrewd

例 The boy has a **keen** mind and can solve most problems easily.

その男の子は頭がよく、ほとんどの問題を簡単に解くことができる。

108

□□□ 0227

funeral

/ fjú:nərəl /

名 a ceremony that is held to honor and remember someone who has died

葬式

≒ memorial

例 Wearing black to a **funeral** is common in many countries.

多くの国では葬式に黒い服を着ていくのが一般的だ。

□□□ 0228

boundary

/ báʊndəri /

名 something, such as a line, that shows where one area ends and another one starts

境界（線）

≒ border

🔑〈bound（境界）+-ary（場所）〉

例 The **boundary** between Tokyo and Kanagawa is marked by the Tama River.

多摩川が東京と神奈川の境界をなしている。

□□□ 0229

initiative

/ ɪníʃətɪv /

名 ① the chance to do something bold (before someone else does it)

主導権、率先

≒ opportunity

例 If you want to go on a date, you'll have to take the **initiative** and ask her out.

デートに行きたいなら、自分から行動を起こして彼女を誘いなさい。

0229語

② a plan that has been designed to solve a problem

構想

≒ procedure, program

例 The mayor proposed some new **initiatives** to reduce poverty in the city.

市長は市内の貧困を減らすための新構想を提案した。

☐☐☐ **0230**

sweep

/ swíːp / 形 sweeping 広範囲な

動 **to use a broom or brush to remove dirt, dust, etc.**

〜を掃く

≒ mop

ⓘ sweep-swept-sweptと活用する。

例 He **swept** the kitchen while his sister vacuumed the living room.

彼はキッチンを掃き、その間、妹は居間に掃除機をかけた。

☐☐☐ **0231**

aggressive

/ əgrésɪv / 名 aggression 攻撃

形 **showing a high amount of energy, anger, or a desire to fight**

攻撃的な

⇔ relaxed, easy-going

🔑 〈ag- (〜に) +gress (進む) + -ive (形容詞)〉

例 The boy was often very **aggressive** with his teacher, pushing her when he wanted something.

その男の子はしばしば先生に対してとても攻撃的で、何かが欲しいと先生を押したりした。

☐☐☐ **0232**

altogether

/ ɔːltəgéðər /

副 ① **completely**

完全に、すっかり

≒ entirely ⇔ partly

ⓘ not altogetherだと「完全に…というわけではない」という部分否定になる。

例 If we don't do something about climate change, the Great Barrier Reef may disappear **altogether**.

気候変動について何かしなければ、グレートバリアリーフは完全に消滅してしまうかもしれない。

② **with everything added together**

全部で

例 They spent 500 dollars **altogether** on their shopping trip.

彼らは買い物に出かけて合計500ドル使った。

□□□ 0233

legislation / lèʤɪsléɪʃən /

動 legislate 法律を制定する
名 legislature 立法府
形 legislative 立法の

名 ① a law or a group of laws that the government has made

法律

例 The world needs more **legislation** that protects the environment.

世界は環境を守る法律をもっと必要としている。

② the act of the government making new laws

立法

例 One of the most important jobs in government is **legislation**.

政治の最も重要な仕事の一つは立法だ。

□□□ 0234

forgive / fərgív /

動 to stop showing anger about something someone did

～を許す

≒ excuse, pardon   ⇔ blame, condemn

ⓘ forgive-forgave-forgivenと活用する。

例 The girl **forgave** her brother for breaking her doll after he said sorry.

その女の子は、兄が謝ると、彼が人形を壊したことを許した。

□□□ 0235

strip / stríp /

動 to take something away from someone with force

～を奪う、剥奪する

0235語

≒ remove, deprive, withdraw

⇔ supply, offer, give

ⓘ 〈strip＋人＋of A〉（人からAを奪う）の形で押さえておこう。

例 The organization **stripped** him of the title when it was discovered he had been using illegal drugs.

その団体は彼が違法薬物を使用していたことがわかると彼のタイトルを剥奪した。

□□□ 0236

welfare

/ wélfèər /

名 ① a program run by the government to give money to people who need it

生活保護

≒ benefit

例 **Welfare** programs help keep people from becoming homeless.

生活保護制度によって人々はホームレスにならずに済む。

② the state of being well

幸福

≒ well-being

例 Parents usually have their children's **welfare** in mind when punishing them.

子どもにお仕置きをするとき、親はふつう子どもの幸福を考えている。

□□□ 0237

cheat

/ tʃíːt /

動 to go against a law or rule to gain an advantage

不正をする

ⓘ テストの文脈では「カンニング（をする）」の意味になる。また「不正をする人」という名詞の意味もある。

例 The country's Olympic team was caught **cheating** on their drug tests.

その国のオリンピックチームは薬物検査で不正をしているところを見つかった。

□□□ 0238

neat

/ níːt /　　副 neatly きちんと

形 clean and in order

きちんとした

≒ tidy, organized

⇔ disorganized, messy

例 Having a **neat** room is important to having a stress-free life.

ストレスのない生活を送るには、部屋をきれいにしておくことが大切だ。

□□□ 0239

exclude / ıksklú:d /

名 exclusion 除外
形 exclusive 排他的な
前 excluding ～を除いて

動 **to leave out something or someone**

～を除外する

⇔ include

🔑 〈ex-（外に）+clude（閉じる）〉

例 The prices written on the packages **exclude** tax.

パッケージについた値段には税金が含まれていない。

□□□ 0240

justify / ʤʌ́stəfàɪ /

形 justified 理にかなった
名 justification 正当化

動 **to be or give a good reason for something**

～を正当化する

≒ rationalize, support, defend

🔑 〈just（正しい）+-ify（～にする）〉

例 She tried to **justify** throwing away the apple by saying it was damaged.

彼女はリンゴが傷んでいたと言ってそれを捨てたことを正当化しようとした。

□□□ 0241

glory / glɔ́:ri /

形 glorious 栄光の、輝かしい
動 glorify ～に栄誉を与える

名 **honor or praise that is received publicly**

栄光、名誉

≒ prestige

⇔ criticism, condemnation

例 John earned **glory** from the village after killing the wolf.

ジョンはそのオオカミを殺して村中からたたえられた。

□□□ 0242

precise / prɪsáɪs /

副 precisely 正確に
名 precision 正確さ

0242語

形 **very accurate**

正確な

≒ exact, specific

⇔ imprecise, vague

例 The dressmaker took **precise** measurements for the bride's wedding dress.

仕立て屋は花嫁のウェディングドレスの寸法を正確に測った。

□□□ **0243**

substantial
/ səbstǽnʃəl /

圖 substantially 相当に

形 large in amount, size, or number
相当な、かなりの

≒ considerable, significant, generous

⇔ inconsiderable, little

例 Changing banks could save us a **substantial** amount of money.

銀行を変えるとかなりの金額を節約できるかもしれない。

□□□ **0244**

mess
/ més /

形 messy 散らかった

名 a very dirty or untidy state
乱雑、散らかった状態

例 Her mother wouldn't let her cook because she always made a **mess** in the kitchen.

彼女はいつもキッチンを散らかしてしまうので、母親は彼女に料理をさせなかった。

□□□ **0245**

ultimate
/ ʌ́ltəmɪ̀y /

圖 ultimately 最終的に、結局

形 the best or most extreme
最大の、究極の

≒ supreme

⇔ inferior, lowest

例 Mr. Smith became known as the **ultimate** baker after winning a contest on TV.

スミスさんはテレビのコンテストで優勝してから、究極のパン職人として知られるようになった。

□□□ **0246**

criticize
/ krítəsàɪz /

形 critical 批評の
名 criticism 批評、批判
名 critic 批評家、評論家

動 to talk about the problems someone or something has
～を批判する

≒ judge, scrutinize

⇔ approve, praise

ⓘ イギリス英語では criticise ともつづる。

例 She did not feel confident because her mother always **criticized** her.

彼女は母親にいつもけなされていたので、自信がなかった。

□□□ **0247**

yield / jíːld /

動 ① to produce something, such as a crop

～を産出する

例 The soil did not **yield** good harvests for many years.

その土壌では長年、実りがよくなかった。

② to make money from something

〈利益など〉を生む

例 The tax increase should **yield** a lot of money for the government.

増税は政府に多額の歳入をもたらすはずだ。

名 the amount that is made by a plant, farm, etc.

収穫量、産出高

≒ harvest

例 Because of the typhoon, this year's apple **yield** wasn't as good as usual.

台風のせいで今年のリンゴの収穫量は例年ほどではなかった。

□□□ **0248**

companion / kəmpǽnjən /

名 a person or animal that you (like to) spend time with

仲間、連れ

≒ friend, comrade, partner

⇔ enemy, stranger

ⓘ companion animalとは「連れ合いの動物」、つまり「ペット」のこと。

🔑〈com- (共に) +pan (パン) + -ion (人)〉

0248語

例 For many people, the person they marry becomes their lifelong **companion**.

多くの人にとって、結婚相手は生涯を共にする人になる。

□□□ **0249**

lean / líːn /

動 to bend or move from a straight position to a sloping position

上体を曲げる

≒ tilt

ⓘ lean on（〜によりかかる）という表現も覚えておこう。

例 They **leaned** forward to smell the roses on the table.

彼らはテーブルの上のバラのにおいをかごうと体をかがめた。

形 having little to no fat

脂肪分の少ない、締まった

⇔ fatty

例 **Lean** meats are more popular in America than in Japan.

赤身の肉は日本よりもアメリカで人気がある。

□□□ **0250**

strain / stréin /

名 ① a feeling of stress and worry caused by trying to do too much

緊張

≒ anxiety, pressure, tension

⇔ ease, relief, relaxation

ⓘ 同じつづりで「（人・生物の）血統」という意味もある。

例 The **strain** of trying to find a new job was causing him to lose sleep.

新しい仕事を見つけようという緊張で彼はよく眠れなかった。

---

② something that is not easy to deal with

負担

≒ burden

例 Starting the new business put a **strain** on their personal finances.

新しい会社の立ち上げは彼らの個人資産の負担になった。

116

□□□ 0251

prior

/ práɪər /

图 priority 優先事項

形 existing at an earlier time

（時間・順番が）前の、先の

≒ previous, preceding

⇔ latter, following

ⓘ prior to（〜に先立って）の形で押さえておこう。

例 **Prior** to meeting her husband, the woman had never tried sushi.

その女性は夫と出会う前にはすしを食べたことがなかった。

□□□ 0252

fabric

/ fǽbrɪk /

图 material that is made by weaving or knitting threads together

布地、織物

≒ cloth, textile

例 The company makes all of their clothes with recycled **fabrics**.

その会社はすべての服をリサイクルされた布地で作っている。

□□□ 0253

regret

/ rɪgrét /

形 regretful 後悔した
形 regrettable 残念な

動 to feel unhappy or sorry about something that you did or did not do

〜を後悔する、残念に思う

≒ lament

例 Mrs. Andrews **regrets** that she didn't go to university when she was young.

アンドリューさんは若いときに大学に行かなかったことを後悔している。

0253 語

图 a feeling of unhappiness or sadness that you did or did not do something

後悔

例 She has no **regrets** about leaving the small town she grew up in.

彼女は自分が育った小さな町を出たことにまったく後悔がない。

□□□ 0254

withdraw

/ wıðdrɔ́ː / 名 withdrawal 撤退、撤兵

動 ① to leave a place and go to a different place

退く、退出する

≒ exit

⇔ remain, stay

ⓘ withdraw-withdrew-withdrawnと活用する。

例 After drinking their tea, they **withdrew** to their rooms to study.

お茶を飲むと、彼らは勉強するために自室へ退いた。

---

② to leave an area (usually refers to soldiers)

撤退する

≒ retreat, pull back

例 The soldiers **withdrew** from their posts after the war was over.

戦争終結後、兵士たちは駐屯地から撤退した。

---

③ to take money out of a bank account

〈預金〉を引き出す

⇔ deposit

例 He forgot his PIN, so he couldn't **withdraw** money at the ATM.

彼は暗証番号を忘れて、ATMでお金をおろせなかった。

□□□ 0255

flame

/ fléɪm /

名 the hot and glowing part that is seen when a fire burns

炎、火炎

≒ blaze

ⓘ -able（できる）のついたflammable（可燃性の）という語も覚えておこう。

例 The **flames** turned blue when the scientist added copper to the fire.

科学者が火に銅を入れると、炎が青くなった。

□□□ **0256**

luxury
/ lʌ́gʒəri /

形 luxurious ぜいたくな、豪華な

名 ① **a condition of great comfort or wealth**

ぜいたく

≒ affluence, opulence

⇔ poverty

例 The little boy's dream was to live in **luxury** when he grew up.

その小さな男の子の夢は、大きくなったらぜいたくに暮らすことだった。

② **something that is expensive and not needed**

ぜいたく品

≒ indulgence, extravagance

例 Most people cannot buy **luxuries** because their salary is too low.

ほとんどの人は給料が少なすぎてぜいたく品を買えない。

□□□ **0257**

bind
/ báind /

名 binder バインダー

動 **to tie something tightly**

〜を縛る

≒ fasten

⇔ untie

ⓘ bind-bound-boundと活用する。

例 They **bound** the branches together to build a small raft.

彼らは小さないかだを作るためにその枝をまとめて縛った。

0258語

□□□ **0258**

fortunate
/ fɔ́:rtʃənət /

副 fortunately 幸いにも
名 fortune 運

形 **having good things happen to you**

幸運な

≒ lucky

⇔ unfortunate

例 She was **fortunate** enough to see the exhibition during her trip to Europe.

彼女は幸運にもヨーロッパ旅行中にその展覧会を見ることができた。

☐☐☐ 0259

quote / kwóut / 图 quotation 引用

動 to exactly repeat something that has been written or said by another person

〜を引用する

≒ cite

例 She **quoted** five different authors in her final essay.

彼女は最後の論文で5人の異なる作家の言葉を引用した。

图 the words of a person that are repeated by someone else in writing or speech

引用 (文)

≒ citation

例 Many fantasy books begin with a **quote** by another famous fantasy novel author.

多くのファンタジー本は、別の有名なファンタジー小説家の言葉を引用して始まる。

☐☐☐ 0260

garbage / gá:rbɪʤ /

图 things that are thrown away because they are not wanted or no longer needed

ごみ

≒ rubbish, trash

ⓘ 不可算名詞。

例 Glass is not considered **garbage** and should be recycled after use.

ガラスはごみとは見なされず、使用後にリサイクルされなければならない。

☐☐☐ 0261

anxious / ǽŋkʃəs / 图 anxiety 心配、不安

形 feeling scared or nervous about things that could happen

心配して、気にして

≒ distressed, uneasy

⇔ confident, relaxed

例 She was very **anxious** for her interview for the job.

彼女は仕事の面接のことでとても不安になっていた。

□□□ 0262

margin
/ mɑ́ːrdʒin / 形 marginal 余白の

名 the empty space or area at or near the edge of something

余白

例 He wrote small notes in the **margins** of the book.

彼は本の余白にちょっとメモ書きをした。

□□□ 0263

silly
/ síli /

形 acting or looking stupid and showing a lack of thought

愚かな

≒ ridiculous

例 That man looks **silly** with his shirt on backwards.

あの男はシャツを後ろ前に着ていて、間抜けに見える。

□□□ 0264

sin
/ sín / 形 sinful 罪深い

名 something that people believe is wrong because of religious or moral rules

罪

例 Murder is considered by all people to be a **sin**.

殺人は誰もが罪だと思っている。

□□□ 0265

asset
/ ǽset /

名 a thing that is owned by a person or a company

資産、財産

0265語

≒ resource

⇔ liability

ⓘ 複数形で使うことが多い。

例 All of his **assets** were taken by the bank because he couldn't pay off a loan.

彼はローンを完済できなかったため、全資産を銀行に取られた。

☐☐☐ **0266**

compose / kəmpóuz / 名 composition 構成

動 ① to come together to form or make something

〜を構成する

≒ make up, constitute

⇔ break up, dismantle

🔑 〈com- (共に) +pose (置く)〉

ⓘ composed (落ち着いた) という使い方も重要。

例 Women **composed** about 90% of the people attending the conference.

その会議の出席者の約90%を女性が占めた。

② to make a piece of music or write something

〜を創作する、作曲する

例 It is hard work to **compose** a new piece of music.

新曲を作るのは大変な仕事だ。

☐☐☐ **0267**

whereas / weərǽz /

接 used to connect two statements that show how something is different

〜であるのに対し

≒ while, although

例 Her sister has beautiful blue eyes, **whereas** hers are brown and dull.

彼女のお姉さんはきれいな青い目をしているのに、彼女の目は茶色でくすんでいる。

☐☐☐ **0268**

fame / féɪm / 形 famous 有名な

名 the condition of being known or recognized by many people

名声

≒ renown

例 **Fame** can cause people to lose all privacy in their lives.

有名になると生活上のプライバシーをすべて失う可能性がある。

□□□ 0269

valid
/ vǽlɪd /

名 validity 妥当性、有効性
動 validate ～の正当性を証明する

形 ① acceptable according to the law
有効な

≒ legitimate, lawful, legal

⇔ invalid, illegal, unacceptable

例 Contracts with conditions that are against the law are not **valid**.
法律に反する条項のある契約は有効ではない。

② within reason or fair
根拠がしっかりとした、正当な

≒ reasonable

例 A death in the family is a **valid** reason to miss work.
家族の不幸は仕事を休む正当な理由だ。

□□□ 0270

wander
/ wάːndər /

動 to move around different places without having a goal
さまよう、歩き回る

≒ meander

ⓘ wonder[wʌ́ndər]（不思議に思う）と混同しないように注意。

例 She **wandered** through the park, sometimes stopping to smell the flowers.
彼女は公園を歩き回り、ときどき立ち止まって花のにおいをかいだ。

□□□ 0271

interrupt
/ ìntərʌ́pt /

名 interruption 妨害、中断

0271語

動 to get in the way of something continuous and make it stop
～の邪魔をする、～を中断する

≒ cut short, hold up

🔑 〈inter-（間に）+rupt（破壊する)〉

例 The teacher kept being **interrupted** by two students that were talking during class.
その先生は授業中にしゃべっている2人の生徒に邪魔され続けた。

☐☐☐ 0272

cruise
/ krúːz /

動 ① to travel to multiple places by boat as a vacation

遊覧航海する、クルージングする

≒ sail

例 They **cruised** down the Mississippi River during summer vacation.

彼らは夏休み中にミシシッピ川を遊覧船で下った。

② to continue moving at a steady speed

巡航速度で走る［飛ぶ］

例 Attention passengers: we are now **cruising** at about 30,000 feet.

ご搭乗の皆さま。当機は現在、高度約3万フィートを飛行中です。

☐☐☐ 0273

heritage
/ hérətɪʤ /

名 the traditions and other parts of the history of a group or nation

遺産、伝統

≒ legacy

ⓘ World Heritage Site（世界遺産）という表現も覚えておこう。

例 Remembering their **heritage** is important to immigrant families.

自分たちの伝統を覚えておくことは移民の家族にとって重要だ。

☐☐☐ 0274

accuse
/ əkjúːz /　名 accusation 告訴

動 to blame someone for doing something wrong or illegal

〜を訴える、告訴する

⇔ pardon

🔑 〈ac-（〜に）+cuse（原因）〉

ⓘ 〈accuse A of B〉（AをBの件で訴える）の形で押さえておこう。

例 The men were both **accused** of the murder of their neighbor.

その男たちはどちらも隣人の殺害で告訴された。

124

□□□ 0275

dedicate
/ dédəkèɪt / 名 dedication 献身、専心

動 ① to spend a lot of time and effort doing something (because you think it is important)

～をささげる

≒ commit, devote

例 Jane Goodall **dedicated** her career to studying chimpanzees.

ジェーン・グドールはチンパンジーの研究に人生をささげた。

② to honor someone by attaching their name to a thing or place

～を献じる、～に献辞を記す

例 The tree in front of our school is **dedicated** to a local war hero.

わが校の前にある木は、戦争で活躍した地元の英雄に奉じられている。

□□□ 0276

mature
/ mətʃúər / 名 maturity 成長、成熟

形 having an adult body or showing that you are emotionally an adult

成長した、成熟した

≒ grown-up, developed

⇔ immature, undeveloped

ⓘ premature（早熟な）という語も覚えておこう。

例 Her daughter is only seven years old but is already very **mature** for her age.

彼女の娘はたった7歳だが、その年齢にしてはすでにとても大人びている。

0276語

動 to become a fully developed adult in both mind and body

成長する、成熟する

≒ grow up

例 His son has **matured** into a very smart young man.

彼の息子はとても賢い若者に成長した。

□□□ 0277

certificate

/ sərtífɪkət /

動 certify ～を保証する
名 certification 証明、保証

名 a piece of paper that is official proof of something

証明書

≒ qualification, authorization

ⓘ certは「確かな」を意味する語根で、certain（確かな）なども同語源語。

例 She was given a **certificate** to show that she had passed the highest level of the exam.

彼女はその試験の最難関レベルに合格したことを示す証明書を授与された。

□□□ 0278

assess

/ əsés /

名 assessment 査定

動 to say the amount or value of something officially

～を査定する

≒ judge, evaluate

例 The painting was **assessed** at a value of 20 million dollars.

その絵は2千万ドルの価値があると査定された。

□□□ 0279

scare

/ skéər /

形 scary 怖い

動 to make someone feel fear

～を怖がらせる

≒ frighten, intimidate, terrify

⇔ soothe, assure, calm

例 The children jumped out from behind the sofa, **scaring** their mother.

子どもたちはソファの後ろから飛び出して、母親を怖がらせた。

名 a feeling of fear that comes suddenly

恐怖

≒ fright, terror

例 He thought he had lost his wallet, and it gave him quite a **scare**.

彼は財布をなくしたと思い、とても恐ろしくなった。

□□□ 0280

harvest　　　　　　　　　　　/ háːrvəst /

動 ① to collect a crop

～を収穫する

≒ pick, gather

ⓘ「収穫（高）」という名詞の意味もある。

例 Small towns need more young people to help **harvest** the crops.

小さな町は作物の収穫を手伝ってくれる若者をもっと必要としている。

② to collect something to use

～を集める

≒ gather

例 The people had to **harvest** wood if they wanted to stay warm in the winter.

その人たちは冬に暖かくしていたければ、まきを集めなければならなかった。

□□□ 0281

fade　　　　　　　　　　　/ féɪd /

動 to disappear slowly or grow less bright over time

〈色が〉あせる、〈記憶などが〉薄れる

≒ vanish, dissolve　　⇔ increase, rise

ⓘ fade out（〈光・音が〉だんだん小さくなって消える）はカタカナ語にもなっている。

例 Her mother's jeans had **faded** from black to gray after many washes.

彼女の母親のジーンズは何度も洗ったために黒からグレーに色あせていた。

□□□ 0282

resemble　　　　　　　　/ rɪzémbl /　图 resemblance 類似

動 to look or act like another person or thing

～に似ている

≒ be similar to

⇔ differ from

ⓘ 他動詞である点に注意。進行形にしない。

例 Her eyes **resemble** her mother's.

彼女の目は母親の目に似ている。

□□□ 0283

restrict

/ rɪstríkt / 名 restriction 制限

動 to limit what someone or something is allowed to do or be

～を制限する、限定する

≒ curb, impede

🔑 〈re- (強意) +strict (引き締める)〉

例 Access to the gym is **restricted** to members only.

そのジムの利用は会員に限定されている。

□□□ 0284

gross

/ gróus /

形 including all things

総計の

≒ total, entire

⇔ net

ⓘ oの発音に注意。

例 Her **gross** income was only 20,000 dollars last year.

彼女の去年の総収入はたった2万ドルだった。

□□□ 0285

dominate

/ dá:mənèit / 名 domination 支配
形 dominant 支配的な、優勢な

動 ① to control or have power over another person or thing

～を支配する、～で優位を占める

≒ rule, command, lead

🔑 〈domin (支配する) +-ate (動詞)〉

⇔ follow, obey

例 The queen wanted to **dominate** all of the surrounding countries.

女王は周辺国すべてを支配することを望んだ。

② to be the most important part of a specific thing

～の最も重要な要素となる

≒ control

例 Haruki Murakami still **dominates** the Japanese literature scene overseas.

村上春樹は今でも海外の日本文学部門でトップに君臨している。

□□□ 0286

harsh / háːrʃ /

形 **severe or unkind**

厳しい、過酷な

≒ grim, nasty

⇔ easy, pleasant

例 Five years in prison is a **harsh** punishment for some stolen food.

食べ物をいくらか盗んで懲役5年というのは厳しい処罰だ。

□□□ 0287

equip / ɪkwíp /

名 equipment 装置、備品

動 **to give someone things that they need**

〜に（必要なものを）装備させる

≒ outfit

(i) be equipped with（〜を装備している）の形で押さえておこう。

例 The doctors were **equipped** with face masks to protect themselves from the virus.

医師たちはウイルスから身を守るためにマスクを装着していた。

□□□ 0288

leisure / líːʒər /

名 ① **time when you can do things that you want to do**

暇、自由な時間

≒ free time

(i) ei の発音に注意。

例 In her **leisure**, she likes to translate news stories.

彼女は暇なときにニュース記事を翻訳するのが好きだ。

0288語

② **fun activities that you can do when you are not working**

余暇、娯楽

≒ recreation, relaxation

例 Single mothers often don't have time for **leisure** because they work a lot.

シングルマザーはたくさん働くので、余暇の時間がないことが多い。

☐☐☐ 0289

clue
/ klúː /

名 a hint that can help someone find or understand something

手がかり

≒ tip, key

例 The author put many **clues** in her book so that readers could solve the mystery.

読者がなぞを解けるように、作者は本の中に多くの手がかりを残した。

☐☐☐ 0290

prompt
/ prάːmpt /

動 to cause something to start or happen

～を引き起こす

≒ incite, motivate

ⓘ 〈prompt + A + to do〉（Aに～するよう促す）の形も押さえておこう。

例 The death of the princess **prompted** a major investigation.

その王女の死を受けて大がかりな捜査が行われた。

☐☐☐ 0291

naked
/ néɪkɪd /

形 not being covered by any clothing

裸の

≒ nude, bare, exposed

⇔ clothed

ⓘ ed の発音に注意。

例 Some people find it hard to be **naked** with other people at hot springs.

温泉には他人がいるので、裸になるのに抵抗を感じる人もいる。

☐☐☐ 0292

stir
/ stə́ːr /

動 to mix something in a circular motion

～をかき混ぜる

≒ shake, blend, beat

例 Please keep **stirring** the curry so it doesn't get burned.

カレーが焦げないようにずっとかき混ぜてください。

☐☐☐ 0293

resort

/ rɪzɔ́ːrt /

動 to do something, especially when you have no other choice

(手段に) 頼る、訴える

≒ turn to

例 Without any money, the children had to **resort** to begging for food in the streets.

お金がまったくなかったので、その子どもたちは路上で食べ物を乞うという手段に出るしかなかった。

名 a place people go to for vacations

リゾート地

例 Having a wedding at a Hawaiian **resort** is popular among Japanese couples.

ハワイのリゾートで結婚式を挙げることは、日本人カップルに人気だ。

☐☐☐ 0294

acknowledge

/ əknáːlɪdʒ /

形 acknowledged 広く認められた
名 acknowledgement 承認

動 to say that you accept that something is true

〜を認める

≒ admit

⇔ reject, deny

🔑 ⟨ac- (〜に) +know (知る) +ledge (行為)⟩

例 It is important to **acknowledge** that everyone deals with pain differently.

痛みへの対処法は人それぞれだと認めることが大事だ。

0295 語

☐☐☐ 0295

fancy

/ fǽnsi /

形 not plain or ordinary (often refers to something expensive or fashionable)

高級な、手の込んだ

≒ extravagant, elegant

⇔ cheap

例 All of the girls wore **fancy** dresses to the dinner party.

女の子たちは皆ディナーパーティーに高級服を着ていった。

☐☐☐ **0296**

govern

/ ɡʌ́vərn /

名 government 政府；政治

🔲 to control and lead people in a way that is official (and connected to the government)

〜を統治する、治める

≒ rule, administer

⇔ serve, obey

例 She was chosen to **govern** the people because of her great speaking skills.

彼女には見事な話術があったので、人々の統治者に選ばれた。

☐☐☐ **0297**

evolve

/ ɪváːlv /

名 evolution 進化
形 evolutionary 進化（論）の

🔲 to change over time into something that is often better or more advanced

進化する

≒ develop, grow ⇔ devolve

🔑 〈e-(外に)+volve(回転する)〉

例 Many scientists now believe that birds **evolved** from dinosaurs.

今では多くの科学者が鳥は恐竜から進化したと考えている。

☐☐☐ **0298**

burst

/ báːrst /

🔲 to (make something) break open or break into many pieces

破裂する；〜を破裂させる

≒ erupt, rupture

ⓘ burst-burst-burstと活用する。

例 The balloon **burst** loudly when the child stepped on it.

風船はその子が踏むと大きな音を立てて破裂した。

📛 the act of breaking something open or breaking it into pieces

爆発、破裂

≒ eruption

例 The **burst** of a bubble is exciting for young children.

泡がはじけると小さな子は大喜びする。

132

□□□ 0299

suburb

/ sʌ́bəːrb / 形 suburban 郊外の

名 an area where people live that is close to a larger city

郊外（の一地区）

≒ outskirts

🔑 〈sub-（近くに）+urb（都市）〉

ⓘ the suburbs で集合的に「郊外、近郊」を表す。

例 He wanted a larger home, so he moved out of the city center and into the **suburbs**.

彼はもっと広い家が欲しかったので、都心から郊外へと引っ越した。

□□□ 0300

attribute

/ 動 ətríbjuːt 名 ǽtrəbjùːt / 名 attribution 帰属；属性

動 ① to say that one thing is because of something or someone else

〜を（…に）帰する

≒ credit, blame

🔑 〈at-（〜に）+tribute（割り当てる）〉

ⓘ 動詞のアクセントは ri の位置。〈attribute A to B〉（A を B のためだとする）の形で使う。

例 Mr. Anderson's doctor **attributed** his heart attack to bad eating habits.

アンダーソンさんの医師は、彼の心臓発作をひどい食習慣によるものとした。

② to consider something as being made by someone

〜を（…の）作品と考える

≒ credit

例 It is possible that some of the plays **attributed** to Shakespeare were not written by him.

シェイクスピアの作品と考えられている戯曲のいくつかは彼が書いていない可能性がある。

0300語

名 a normally good quality that someone or something has

特質、特性

例 Both interview candidates have the right **attributes** for the job.

どちらの面接候補者もその職への適性がある。

133

章末ボキャブラリーチェック

次の語義が表す英単語を答えてください。

語義	解答	連番
❶ used to stress that something said is true (even if it is hard to believe)	literally	0222
❷ to give up on doing or having something	abandon	0225
❸ to come together to form or make something	compose	0266
❹ very excited and having a lot of interest in something	keen	0226
❺ the best or most extreme	ultimate	0245
❻ happening at the start of something	initially	0215
❼ to do something, especially when you have no other choice	resort	0293
❽ happening or existing without stopping	continuous	0220
❾ the traditions and other parts of the history of a group or nation	heritage	0273
❿ to leave out something or someone	exclude	0239
⓫ the money a person needs to pay to travel on buses, boats, etc.	fare	0208
⓬ existing at an earlier time	prior	0251
⓭ something, such as a line, that shows where one area ends and another one starts	boundary	0228
⓮ the act of introducing new ideas or methods	innovation	0206
⓯ to use a broom or brush to remove dirt, dust, etc.	sweep	0230
⓰ to (strongly) try to convince someone to do something	urge	0204
⓱ a program run by the government to give money to people who need it	welfare	0236
⓲ a feeling of stress and worry caused by trying to do too much	strain	0250
⓳ to look or act like another person or thing	resemble	0282
⓴ not being covered by any clothing	naked	0291

語義	解答	連番
㉑ time when you can do things that you want to do	l e i s u r e	0288
㉒ to go against a law or rule to gain an advantage	c h e a t	0237
㉓ to talk about the problems someone or something has	c r i t i c i z e	0246
㉔ a law or a group of laws that the government has made	l e g i s l a t i o n	0233
㉕ to follow something back to where it came from	t r a c e	0218
㉖ to (make something) break open or break into many pieces	b u r s t	0298
㉗ something wrong with your body or mind that is not normal or healthy	d i s o r d e r	0207
㉘ to bend or move from a straight position to a sloping position	l e a n	0249
㉙ an idea or opinion	n o t i o n	0224
㉚ the condition of being known or recognized by many people	f a m e	0268
㉛ having an adult body or showing that you are emotionally an adult	m a t u r e	0276
㉜ a piece of paper that is official proof of something	c e r t i f i c a t e	0277
㉝ a shop that sells food and household supplies	g r o c e r y	0213
㉞ to mix something in a circular motion	s t i r	0292
㉟ acting or looking stupid and showing a lack of thought	s i l l y	0263
㊱ showing a high amount of energy, anger, or a desire to fight	a g g r e s s i v e	0231
㊲ completely	a l t o g e t h e r	0232
㊳ able to be trusted to help or do things that are needed	r e l i a b l e	0203
㊴ to say something without directly saying it	i m p l y	0219
㊵ to move around different places without having a goal	w a n d e r	0270
㊶ to travel to multiple places by boat as a vacation	c r u i s e	0272
㊷ to give someone things that they need	e q u i p	0287

語義	解答	連番
❸ to be or give a good reason for something	j u s t i f y	0240
❹ to produce something, such as a crop	y i e l d	0247
❺ to leave a place and go to a different place	w i t h d r a w	0254
❻ including all things	g r o s s	0284
❼ a new thing you start that is usually risky, such as a project or business	v e n t u r e	0212
❽ the written part of things such as movies and plays	s c r i p t	0217
❾ to limit your business or what you study to a specific thing	s p e c i a l i z e	0211
❺⓪ a ceremony that is held to honor and remember someone who has died	f u n e r a l	0227
❺❶ to stop showing anger about something someone did	f o r g i v e	0234
❺❷ something that people believe is wrong because of religious or moral rules	s i n	0264
❺❸ the chance to do something bold (before someone else does it)	i n i t i a t i v e	0229
❺❹ very bad and not pleasant	a w f u l	0221
❺❺ to feel unhappy or sorry about something that you did or did not do	r e g r e t	0253
❺❻ to collect a crop	h a r v e s t	0280
❺❼ to disappear slowly or grow less bright over time	f a d e	0281
❺❽ to tie something tightly	b i n d	0257
❺❾ to take something away from someone with force	s t r i p	0235
❻⓪ a hint that can help someone find or understand something	c l u e	0289
❻❶ large in amount, size, or number	s u b s t a n t i a l	0243
❻❷ to control or have power over another person or thing	d o m i n a t e	0285
❻❸ very different from something that is seen to be normal	e x t r a o r d i n a r y	0205
❻❹ having good things happen to you	f o r t u n a t e	0258

語義	解答	連番
㊺ space where you put things that are not currently being used	s t o r a g e	0210
㊻ to make someone feel fear	s c a r e	0279
㊼ severe or unkind	h a r s h	0286
㊽ feeling scared or nervous about things that could happen	a n x i o u s	0261
㊾ the hot and glowing part that is seen when a fire burns	f l a m e	0255
㊿ used to connect two statements that show how something is different	w h e r e a s	0267
㉛ to change over time into something that is often better or more advanced	e v o l v e	0297
㉜ a condition of great comfort or wealth	l u x u r y	0256
㉝ not plain or ordinary (often refers to something expensive or fashionable)	f a n c y	0295
㉞ to say that you accept that something is true	a c k n o w l e d g e	0294
㉟ to say that one thing is because of something or someone else	a t t r i b u t e	0300
㊱ very accurate	p r e c i s e	0242
㊲ to get in the way of something continuous and make it stop	i n t e r r u p t	0271
㊳ to say the amount or value of something officially	a s s e s s	0278
㊴ a thing that is owned by a person or a company	a s s e t	0265
㊵ giving and sharing things with others even though you do not have to	g e n e r o u s	0223
㊶ honor or praise that is received publicly	g l o r y	0241
㊷ main, or most important	p r i m e	0201
㊸ material that is made by weaving or knitting threads together	f a b r i c	0252
㊹ an area where people live that is close to a larger city	s u b u r b	0299
㊺ not afraid of danger or difficult situations	b o l d	0216
㊻ a very dirty or untidy state	m e s s	0244

語義	解答	連番
❸ the empty space or area at or near the edge of something	m a r g i n	0262
❸ to leave somewhere	d e p a r t	0214
❸ to cause something to start or happen	p r o m p t	0290
❹ to exactly repeat something that has been written or said by another person	q u o t e	0259
❹ to control and lead people in a way that is official (and connected to the government)	g o v e r n	0296
❹ things that are thrown away because they are not wanted or no longer needed	g a r b a g e	0260
❹ acceptable according to the law	v a l i d	0269
❹ to limit what someone or something is allowed to do or be	r e s t r i c t	0283
❹ to press two things together and move them back and forth	r u b	0209
❹ to spend a lot of time and effort doing something (because you think it is important)	d e d i c a t e	0275
❹ clean and in order	n e a t	0238
❹ to blame someone for doing something wrong or illegal	a c c u s e	0274
❹ a person or animal that you (like to) spend time with	c o m p a n i o n	0248
❿ something that controls how much of something is possible or allowed	l i m i t a t i o n	0202

Stage 4

Slow and steady wins the race.
急がば回れ。

☐☐☐ 0301

furthermore / fə́ːrðərmɔ̀ːr /

副 in addition to something already said　　さらに

≒ moreover, besides

例 She is never late for work. **Furthermore**, her work is always done perfectly.

彼女は一度も仕事に遅れたことがない。それに、常に仕事を完ぺきに行う。

☐☐☐ 0302

thorough / θə́ːrou /　副 thoroughly 徹底的に

形 complete or absolute　　徹底的な、完全な

≒ detailed, exhaustive

⇔ incomplete, unfinished

ⓘ 発音に注意。

例 The child was being a **thorough** nuisance, and her mother couldn't get anything done.

その子は徹底的に邪魔をしていたので、母親は何も終えることができなかった。

☐☐☐ 0303

explode / ɪksplóud /

名 explosion 爆発
形 explosive 爆発性の

動 to break apart suddenly and violently　　爆発する

≒ burst

例 The airplane **exploded** as it crashed into the ground.

その飛行機は地面に激突するのと同時に爆発した。

☐☐☐ 0304

shortage / ʃɔ́ːrtɪʤ /　形 short 不足した

名 a state in which there is a lack of something that is needed　　不足

≒ shortfall

⇔ surplus, extra

例 Water **shortage** is one of the biggest problems of this century.

水不足は今世紀最大の問題の一つだ。

□□□ 0305

stare / stéər /

動 **to look directly at something or someone for a long time without looking somewhere else**

じっと見る、凝視する

≒ glare

(i) stare at (〜を凝視する) の形で押さえておこう。

例 The dog **stared** at the television after he heard dogs barking from the speakers.

その犬は、スピーカーから犬の ほえ声が聞こえると、テレビを じっと見た。

□□□ 0306

insight / ínsàɪt / 形 insightful 洞察に富んだ

名 the ability to understand things deeply

洞察力、識見

≒ intuition

🔑 〈in- (中) +sight (見ること)〉

⇔ ignorance

例 It is important for leaders to have knowledge and **insight** so they can solve problems.

リーダーは問題を解決できるよ うに知識と洞察力を持つことが 重要だ。

□□□ 0307

accommodate / əká:mədèɪt / 名 accommodation 宿泊設備

動 ① to have room for someone or something

〜を収容できる

≒ contain

0307語

例 This restaurant can **accommodate** 150 guests at one time.

このレストランは一度に150人 の客を入れられる。

② to give something that is needed or wanted, such as time or consideration

〈要求など〉に応じる、 便宜を図る

例 Changing his schedule to **accommodate** client needs wasn't always easy.

彼が顧客の要望に合わせてス ケジュールを変更することは必 ずしも簡単ではなかった。

□□□ **0308**

entitle

/ ɪntáɪtl /

名 entitlement 資格

動 ① to title something

〜に（…と）表題をつける

≒ designate, call, dub

例 The book was **entitled** *My Biggest Dream* in memory of the author's grandfather.

その本は著者の祖父をしのんで『私の最大の夢』という書名がつけられた。

② to give someone a right to do something

〈人〉に資格を与える

≒ authorize, enable

例 This membership card **entitles** you to a 5% discount on all purchases.

この会員カードですべての購入品が5%割引になります。

□□□ **0309**

mere

/ míər /

副 merely ただ、単に

形 used when talking about something or someone that is small or not very important

ほんの、単なる

≒ insignificant, minor

例 The girl was a **mere** child when she lost her whole family in a fire.

火事で家族全員を失ったとき、その女の子はまだほんの子どもだった。

□□□ **0310**

grave

/ gréɪv /

名 the place in the ground where a dead body is buried

墓、墓場

≒ tomb

ⓘ 同じつづりで「重大な」という意味の形容詞もある。

例 Japanese people often visit family members' **graves** in March.

日本人はよく3月に家族の墓を訪れる。

□□□ 0311

shield / ʃíːld /

名 something that is used to protect or defend someone or something

防御物、盾

≒ protection, armor

例 The knight lifted his **shield** to block the sword.

騎士は剣を食い止めるために盾を持ち上げた。

動 to protect someone or something from an attack or experience

～を保護する、かばう

≒ cover, defend

例 The man put his hand above his eyes to **shield** them from the sun.

その男性は日光から目を守るために、両目の上に手をかざした。

□□□ 0312

perceive / pərsíːv /

名 perception 知覚；認識
形 perceptible 知覚できる

動 to realize or notice something

～に気づく、～を知覚する

≒ identify, distinguish

⇔ miss, overlook

例 Her father easily **perceived** that she had been crying because of her red eyes.

彼女の赤い目から、父親は彼女が泣いていたことにすぐに気づいた。

□□□ 0313

delight / dıláıt /

形 delighted 喜んでいる
形 delightful 愉快な

名 a very strong feeling of happiness or pleasure

大喜び

≒ joy

⇔ sorrow

例 The children watched the fireworks with pure **delight**.

子どもたちは心から喜んで花火を見物した。

0313語

☐☐☐ 0314

genetic
/ dʒənétɪk /

名 gene 遺伝子
副 genetically 遺伝子的に

形 relating to biological information passed from generation to generation

遺伝の、遺伝的な

≒ hereditary

⇔ acquired

例 Breast cancer is a type of **genetic** disease that can be passed from mother to daughter.

乳がんは母から娘に受け継がれる可能性がある一種の遺伝性疾患だ。

☐☐☐ 0315

overlook
/ òʊvərlók /

動 ① to fail to notice or see something

〜を見落とす、見過ごす

≒ pass over, miss

例 The police **overlooked** an important clue at the crime scene.

警察は犯行現場にあった重要な手がかりを見落とした。

② to not pay attention to something or someone

〜を大目に見る

≒ ignore, neglect

例 He had a habit of **overlooking** the faults in his girlfriends until it was too late.

彼にはガールフレンドの欠点を手遅れになるまでずっと大目に見る傾向があった。

③ to have a view of something (that is lower)

〜を見下ろす

例 The couple stayed at a hotel that **overlooked** the ocean for their honeymoon.

その夫婦はハネムーンで海を見下ろすホテルに泊まった。

□□□ 0316

disadvantage

/ dìsədvǽntɪʤ / 形 disadvantageous 不利な

名 ① something that makes something harder to do than it is for others

不利な状況

≒ handicap

⇔ advantage

例 He was at a **disadvantage** in the race because his shoes were damaged.

彼はシューズが損傷したためそのレースで不利な状況になった。

② a feature of something that is bad or unwanted

不都合なこと、デメリット

≒ downside

⇔ advantage, upside

例 There are many **disadvantages** to the new tax payment system.

新納税制度には多くのデメリットがある。

□□□ 0317

stake

/ stéɪk /

名 ① an interest or share that someone can hold in a business

出資(金)、株保有

ⓘ at stake (危険にさらされて) という表現も重要。

例 He had a **stake** in the company that just went bankrupt.

彼は倒産したばかりの会社の株を持っていた。

0317語

② something that you can win or lose in a game or contest

賭け金

≒ bet

例 The poker game had high **stakes**, and the winner would go home very rich.

そのポーカーゲームは賭け金が高く、勝者は大金を持ち帰ることになった。

☐☐☐ **0318**

glance / glǽns /

名 a quick look at someone or something

ちらりと見ること

≒ peek, glimpse

ⓘ at a glance（一目見ただけで）という表現も覚えておこう。

例 The girl took one last **glance** at her notes before the test started.

その女の子は試験が始まる前、最後にノートをちょっと見返した。

☐☐☐ **0319**

seemingly / síːmɪŋli / 形 seeming 見せかけの

副 appearing to be true, but without certainty

外見上は、見たところ

≒ apparently

例 There is **seemingly** no reason for that girl to be late for school every day.

あの女子生徒が毎日学校に遅刻する理由は何もないように思われる。

☐☐☐ **0320**

pregnant / prégnənt / 名 pregnancy 妊娠

形 having a baby or babies growing inside the body

妊娠した

≒ expecting, carrying

例 **Pregnant** women are at more risk of health problems than others.

妊婦はほかの人より健康上の問題を起こす危険性が高い。

☐☐☐ **0321**

tackle / tǽkl /

動 to deal with something that is not easy

〈問題など〉に取り組む

≒ confront, engage

ⓘ 他動詞である点に注意。ラグビーなどの「タックル」もtackle。

例 The boy decided to **tackle** his math homework after eating a snack.

その男の子はおやつを食べてから数学の宿題に取り組むことにした。

□□□ 0322

innocent

/ ínəsnt /

图 innocence 無罪

形 not guilty of doing something wrong, such as a crime

無実の、無罪の

≒ blameless

🔑 〈in-(否定)+noc(害のある)+ -ent(形容詞)〉

例 The woman was clearly **innocent** because she was at home when the crime occurred.

犯罪が起きたとき家にいたので、その女性は明らかに無実だった。

□□□ 0323

burden

/ bə́:rdn /

形 burdensome 重荷となる

名 something heavy that is being carried, or a thought or feeling that is hard to accept

負担、荷物

≒ difficulty, hardship

例 The man had to shoulder the **burden** of caring for his aging parents alone.

その男性は年老いた両親を一人で介護する重荷を背負わなければならなかった。

□□□ 0324

spill

/ spíl /

動 to make something come out of a container, usually by mistake

～をこぼす

ⓘ spill-spilled/spilt-spilled/spiltと活用する。

0325 語

例 The child tripped and **spilled** his milk all over the floor.

その子はつまずいて、牛乳を床中にこぼした。

□□□ 0325

excessive

/ ɪksésɪv /

名 excess 超過
副 excessively 過度に

形 doing more than what is normal or proper

過度な

≒ superfluous

⇔ moderate, appropriate

例 She has trouble sleeping because she drinks **excessive** amounts of coffee.

彼女はコーヒーを過度に飲むので、眠れなくて困っている。

☐☐☐ **0326**

concrete

/ káːnkriːt /

形 connected to something specific, not a broad or general idea

具体的な、有形の

≒ solid, real

⇔ abstract, indefinite

例 **Concrete** examples of word use are important for language learners.

単語の具体的な使用例は言語を学ぶ人にとって重要だ。

名 a material made of cement, sand, broken rocks, and water that is used to build things

コンクリート

例 They built the bridge out of **concrete**.

その橋はコンクリートで造られた。

☐☐☐ **0327**

spoil

/ spɔ́ɪl /

動 ① to have a bad effect on something or ruin it

～を台なしにする、だめにする

≒ harm, destroy

⇔ fix, repair

例 The party was **spoiled** by the host's bad mood.

そのパーティーは主催者が不機嫌だったために台なしになった。

② to give someone everything that they want (usually a child)

〈子供など〉を甘やかす

≒ pamper

例 His grandparents **spoiled** him when he was a child.

彼は子どものころ、祖父母に甘やかされた。

□□□ 0328

nod / ná:d /

動 to move your head up and down to show that you agree or understand

うなずく

(i) 首を横に振るは shake *one's* head。

例 His aunt asked him if he wanted some chocolate, and he **nodded**.

彼はおばにチョコレートが欲しいか聞かれてうなずいた。

□□□ 0329

sustain / səstéin /

形 sustainable 持続できる
名 sustenance 生命の維持

動 to provide the things needed for something or someone to exist or continue

～を維持する

≒ preserve, supply, maintain

⇔ stop, hinder, deny

🔑 〈sus-（下から）+tain（保つ）〉

(i) SDGs は Sustainable Development Goals（持続可能な開発目標）の略。

例 There isn't enough oxygen at the top of Mt. Everest to **sustain** life.

エベレストの山頂には生命を維持するのに十分な酸素がない。

□□□ 0330

collapse / kəlǽps /

動 to break and fall down without warning

崩壊する

0330語

≒ fall apart, crash

🔑 〈col-（共に）+lapse（すべる）〉

例 The bridge **collapsed** under the weight of the truck trying to cross it.

その橋は渡ろうとしたトラックの重みで崩れた。

名 a situation in which something breaks and falls down without warning

崩壊

例 The earthquake yesterday caused the **collapse** of the tower.

昨日の地震で塔が倒壊した。

desirable

/ dɪzáɪərəbl /

動 desire 〜を強く望む

形 having qualities that are good or pleasant and worth getting

望ましい、価値のある

≒ enticing, tempting

⇔ undesirable, repulsive

例 Apartments that are in **desirable** locations usually have higher rents.

望ましい場所にあるアパートはたいてい家賃が高めだ。

cattle

/ kǽtl /

名 cows that are kept on a farm for their meat or milk

牛、畜牛

≒ livestock

ⓘ 集合的に畜牛を表す。a cattle、cattlesとは言わない。

例 Her family had raised **cattle** on their farm for over 100 years.

彼女の家族は100年以上にわたって農場で牛を飼育していた。

regulate

/ régjəlèɪt /

名 regulation 規制

動 ① to make rules or laws to control something

〜を規制する

≒ administer

⇔ deregulate

例 The government **regulates** the cost of tobacco in many countries.

多くの国では政府がたばこの価格を規制している。

② to control the amount of something

〜を制御する、調整する

例 The flow of the river is **regulated** by a dam further up stream.

その川の流れはずっと上流にあるダムが調整している。

□□□ 0334

personnel / pə̀:rsənél /

名 ① a department at a company that manages the people who work for it

人事部［課］

≒ human resources, HR

ⓘ アクセントはnelの位置。personal（個人の）と混同しないように注意。

例 She contacted the **personnel** department about her manager's inappropriate behavior.

彼女は部長の不適切な行為のことで人事部に連絡した。

② people who work for a company or organization

職員、社員

≒ staff, employee

例 Only medical **personnel** were allowed to enter the hospital during the outbreak.

病気の流行中は医療従事者だけがその病院に入ることを許された。

□□□ 0335

occupation / à:kjəpéiʃən / 形 occupational 職業の

名 what a person does as their job

職業、仕事

≒ work, profession

例 She wrote her **occupation** as "nurse" when she filled out her tax forms.

彼女は納税書類に記入するときに職業を「看護師」と書いた。

0336語

□□□ 0336

insert / insə́:rt / 名 insertion 挿入

動 to put something inside of something else

～を差し込む、挿入する

≒ inject, put in

⇔ remove, withdraw

例 He **inserted** the key into the lock and turned it to open the door.

彼はドアを開けるために鍵を錠に差し込んで回した。

□□□ 0337

liberal

/ líbərəl /

名 **liberty** 自由
動 **liberate** ～を解放する

形 ① **accepting new ideas or behavior, even if they are not widely accepted**

進歩的な

≒ open, progressive

⇔ limited, conservative, narrow

例 Her parents had a **liberal** attitude about education, so they were not upset when she decided to quit school.

彼女の両親は教育に対して進歩的な考えで、彼女が学校をやめることにしたときも動揺しなかった。

② **believing that governments should actively support social and political change**

自由主義の

⇔ conservative

例 Many **liberal** voters are asking for free university education for everyone.

多くのリベラル派の有権者は、国民全員に対する大学教育の無償化を求めている。

□□□ 0338

instruct

/ ɪnstrʌ́kt /

名 **instruction** 教育、指示
名 **instructor** 教官
形 **instructive** 教育的な

動 ① **to order or command someone to do something**

～に指示する

≒ direct

例 The soldiers were **instructed** to leave the people alone as they passed through the town.

兵士たちはその町を通過するときに住民に手を出さないよう指示された。

② **to teach someone about something**

〈人〉に教える

≒ educate, train

例 Her mother **instructed** her in sewing so that she could fix her clothes.

彼女の母親は彼女が自分の服を繕えるように裁縫を教えた。

152

□□□ 0339

boost

/ búːst /

動 ① **to make something increase or become better**

～を増やす、高める

≒ improve

⇔ diminish, lessen

例 Getting a promotion at work really **boosted** his confidence.

彼は仕事で昇進したことで非常に自信を深めた。

---

② **to push something or someone up**

～を押し上げる、上昇させる

≒ lift, raise

⇔ lower, drop

例 His mother **boosted** him up onto his grandfather's shoulders.

母親は彼を持ち上げて祖父の肩に載せた。

名 **an increase in the amount of something**

増加

例 A **boost** in mask production is needed to keep everyone safe from the virus.

皆をウイルスから守るためにマスクを増産する必要がある。

□□□ 0340

persuade

/ pərswéid /

形 persuasive 説得力のある
名 persuasion 説得

動 **to make someone believe something**

～を説得する

≒ convince, influence

⇔ dissuade, repel

ⓘ 説得した行為が行われたことまでを含意する。「説得を試みる」の意味では try to persuade と言う。〈persuade ＋人＋ to *do*〉（人を説得して～させる）の形で押さえておこう。

例 Sarah **persuaded** her mother to let her go to the concert by promising to come home early.

サラは早く帰宅すると約束することで、コンサートに行かせてもらえるように母親を説得した。

☐☐☐ **0341**

interfere
/ ìntərfíər / 图 interference 干渉、妨害

動《interfere in》to involve yourself in something when your action is not wanted

〜に干渉する

≒ intrude, impede

ⓘ interfere with（〜を妨げる）の形も押さえておこう。

例 Rich countries should stop **interfering in** the politics of poorer developing countries.

豊かな国は貧しい発展途上国の政治に干渉するのをやめるべきだ。

☐☐☐ **0342**

treaty
/ trí:ti /

名 an agreement that is made officially between two or more countries or groups

条約、協定

≒ accord

例 The two countries have agreed to sign a peace **treaty** and end the war.

2国は和平条約を締結して戦争を終結することに合意した。

☐☐☐ **0343**

recruit
/ rɪkrú:t / 图 recruitment 人員補充
图 recruiter 採用担当者

動 to find people to join a company or specific group

〜を募集する、採用する

≒ hire, enlist

例 In North America, most large corporations **recruit** new staff year round.

北米では、ほとんどの大企業は新社員を通年採用している。

名 a person who is new to a company or specific group

新人

≒ newcomer, rookie

⇔ veteran

例 She is only a new **recruit**, but she is more skilled than most of the senior staff.

彼女は新人にすぎないが、ほとんどの先輩スタッフより有能だ。

□□□ 0344

exceptional / ɪksépʃənl /

前 except 〜を除いて
副 exceptionally 例外的に
名 exception 例外

形 ① much better than usual

特に優れた

≒ remarkable, fantastic

⇔ unremarkable, normal

例 The food at his restaurant is **exceptional**.

彼のレストランの料理は格別だ。

② not common or usual

例外的な、特別な

≒ noteworthy

⇔ commonplace, regular

例 There has been an **exceptional** amount of rain this year.

今年は例年にない量の雨が降っている。

□□□ 0345

await / əwéɪt /

動 to wait for something or someone to come or something to happen

〜を待つ、待ち受ける

≒ anticipate, look forward to

🔑 〈a- (〜を) +wait (待つ)〉

例 The woman was arrested, and she is now **awaiting** trial.

その女は逮捕され、現在は裁判を待っている。

0346語

□□□ 0346

pretend / prɪténd /

名 pretense ふり、見せかけ
名 pretender 偽善者

動 to act like something is true even if it is not

〜のふりをする

≒ fake　⇔ be honest, tell the truth

ⓘ 〈pretend (that).../to do〉(…である／〜するふりをする) の形で押さえておこう。

例 The friends agreed to **pretend** that they were a couple to get a special discount.

その友人同士は特別割引を受けるためにカップルのふりをすることにした。

□□□ 0347

steep / stíːp /

形 rising or falling very sharply

険しい、急な

例 The mountain road is very **steep**, so cars cannot get up the mountain in the winter.

その山道はとても急なので、冬になると車は山を登れない。

□□□ 0348

genuine / ʤénjuɪn /

形 real and not fake

本物の

≒ authentic, legitimate

⇔ counterfeit

ⓘ アクセントは ge の位置。

例 Ichiro's autograph on this baseball is **genuine**.

この野球ボールのイチローのサインは本物だ。

□□□ 0349

motivate / móʊtəvèɪt /

名 motivation 動機づけ
名 motive 動機

動 to give or help someone find a reason to do something

〜に動機を与える

≒ inspire

⇔ discourage

例 Her teacher **motivated** her to go after her dreams.

先生から刺激を受けて、彼女は自分の夢を追おうと思った。

□□□ 0350

arise / əráɪz /

動 to start to happen or exist

起こる

≒ appear, emerge

🔑 〈a-（上に）+rise（立つ）〉

⇔ disappear, vanish

ⓘ arise-arose-arisen と活用する。

例 Problems at companies **arise** when people ignore their responsibilities.

会社の問題は社員が自らの責任を無視するときに起こる。

☐☐☐ 0351

anticipate
/ æntísəpèit /　图 anticipation 予想、期待

動 to think about or look forward to something in the future

～を予想する、期待する

≒ forecast, predict

例 She **anticipated** the arrival of her boyfriend for their winter vacation.

彼女はボーイフレンドが冬休みを過ごすために来てくれることを期待した。

☐☐☐ 0352

monument
/ mɑ́:njəmənt /　形 monumental 記念碑的な

名 a structure that is built to honor someone or an event

(記念) 碑

例 The statue in the park is a **monument** to the country's first king.

公園の像はその国の初代の王の記念碑だ。

☐☐☐ 0353

donate
/ dóuneit /　图 donation 寄付

動 ① to give something to help a person or group

～を寄付する

≒ give away, contribute

ⓘ 〈donate A to B〉(AをBに寄付する) の形で押さえておこう。

🔑 〈don (与える) +-ate (動詞)〉

0353語

例 Every year at Christmas, the school **donates** winter jackets to the homeless.

その学校は毎年クリスマスに、ホームレスに冬用上着を寄付している。

② to give blood or a part of your body to a hospital or medical group to help someone else

〈血液・臓器など〉を提供する

例 All citizens are encouraged to **donate** blood to help others.

人助けのために献血するよう全国民に呼びかけられている。

☐☐☐ 0354

prohibit / prouhíbət /

形 prohibitive 禁止するための
名 prohibition 禁止

動 to tell someone they are not allowed to use or do something

〈法・団体などが〉〜を禁止する

≒ ban, limit, block, forbid

⇔ permit

🔑〈pro- (前に) +hibit (保つ)〉

ⓘ〈prohibit A from *doing*〉(Aが〜するのを禁止する)という形も押さえておこう。

例 Alcohol was **prohibited** in the United States for many years.

アメリカでは長年、酒が禁じられていた。

☐☐☐ 0355

neglect / nɪglékt /

名 negligence 怠慢、不注意
形 negligent 怠慢な、不注意な

動 ① to fail to look after someone or something

〜を無視する、なおざりにする

≒ overlook, disregard

⇔ pay attention to, focus on

🔑〈neg (否定) +lect (集める)〉

例 The **neglected** building finally fell during the typhoon.

その放置されていた建物は台風のときについに倒壊した。

② to fail to do something

(無関心・不注意から)〜しない

例 The man **neglected** to tell his wife that he had lost his job.

その男性は失業したことを妻に言わなかった。

名 lack of attention or care for someone or something

無視

≒ carelessness, disregard

例 They were charged with child **neglect** after their son died of hunger.

彼らは息子が飢え死にした後、育児放棄で告発された。

□□□ 0356

mutual
/ mjúːtʃuəl /

剾 mutually 相互に
名 mutuality 相互関係

形 shared by two or more people or groups

相互の

≒ connected, reciprocal

⇔ detached, disconnected

例 **Mutual** love and respect is the key to any healthy relationship.

相互に愛し尊敬することがあらゆる健全な関係に大事なことだ。

□□□ 0357

scope
/ skóup /

名 the range of an area that is included in or handled by something

（議論などで扱う）範囲

≒ breadth, sphere

ⓘ microscope（顕微鏡）、telescope（望遠鏡）も覚えておこう。

例 The broad **scope** of her essay impressed all her teachers.

教師は皆、彼女の論文の視野の広さに感心した。

□□□ 0358

sequence
/ síːkwəns /

形 sequential 連続して起こる

名 a set of things that follow one after the other

連続、並び

0358語

≒ series

♥ 〈sequ（ついていく）+-ence（状態）〉

例 His lawyer asked him to explain the **sequence** of events that followed the robbery.

弁護士は彼に強盗の後の一連の出来事を説明するよう求めた。

動 to put things in a specific order

〜を並べる

≒ arrange

例 The librarians were responsible for deciding how to **sequence** books without an author.

その図書館員たちは著者名のない本の並べ方を決めるのを任された。

□□□ 0359

remark
/ rɪmάːrk /

形 remarkable 注目すべき
副 remarkably 目立って

動 to say something about someone or something

（意見などを）言う、述べる

≒ comment, mention

例 The engineer **remarked** on how quickly the bridge was being built.

その技師は橋がいかに急ピッチで建設されているかを述べた。

名 something that someone says or writes to show their ideas or opinions

発言

≒ comment

例 The author offended many with her **remarks** about poor people.

その作家は貧しい人々についての発言で多くの人の気持ちを傷つけた。

□□□ 0360

flesh
/ fléʃ /

名 the parts of the body that are soft

（動物・人間の）肉

ⓘ fresh（新鮮な）と混同しないように注意。

例 The dog's teeth bit deep into the man's **flesh**, drawing blood.

その犬の歯が男性の肉に深く食い込んで、血が流れた。

□□□ 0361

exaggerate
/ ɪgzǽdʒərèɪt /

名 exaggeration 誇張

動 to consider or describe something as being greater than it actually is

（〜を）誇張する

≒ amplify, inflate

⇔ play down

ⓘ アクセントは xa の位置。

例 She always **exaggerates** when she talks about how smart her son is.

彼女は、自分の息子がいかに賢いか話すときはいつも大げさに言う。

□□□ 0362

consent / kənsént /

動 to agree to something or give permission for something

同意する、承諾する

≒ approve, permit

🔑 〈con-(共に)+sent(感じる)〉

⇔ disapprove, deny

例 She didn't like it, but eventually she **consented** to having her picture in the newspaper.

彼女は気が進まなかったが、結局、自分の写真を新聞に載せることを承諾した。

名 agreement for something to be done or happen

同意、承諾

≒ permission

ⓘ カタカナ語の「コンセント」は英語では outlet。

例 Parents need to give written **consent** for their child's pictures to be used by the school.

親は子どもの写真を学校が使うための同意書を提出する必要がある。

□□□ 0363

evil / íːvl /

形 considered bad based on common morals

(道徳上)悪い

≒ malicious

⇔ good, righteous

例 Every superhero story has an **evil** character for the superhero to defeat.

どんなスーパーヒーローの物語にもスーパーヒーローがやっつける悪者がいる。

0364語

□□□ 0364

colony / káːləni /

形 colonial 植民地の
動 colonize 〜を植民地化する

名 an area that is controlled by a country that is not close to it

植民地

例 Both Canada and the United States used to be **colonies** of England.

カナダもアメリカもかつてはイギリスの植民地だった。

☐☐☐ **0365**

charm
/ tʃɑ́ːrm /

形 charming 魅力的な

動 to attract people or get them to do what you want by being beautiful, friendly, etc.

〜をうっとりさせる

≒ captivate, delight

⇔ disgust, displease

例 The young couple was **charmed** by the cottages along the lake.

その若いカップルは湖沿いに並ぶコテージに魅了された。

名 something that makes a person or an object likeable

魅力

≒ appeal

例 The location of the house was part of its **charm**.

立地がその家の魅力の一部だった。

☐☐☐ **0366**

yell
/ jél /

動 to say something using a very loud voice

叫ぶ

≒ shout, scream

⇔ whisper, mutter

ⓘ 「エールを送る」の「エール」もこのyellから。

例 She was **yelling** at her husband so loudly that her neighbors called the police.

彼女はすごい大声で夫に怒鳴っていたので、近所の人が警察に通報した。

☐☐☐ **0367**

scenery
/ síːnəri /

名 scene 場面、光景
形 scenic 景色の美しい

名 a view of things in nature that are nice to look at

景色、風景

≒ landscape

例 The **scenery** of the Scottish Highlands is rough and beautiful.

スコットランドのハイランド地方の風景は荒涼としていて美しい。

□□□ 0368

radical
/ rǽdɪkl /

剾 radically 抜本的に
名 radicalism 急進主義

形 ① having very strong views that are not shared by the majority of people

急進的な、過激な

≒ revolutionary

⇔ normal, typical, common

🔑〈radi (根) +-cal (形容詞)〉

例 Recently, there has been a rise in **radical** movements throughout the world.

近頃は世界中で急進的な運動が盛り上がっている。

② important at a base level

根本的な、抜本的な

≒ essential

例 There are **radical** differences between each person running for president.

大統領選挙の各立候補者の間には根本的な違いがある。

□□□ 0369

supreme
/ suprí:m /

名 supremacy 至高、最高

形 having the highest rank

最高の、この上ない

≒ absolute, best, chief

⇔ lowest, inferior, minor

ⓘ 語源は super の最上級。

例 The **supreme** commander of the military is in charge of everyone.

軍隊の最高司令官は全隊員に対する責任を持つ。

□□□ 0370

assemble
/ əsémbl /

名 assembly 組み立て；集会

動 to put together parts to complete something

～を組み立てる

≒ combine, collect

⇔ disassemble, take apart

🔑〈as-(～に)+semble(一緒に)〉

例 Three people were needed to **assemble** the table.

そのテーブルを組み立てるのに3人必要だった。

☐☐☐ 0371

moderate

/ máːdərət /

名 moderation 節度

形 not too much or too little

穏やかな、適度の

≒ adequate, balanced

⇔ excessive

ⓘ 音楽用語のmoderato（モデラート。中くらいの速さで）と同語源語。

例 Drinking **moderate** amounts of coffee isn't bad for your health.

適度な量のコーヒーを飲むことは健康に悪いことではない。

☐☐☐ 0372

oral

/ ɔ́ːrəl /

形 spoken instead of being written

口頭の、口述の

≒ vocal, lingual

🔑 〈or（口）+-al（形容詞）〉

例 Some English language exams have an **oral** section.

英語の試験には口述問題があるものもある。

☐☐☐ 0373

hesitate

/ hézətèɪt /

名 hesitation ためらい
形 hesitant ためらった

動 to pause before doing something, especially when you are nervous or unsure

ためらう、躊躇する

≒ delay, waver

例 He **hesitated** for a moment before accepting the cake.

彼はそのケーキを受け取る前にちょっとためらった。

☐☐☐ 0374

sacred

/ séɪkrəd /

形 holy and worthy of worship or respect in religious situations

神聖な

例 Mecca is a **sacred** place for Muslims.

メッカはイスラム教徒にとって神聖な場所だ。

□□□ 0375

ratio / réɪʃiòʊ /

名 a relationship between two things that is usually shown using two numbers

比率、割合

≒ proportion

ⓘ 発音に注意。

例 The **ratio** of girls to boys in the class is two to one.

そのクラスの女子と男子の割合は2対1だ。

□□□ 0376

squeeze / skwíːz /

動 to press the parts of something or multiple things together, especially from opposite sides

～を絞る、圧搾する

≒ pinch, compress

⇔ release, let go

例 She **squeezed** the tube of toothpaste too hard, and toothpaste got everywhere.

彼女は歯磨き粉のチューブをあまりにも強く押したため、歯磨き粉があちこちについてしまった。

□□□ 0377

intent / ɪntént /

0377語

名 something that you plan to do or achieve

意思、意向

≒ intention

例 The **intent** of the author was to educate others about women's rights.

著者の意図は、女性の権利についてほかの人々を啓発することだった。

形 showing concentration or paying close attention to something

没頭した、集中した

⇔ distracted

例 He had an **intent** look on his face as he studied the book.

その本を読み込んでいるとき、彼は集中した表情をしていた。

□□□ **0378**

cite

/ sáɪt / 名 citation 引用、例証

動 ① to use something as an example to support an idea

～を挙げる、引き合いに出す

≒ refer to, mention, quote

ⓘ site（用地；サイト）、sight（見ること）と同音。

例 The police **cited** evidence to prove that the woman had been at the crime scene.

警察はその女が犯罪現場にいたことを証明する証拠を挙げた。

② to use the words or work of someone else in your own (written) work

～を引用する

≒ quote

例 She **cited** a passage from Shakespeare's *Hamlet* in her paper.

彼女はレポートでシェイクスピアの『ハムレット』の1節を引用した。

□□□ **0379**

alien

/ éɪliən /

形 from a country different from the one you are in

外国の、外来の

≒ foreign

⇔ native

例 **Alien** residents are required to carry these identification cards at all times.

外国人居住者は常にこれらの身分証明書を携帯することが義務づけられている。

名 a being from somewhere that is not the planet Earth

宇宙人

≒ extraterrestrial

例 There are many stories about **aliens** living on Mars and coming to Earth.

火星に住んでいて地球にやってくる宇宙人についての話はたくさんある。

□□□ 0380

prominent

/ prá:mənənt /

名 prominence 目立つこと、卓越

形 ① standing out and easily seen

目立つ、顕著な

≒ outstanding, obvious

⇔ obscure, hidden

🔑〈pro-(前に)+min(突き出る)+-ent(形容詞)〉

例 She liked to think that her **prominent** nose gave her a great sense of smell.

彼女は、高い鼻のおかげで自分は嗅覚がすごくいいのだと考えるのが好きだった。

② well known to many people

有名な、著名な

≒ distinguished, renowned

例 Michael Jackson was a **prominent** member of the music industry before he died.

マイケル・ジャクソンは亡くなる前、音楽業界で傑出した人物だった。

□□□ 0381

seize

/ síːz /

名 seizure つかむこと

動 ① to take someone or something using force

～をつかむ、捕らえる

≒ catch, grab

⇔ let go

ⓘ ei の発音に注意。

0381語

例 The police officer **seized** the gun from the fallen man.

警官は倒れた男から銃をつかみ取った。

② to take something using legal or official power

～を押収する、差し押さえる

≒ confiscate, apprehend

例 Her house was **seized** by the bank after she stopped paying her bills.

彼女が支払うべきお金を支払わなくなると、家は銀行に差し押さえられた。

sore / sɔ́ːr /

形 feeling pain, especially a dull and consistent pain

痛い、ひりひりする

≒ aching

ⓘ 「のどが痛い」は have a sore throatと言う。

例 The soccer player had **sore** muscles after a long and hard practice.

そのサッカー選手は長時間の きついうつ練習で筋肉痛になった。

ancestor / ǽnsestər / 名 ancestry 祖先(全体)

名 a person who was part of your family in the distant past

祖先、先祖

≒ forefather

⇔ descendant

 ⟨an-(先に)+cest(行く)+-or (人)⟩

ⓘ アクセントはaの位置。

例 Her **ancestors** traveled from Europe to settle in America in 1830.

彼女の祖先は1830年にアメリカに定住するためにヨーロッパから移ってきた。

terminal / tə́ːrmənl / 動 terminate 〜を終わらせる

形 leading to eventual death

〈病気などが〉末期の

≒ fatal, incurable

⇔ curable, survivable

 ⟨term(境界)+-inal(形容詞)⟩

例 She was told she had **terminal** cancer when she was still a child.

彼女はまだ子どもだったころに末期がんだと告げられた。

名 a place where passengers can get on and off, such as a bus stop or airport

発着駅、(空港の)ターミナル

例 You cannot enter the **terminal** without a plane ticket.

航空券がないとターミナルに入れません。

□□□ 0385

accordingly / əkɔ́ːrdɪŋli /

副 in the way that meets the needs of a situation

それに応じて

≒ corresponding

例 That lawyer is the best in his field and is paid **accordingly**.

その弁護士は彼の専門において最も腕がよく、それ相応の料金を取っている。

□□□ 0386

scent / sént /

名 a nice smell that is made by something

(快い) におい、香り

≒ aroma, fragrance

例 The **scent** of roses drifted through the park.

バラの香りが公園中に漂っていた。

□□□ 0387

rob / rάːb /

名 robber 強盗(犯)
名 robbery 強盗(事件)

動 to steal money or objects from someone, usually using force

〈人・場所〉から奪う

ⓘ 人や場所が目的語になる。〈rob A of B〉(AからBを奪う)の形も押さえておこう。

0388語

例 The men **robbed** a bank to get money to pay for their friend's hospital bills.

その男たちは友人の医療費として払う金を得るために銀行強盗をした。

□□□ 0388

dull / dʌ́l /

形 not fun or interesting

退屈な

≒ boring, unexciting

⇔ exciting, inspiring, lively

例 The lecture was very **dull**, and soon all the students fell asleep.

その講義はとても退屈で、間もなく学生は全員眠りに落ちた。

☐☐☐ 0389

partial / pɑ́ːrʃəl /

名 part 部分
副 partially 部分的に

形 ① not complete

部分的な

≒ incomplete, limited

⇔ total

例 Some plants grow better if they have **partial** shade.

部分的に日陰になっている方がよく育つ植物もある。

② treating someone or something better than another or liking them more

ひいきする、偏愛する

例 She told her friend that she was **partial** to tall men with dark hair.

彼女は背の高い黒髪の男性が特に好きだと友達に言った。

☐☐☐ 0390

breakdown / bréɪkdàun /

名 a failure of a car or machine to continue to work

(車・機械などの) 故障

≒ disruption, interruption

ⓘ 「(制度・事業などの) 崩壊、破たん」という意味もある。

例 They suffered a **breakdown** on the way to the concert and had to call a tow truck.

彼らはコンサートに行く途中で車が故障し、レッカー車を呼ばなければならなかった。

☐☐☐ 0391

loyal / lɔ́ɪəl /

副 loyally 誠実に
名 loyalty 忠誠

形 having or showing complete support for someone or something

忠実な、義理堅い

≒ devoted, dependable

⇔ disloyal, untrustworthy, undependable

🔑 〈loy (法律) +-al (形容詞)〉

ⓘ royal (王の) と混同しないように注意。

例 The dog was **loyal** to his master even after his death.

その犬は飼い主が死んだ後も主人に忠実だった。

コ□□ **0392**

peer / píər /

名 someone with the same status or in the same group as someone else

同等の人、仲間

≒ associate, rival

⇔ inferior, superior

(i) 原義は「同等の人」で、pair (一対) やcompare (〜を比較する) などと同語源語。

例 Anna didn't get along well with her **peers** and played with older kids instead.

アナは同じ年頃の子たちとうまく付き合えず、代わりに年上の子たちと遊んだ。

コ□□ **0393**

outlook / áʊtlùk /

名 ① the possible future condition of someone or something

(将来の) 展望、見通し

≒ prospect

🔑 〈out- (外を) +look (見る)〉

例 The country's economic **outlook** isn't very good right now.

その国の経済の見通しは今のところかんばしくない。

② a person's way of thinking

見解、ものの見方

≒ attitude, perspective, viewpoint

例 She has a very positive **outlook** on life.

彼女は人生をとても前向きに考えている。

③ a place where people can see a wide area all at once

見晴らしのいい場所

≒ viewpoint

例 There are many scenic **outlooks** along highways in the U.S.

アメリカの幹線道路沿いには景色のいい開けた場所がたくさんある。

□□□ 0394

crush / krʌ́ʃ /

動 to press something together hard enough that it breaks or loses its shape

～を押しつぶす、粉々にする

≒ smash

例 Cans are **crushed** so they can be recycled more easily.

缶はより簡単にリサイクルできるように押しつぶされる。

□□□ 0395

urgent / ə́ːrdʒənt /

副 urgently 緊急に
名 urgency 緊急

形 important and needing attention right away

急を要する、緊急の

≒ critical, crucial, pressing
⇔ unimportant

💡 〈urg（駆り立てる）+-ent（形容詞）〉

例 Areas hit by the tornado are in **urgent** need of help.

竜巻に襲われた地域は緊急に援助を必要としている。

□□□ 0396

obstacle / ɑ́ːbstəkl /

名 something that makes it hard to do a task or blocks the way

障害（物）、支障

≒ obstruction, barrier

💡 〈ob-（反対に）+sta（立つ）+-cle（指小辞）〉

例 There will be many **obstacles** in the way of opening your new restaurant.

あなたが新しいレストランを開店する過程で多くの障害があるだろう。

□□□ 0397

contrary / kɑ́ːntrèri /

形 completely different from something else

反対の、逆の

≒ opposite to, contradictory

ⓘ on the contrary（それどころか）という表現も重要。

💡 〈contr（反対）+-ary（形容詞）〉

例 **Contrary** to what you may think, he actually hates strawberries.

きみが思いそうなこととは逆に、彼は実はイチゴが嫌いだ。

□□□ 0398

sacrifice
/ sǽkrəfàɪs /

動 to give up something you want to keep so that you can help others or do something else

～を犠牲にする

🔑 〈sacr (聖なる) +-ifice (～にする)〉

例 His wife **sacrificed** her career to raise their children.

彼の妻は子育てのためにキャリアを犠牲にした。

名 the act of giving up something you want to keep so that you can help others or do something else

犠牲

例 People had to make many **sacrifices** to survive during the war.

戦時中、人々は生き延びるために多くの犠牲を払わなければならなかった。

□□□ 0399

strive
/ stráɪv /

動 to work very hard to do or achieve something

(懸命に) 努力する

≒ endeavor

ⓘ strive-strove/strived-striven/strivedと活用する。

例 As a dancer, she **strives** for perfection.

彼女はダンサーとして完べきを目指して努力している。

0400語

□□□ 0400

devote
/ dɪvóʊt /   名 devotion 献身

動 to use your time, money, or energy to do something

〈時間・努力・金など〉を (～に) ささげる

≒ dedicate

ⓘ devote *oneself* to (～に献身する) という表現も覚えておこう。

例 He **devoted** his whole life to saving honeybees.

彼はミツバチの保護に一生をささげた。

章末ボキャブラリーチェック

次の語義が表す英単語を答えてください。

語義	解答	連番
❶ the possible future condition of someone or something	o u t l o o k	0393
❷ someone with the same status or in the same group as someone else	p e e r	0392
❸ to steal money or objects from someone, usually using force	r o b	0387
❹ from a country different from the one you are in	a l i e n	0379
❺ an interest or share that someone can hold in a business	s t a k e	0317
❻ standing out and easily seen	p r o m i n e n t	0380
❼ to work very hard to do or achieve something	s t r i v e	0399
❽ to wait for something or someone to come or something to happen	a w a i t	0345
❾ to press something together hard enough that it breaks or loses its shape	c r u s h	0394
❿ a view of things in nature that are nice to look at	s c e n e r y	0367
⓫ the place in the ground where a dead body is buried	g r a v e	0310
⓬ appearing to be true, but without certainty	s e e m i n g l y	0319
⓭ to put something inside of something else	i n s e r t	0336
⓮ to break and fall down without warning	c o l l a p s e	0330
⓯ a structure that is built to honor someone or an event	m o n u m e n t	0352
⓰ to deal with something that is not easy	t a c k l e	0321
⓱ complete or absolute	t h o r o u g h	0302
⓲ having or showing complete support for someone or something	l o y a l	0391
⓳ to say something using a very loud voice	y e l l	0366
⓴ holy and worthy of worship or respect in religious situations	s a c r e d	0374

語義	解答	連番
㉑ much better than usual	e x c e p t i o n a l	0344
㉒ to make rules or laws to control something	r e g u l a t e	0333
㉓ to give or help someone find a reason to do something	m o t i v a t e	0349
㉔ a state in which there is a lack of something that is needed	s h o r t a g e	0304
㉕ to have room for someone or something	a c c o m m o d a t e	0307
㉖ considered bad based on common morals	e v i l	0363
㉗ not too much or too little	m o d e r a t e	0371
㉘ something that makes something harder to do than it is for others	d i s a d v a n t a g e	0316
㉙ connected to something specific, not a broad or general idea	c o n c r e t e	0326
㉚ something that is used to protect or defend someone or something	s h i e l d	0311
㉛ to make something come out of a container, usually by mistake	s p i l l	0324
㉜ something heavy that is being carried, or a thought or feeling that is hard to accept	b u r d e n	0323
㉝ to title something	e n t i t l e	0308
㉞ rising or falling very sharply	s t e e p	0347
㉟ to tell someone they are not allowed to use or do something	p r o h i b i t	0354
㊱ not complete	p a r t i a l	0389
㊲ 《--------- in》 to involve yourself in something when your action is not wanted	i n t e r f e r e	0341
㊳ a set of things that follow one after the other	s e q u e n c e	0358
㊴ used when talking about something or someone that is small or not very important	m e r e	0309
㊵ to give something to help a person or group	d o n a t e	0353
㊶ the ability to understand things deeply	i n s i g h t	0306
㊷ something that you plan to do or achieve	i n t e n t	0377

語義	解答	連番
❸ having very strong views that are not shared by the majority of people	r a d i c a l	0368
❹ to attract people or get them to do what you want by being beautiful, friendly, etc.	c h a r m	0365
❺ in addition to something already said	f u r t h e r m o r e	0301
❻ doing more than what is normal or proper	e x c e s s i v e	0325
❼ to find people to join a company or specific group	r e c r u i t	0343
❽ a department at a company that manages the people who work for it	p e r s o n n e l	0334
❾ feeling pain, especially a dull and consistent pain	s o r e	0382
❺ having the highest rank	s u p r e m e	0369
❶ what a person does as their job	o c c u p a t i o n	0335
❷ not guilty of doing something wrong, such as a crime	i n n o c e n t	0322
❸ to look directly at something or someone for a long time without looking somewhere else	s t a r e	0305
❹ cows that are kept on a farm for their meat or milk	c a t t l e	0332
❺ the parts of the body that are soft	f l e s h	0360
❻ having a baby or babies growing inside the body	p r e g n a n t	0320
❼ an area that is controlled by a country that is not close to it	c o l o n y	0364
❽ to put together parts to complete something	a s s e m b l e	0370
❾ to order or command someone to do something	i n s t r u c t	0338
❻ to fail to look after someone or something	n e g l e c t	0355
❶ to act like something is true even if it is not	p r e t e n d	0346
❷ to use your time, money, or energy to do something	d e v o t e	0400
❸ something that makes it hard to do a task or blocks the way	o b s t a c l e	0396
❹ to consider or describe something as being greater than it actually is	e x a g g e r a t e	0361
❺ to press the parts of something or multiple things together, especially from opposite sides	s q u e e z e	0376

語義	解答	連番
⑥⑥ to say something about someone or something	r e m a r k	0359
⑥⑦ to realize or notice something	p e r c e i v e	0312
⑥⑧ to have a bad effect on something or ruin it	s p o i l	0327
⑥⑨ to make someone believe something	p e r s u a d e	0340
⑦⓪ shared by two or more people or groups	m u t u a l	0356
⑦① to use something as an example to support an idea	c i t e	0378
⑦② a nice smell that is made by something	s c e n t	0386
⑦③ to start to happen or exist	a r i s e	0350
⑦④ real and not fake	g e n u i n e	0348
⑦⑤ in the way that meets the needs of a situation	a c c o r d i n g l y	0385
⑦⑥ to provide the things needed for something or someone to exist or continue	s u s t a i n	0329
⑦⑦ relating to biological information passed from generation to generation	g e n e t i c	0314
⑦⑧ to make something increase or become better	b o o s t	0339
⑦⑨ a quick look at someone or something	g l a n c e	0318
⑧⓪ to agree to something or give permission for something	c o n s e n t	0362
⑧① leading to eventual death	t e r m i n a l	0384
⑧② the range of an area that is included in or handled by something	s c o p e	0357
⑧③ a very strong feeling of happiness or pleasure	d e l i g h t	0313
⑧④ accepting new ideas or behavior, even if they are not widely accepted	l i b e r a l	0337
⑧⑤ to break apart suddenly and violently	e x p l o d e	0303
⑧⑥ to pause before doing something, especially when you are nervous or unsure	h e s i t a t e	0373
⑧⑦ spoken instead of being written	o r a l	0372
⑧⑧ to give up something you want to keep so that you can help others or do something else	s a c r i f i c e	0398
⑧⑨ completely different from something else	c o n t r a r y	0397

❾⓪ to fail to notice or see something — <u>o v e r l o o k</u> — 0315

❾① an agreement that is made officially between two or more countries or groups — <u>t r e a t y</u> — 0342

❾② important and needing attention right away — <u>u r g e n t</u> — 0395

❾③ not fun or interesting — <u>d u l l</u> — 0388

❾④ a relationship between two things that is usually shown using two numbers — <u>r a t i o</u> — 0375

❾⑤ a failure of a car or machine to continue to work — <u>b r e a k d o w n</u> — 0390

❾⑥ having qualities that are good or pleasant and worth getting — <u>d e s i r a b l e</u> — 0331

❾⑦ to think about or look forward to something in the future — <u>a n t i c i p a t e</u> — 0351

❾⑧ to take someone or something using force — <u>s e i z e</u> — 0381

❾⑨ a person who was part of your family in the distant past — <u>a n c e s t o r</u> — 0383

❿ to move your head up and down to show that you agree or understand — <u>n o d</u> — 0328

Stage 5

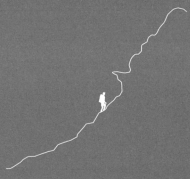

Never put off till tomorrow what you can do today.
今日できることを明日まで延ばすな。

□□□ 0401

undertake / ʌ̀ndərtéɪk /

動 to begin or agree to do some kind of task

〜を引き受ける、
〜に着手する

≒ take up, accept

🔑 〈under-(下から)+take(とる)〉

⇔ refuse

ⓘ undertake-undertook-undertakenと活用する。

例 The teacher **undertook** the task of cleaning the whole classroom by himself.

その先生は教室中を一人で掃除する仕事を引き受けた。

□□□ 0402

beast / bíːst /

名 a wild animal that is large and maybe dangerous

獣

≒ monster

ⓘ 「百獣の王」は the king of beastsと言う。

例 There are many stories of magical **beasts** with multiple heads.

複数の頭を持つ不思議な獣の物語は多い。

□□□ 0403

namely / néɪmli /

副 used when adding detailed information to something already said

すなわち、換言すると

≒ that is (to say)

例 The nurse brought lunch to the patient, **namely** soup and some salad.

看護師は患者に昼食、つまりスープとサラダを持ってきた。

□□□ 0404

originate / ərídʒənèɪt /

形 original 最初の、元の
名 origin 起源

動 to start existing or be made

起こる、生じる

⇔ end, finish

例 The story is believed to have **originated** in India hundreds of years ago.

その物語は何百年も前にインドで生まれたと考えられている。

□□□ 0405

swell
/ swél /

動 ① to grow larger than normal
腫れる

≒ expand

⇔ shrink

ⓘ swell-swelled-swelled/swollenと活用する。

例 Many women's ankles or feet **swell** when they are pregnant.
多くの女性は妊娠するとかかとや足が腫れる。

---

② to get bigger in size or number
増える

≒ increase

例 Her Instagram followers **swelled** to thousands in a few days.
彼女のインスタグラムのフォロワーは2、3日で数千人に増えた。

□□□ 0406

leak
/ líːk /

形 leaky 漏れる
名 leakage 漏れ

動 ① to tell someone secret information so that it will be shared with the public
〈情報〉を漏洩する

≒ slip, spill

⇔ hide

ⓘ 「(情報などを) リークする」はカタカナ語にもなっている。

例 The true cost of the new stadium was **leaked** to the press by a top official in the government.
新スタジアムの本当のコストが政府の高官によってメディアに漏れた。

0406語

---

② to let something in or out of something through a hole
〈屋根・船などが〉漏る

例 The boat was **leaking** and soon filled up with water and sank.
そのボートは水漏れしていて、すぐに水でいっぱいになって沈没した。

181

□□□ 0407

literary

/ lítərèri /

名 literature 文学

形 connected to literature

文学の、文学的な

例 **Literary** translation is one of the hardest types of translation there is.

文学の翻訳は世にある翻訳の中で最も難しいタイプの一つだ。

□□□ 0408

decent

/ díːsnt /

名 decency 上品さ

形 good or appropriate

適正な、まともな

≒ suitable, proper

⇔ inappropriate, improper

ⓘ 発音に注意。

例 Going to bed at a **decent** hour is really important the day before a test.

テストの前日はちょうどいい時間に寝るのが非常に大事だ。

□□□ 0409

supplement

/ 動 sʌ́pləmènt　名 sʌ́pləmənt /

形 supplementary 補足の、追加の

動 to add something to another thing to make it complete

～を補う、補足する

⇔ detract

🔑〈sup-（下に）+ple（満たす）+-ment（名詞）〉

例 The young woman started to do freelance work on the side to **supplement** her income.

その若い女性は収入を補うために副業でフリーランスの仕事をし始めた。

名 something that you add to another thing to finish it or make it complete

補足；栄養補助食品

ⓘ カタカナ語の「サプリメント」はこの supplement。

例 Most American women take vitamin **supplements** when they are pregnant.

アメリカの女性はほとんどが妊娠するとビタミン補助剤を摂取する。

☐☐☐ 0410

bump / bʌ́mp / 名 bumper（車の）バンパー

名 ① a small area on a surface that is raised up

突起

ⓘ 元は擬音語。

例 The **bump** in the road caused the car to fly into the air.　道路が隆起していたために、その車は空中に飛んだ。

② the act of something hitting something else

（軽く）ぶつかること

例 The airplane landed with a **bump** onto the runway.　飛行機は滑走路にどすんと着陸した。

動 to hit or move against someone or something, often by mistake

〜にぶつかる

例 The waiter accidentally **bumped** the woman's drink off the table and into her lap.　ウェイターは誤ってその女性の飲み物に当たり、それをテーブルから女性の膝に落としてしまった。

0411語

☐☐☐ 0411

outlet / áʊtlèt /

名 an opening or activity through which something can be released (e.g. feelings, air, etc.)

はけ口；（気体などの）出口

≒ channel

ⓘ let out（出してやる）ための場所。「（電気の）コンセント」「（メーカーの）直販店」の意味もある。

例 The boy said that he used violent video games as an **outlet** for his anger.　少年は怒りのはけ口に暴力的なテレビゲームを利用していると言った。

☐☐☐ **0412**

convey
/ kənvéɪ / 图 conveyance 輸送

動 ① to give information to someone

〈意思・情報など〉を
伝える

≒ transmit, share

例 Words are not the only way to **convey** your feelings to others.

言葉は自分の気持ちを他人に
伝える唯一の方法ではない。

② to move someone or something from one place to another

〜を運ぶ、輸送する

≒ transport

ⓘ 「ベルトコンベア」は conveyor belt。

例 Pipelines are a dangerous way to **convey** oil across the country.

パイプラインは、国を横断して
石油を輸送する危険な方法だ。

☐☐☐ **0413**

divorce
/ dɪvɔ́ːrs /

图 the end of a marriage done through legal means

離婚

≒ separation

ⓘ get divorced（離婚する）という表現も覚えておこう。

例 After the **divorce** of his parents, Bobby never saw his father again.

両親の離婚後、ボビーが父親
と会うことは二度となかった。

☐☐☐ **0414**

profitable
/ prɑ́ːfətəbl / 图 profit 利益

形 earning money

利益をもたらす

⇔ unprofitable

例 Because the movie wasn't **profitable**, the sequel was canceled.

その映画は利益が出なかった
ので、続編は中止になった。

□□□ 0415

sole

/ sóʊl / 副 solely もっぱら

形 only one

唯一の、ただ一人の

≒ single, lone

ⓘ soul（魂）と同音。同じつづりで「足の裏」という意味の名詞もある。

例 The dog was the **sole** survivor of the fatal airplane accident last week.

その犬は、死亡者の出た先週の航空事故の唯一の生き残りだった。

□□□ 0416

sensation

/ senséɪʃən / 形 sensational 感動させる

名 ① the ability to feel using your physical senses

感覚、知覚

≒ feeling

例 After being hit by the truck, the girl had no **sensation** in her legs.

トラックにひかれた後、その女の子は脚の感覚がなくなった。

② a feeling that your body experiences

感じ、気持ち

0416語

例 The vodka left a burning **sensation** in her throat after she swallowed it.

彼女がウォッカを飲むと、のどが焼けつくような感じが残った。

③ a person or thing that causes excitement and interest

大評判（の人［もの］）

ⓘ カタカナ語の「センセーション」はこの sensation から。

例 *Harry Potter* became a worldwide **sensation** and is now available in many languages.

『ハリー・ポッター』は世界中で大評判になり、今では多くの言語で読むことができる。

□□□ 0417

renew

/ rɪn(j)úː /

動 ① to extend the valid time period of something

〈契約など〉を更新する

≒ prolong

⇔ finish, halt

ⓘ renewable energy (再生可能エネルギー) という表現も覚えておこう。

例 Everyone must **renew** their driver's license every three years if they want to continue driving.

運転を続けたければ、誰もが3年ごとに運転免許を更新しなければならない。

② to make something feel new and fresh again

〜を新たにする、取り戻す

例 Sleep gives your body a chance to **renew** itself for a new day.

睡眠は新しい日に備えて回復する機会を体に与える。

□□□ 0418

alert

/ əlɔ́ːrt /

名 alertness 用心深さ、注意力

動 to give information about something or warn someone of something

〜に警告する

例 They **alerted** the police when they saw someone trying to break into their neighbor's house.

彼らは誰かが隣家に侵入しようとしているのを見て、警察に通報した。

形 able to think about and notice things clearly

警戒した、油断のない

≒ attentive

例 An **alert** dog quickly stopped the kidnapper from taking the child.

油断のない犬が、誘拐犯がその子どもを連れ去るのをすぐに阻止した。

□□□ 0419

scatter

/ skǽtər /

動 ① to make things or people go away from each other

～をまき散らす、散り散りにさせる

≒ spread, disperse

例 The wind **scattered** the cherry blossoms across the schoolyard.

風が桜の花を校庭中に散らした。

② to go away from each other

散り散りになる

≒ disperse

例 The protestors **scattered** when they saw that the police had arrived.

警察がやって来たのを見ると、抗議者たちは散り散りになった。

□□□ 0420

passive

/ pǽsɪv /

形 accepting something that happens or what people do without trying to change anything

受動的な、消極的な

0421語

⇔ active

ⓘ 「受動態」は passive voice [form] と言う。

例 Women are often **passive** characters in older books.

昔の本に出てくる女性は受動的な人であることが多い。

□□□ 0421

ethnic

/ éθnɪk /

名 ethnicity 民族性

形 regarding a group of people or the things connected to a group of people who have a culture that is usually different from the main one

民族の、民族的な

例 The Ainu people were finally recognized as an **ethnic** minority in Japan.

アイヌの人々はついに日本の少数民族として認められた。

□□□ 0422

sew
/ sóʊ /

動 to make or fix something using a needle and thread

〜を縫う、繕う

≒ stitch, tailor

ⓘ ew の発音に注意。sew-sewed-sewn/sewed と活用する。

例 Bonnie decided to **sew** her own wedding dress to save money.

ボニーはお金を節約するために自分のウェディングドレスを縫うことにした。

□□□ 0423

evident
/ évədənt /

形 clear to the mind or by sight

明白な、はっきりわかる

副 evidently 明らかに
名 evidence 証拠

≒ apparent, obvious

⇔ obscure, vague

🔑 〈e- (外に) +vid (見る) +-ent (形容詞)〉

例 It was **evident** from her stare that the woman had never seen such a large dog before.

その女性は犬をまじまじと見ていたので、そんなに大きな犬をそれまで見たことがなかったことは明らかだった。

□□□ 0424

interact
/ ìntərǽkt /

動 ① to talk to others and/or do things with them

（人と）交流する

名 interaction 交流、相互作用
形 interactive 相互に作用する

例 Children need to **interact** with other children their own age to learn and grow.

子どもは学んで成長するために、同年齢のほかの子と交流する必要がある。

② to come together and have an effect of some kind

相互に作用する

例 When some medicines **interact** with each other, the side effects can be deadly.

薬の中には、相互に作用するとその副作用で死に至るものもある。

□□□ 0425

provision
/ prəvíʒən / 動 provide ～を供給する

名 ① the act of making something available that is wanted or needed

供給

≒ allowance, arrangement

🔑 〈pro-（前に）+vis（見る）+ -ion（名詞）〉

例 The **provision** of healthcare is the responsibility of the government.

医療の提供は政府の責任だ。

② something done to prepare for something in advance

準備、用意

≒ preparation

例 He made **provisions** for a natural disaster by buying large amounts of water and canned foods.

彼は自然災害に備えて、大量の水と缶詰を買った。

□□□ 0426

exhaust
/ ɪgzɔ́ːst / 名 exhaustion 消耗

動 to use all of someone's physical or mental energy

～を疲れ果てさせる

0427語

≒ fatigue, wear out, tire

例 Working without a break for over 12 hours **exhausted** him.

休憩なしに12時間以上働いて彼は疲労困憊した。

□□□ 0427

sophisticated
/ səfístɪkèɪtɪd / 動 sophisticate ～を洗練させる
名 sophistication 洗練；精巧さ

形 having or showing experience and knowledge about many things

洗練された、教養のある

≒ worldly, refined

⇔ unsophisticated, unrefined

例 She was a **sophisticated** woman who could speak six different languages.

彼女は6か国語を話せる教養のある女性だった。

□□□ 0428

fossil
/ fáːsl /

名 **something from a plant or an animal from thousands or millions of years ago that you can find in some rocks**

化石

ⓘ fossil fuel（化石燃料）という表現も覚えておこう。

例 The oldest bird **fossil** in Japan was found in Fukui.

日本最古の鳥の化石は福井で見つかった。

□□□ 0429

sue
/ s(j)úː /

動 **to try to legally force a person or organization to give you something that you should receive**

〜を訴える、告訴する

例 Bob Murray **sued** a comedy show for their comments about him, but he lost.

ボブ・マレーは自分に関する発言を理由に、あるコメディー番組を訴えたが、敗訴した。

□□□ 0430

retreat
/ rɪtríːt /

動 **to move away from a place or situation, usually because it is dangerous or not enjoyable**

逃げる、退く

≒ flee, withdraw

⇔ invade

🔑 〈re-（元に）+treat（引く）〉

例 The soldiers **retreated** into the forest to protect themselves from the gunfire.

兵士たちは銃撃から身を守るために森に逃げ込んだ。

名 **movement away from a place or situation that is dangerous, unpleasant, etc.**

退却

例 The woman made a quick **retreat** when she realized that she had entered the men's bathroom by mistake.

その女性は間違って男性トイレに入ってしまったことに気づくと、さっと出た。

□□□ 0431

enthusiastic

/ ɪnθ(j)ùːziǽstɪk /

名 enthusiasm 熱狂
副 enthusiastically 熱狂的に

形 being excited about something

熱狂的な

≒ zealous, eager

⇔ indifferent

例 The cast of *Parasite* received an **enthusiastic** welcome to the Oscars.

『パラサイト』の出演者たちはアカデミー賞で熱狂的な歓迎を受けた。

□□□ 0432

violate

/ váɪəlèɪt /

名 violation 違反

動 to do something that is against a rule or law

～に違反する

≒ break, disregard

⇔ follow, obey

例 The student was punished for **violating** the no-smoking-on-campus rule.

その学生はキャンパスでは禁煙という規則に違反したために罰せられた。

□□□ 0433

inherit

/ ɪnhérət /

名 inheritance 相続；遺産

0433語

動 ① to receive something from someone when they die

～を相続する

例 Some houses in Japan are abandoned because no one wanted to **inherit** them.

日本には相続したい人がいなかったために放置された家がある。

② to have a part of you that you got from your parents when you were born

（遺伝的に）～を受け継ぐ

⇔ pass on

例 His son **inherited** his very large nose.

彼の息子は彼のとても大きな鼻を受け継いだ。

☐☐☐ 0434

pioneer / pàiəníər /

名 a person who helps make something based on new ideas or methods

先駆者、パイオニア

⇔ follower

ⓘ アクセントはneerの位置。

例 Bill Gates was one of the **pioneers** of the computer industry.

ビル・ゲイツはコンピュータ産業の先駆者の一人だった。

動 to help make something new

～を開拓する、～の先駆者となる

例 YouTube **pioneered** a new way of sharing videos with others.

ユーチューブは動画をほかの人と共有する新しい方法を開拓した。

☐☐☐ 0435

quest / kwést /

名 a long and difficult effort or journey to find or do something

探求、追求

≒ expedition

ⓘ 原義は「求める」で、question（質問）やrequest（要請）などにも含まれる。

例 Amelia went on a **quest** to find her real mother.

アメリアは実の母を探す旅に出た。

☐☐☐ 0436

suspend / səspénd /

名 suspension （一時的な）停止
名 suspense 未決定；不安

動 to stop something, such as a service, for a short period of time

～を一時停止する、中止する

≒ delay, postpone

⇔ carry on, continue, keep going

🔑 〈sus-(下に)+pend(つるす)〉

例 Sales of the new game have been **suspended** until the factories open again.

新しいゲームの販売は工場が再開するまで一時停止されている。

192

□□□ 0437

constitute

/ ká:nstət(j)ù:t /

名 constitution 構成
形 constituent 構成する

動 to be the same as another thing

〜を構成する、〜に等しい

≒ equal

ⓘ constitution には「憲法」という意味もある。

例 The court decided that searching their apartment **constituted** breaking into their home.

裁判所は、彼らのアパートを捜索したことは家屋への侵入と見なされる、と判断した。

□□□ 0438

stimulate

/ stímjəlèit /

名 stimulation 刺激
名 stimulus 刺激（の原因）

動 to cause activity in something

〜を刺激する

≒ arouse

⇔ block, dampen

例 Drinking coffee **stimulates** the body and gives you more energy.

コーヒーを飲むと体が刺激され、より多くのエネルギーが得られる。

□□□ 0439

reproduce

/ rì:prəd(j)ú:s /

形 reproductive 生殖の
名 reproduction 繁殖；再現

0439語

動 ① to make babies, new plants, etc.

繁殖する、生殖する

≒ breed, mate

例 Salmon travel upriver every year to **reproduce**.

サケは繁殖するために毎年川を上る。

② to make something that is the same or almost the same as another thing

〜を再現する、再生する

≒ mimic, replicate

例 The sound of many different instruments can be **reproduced** using a computer.

さまざまな楽器の音はコンピュータを使って再現できる。

□□□ 0440

instinct

/ ínstiŋkt /

形 instinctive 本能的な

名 **an action or way of thinking that you do naturally or without learning it**

本能、直感

例 Cats have a natural **instinct** to hunt smaller animals.

猫には小動物を狩る生まれながらの本能がある。

□□□ 0441

soak

/ sóuk /

動 **to leave something in a liquid for some time**

～を浸す

≒ submerge, bathe

ⓘ get soaking wetで「びしょぬれになる」という意味。

例 To remove blood stains from clothes, they must be **soaked** before being washed.

衣服から血の染みを取り除くためには、衣服を洗う前に水に浸さなければならない。

□□□ 0442

tender

/ téndər /

副 tenderly やさしく
名 tenderness やさしさ

形 **being gentle, or showing love and kindness to someone or something**

やさしい、思いやりのある

≒ sweet, affectionate

⇔ rough, violent

ⓘ 「(肉・野菜が) やわらかい」という意味もある。

例 The groom gave a **tender** kiss to his future wife.

花婿は未来の妻にやさしくキスをした。

□□□ 0443

influential

/ ìnfluénʃəl /

名 influence 影響

形 **having the power to make change happen or control people's feelings**

影響力の大きい

⇔ insignificant, trivial

例 The most **influential** person in her life was her mother.

彼女の人生で最も影響力が大きかった人は彼女の母親だった。

□□□ **0444**

progressive

/ prəgrésɪv /

名 progress 進歩、前進

形 using, believing, or interested in new or modern ideas

進歩的な

≒ radical

⇔ conservative

例 The **progressive** school decided to stop giving students tests.

その進歩的な学校は生徒に試験を行うことをやめることにした。

□□□ **0445**

saint

/ séɪnt /

名 a person who has been named by the Christian church as being holy because of the things they did

聖人

ⓘ Saint Augustine（聖アウグスティヌス）のような使い方もある。

例 She was made a **saint** in 2019 for the great things she did during her life.

彼女は生前に行った善行により2019年に聖人に叙せられた。

□□□ **0446**

0446 語

virtue

/ vɚ́ːrtʃuː /

名 ① a quality that is seen as good and moral

徳、美徳

⇔ vice

ⓘ by virtue of（～の理由で）という表現も覚えておこう。

例 It is commonly said that patience is a **virtue**.

一般的に忍耐は美徳とされる。

② a point that is seen as good

長所、利点

≒ advantage, benefit

例 Her apartment has the **virtue** of being close to the train station.

彼女のアパートには駅に近いという利点がある。

□□□ **0447**

abstract
/ 形 ǽbstrækt 動 æbstrǽkt /

名 abstraction 抽象化

形 relating to general ideas

抽象的な、概念上の

≒ vague

🔑 〈abs-(離れて)+tract(引く)〉

⇔ concrete, specific

例 **Abstract** ideas like love and hate aren't easy to define.

愛や憎しみのような抽象的な概念は定義するのが簡単ではない。

動 to get or take something from something else

〜を抽出する

例 Data for the study was **abstracted** from the school's records.

その研究のためのデータは学校の記録から抽出された。

□□□ **0448**

flee
/ flíː /

動 to run away from something that is dangerous

逃げる

≒ escape

ⓘ flee-fled-fledと活用する。free（自由な）と混同しないように注意。

例 The bushfires in Australia were so bad that a lot of animals couldn't **flee** to safety.

オーストラリアの山火事はあまりにもひどくて、多くの動物が安全な場所に逃げることができなかった。

□□□ **0449**

appliance
/ əpláɪəns /

名 a machine that uses electricity and is found in people's homes

電化製品、器具

例 There are many household **appliances** now that are not needed to live a normal life.

普通の生活を送るのに必要のない家電が今ではたくさんある。

□□□ 0450

agenda

/ əʤéndə /

名 ① a list of things that have to be done or considered

（会議などの）議題、
予定表

≒ plan, schedule

例 There are three items on the **agenda** for tonight.

今夜の議題は 3 つある。

② a plan that guides a person's or group's actions

意図、思惑

例 The queen will push her personal **agenda** no matter what anyone says.

誰が何と言おうと、女王は自分の思惑を押し通すだろう。

□□□ 0451

boast

/ bóʊst /

動 to show too much confidence in something you have or have done

〜を誇る、自慢する

≒ brag, show off

ⓘ boast of [about]（〜を自慢する）の形も押さえておこう。

例 The Suzukis **boasted** to everyone they knew that their son had gotten into a famous orchestra.

スズキ夫妻は息子が有名なオーケストラに入ったことを知人全員に自慢した。

0452 語

□□□ 0452

given

/ gívn /

前 used to show something that is assumed

〜を考えると

≒ considering

ⓘ 〈given (that)...〉（…ということを考えると）という接続詞的な使い方も押さえておこう。

例 **Given** the age of the house and its location, this price is excellent.

家の築年数と立地を考えると、この値段は破格だ。

endure

/ ɪnd(j)úər /

名 endurance 忍耐（力）；耐久

動 ① to experience or put up with something unpleasant or painful for a long time (without giving up)

～に耐える

≒ bear, tolerate, deal with

🔑 〈en-(中に)+dure(継続する)〉

例 Many Syrian refugees have **endured** more hardship than anyone can imagine.

多くのシリア難民は、誰もが想像する以上の苦難に耐えている。

② to continue to exist without changing

持ちこたえる

≒ persist

例 The traditional wedding has **endured** for hundreds of years.

伝統的な結婚式は何百年も変わらず続いてきた。

descend

/ dɪsénd /

名 descent 下降

動 to go down from a higher place

下る

⇔ ascend, climb

🔑 〈de-(下に)+scend(登る)〉

ⓘ descendant（子孫）は「世代を下ったもの」という意味。

例 When an airplane **descends**, everyone must put their seatbelt on.

飛行機が降下するときは全員がシートベルトをしなければならない。

terror

/ térər /

名 terrorism テロ行為
名 terrorist テロリスト

名 a very strong feeling of being scared

恐怖、恐ろしさ

≒ fear, horror

🔑 〈terr(驚かす)+-or(名詞)〉

ⓘ terrible（恐ろしい）、terrify（～をおびえさせる）なども同語源語。

例 Everyone ran away in **terror** as the tsunami approached land.

津波が岸に近づいてくると、誰もが恐ろしくなって逃げた。

□□□ **0456**

consequently

/ ká:nsəkwèntli / 图 consequence 結果

圖 happening because of something else

その結果

≒ as a result

例 She overslept and was **consequently** late for work.

彼女は寝過ごし、その結果、仕事に遅刻した。

□□□ **0457**

privilege

/ prívəlɪʤ / 形 privileged 特権を持つ

图 a right that some people have and others do not

特権、恩恵

≒ advantage

⇔ disadvantage

例 Not everyone in the world has the **privilege** of having access to good healthcare.

世界の誰もがよい医療を受ける恩恵にあずかっているわけではない。

□□□ **0458**

fulfill

/ fʊlfíl / 图 fulfillment 実行、達成

圖 ① to do what is required to complete something, such as a contract

～を果たす、履行する

≒ carry out

🍀 〈ful (十分に) +fill (満たす)〉

ⓘ イギリス英語では fulfil とつづる。

例 She **fulfilled** her promise to her mother by graduating university.

彼女は大学を卒業することで、母親との約束を果たした。

② to achieve something that you wanted

～を実現する

≒ realize

例 He **fulfilled** his dream of becoming an actor when he was an old man.

彼は年老いてから、俳優になるという夢を実現した。

□□□ 0459

drown
/ dráʊn /

動 to die from being underwater too long, or to cause someone or something to die in this way

溺れ死ぬ；〜を溺死させる

ⓘ owの発音に注意。

例 Many people **drowned** in an accident at sea.

海難事故で多くの人が溺死した。

□□□ 0460

delete
/ dɪlíːt /

動 to remove something from something else

〜を削除する

≒ erase

例 It is important to **delete** all your personal information from your phone before you sell it.

電話を売る前にそこから個人情報をすべて削除することが重要だ。

□□□ 0461

swear
/ swéər /

動 ① to state or promise very strongly that something is a certain way, or that you will or will not do something

誓う

≒ vow

ⓘ swear-swore-swornと活用する。

例 She **swore** that she wouldn't tell anyone his secret.

彼女は誰にも彼の秘密を言わないと誓った。

② to use words that offend others when speaking

ののしる

≒ curse

例 He **swore** at the players on the TV when they lost the soccer match.

サッカーの試合に負けると、彼はテレビに映る選手たちに悪態をついた。

□□□ 0462

premise / prémɪs /

名 ① **an idea that people believe is true and use in arguments**

前提、根拠

≒ assumption, presumption

🔑 〈pre-(前に)+mise(置く)〉

例 The building was designed on the **premise** that people enjoy being in nature.

その建物は人々が自然の中にいることを楽しむという前提で設計された。

② **an area of land and the building(s) on it**

敷地、構内

≒ ground(s)

ⓘ ふつう複数形で使う。

例 They were asked to leave the **premises** until all rooms had been checked for rats.

彼らはネズミがいないか全室のチェックが済むまで構内から出るように言われた。

□□□ 0463

sympathy / símpəθi /

形 sympathetic 同情的な
動 sympathize 同情する

0464語

名 **the feeling of being sorry for or caring about another person's troubles**

同情、思いやり

≒ empathy, compassion

🔑 〈sym-(共に)+pathy(感情)〉

例 Letters of **sympathy** were sent to all the families who had lost loved ones in the shooting.

銃撃事件で愛する人を失ったすべての家族にお悔やみの手紙が送られた。

□□□ 0464

uncover / ʌnkʌ́vər /

動 **to find something that was not known**

～を発見する、明らかにする

≒ reveal, discover, unearth

🔑 〈un-(否定)+cover(覆う)〉

例 After a long search, the pirates were able to **uncover** their lost treasure.

長い間探した結果、海賊たちは失われた財宝を見つけることができた。

☐☐☐ 0465

lease
/ líːs /

動 to let someone use something for a certain amount of time if they give you money

～を賃貸しする

ⓘ rent（賃貸しする；賃借りする）は類義語にも反意語にもなる。

例 She decided to **lease** her room to a friend for the two months she was studying abroad.

彼女は留学する2か月の間、自分の部屋を友達に賃貸することにした。

名 a legal agreement made to let someone use something for a certain amount of time for money

賃貸借契約

例 The **lease** for most Japanese apartments is two years.

ほとんどの日本のアパートの賃貸借契約は2年だ。

☐☐☐ 0466

modest
/ máːdəst /　名 modesty 謙虚さ

形 not too proud or confident about your skills or yourself

謙虚な

≒ humble

⇔ boastful

例 It is unusual for such a successful woman to be so **modest** about her success.

あれほど成功した女性が自分の成功にあれほど謙虚なのは珍しい。

☐☐☐ 0467

shed
/ ʃéd /

動 to lose something off your body naturally

〈動植物が〉〈皮・毛・葉など〉を落とす

ⓘ shed-shed-shedと活用する。

例 Dogs **shed** their winter fur in the spring to be cooler.

犬の冬毛は春になると体が涼しくなるように抜ける。

]□□ 0468

noble

/ nóʊbl / 名 nobility 気高さ；上流階級

形 having or showing qualities that are respected by others

崇高な、気高い

≒ dignified

⇔ base, low

例 It was **noble** of the prince to admit that he had made a mistake.

自分が誤りを犯したと王子が認めたのは気高いことだった。

□□□ 0469

classify

/ klǽsəfàɪ /

名 classification 分類
形 classified 分類された；
機密の

動 to put things into groups based on what they are like

～を分類する

≒ categorize, bundle

例 Books in libraries are **classified** by both author and subject.

図書館の本は作者とテーマの両方によって分類されている。

□□□ 0470

0470語

span

/ spǽn /

名 the period of time between two different things

(ある一定の) 期間

≒ interval, term

ⓘ 「スパン」はカタカナ語にもなっている。

例 Beethoven's 9th Symphony was composed over a **span** of two years.

ベートーベンの交響曲第9番は2年という期間をかけて作曲された。

動 to continue over a period of time

〈ある期間〉にわたる

例 His political career **spanned** over 30 years.

彼の政治家としてのキャリアは30年以上に及んだ。

□□□ 0471

overwhelming

/ òʊvərwélmɪŋ / 動 overwhelm ～を圧倒する

形 very large in number or effect

圧倒的な、抗しがたい

≒ astounding, staggering

例 An **overwhelming** number of people showed up to protest the new pipeline.

おびただしい数の人が新しいパイプラインに抗議するために集まった。

□□□ 0472

leap

/ líːp /

動 to jump from something

跳ぶ

ⓘ leap-leaped/leapt-leaped/leaptと活用する。

例 The director **leapt** into the air to show his happiness.

監督は喜びを表すために空中に跳び上がった。

□□□ 0473

cease

/ síːs /

動 to stop (doing something)

終わる；～をやめる

≒ end, halt

⇔ begin, commence

ⓘ seの発音に注意。ceaseless（絶え間ない）、cease-fire（停戦）という語も覚えておこう。

例 When the door to the classroom opened, the conversation between the students **ceased**.

教室のドアが開くと、生徒たちのおしゃべりがやんだ。

□□□ 0474

remedy

/ rémədi / 形 remedial 治療の（ための）

名 a medicine or something else that helps fix pain or sickness

治療薬

≒ cure

🔑 〈re-（再び）+medy（癒す）〉

例 Natural **remedies** are becoming popular again to protect the body naturally.

体を自然に守るために、天然薬が再び人気になりつつある。

204

]□□ 0475

nasty

/ nǽsti /

形 ① not nice to see, smell, taste, or hear

不快な、嫌な

≒ unpleasant, disgusting

例 She couldn't take her medicine because it smelled too **nasty**.

その薬はひどく不快なにおいがしたので、彼女はそれを飲めなかった。

② not proper

みだらな、不愉快な

≒ indecent, improper, vulgar

⇔ decent, respectable

例 Children are not allowed to see movies that have a lot of **nasty** language.

子どもは下品な言葉がたくさん出てくる映画を見ることが許されていない。

□□□ 0476

inspect

/ ɪnspékt /

名 inspection 検査、点検

動 to look at something to learn more about it or find problems

～を詳しく調べる、検査する

≒ examine

🔑 〈in- (中) +spect (見る)〉

例 The car was **inspected** for any damage before being sold.

その車は売却される前に損傷しているところがないかどうか検査された。

□□□ 0477

shallow

/ ʃǽloʊ /

形 having a short distance between the top and bottom

(物理的に)浅い

⇔ deep

ⓘ a shallow understanding（浅い理解）のような比喩的な使い方もある。

例 The river was too **shallow** for anyone to swim in.

その川は誰が泳ぐにも浅すぎた。

□□□ 0478

ally / ǽlaɪ /

名 alliance 同盟
形 allied 同盟している

名 ① a country that supports another country during a war

同盟国

⇔ enemy

🔑 〈al-(〜に)+ly(結びつける)〉

ⓘ yの発音に注意。

例 Germany's biggest **ally** today is France.

今のドイツの最大の同盟国はフランスだ。

② a person or group that helps another

同盟者、味方

≒ friend, supporter

例 The mayor was lucky to have a powerful **ally** in the city council.

その市長には幸運にも市議会に強力な味方がいた。

□□□ 0479

accidentally / æ̀ksədéntəli /

形 accidental 偶然の
名 accident 事故；偶然

副 ① happening or done by mistake or unintentionally

誤って、うっかり

≒ unwittingly

⇔ deliberately, intentionally, on purpose

例 The older man **accidentally** pressed the gas pedal instead of the brake and drove into a building.

その高齢の男性は誤ってブレーキの代わりにアクセルペダルを踏み、ビルに突っ込んだ。

② happening or done in a way that was not planned

偶然に

≒ coincidentally, by accident

例 She **accidentally** hit the man with her purse when she turned around.

彼女は振り返ったときにたまたまその男性にバッグをぶつけてしまった。

□□□ 0480

dense / déns /

副 densely 密集して
名 density 密度、密集

形 having things very close together

密集した

≒ packed, compact

⇔ sparse, scattered

例 A sea otter's **dense** fur protects it from the cold water in which it swims.

ラッコの密生した毛は、それが泳ぐ冷たい水からラッコを守っている。

□□□ 0481

likewise / láɪkwàɪz /

副 in the same way

同じように

🔑 〈like（似た）+-wise（ように）〉

例 All of your brothers have started their homework, and you should do **likewise**.

お兄ちゃんたちはみんな宿題を始めたんだから、あなたも同じようにしなさい。

□□□ 0482

scary / skéəri /

動 scare ～を怖がらせる

0483語

形 making someone feel fear

怖い、恐ろしい

≒ terrifying, horrifying

⇔ comforting

例 The man looked **scary** with his bright red eyes.

その男は赤い目がぎらぎらしていて恐ろしく見えた。

□□□ 0483

dye / dáɪ /

名 something that is used to change the color of something for a short time or permanently

染料

ⓘ die（死ぬ）と同音。「〈髪・布など〉を染める」という動詞の意味もある。

例 Teachers shouldn't use **dye** to make their hair an unnatural color.

教員は髪の色を不自然な色に染めるべきではない。

☐☐☐ **0484**

offend

/ əfénd /

图 offense 犯罪；侮辱
形 offensive 失礼な

🎬 to make someone feel hurt, angry, or upset

〜の感情を害する

≒ irritate, outrage

🔑 ⟨of-⟨〜に対して⟩+fend⟨打つ⟩⟩

⇔ please

例 Reporters must be careful with their words so they don't **offend** any listeners.

リポーターはどのリスナーの感情も害さないよう、言葉に注意しなければならない。

☐☐☐ **0485**

isolate

/ áɪsəlèɪt /

形 isolated 孤立した
图 isolation 隔離、孤立

🎬 to put or keep something or someone away from others

〜を隔離する、孤立させる

≒ separate, alienate, confine

🔑 ⟨isol⟨島⟩+-ate⟨動詞⟩⟩

例 They had no choice but to keep the sick people **isolated** from the healthy people.

彼らは病人を健康な人々から隔離しておくしかなかった。

☐☐☐ **0486**

commodity

/ kəmá:dəti /

图 ① a person or a thing that is useful or valued by others

（価値のある）もの

例 That actress is a hot **commodity** in Hollywood right now.

その女優はハリウッドで今、大人気だ。

② a thing that is bought and sold for money

商品、売買品

≒ product, goods, item

例 Oil is still a major worldwide **commodity**.

石油はいまだに主要な世界的商品だ。

□□□ 0487

weave / wíːv /

動 ① to make something by crossing threads or materials over each other

～を編む

ⓘ weave-wove-wovenと活用する。

例 The young girl **wove** a hat out of straw.

その若い娘はわらで帽子を編んだ。

② to create something new by putting different things together

～を作り上げる、まとめ上げる

≒ piece together

例 The musicians **wove** together a beautiful and heartbreaking song.

そのミュージシャンたちは美しく切ない歌を一緒に作り上げた。

□□□ 0488

invade / ɪnvéɪd /

图 invasion 侵略
图 invader 侵略者

動 to enter a place and try to take control by force

～を侵略する、～に侵入する

≒ attack

🔑 〈in- (中に) +vade (行く)〉

⇔ retreat, withdraw, defend

例 The British and the French **invaded** each others' countries for hundreds of years.

イギリス人とフランス人は何百年もの間、互いの国を侵略した。

□□□ 0489

chaos / kéɪɑːs /

形 chaotic 無秩序な

图 a state in which everything is out of control

無秩序、大混乱

≒ disorder, anarchy

⇔ order, harmony

ⓘ 「カオス」はカタカナ語にもなっている。aの発音に注意。

例 The train station was in complete **chaos** after people heard the gunshots.

人々が銃声を聞くと、駅は完全な混乱状態になった。

☐☐☐ 0490

demanding

/ dɪmǽndɪŋ /

動 demand 〜を要求する

形 needing a lot of time, attention, or energy

要求の多い、厳しい

≒ stringent

例 Being a doctor can be very **demanding** because you must work long hours.

医者になると長時間働かなければならないので、とても大変な場合がある。

☐☐☐ 0491

probable

/ prɑ́:bəbl /

副 probably たぶん
名 probability 可能性、見込み

形 having a high chance of happening or being true

〈物事が〉ありそうな、起こりそうな

≒ likely, possible

⇔ improbable, unlikely

例 Unfortunately, it is **probable** that the wolves have disappeared from this forest forever.

残念ながら、オオカミがこの森から永久に姿を消した可能性が高い。

☐☐☐ 0492

domain

/ doʊméɪn /

名 ① an area of knowledge or skill in something

領域、分野

≒ field

例 In many parts of the world, childcare is no longer seen as only a woman's **domain**.

世界の多くの地域で、子育てはもはや女性だけの領域と見なされていない。

② the land controlled by a ruler or government

領地、領土

≒ territory

例 The British **domain** once spread across the whole world.

イギリスの領土はかつて全世界に広がっていた。

□□□ 0493

acute / əkjúːt / 副 acutely 強く、激しく

形 ① very serious and needing attention or action

深刻な

≒ severe

⇔ minor

例 An **acute** fuel shortage was caused by the war.

その戦争によって深刻な燃料不足が引き起こされた。

② having or showing skill in thinking clearly and understanding difficult things

〈考察などが〉鋭い

≒ keen

例 Even as a child, she had an **acute** understanding of politics.

子どもながら、彼女は政治を鋭く理解していた。

□□□ 0494

cough / kɔ́(ː)f /

動 to force air out of your throat, often because you are sick

咳をする

ⓘ gh の発音に注意。

例 The poor girl couldn't stop **coughing** and wasn't able to sleep.

そのかわいそうな女の子は咳が止まらず、眠れなかった。

□□□ 0495

awkward / ɔ́ːkwərd / 副 awkwardly 不器用に

形 not having skill, or made without skill

不器用な、下手な

≒ clumsy

例 The English translation of the book was very **awkward**, so no one read it.

その本の英訳はとても下手だったので、誰も読まなかった。

☐☐☐ 0496

transmit
/ trænsmít /

名 transmission 伝送、伝達
名 transmitter 送信器

動 ① to give or pass something from one person to another

〈情報など〉を伝える、
伝達する

≒ convey

⇔ receive

🔑 〈trans-(越えて)+mit(送る)〉

例 Parents often **transmit** the things they believe to their children.

親はしばしば自分が信じること
を子どもに伝える。

② to send something as an electrical signal to things, such as radios and televisions

〜を送信する、伝送する

≒ broadcast

例 The radio station **transmits** their broadcasts on two different frequencies.

そのラジオ局は放送を2つの
異なる周波数で送っている。

☐☐☐ 0497

drift
/ dríft /

動 to move slowly and freely on water or wind

漂う、漂流する

≒ float (away)

例 The balloon **drifted** away on the wind until it was no longer visible.

風船は見えなくなるまで風に
乗って遠ざかっていった。

☐☐☐ 0498

appetite
/ ǽpətàɪt /

名 a desire for something, especially food

食欲、欲求

⇔ dislike, indifference

🔑 〈ap-(〜に)+pet(求める)+
-ite(名詞)〉

例 Everyone had a big **appetite** after working hard in the fields all day.

畑で一日中重労働をしたので、
みんなとても食欲があった。

□□□ 0499

navigate

/ nǽvəgèɪt /

名 navigation 航海、航行
名 navigator 航海者

動 ① to direct something, such as a ship or airplane

～を操縦する、あやつる

≒ operate, maneuver

〈navi（船）+gate（進める）〉

例 The captain was able to safely **navigate** the ship into the harbor.

船長は船を安全に港の中まで航行させることができた。

② to find your way somewhere when traveling

航海する、進む

≒ sail

例 Before GPS, sailors had to **navigate** using the stars or a compass.

GPSが出てくる前は、船員は星や羅針盤を使って航海しなければならなかった。

□□□ 0500

discourage

/ dɪskə́ːrɪʤ /

名 discouragement 落胆

動 ① to try to make someone not want to do something

～を妨げる、思いとどまらせる

≒ dissuade

⇔ encourage

〈dis-(離れて)+courage(勇気)〉

ⓘ 〈discourage A from *doing*〉（Aが～するのを妨げる、思いとどまらせる）の形で押さえておこう。

例 The tax system in Japan **discourages** women from working full-time jobs once they are married.

日本の税制は女性が結婚後に常勤の仕事をするのを妨げる。

② to make someone feel less confident, hopeful, etc.

〈人〉を失望させる

⇔ encourage

例 Language learners can be **discouraged** by the amount of things they still don't know.

言語学習者は、自分がまだ知らないことの多さにくじけることがある。

0500語

章末ボキャブラリーチェック

次の語義が表す英単語を答えてください。

語義	解答	連番
❶ an action or way of thinking that you do naturally or without learning it	i n s t i n c t	0440
❷ to tell someone secret information so that it will be shared with the public	l e a k	0406
❸ to give information about something or warn someone of something	a l e r t	0418
❹ a quality that is seen as good and moral	v i r t u e	0446
❺ to try to make someone not want to do something	d i s c o u r a g e	0500
❻ to lose something off your body naturally	s h e d	0467
❼ having the power to make change happen or control people's feelings	i n f l u e n t i a l	0443
❽ to make or fix something using a needle and thread	s e w	0422
❾ to go down from a higher place	d e s c e n d	0454
❿ to enter a place and try to take control by force	i n v a d e	0488
⓫ to make someone feel hurt, angry, or upset	o f f e n d	0484
⓬ regarding a group of people or the things connected to a group of people who have a culture that is usually different from the main one	e t h n i c	0421
⓭ to do what is required to complete something, such as a contract	f u l f i l l	0458
⓮ making someone feel fear	s c a r y	0482
⓯ something from a plant or an animal from thousands or millions of years ago that you can find in some rocks	f o s s i l	0428
⓰ the act of making something available that is wanted or needed	p r o v i s i o n	0425
⓱ a person who helps make something based on new ideas or methods	p i o n e e r	0434
⓲ an opening or activity through which something can be released (e.g. feelings, air, etc.)	o u t l e t	0411
⓳ to make things or people go away from each other	s c a t t e r	0419

語義	解答	連番
⑳ very serious and needing attention or action	a c u t e	0493
㉑ a right that some people have and others do not	p r i v i l e g e	0457
㉒ a desire for something, especially food	a p p e t i t e	0498
㉓ clear to the mind or by sight	e v i d e n t	0423
㉔ to die from being underwater too long, or to cause someone or something to die in this way	d r o w n	0459
㉕ a machine that uses electricity and is found in people's homes	a p p l i a n c e	0449
㉖ to look at something to learn more about it or find problems	i n s p e c t	0476
㉗ to move away from a place or situation, usually because it is dangerous or not enjoyable	r e t r e a t	0430
㉘ a person who has been named by the Christian church as being holy because of the things they did	s a i n t	0445
㉙ to stop (doing something)	c e a s e	0473
㉚ to add something to another thing to make it complete	s u p p l e m e n t	0409
㉛ to start existing or be made	o r i g i n a t e	0404
㉜ to do something that is against a rule or law	v i o l a t e	0432
㉝ in the same way	l i k e w i s e	0481
㉞ to move slowly and freely on water or wind	d r i f t	0497
㉟ to be the same as another thing	c o n s t i t u t e	0437
㊱ used to show something that is assumed	g i v e n	0452
㊲ to find something that was not known	u n c o v e r	0464
㊳ something that is used to change the color of something for a short time or permanently	d y e	0483
㊴ to cause activity in something	s t i m u l a t e	0438
㊵ to stop something, such as a service, for a short period of time	s u s p e n d	0436
㊶ to run away from something that is dangerous	f l e e	0448
㊷ to grow larger than normal	s w e l l	0405

❸ good or appropriate — d e c e n t — 0408

❹ a country that supports another country during a war — a l l y — 0478

❺ having or showing experience and knowledge about many things — s o p h i s t i c a t e d — 0427

❻ connected to literature — l i t e r a r y — 0407

❼ a very strong feeling of being scared — t e r r o r — 0455

❽ not nice to see, smell, taste, or hear — n a s t y — 0475

❾ being gentle, or showing love and kindness to someone or something — t e n d e r — 0442

❺ to use all of someone's physical or mental energy — e x h a u s t — 0426

❺ used when adding detailed information to something already said — n a m e l y — 0403

❺ to state or promise very strongly that something is a certain way, or that you will or will not do something — s w e a r — 0461

❺ to receive something from someone when they die — i n h e r i t — 0433

❺ having a short distance between the top and bottom — s h a l l o w — 0477

❺ a long and difficult effort or journey to find or do something — q u e s t — 0435

❺ a list of things that have to be done or considered — a g e n d a — 0450

❺ a wild animal that is large and maybe dangerous — b e a s t — 0402

❺ using, believing, or interested in new or modern ideas — p r o g r e s s i v e — 0444

❺ having things very close together — d e n s e — 0480

❻ to extend the valid time period of something — r e n e w — 0417

❻ earning money — p r o f i t a b l e — 0414

❻ needing a lot of time, attention, or energy — d e m a n d i n g — 0490

❻ happening because of something else — c o n s e q u e n t l y — 0456

❻ a person or a thing that is useful or valued by others — c o m m o d i t y — 0486

❻ not too proud or confident about your skills or yourself — m o d e s t — 0466

語義	解答	連番
⑥ relating to general ideas	a b s t r a c t	0447
⑥ to experience or put up with something unpleasant or painful for a long time (without giving up)	e n d u r e	0453
⑥ accepting something that happens or what people do without trying to change anything	p a s s i v e	0420
⑥ being excited about something	e n t h u s i a s t i c	0431
⑦ a small area on a surface that is raised up	b u m p	0410
⑦ to put or keep something or someone away from others	i s o l a t e	0485
⑦ to leave something in a liquid for some time	s o a k	0441
⑦ happening or done by mistake or unintentionally	a c c i d e n t a l l y	0479
⑦ the feeling of being sorry for or caring about another person's troubles	s y m p a t h y	0463
⑦ to remove something from something else	d e l e t e	0460
⑦ to jump from something	l e a p	0472
⑦ to give or pass something from one person to another	t r a n s m i t	0496
⑦ the end of a marriage done through legal means	d i v o r c e	0413
⑦ to make something by crossing threads or materials over each other	w e a v e	0487
⑧ a medicine or something else that helps fix pain or sickness	r e m e d y	0474
⑧ an idea that people believe is true and use in arguments	p r e m i s e	0462
⑧ to force air out of your throat, often because you are sick	c o u g h	0494
⑧ to direct something, such as a ship or airplane	n a v i g a t e	0499
⑧ to try to legally force a person or organization to give you something that you should receive	s u e	0429
⑧ to give information to someone	c o n v e y	0412
⑧ to begin or agree to do some kind of task	u n d e r t a k e	0401
⑧ very large in number or effect	o v e r w h e l m i n g	0471

㊱ having or showing qualities that are respected by others — <u>n o b l e</u> — 0468

㊲ not having skill, or made without skill — <u>a w k w a r d</u> — 0495

㊳ to talk to others and/or do things with them — <u>i n t e r a c t</u> — 0424

㊴ to make babies, new plants, etc. — <u>r e p r o d u c e</u> — 0439

㊵ to let someone use something for a certain amount of time if they give you money — <u>l e a s e</u> — 0465

㊶ only one — <u>s o l e</u> — 0415

㊷ to put things into groups based on what they are like — <u>c l a s s i f y</u> — 0469

㊸ the period of time between two different things — <u>s p a n</u> — 0470

㊹ an area of knowledge or skill in something — <u>d o m a i n</u> — 0492

㊺ to show too much confidence in something you have or have done — <u>b o a s t</u> — 0451

㊻ the ability to feel using your physical senses — <u>s e n s a t i o n</u> — 0416

㊼ a state in which everything is out of control — <u>c h a o s</u> — 0489

㊽ having a high chance of happening or being true — <u>p r o b a b l e</u> — 0491

Stage 6

When the going gets tough, the tough get going.
困難なときが力の見せどき。

□□□ 0501

segment

/ 名 ségmənt 動 ségment /

名 segmentation 分割

名 one of the parts into which something can be divided

部分、区分

≒ section, portion

例 In the final **segment** of the novel, the main character dies.

その小説の最後の部分で主人公は死ぬ。

動 to divide something into parts or pieces

〜を分割する

例 The population of the world is **segmented** into different age groups when studied.

世界人口は、研究されるとき、異なる年齢層に分割される。

□□□ 0502

mercy

/ mə́:rsi /

形 merciful 慈悲深い
形 merciless 無慈悲な

名 kind or forgiving treatment of someone you have the power to harm or punish

慈悲、情け

≒ compassion, sympathy

⇔ cruelty

ⓘ at the mercy of (〜のなすがままに) という表現も覚えておこう。

例 The hungry woman begged for **mercy** after she was caught stealing food.

腹をすかせたその女性は食べ物を盗んで捕まると慈悲を乞うた。

□□□ 0503

consensus

/ kənsénsəs /

名 a way of thinking that is shared by all the people in a group

合意、総意

≒ accord ⇔ disagreement

ⓘ 「コンセンサス」はカタカナ語にもなっている。

例 There is a growing **consensus** throughout the world that something needs to be done about climate change.

気候変動に関して何かしなければならないという一致した考えが世界中で拡大している。

□□□ 0504

hence / héns /

副 for the reason said

それゆえ、従って

≒ thus

ⓘ 文章で用いられる堅い語。

例 The woman was new to the neighborhood and **hence** had no friends there.

女性はその地区に引っ越してきたばかりで、そのため、そこには友人がいなかった。

□□□ 0505

neutral / n(j)úːtrəl /

名 neutrality 中立
動 neutralize ～を中立化する

形 not supporting anything or anyone in a fight or war

中立の

≒ unbiased

⇔ biased

例 Switzerland remained **neutral** during the fighting of World War II.

スイスは第二次世界大戦の戦闘中、中立を保った。

0506 語

□□□ 0506

desperate / déspərət /

副 desperately 必死に
名 despair 絶望

形 ① done with all your energy but with low chances of success

必死の、死に物狂いの

🔑 〈de-(～のない)+sper(希望)+-ate(形容詞)〉

例 He made a **desperate** attempt to save his job but was fired anyway.

彼は必死になって自分の仕事を守ろうとしたが、結局解雇されてしまった。

② strongly wanting (to do) something

欲しくてたまらない

≒ eager

例 He was **desperate** to see his favorite band play before he died.

彼は死ぬまでに大好きなバンドの演奏をどうしても見たかった。

☐☐☐ 0507

scold
/ skóʊld /

動 to speak in an upset or angry way to someone who has done something wrong

～を叱る

≒ admonish, reprimand

⇔ praise, commend, compliment

ⓘ 〈scold A for B〉（BのことでAを叱る）の形で押さえておこう。

例 The children were **scolded** for running through the house with muddy shoes on.

子どもたちは泥のついた靴を履いたまま家中を走り回って叱られた。

☐☐☐ 0508

disclose
/ dɪsklóʊz /

名 disclosure 暴露

動 to share information with the public

～を公表する、暴く

≒ reveal, state

🔑 〈dis-（否定）+close（閉じる）〉

例 The name of the train accident victim was never **disclosed** to the public.

その鉄道事故の犠牲者の名前が世間に公表されることはなかった。

☐☐☐ 0509

dump
/ dʌmp /

動 to throw away something, usually in secret or illegally

〈ごみなど〉を捨てる

≒ dispose of

ⓘ 「～を投げ売りする」の意味もあり、そのing形がdumping（ダンピング）。

例 Many people used to **dump** their garbage in the river.

昔は多くの人がごみをその川に捨てていた。

名 a place where garbage is taken and left

ごみ捨て場

例 If you are willing to look, many treasures can be found at the **dump**.

探す気があれば、ごみ捨て場でたくさんの掘り出し物を見つけられる。

☐☐☐ 0510

ritual

/ ríʧuəl / 形 ritualistic 儀式の

名 a formal ceremony or actions that are always done in the same way

儀式

例 The Shinto priest performed a special **ritual** to keep away evil spirits.

神主は悪霊を寄せつけないための特別な儀式を行った。

☐☐☐ 0511

bounce

/ báuns /

動 to hit a surface and move quickly in a different direction

〈音などが〉反響する、反射する

≒ rebound

例 The sound of the children's voices **bounced** off the walls of the cave.

子どもたちの声の音が洞窟の壁に反響した。

☐☐☐ 0512

0512 語

cater

/ kéɪtər /

動 ① to provide something that is wanted or needed by someone or something

要望に応える

⇔ ignore, neglect

ⓘ cater to（〜に必要なものを提供する）の形で押さえておこう。

例 The easy-to-use online school **caters** to older students who are not good with computers.

その使いやすいオンラインスクールは、コンピュータの扱いがうまくない年配の学生の要望に応える。

② to provide food and drinks at a gathering for money

料理をまかなう

ⓘ 「ケータリング」はカタカナ語にもなっている。

例 The Italian restaurant mostly **caters** for formal events such as weddings.

そのイタリア料理店は主に結婚式のようなフォーマルな行事に飲食物を提供する。

☐☐☐ 0513

sensible / sénsəbl /

副 sensibly 賢明にも
名 sensibility 感受性

形 having or showing good reason or judgement

賢明な

≒ reasonable

⇔ unreasonable, irrational, foolish

🔑 ⟨sens(感じる)+-ible(できる)⟩

例 Grandma was **sensible** enough to stop driving after her eyesight got bad.

祖母は視力が悪くなると、賢明にも運転するのをやめた。

☐☐☐ 0514

attain / ətéɪn /

名 attainment 達成

動 to gain or finish something

～を達成する、成し遂げる

≒ achieve, obtain

⇔ give up

🔑 ⟨at-(～に)+tain(保つ)⟩

例 She promised nothing would stop her from **attaining** her goal.

彼女は、自分が目標を達成するのを妨げるものは何もないと断言した。

☐☐☐ 0515

frankly / frǽŋkli /

形 frank 率直な

副 in an honest and direct way

率直に、正直に言って

≒ honestly

例 The therapist told all of her patients to speak to her **frankly**.

そのセラピストは、私に率直に話してください、と患者全員に言った。

☐☐☐ 0516

voluntary / vá:ləntèri /

副 voluntarily 自発的に

形 done by choice and without being forced

自発的な、任意の

≒ willing, independent

⇔ involuntary

例 Giving blood is a **voluntary** act that helps many people.

献血は多くの人を助ける自発的な行為だ。

□□□ 0517

sour / sáʊər /

形 ① having an acidic taste that is close to the taste of a lemon or lime

酸っぱい

ⓘ ourの発音に注意。

例 Citric acid is used to make candy **sour** like a lemon.

クエン酸は、あめをレモンのように酸っぱくするのに使われる。

② not nice or kind

不機嫌な

≒ bitter, unpleasant

⇔ pleasant, enjoyable

例 Nobody wants to be friends with someone who is **sour** and unhappy all the time.

いつも不機嫌で不満げな人とは誰も友達になりたくない。

動 to make something less good or pleasant

〈物事〉を気まずくする

≒ spoil, ruin

例 The rugby team's victory was **soured** by the fact that their captain was seriously injured during the match.

そのラグビーチームは勝ったものの、試合中にキャプテンが大けがをしたことで、苦い勝利になった。

□□□ 0518

confess / kənfés / 名 conféssion 告白

動 to admit to someone that you did something bad or illegal

白状する、認める

≒ profess, reveal

⇔ deny

ⓘ 〈confess to A/doing〉（A／〜したことを白状する）のほか、〈confess (that)...〉（…ということを白状する）という他動詞の使い方も押さえておこう。

例 None of the children would **confess** to stealing the cookies that had been on the counter.

子どもは誰もカウンターにあったクッキーを盗んだことを認めようとしなかった。

225

□□□ **0519**

assert

/ əsə́ːrt /

名 assertion 主張
形 assertive 断定的な

動 to say something strongly

〜を言い張る、断言する

≒ declare, stress

🔑 〈as- (〜に) +sert (結ぶ)〉

ⓘ 〈assert (that)...〉(…だと言い張る) の形で押さえておこう。

例 The man **asserted** that he had not stolen his mother's watch.

その男は自分の母親の腕時計を盗んでいないと言い張った。

□□□ **0520**

abundant

/ əbʌ́ndənt /

名 abundance 豊富さ
副 abundantly 豊富に
動 abound たくさんある

形 existing or happening in large amounts

豊富な、たくさんの

≒ ample, sufficient

⇔ insufficient, lacking

例 Tropical plants grow in areas with **abundant** rainfall.

熱帯の植物は豊かな降雨に恵まれた地域で育つ。

□□□ **0521**

insure

/ ɪnʃúər /

名 insurance 保険

動 to buy insurance for something to be financially protected

〜に保険をかける

≒ guarantee

🔑 〈in- (中に) +sure (確かな)〉

例 It is against the law in Canada to drive a car that isn't **insured**.

保険をかけていない車を運転することはカナダでは法律違反だ。

□□□ **0522**

portray

/ pɔːrtréɪ /

名 portrait 肖像画
名 portrayal 描写

動 to show a likeness of someone or something using images or words

〜を描写する、言葉で書く

≒ depict, illustrate

例 King Henry VIII is **portrayed** as a greedy and unkind man in many books about him.

国王ヘンリー8世は彼について書かれた多くの本で強欲で冷酷な男として描かれている。

□□□ 0523

accumulate

/ əkjú:mjəlèɪt /

名 accumulation 蓄積、積み立て
形 accumulative 累積する

動 ① **to gather something little by little over time**

～を蓄積する、ためる

⇔ decrease, diminish, lose

🔑 〈ac-(～に)+cuml(集める)+-ate(動詞)〉

例 In three years, the librarian has **accumulated** over 6,000 new books for the library.

その図書館員は図書館のために3年で6千冊以上の新しい本をためた。

② **to grow larger as time passes**

蓄積する、たまる

≒ pile up

⇔ shrink

例 The dust covering the books had **accumulated** after years of neglect.

本を覆うほこりは何年も放っておいたために蓄積したものだった。

0525 語

□□□ 0524

tempt

/ témpt /

名 temptation 誘惑、衝動
形 tempting 魅力的な

動 to make someone want (to do) something even though it may be bad

～を誘惑する、そそのかす

≒ entice, persuade

ⓘ 〈tempt A to *do*/into *do*ing〉(Aを～するよう誘惑する) の形で押さえておこう。

例 It is the job of a salesperson to **tempt** people into buying something.

人々にものを買ってもらうよう誘導するのが販売員の仕事だ。

□□□ 0525

ridiculous

/ rɪdíkjələs /

動 ridicule ～を嘲笑する

形 very silly

ばかげた、滑稽な

≒ absurd, outrageous, unreasonable

例 The dog looked **ridiculous** wearing a clown costume.

その犬はピエロの衣装を身につけていて、滑稽に見えた。

□□□ 0526

nightmare

/ náɪtmèər /

名 a dream that is bad or scares the person dreaming

悪夢

🔑〈night（夜）+mare（悪霊）〉

例 She had **nightmares** about her cat's death every night for one year.

彼女は1年間、毎晩、飼い猫が死ぬ悪夢を見た。

□□□ 0527

voyage

/ vɔ́ɪɪʤ /

名 a long trip that is made over water or through space

（特に船・空の長い）旅

≒ journey

ⓘ aの発音に注意。

例 The Titanic sank off the Canadian coast on its first **voyage** across the Atlantic Ocean.

タイタニック号は大西洋を渡る初航海でカナダ沖に沈んだ。

□□□ 0528

triumph

/ tráɪəmf /

形 triumphant 勝ち誇った

名 ① a great victory

（大）勝利

⇔ loss, defeat

ⓘ 発音に注意。「（苦労の末）勝利する」という動詞の意味もある。

例 The army celebrated their **triumph** with a parade.

その軍隊はパレードをして勝利を祝った。

② a great success

大成功

≒ achievement

⇔ failure

例 Quitting gambling was a **triumph** for her father.

賭け事をやめたことは彼女の父にとって大きな意味があった。

□□□ 0529

clarify

/ klǽrəfàɪ /

图 clarity 明快さ
图 clarification 明確化

動 to make something clear or easy to understand

〈意味など〉を明らか
にする

≒ define

♥〈clar (はっきりした) +ify (〜
にする)〉

例 The teacher's explanation did not **clarify** the meaning of the word.

先生の説明ではその単語の意
味は明らかにならなかった。

□□□ 0530

whisper

/ wíspər /

動 to speak using a very quiet voice

ささやく、小声で話す

≒ murmur

例 The students **whispered** to each other to hide their conversation from the teacher.

生徒たちは会話が先生に聞こ
えないようにささやき合った。

0531語

□□□ 0531

illusion

/ ɪlúːʒən /

形 illusory 錯覚による

名 ① something that looks different from what it really is

錯覚、幻想

≒ fantasy

⇔ reality

例 The paper on the cover of the notebook gives the **illusion** that it is leather.

そのノートの表紙はそれが革
であるかのような錯覚を与える。

② an idea about something that is untrue

思い違い

≒ misconception

⇔ fact, truth

例 The man was under the **illusion** that he was a great lawyer even though no one would hire him.

その男は、誰も彼を雇おうとし
ないのに、自分は素晴らしい弁
護士だと思い違いをしていた。

□□□ **0532**

ashamed / əʃéɪmd /

形 feeling guilty or shameful about something

恥じている

≒ embarrassed ⇔ unashamed

ⓘ shame（恥）、shameful（恥ずべき）という語も覚えておこう。

例 She still feels **ashamed** that she hit her brother when he was a baby.

彼女は弟が赤ん坊だったころに弟をたたいたことをいまだに恥ずかしく思っている。

□□□ **0533**

intensive / ɪnténsɪv /

副 intensively 集中的に
名 intensity 強烈さ
動 intensify ～を強くする

形 involving a lot of energy or effort

集中的な

≒ comprehensive

ⓘ 病院のICU（集中治療室）は、intensive care unit の略。

例 It is common for Japanese students to take **intensive** study programs to help them pass exams.

日本の学生は試験に通るのを助けてもらうために、集中学習プログラムを受講することがよくある。

□□□ **0534**

decay / dɪkéɪ /

動 to slowly break down because of natural processes

腐る、朽ちる

≒ corrode, rot

🔑 〈de-（下に）+cay（落ちる）〉

例 The fallen leaves in the forest will slowly **decay** before becoming part of the soil.

森の落ち葉は土の一部になるまでゆっくりと腐る。

名 the act or result of decaying

腐敗、虫歯

≒ corrosion

例 The dentist had to take out several of her teeth because there was too much **decay** to save them.

彼女の虫歯はひどくて手の施しようがなかったため、歯科医は何本かの歯を抜かなければならなかった。

□□□ 0535

cruel

/ krúːəl /

副 cruelly 残酷に、意地悪に
名 cruelty 残酷さ

形 having a desire to be unkind to others without feeling sorry about it

残酷な

≒ mean

⇔ kind, sympathetic

例 It is surprising how **cruel** children can be to others.

子どもが他人にいかに残酷になり得るかは驚くべきことだ。

□□□ 0536

tolerate

/ tάːlərèit /

名 tolerance 許容、寛容
形 tolerant 寛容な

動 to let something exist or be done, even if you do not like it

〜を許容する、大目に見る

≒ accept, permit ⇔ reject

例 His bad temper was **tolerated** because he was a great musician.

彼は偉大な音楽家だったので、気難しさは大目に見られた。

0538語

□□□ 0537

implication

/ ìmpləkéiʃən /

動 imply 〜を含意する

名 a possible future result caused by something done now

(予想される)影響、結果

≒ consequence

ⓘ ふつう複数形で使う。「含意」の意味もある。

例 The **implications** of oil pollution are only now becoming known to the public.

原油による汚染の影響は今になってようやく世間に知られ始めている。

□□□ 0538

racial

/ réiʃəl /

名 race 人種
名 racism 人種差別主義

形 connected to race

人種の

≒ ethnic

例 It is important not to let **racial** stereotypes control how you think about someone.

誰かについてどう思うかを、人種への固定観念に左右されないようにすることが重要だ。

□□□ 0539

flock

/ flá:k /

名 a group of birds or animals (such as sheep) that move together

（鳥・ヒツジなどの）群れ

≒ herd

例 The shepherd led his **flock** of sheep back to the barn every night.

その羊飼いは毎晩、ヒツジの群れを小屋に戻した。

動 to gather in one place or move together in a group

群がる、詰めかける

≒ converge

⇔ disperse, scatter

例 Hundreds of people **flocked** to the beach to see the baby turtles.

何百人もの人々が子ガメを見るために浜辺に詰めかけた。

□□□ 0540

carve

/ ká:rv /

名 carving 彫刻（した像）

動 to make something by cutting off pieces of its original form

〜を刻む、彫る

≒ sculpt

ⓘ curve は「曲がる」、curb は「縁石；〜を抑える」。

例 His mother **carved** him a toy horse out of wood.

母親は彼におもちゃの馬を木から彫ってやった。

□□□ 0541

magnificent

/ mægnífəsənt /

名 magnificence 壮大
動 magnify 〜を拡大する

形 very beautiful, impressive, or great

〈外観・景色などが〉壮大な

≒ brilliant, splendid

例 The view of Mt. Fuji from Lake Kawaguchiko is **magnificent**.

河口湖からの富士山の眺めは素晴らしい。

□□□ 0542

enclose

/ ɪnklóʊz / 名 enclosure 包囲

動 ① **to put something completely around another thing**

～を囲む、包囲する

♥〈en- (中に) +close (閉じる)〉

例 A high wooden fence **encloses** the garden and hides it from view.

高い木製の柵がその庭を取り囲んで、中が見えないようにしている。

② **to include something with a letter or in a package**

～を同封する

≒ insert

例 Their daughter **enclosed** pictures of their grandchildren with the letter.

彼らの娘は手紙に孫たちの写真を同封した。

0544語

□□□ 0543

destiny

/ déstəni / 動 destine ～を運命づける
形 destined 運命づけられた

名 **the things that will happen (to someone) in the future**

運命、宿命

≒ fate, inevitability

例 She believed that it was her **destiny** to marry a rich man.

彼女は、自分が金持ちと結婚する運命にあると信じていた。

□□□ 0544

conceive

/ kənsíːv / 形 conceivable 考えられる
名 concept 概念

動 **to think of or make something in your mind**

～を思いつく、考え出す

≒ envision, devise

♥〈con- (完全に) +ceive (つかむ)〉

例 When the scriptwriter **conceived** this role, he knew that Angelina Jolie had to play it.

脚本家は、この役を構想したとき、演じるのはアンジェリーナ・ジョリーしかいないと思った。

□□□ 0545

realm / rélm /

名 ① an area of an activity or interest 領域、範囲

≒ field, territory, domain

ⓘ ea の発音に注意。

例 New discoveries are made in the **realm** of medicine every day.　医学の分野では毎日、新発見がある。

② a country with a king or queen as its ruler 王国

≒ kingdom, domain

例 The **realm** has been peaceful for over 100 years.　その王国は100年以上にわたって平和だ。

□□□ 0546

render / réndər /

動 to make someone or something be a certain way 〜を(ある状態に)する

ⓘ 〈render A B〉で「AをBにする」。

例 The beauty of the song **rendered** the audience speechless.　その歌は美しく、聴衆は言葉を失った。

□□□ 0547

courtesy / kə́ːrtəsi / 形 courteous 礼儀正しい

名 behavior that shows respect to others and is polite 礼儀正しいこと

≒ manners, politeness

⇔ disrespect

ⓘ 原義は「court(宮廷)の作法を身につけていること」。

例 The doctor did not even have the common **courtesy** to introduce himself before starting the examination of the patient.　その医者には、患者の診察を始める前に自己紹介をするという一般的な礼儀さえなかった。

☐☐☐ **0548**

bore
/ bɔ́ːr /

形 boring 退屈な
名 boredom 退屈

動 to make someone feel tired or annoyed by being uninteresting

〈人〉を退屈させる

⇔ interest

例 A good writer will never **bore** their readers.

上手な書き手は読み手を決して退屈させない。

☐☐☐ **0549**

comply
/ kəmpláɪ /

名 compliance 遵守

動 to do the task you have been asked or ordered to do

従う、応じる

≒ adhere to, obey

⇔ disregard, violate

ⓘ comply with の形で使う。

例 People that don't **comply** with the rules will be punished.

規則に従わない人は罰せられる。

☐☐☐ **0550**

cultivate
/ kʌ́ltəvèɪt /

名 cultivation 栽培

動 ① to get soil ready and use it to grow plants

〈土地〉を耕す、〜を栽培する

例 Towns and villages started to form when people began to **cultivate** the land.

人々がその土地を開拓し始めると、町や村が形成されだした。

② to make something better through careful attention, training, or study

〈技能・心身〉を養う、育成する

≒ nourish, foster

ⓘ cult は「耕す」を意味する語根で、culture（文化、教養）、agriculture（農業）なども同語源語。

例 The young man **cultivated** his imagination by reading different kinds of books.

その若者はさまざまな本を読んで想像力を養った。

□□□ 0551

frustrate

/ frʌ́streɪt / 　名 frustration 挫折；欲求不満

動 to make someone feel angry or upset because of something they cannot do

〜をいらいらさせる

≒ annoy

⇔ comfort

例 Toddlers often get **frustrated** when adults cannot understand what they want.

幼児は自分が欲しいものを大人が理解できないとしばしば機嫌が悪くなる。

□□□ 0552

stain

/ stéɪn /

動 to leave a mark on something (usually fabric)

〜を汚す、しみをつける

≒ tarnish

ⓘ「汚れ、しみ」という名詞の意味もある。

例 The actress got spaghetti sauce all over her T-shirt and **stained** it red.

その女優はスパゲティソースをTシャツ中に飛ばして、赤いしみをつけた。

□□□ 0553

idle

/ áɪdl /

形 ① not doing much

〈人が〉仕事のない、何もしていない

⇔ active

ⓘ idol（アイドル、偶像）と同音。

例 The students sat **idle** at their desks, waiting for the teacher to return.

生徒たちは手持ちぶさたで席に座って、先生が戻ってくるのを待っていた。

② not being used

〈機械などが〉動いていない

≒ unused, inactive

ⓘ 動名詞形の idling（アイドリング）はカタカナ語にもなっている。

例 The factory has been **idle** since the owner died two weeks ago.

その工場はオーナーが2週間前に死んでから稼働していない。

□□ 0554

coordinate

/ kouɔ́:rdənèit /

名 coordination 調整、調和

動 to arrange things so that different groups of people can work together well

～を調整する、まとめる

≒ organize, regulate

ⓘ 「coordinate する人」が coordinator（コーディネーター）。

🔑〈co-（共に）+ordin（命令）+ -ate（動詞）〉

例 The military **coordinated** the clean-up effort after the earthquake.

地震の後、軍が清掃活動の調整をした。

□□ 0555

intermediate

/ ìntərmíːdiət /

形 at a level that is in between beginner and advanced

中間の、中級の

🔑〈inter-（間に）+medi（中間）+ -ate（形容詞）〉

0556語

例 You need to complete the beginner course before moving to the **intermediate** one.

中級コースに進む前に入門コースを終える必要がある。

□□ 0556

mold

/ móuld /

名 ① a fungus that grows on damp or rotting things

かび

ⓘ イギリス英語では mould とつづる。

例 After three weeks in the fridge, the food was covered in **mold**.

3週間冷蔵庫に入れておいたら、その食品はかびに覆われた。

② a container that gives a shape to something that is put into it

鋳型
いがた

≒ cast, model

例 The candles for the wedding were made in heart-shaped **molds**.

その結婚式のキャンドルはハート形の鋳型で作られた。

□□□ 0557

bleed

/ blíːd / 名 blood 血

動 to lose blood from your body because of a cut or injury

出血する

ⓘ bleed-bled-bledと活用する。

例 Her nose began **bleeding** after the ball hit her in the face.

ボールが彼女の顔に当たって、鼻血が出始めた。

□□□ 0558

grasp

/ grǽsp /

動 ① to grab something and hold onto it

〜を(しっかり)つかむ

≒ clutch, grip

⇔ let go, release

例 As people get older, they have a hard time **grasping** small objects like pencils.

人は年を取るにつれて、鉛筆のような小さいものをつかむのが大変になる。

② to understand something that is not simple

〜を理解する

≒ comprehend

⇔ misinterpret, misunderstand

例 Many people fail to **grasp** how important dealing with climate change is.

気候変動に対処することがいかに重要か、多くの人が理解していない。

名 a strong hold onto something, or a good understanding of a topic

把握、理解

例 The author's writing shows a weak **grasp** of basic writing techniques.

その著者の作品を読むと、基本的な文章作成技法をあまり理解していないことがわかる。

□□□ 0559

amaze / əméɪz /

形 amazing 驚くべき、素晴らしい
名 amazement 驚嘆

動 to surprise someone and sometimes make them confused

～を驚嘆させる、感心させる

≒ astonish, astound, impress　⇔ bore, tire

例 As a teacher, she was **amazed** by the progress that her students had made in only one year.

教師として、彼女は自分の生徒たちがわずか1年で遂げた進歩に驚いた。

□□□ 0560

digest / daɪdʒést /

名 digestion 消化
形 digestive 消化の

動 to change what you have eaten by natural processes into something that can be used by your body

～を消化する

ⓘ 「要約、ダイジェスト」という名詞の使い方もある。その場合、発音は [dáɪdʒest]。

🔑 〈di- (離れて) +gest (運ぶ)〉

0562語

例 Beef takes longer to **digest** than other meats like chicken.

牛肉は鶏肉などのほかの肉より、消化するのに時間がかかる。

□□□ 0561

bulk / bʌlk /

形 bulky かさばる

名 the large size of a person or object

容積、大きさ

例 The box's **bulk** made it impossible to move with only one person.

それらの箱は大きくて、一人だけでは動かせなかった。

□□□ 0562

refine / rɪfáɪn /

形 refined 洗練された；精製された
名 refinement 洗練

動 to make something better by changing small things

～を洗練する、〈技術など〉を磨く

≒ improve

🔑 〈re- (再び) +fine (完成する)〉

例 She started taking classes at night to **refine** her Spanish skills.

彼女はスペイン語を向上させるために夜間授業を受け始めた。

□□□ 0563

worship / wə́ːrʃəp /

動 to pray to, honor, or respect someone or something as a god

〜を崇拝する、あがめる

≒ revere, venerate

🔑 〈wor（価値のある）+ship（状態）〉

例 Followers of Buddhism are technically not supposed to **worship** the Buddha.

仏教の信徒は厳密には仏陀を崇拝しないことになっている。

名 the act of showing love for a god, usually done by praying with others

崇拝、礼拝

≒ veneration

例 Wedding ceremonies are traditionally held at places of **worship**.

結婚式は伝統的に礼拝所で行われる。

□□□ 0564

durable / d(j)úərəbl /

副 durably 丈夫に
名 durability 耐久性

形 staying in good condition even after a long time has passed

耐久性のある

≒ resilient　⇔ weak, fragile

ⓘ durは「継続する」を意味する語根で、during（〜の間）、endure（耐える）なども同語源語。

例 Very **durable** fabrics are used to make a soldier's uniform.

非常に耐久性のある生地が軍服を作るのに使われる。

□□□ 0565

lump / lʌ́mp /

名 a small piece of an object

（小さい）塊、かけら

≒ chunk, clump

例 It is said that Santa Claus gives **lumps** of coal to children who are bad.

サンタクロースは悪い子には石炭の塊をプレゼントすると言われている。

□□□ 0566

fake / féɪk /

形 not true or real

偽の

≒ fabricated, fictitious, forged

⇔ genuine, authentic

例 The blood used on movie sets is **fake**.

映画の撮影現場で使われる血は偽物だ。

名 a copy of something that looks like the real thing to trick people

偽物

≒ counterfeit

例 The woman was very upset when she found out the Louis Vuitton bag she had bought was a **fake**.

その女性は、自分が買ったルイ・ヴィトンのバッグが偽物だとわかって憤慨した。

0568 語

□□□ 0567

mainstream / méɪnstrìːm /

形 thought to be normal because most people do it

主流の

≒ dominant, conventional

⇔ unusual, unconventional

例 Not all illnesses can be treated with **mainstream** medicine alone.

すべての病気が主流の医療だけで治療できるわけではない。

□□□ 0568

vivid / vívɪd /

形 seeming like it is real because of clear details

生き生きとした、鮮明な

⇔ vague

🍭〈viv(生命)+-id(形容詞)〉

例 The ship captain's story of pirates was so **vivid** that everyone could imagine the scene perfectly.

海賊についての船長の話は真に迫っていたので、みんながその場面を完ぺきに想像できた。

□□□ 0569

sorrow

/ sάːrou / 形 sorrowful 悲嘆にくれた

名 a feeling of deep sadness that is usually caused by losing someone or something important

悲しみ

≒ grief　⇔ happiness, joy

ⓘ sor(r)は「痛み」を意味する語根で、sore（ひりひりする）、sorry（気の毒な）なども同語源語。

例 The girl felt great **sorrow** over the loss of her grandmother.

少女は祖母を失って大きな悲しみを感じた。

□□□ 0570

expedition

/ èkspədíʃən /

名 a trip that is made to do something specific

探検、遠出

≒ trek, quest

例 The **expedition** to reach the South Pole finally took place in 1911.

南極に達する探検は1911年についに実現した。

□□□ 0571

profound

/ prəfáʊnd / 副 profoundly 深く；心から

形 ① felt or experienced very strongly

深い、大きな

≒ deep

🔑 〈pro-（の方に）+found（底）〉

例 The major earthquake had a **profound** effect on the small town's economy.

大地震はその小さな町の経済に大きな影響を与えた。

② having a deep understanding of or a lot of knowledge about something

〈知識・理解が〉深い

⇔ superficial

例 The professor's **profound** knowledge of psychology helped his students understand their own minds.

教授の心理学に関する深い知識は、学生たちが自らの心を理解するのに役立った。

□□□ 0572

fatigue / fətí:g /

名 a state of being very tired

疲労、倦怠感

≒ tiredness, exhaustion　⇔ vigor, liveliness

ⓘ フランス語から来た語。アクセントは ti の位置。

例 The sailors were overcome with **fatigue** after their long trip.

船員たちは長旅の後で疲労困ばいしていた。

□□□ 0573

vanish / vǽnɪʃ /

動 to disappear completely without any explanation

（突然・わけもなく）消える、消え失せる

⇔ appear

❢〈van (からの) +-ish (動詞)〉

0575語

ⓘ 「(遠近画法の) 消尽点」は vanishing point と言う。

例 The missing women all seem to have **vanished** without a trace.

行方不明の女性たちは全員跡形もなく消えてしまったようだ。

□□□ 0574

crawl / krɔ́:l /

動 to move by using your hands and knees

はう、腹ばいで進む

ⓘ 水泳の「クロール」はこの crawl。

例 The baby **crawled** for the first time when he was only six months old.

その赤ちゃんはわずか6か月で初めてはいはいした。

□□□ 0575

deficit / défəsɪt /

形 deficient 不足した
名 deficiency 不足

名 an amount of something that is less than what is needed

不足額、赤字

≒ lack, insufficiency

⇔ surplus

例 The new government is facing a two billion dollar **deficit** this year.

新政府は今年、20億ドルの赤字に直面している。

□□□ 0576

stumble

/ stʌ́mbl /

動 to hit your foot when walking or running and almost fall

つまずく

≒ trip, stagger

ⓘ 比喩的に「とちる、間違える」という意味でも使われる。

例 The horse **stumbled** on the uneven ground, and the rider almost fell off.

その馬はでこぼこの地面でつまずき、騎手はあやうく落馬しそうになった。

□□□ 0577

compromise

/ ká:prəmàɪz /

動 ① to give up on something that you want so that you can make an agreement with another person

妥協する、譲歩する

ⓘ mise の発音に注意。

🔑 〈com- (共に) +promise (約束)〉

例 The brothers would not **compromise** with each other about how to share the new video game.

その兄弟は新しいテレビゲームの共有の仕方について互いに譲ろうとしなかった。

② to risk putting something in danger

～を危険にさらす

≒ endanger

例 The house cannot be remodeled without **compromising** the strength of the foundation.

その家は改築すれば必ず土台の強度が損なわれる。

名 a way to reach an agreement between two people by each person giving up something they want

妥協、譲歩

例 Their **compromise** was that she could only go to the concert if she cleaned her room.

彼らの妥協案は、自分の部屋を掃除したら彼女はコンサートに行ってよいというものだった。

□□□ 0578

immense

/ ɪméns /

🗾 immensely とても

形 very great in size or amount

巨大な、莫大な

≒ huge, enormous

💡 〈im-（否定）+mense（測る）〉

⇔ small, tiny

例 Elvis Presley's music continues to have **immense** popularity long after his death.

エルヴィス・プレスリーの音楽は、彼の死後も長く絶大な人気を保ち続けている。

□□□ 0579

infect

/ ɪnfékt /

名 infection 伝染
形 infectious 伝染性の

動 to pass an illness on to someone else

〈人など〉に伝染する、感染する

💡 〈in-（中に）+fect（置く）〉

例 Hundreds of people in the church were **infected** by a single sick person.

たった一人の病人から、教会にいた何百もの人に感染した。

□□□ 0580

substitute

/ sʌ́bstət(j)ùːt /

名 substitution 代用

動 to use a thing or person instead of another thing or person

〜を代わりにする

(i) アクセントはsubの位置。〈substitute A for B〉（Bの代わりにAを使う）の形で押さえておこう。

例 You can **substitute** maple syrup for sugar to make the recipe healthier.

より健康的に調理するには、砂糖の代わりにメープルシロップを使うとよい。

名 a person or thing that does something in the place of someone or something else

代わり、代用品

≒ alternative

例 Many burger restaurants have started to sell burgers made with meat **substitutes**.

多くのバーガー店が代用肉を使って作られたバーガーを売り始めている。

□□□ **0581**

distract

/ dɪstrǽkt /

形 **distracted** 気が散った
名 **distraction** 気晴らし

動 **to make someone think about something different from what they were thinking about before**

〈人・注意など〉をそらす、紛らす

≒ divert (*someone's* attention)

🔑 〈dis- (離れて) +tract (引く)〉

⇔ focus

例 The children in the classroom were **distracted** by the large dog standing outside the window.

教室の子どもたちは窓の外に立っている大きな犬に気をとられた。

□□□ **0582**

shrink

/ ʃríŋk /

動 **to become smaller**

縮む、縮小する

⇔ enlarge, expand, swell

ⓘ shrink-shrank/shrunk-shrunk(en)と活用する。

例 Some clothes will **shrink** if you put them in the dryer.

乾燥機に入れると縮む服もある。

□□□ **0583**

publicity

/ pʌblísəti /

動 **publicize** ～を宣伝する

名 ① **(something that attracts) people's attention, especially for a product**

注目、評判

例 The novel received a lot of good **publicity** thanks to the author's marketing efforts.

著者の売り込みのおかげで、その小説は多くの注目を浴びた。

② **the activity or business of getting people to pay attention to someone or something**

広告、宣伝

≒ advertising

例 Both the studio and the movie theater spent a lot of money on **publicity** for the movie.

制作会社も映画館もその映画の宣伝に大金を費やした。

□□□ 0584

miserable
/ mízərəbl / 名 misery みじめさ

形 not happy at all
みじめな、不幸な

≒ gloomy, depressed

⇔ cheerful, joyful

ⓘ フランスのユゴーの小説『レ・ミゼラブル』(Les Miserables) は直訳すると「悲惨な人たち」という意味。

例 Many people become lonely and **miserable** after their divorce.
多くの人は離婚後に寂しくなって落ち込む。

□□□ 0585

designate
/ dézɪgnèɪt / 名 designation 指定

動 to choose someone or something officially for a purpose
～を指定する、指名する

≒ nominate

ⓘ designと違い、gを発音する。

例 Hiraizumi was **designated** as a UNESCO World Heritage Site in 2011.
平泉は2011年にユネスコの世界遺産として登録された。

□□□ 0586

distress
/ dɪstrés / 形 distressful 苦しい

動 to make someone worry or get upset
～を悩ませる、悲しませる

≒ torment

例 They felt **distressed** after reading the news of the plane being shot down.
航空機が撃墜されたという記事を読んで、彼らは悲しみに沈んだ。

名 unhappiness that affects the mind or body and causes pain
悩み、嘆き

≒ anxiety, suffering

例 The citizens voiced their **distress** over the raise in taxes for months.
国民は何か月も増税に対する嘆きを表明した。

☐☐☐ 0587

motive

/ móʊtɪv /

動 motivate ～に動機を与える
名 motivation 動機づけ

名 a reason that someone has to do something

動機

≒ purpose, aim

例 The police were not able to find a **motive** for the murder.

警察はその殺人の動機を解明
できなかった。

☐☐☐ 0588

cautious

/ kɔ́:ʃəs /

副 cautiously 用心して、慎重に
名 caution 注意、警戒

形 careful to avoid danger or risk

慎重な

≒ watchful　　⇔ careless, inattentive, reckless

例 **Cautious** tourists will make sure that their passport is always close to their body.

慎重な旅行者はパスポートを
常に肌身離さず持っているよう
に気をつける。

☐☐☐ 0589

respective

/ rɪspéktɪv /

副 respectively それぞれ

形 belonging to or relating to each thing that has already been said

それぞれの、めいめいの

≒ corresponding

例 All the Olympic athletes will return to their **respective** countries after the Games are over.

オリンピック選手は皆、オリン
ピックが終わればそれぞれの
国に戻る。

☐☐☐ 0590

compensate

/ ká:mpənsèɪt /

形 compensatory 補償の、
埋め合わせの
名 compensation 補償

動 to give something of value to another person in return for something of equal value

〈人〉に補償する、報いる

≒ reimburse

🔑〈con-（共に）+pens（釣り合
い）+-ate（動詞）〉

例 Not all Japanese office workers are **compensated** for overtime.

すべての日本の会社員が残業
代を支払ってもらっているわけ
ではない。

248

☐☐☐ 0591

correspond

/ kɔ̀ːrəspáːnd /

形 **corresponding** 結果として起こる；対応する

動 ① to be like another thing

相当する

≒ correlate

⇔ differ

🔑 〈cor- (共に) +respond (応じる)〉

例 The role of the prime minister **corresponds** to the role of the president in some countries.

国によっては、総理大臣の役割は大統領の役割に相当する。

② to have a relationship to or with another thing

一致する、合致する

≒ coincide

⇔ disagree, conflict

例 The statements of the stabbing suspect don't **correspond** with the video evidence.

刺傷事件の容疑者の陳述は映像の証拠と合致しない。

☐☐☐ 0592

resign

/ rɪzáɪn /

名 **resignation** 辞職

動 to formally leave a job or position

辞職する

≒ step down, quit

ⓘ 「役職を (途中で) やめる」の意。定年で退職するときは retire。

例 The director of the company **resigned** after working there for 30 years.

その会社の取締役はそこで30年間勤務した後辞職した。

☐☐☐ 0593

semester

/ səméstər /

名 one of usually two periods of time that make up the school year at a school or university

(2学期制の) 学期

ⓘ 「(3期制の) 学期」は term と言う。

例 International students usually start classes in the summer **semester**.

留学生は通常、夏学期に授業を受け始める。

☐☐☐ 0594

annoy
/ ənɔ́ɪ /

名 annoyance いらだち
形 annoyed いらいらした
形 annoying いらいらさせる

動 to make someone feel a little angry　～をいらいらさせる

≒ irritate　⇔ calm, soothe

例 The actress was **annoyed** by reporters who asked too many questions about her private life.

その女優は私生活についてあまりにも多くの質問をするリポーターたちにいらいらした。

☐☐☐ 0595

nonetheless
/ nʌ̀nðəlés /

副 regardless of what was just said　それにもかかわらず

≒ however, nevertheless

ⓘ アクセントはlessの位置。

例 Everyone agreed that the hike had been fun, but **nonetheless** very tiring.

ハイキングは楽しかったけれど、それでもすごく疲れたということで、みんなの意見が一致した。

☐☐☐ 0596

browse
/ bráʊz /

動 ① to look at things in a store to see if there is something you want to buy or that looks interesting　（店で商品を）見て回る

≒ look through, scan

ⓘ owの発音に注意。

例 There were many people **browsing** in the bookstore.

その書店ではたくさんの人が見て回っていた。

② to use a program to find information on the Internet　〈ウェブサイト〉をあちこち見る

≒ surf, search

ⓘ ネット上の情報を「見て回る」ためのものがbrowser（ブラウザー）。

例 She **browsed** the Internet, looking for a new apartment.

彼女はネットをあちこち見て新しいアパートを探した。

□□□ 0597

narrative

/ nǽrətɪv /

動 narrate ～を語る
名 narration 語り、ナレーション

名 a written or spoken story

話、物語

≒ plot, account

例 Famous people often write a **narrative** of their life once they grow older.

有名人は年を取るとよく自分の人生の物語を書く。

□□□ 0598

reluctant

/ rɪlʌ́ktənt /

副 reluctantly いやいや
名 reluctance 気が進まないこと

形 feeling or showing a desire not to do something (yet)

気乗りがしない、しぶしぶの

≒ hesitant　⇔ willing, eager

0600 語

例 The dog was **reluctant** to go outside in the rain.

その犬は雨の中、外に出るのを嫌がった。

□□□ 0599

jealous

/ ʤéləs /

名 jealousy 嫉妬

形 feeling or showing an unhappy desire to have what another person has

嫉妬して、ねたんで

≒ envious

ⓘ jea の発音に注意。

例 Seeing the success of her friends made the failing actress **jealous** and unhappy.

友人たちの成功を目にして、うまくいっていない女優は嫉妬し、みじめだった。

□□□ 0600

impulse

/ ímpʌls /

形 impulsive 衝動的な

名 a desire to do something that appears suddenly

衝動

ⓘ 〈impulse to *do*〉（～したい衝動）の形で押さえておこう。

🔑 〈im-（上に）+pulse（駆り立てる）〉

例 She had to resist the **impulse** to scream when she saw her favorite singer.

大好きな歌手を見かけたとき、彼女は叫びたい衝動を抑えなければならなかった。

章末ボキャブラリーチェック

次の語義が表す英単語を答えてください。

語義	解答	連番
❶ an area of an activity or interest	r e a l m	0545
❷ done by choice and without being forced	v o l u n t a r y	0516
❸ to make something better by changing small things	r e f i n e	0562
❹ to disappear completely without any explanation	v a n i s h	0573
❺ one of the parts into which something can be divided	s e g m e n t	0501
❻ belonging to or relating to each thing that has already been said	r e s p e c t i v e	0589
❼ a possible future result caused by something done now	i m p l i c a t i o n	0537
❽ to make someone feel tired or annoyed by being uninteresting	b o r e	0548
❾ to pass an illness on to someone else	i n f e c t	0579
❿ something that looks different from what it really is	i l l u s i o n	0531
⓫ a dream that is bad or scares the person dreaming	n i g h t m a r e	0526
⓬ a fungus that grows on damp or rotting things	m o l d	0556
⓭ having or showing good reason or judgement	s e n s i b l e	0513
⓮ to move by using your hands and knees	c r a w l	0574
⓯ existing or happening in large amounts	a b u n d a n t	0520
⓰ to let something exist or be done, even if you do not like it	t o l e r a t e	0536
⓱ an amount of something that is less than what is needed	d e f i c i t	0575
⓲ to lose blood from your body because of a cut or injury	b l e e d	0557
⓳ a state of being very tired	f a t i g u e	0572
⓴ to gather something little by little over time	a c c u m u l a t e	0523
㉑ to make something clear or easy to understand	c l a r i f y	0529

語義	解答	連番
㉒ one of usually two periods of time that make up the school year at a school or university	s e m e s t e r	0593
㉓ a trip that is made to do something specific	e x p e d i t i o n	0570
㉔ to hit a surface and move quickly in a different direction	b o u n c e	0511
㉕ to think of or make something in your mind	c o n c e i v e	0544
㉖ to get soil ready and use it to grow plants	c u l t i v a t e	0550
㉗ to formally leave a job or position	r e s i g n	0592
㉘ not doing much	i d l e	0553
㉙ a feeling of deep sadness that is usually caused by losing someone or something important	s o r r o w	0569
㉚ feeling or showing a desire not to do something (yet)	r e l u c t a n t	0598
㉛ to hit your foot when walking or running and almost fall	s t u m b l e	0576
㉜ a formal ceremony or actions that are always done in the same way	r i t u a l	0510
㉝ feeling guilty or shameful about something	a s h a m e d	0532
㉞ not happy at all	m i s e r a b l e	0584
㉟ to speak in an upset or angry way to someone who has done something wrong	s c o l d	0507
㊱ a small piece of an object	l u m p	0565
㊲ careful to avoid danger or risk	c a u t i o u s	0588
㊳ to choose someone or something officially for a purpose	d e s i g n a t e	0585
㊴ to buy insurance for something to be financially protected	i n s u r e	0521
㊵ connected to race	r a c i a l	0538
㊶ to put something completely around another thing	e n c l o s e	0542
㊷ to make something by cutting off pieces of its original form	c a r v e	0540
㊸ to leave a mark on something (usually fabric)	s t a i n	0552

❹ to admit to someone that you did something bad or illegal — c o n f e s s — 0518

❺ a group of birds or animals (such as sheep) that move together — f l o c k — 0539

❻ behavior that shows respect to others and is polite — c o u r t e s y — 0547

❼ to give up on something that you want so that you can make an agreement with another person — c o m p r o m i s e — 0577

❽ to surprise someone and sometimes make them confused — a m a z e — 0559

❾ staying in good condition even after a long time has passed — d u r a b l e — 0564

❺⓪ a written or spoken story — n a r r a t i v e — 0597

❺① to share information with the public — d i s c l o s e — 0508

❺② kind or forgiving treatment of someone you have the power to harm or punish — m e r c y — 0502

❺③ to give something of value to another person in return for something of equal value — c o m p e n s a t e — 0590

❺④ in an honest and direct way — f r a n k l y — 0515

❺⑤ to speak using a very quiet voice — w h i s p e r — 0530

❺⑥ not supporting anything or anyone in a fight or war — n e u t r a l — 0505

❺⑦ involving a lot of energy or effort — i n t e n s i v e — 0533

❺⑧ to look at things in a store to see if there is something you want to buy or that looks interesting — b r o w s e — 0596

❺⑨ very silly — r i d i c u l o u s — 0525

❻⓪ (something that attracts) people's attention, especially for a product — p u b l i c i t y — 0583

❻① not true or real — f a k e — 0566

❻② to make someone feel a little angry — a n n o y — 0594

❻③ to make someone worry or get upset — d i s t r e s s — 0586

❻④ a great victory — t r i u m p h — 0528

❻⑤ to pray to, honor, or respect someone or something as a god — w o r s h i p — 0563

語義	解答	連番
❻ for the reason said	h e n c e	0504
❼ to become smaller	s h r i n k	0582
❽ regardless of what was just said	n o n e t h e l e s s	0595
❾ the things that will happen (to someone) in the future	d e s t i n y	0543
❼⓿ at a level that is in between beginner and advanced	i n t e r m e d i a t e	0555
❼❶ very great in size or amount	i m m e n s e	0578
❼❷ thought to be normal because most people do it	m a i n s t r e a m	0567
❼❸ a desire to do something that appears suddenly	i m p u l s e	0600
❼❹ done with all your energy but with low chances of success	d e s p e r a t e	0506
❼❺ to arrange things so that different groups of people can work together well	c o o r d i n a t e	0554
❼❻ having an acidic taste that is close to the taste of a lemon or lime	s o u r	0517
❼❼ seeming like it is real because of clear details	v i v i d	0568
❼❽ to gain or finish something	a t t a i n	0514
❼❾ to provide something that is wanted or needed by someone or something	c a t e r	0512
❽⓿ to change what you have eaten by natural processes into something that can be used by your body	d i g e s t	0560
❽❶ to throw away something, usually in secret or illegally	d u m p	0509
❽❷ felt or experienced very strongly	p r o f o u n d	0571
❽❸ feeling or showing an unhappy desire to have what another person has	j e a l o u s	0599
❽❹ to make someone feel angry or upset because of something they cannot do	f r u s t r a t e	0551
❽❺ to use a thing or person instead of another thing or person	s u b s t i t u t e	0580
❽❻ having a desire to be unkind to others without feeling sorry about it	c r u e l	0535

❽ very beautiful, impressive, or great — m a g n i f i c e n t — 0541

❽ to be like another thing — c o r r e s p o n d — 0591

❽ a reason that someone has to do something — m o t i v e — 0587

❾ to make someone or something be a certain way — r e n d e r — 0546

❾ to slowly break down because of natural processes — d e c a y — 0534

❾ to say something strongly — a s s e r t — 0519

❾ to make someone want (to do) something even though it may be bad — t e m p t — 0524

❾ to do the task you have been asked or ordered to do — c o m p l y — 0549

❾ to grab something and hold onto it — g r a s p — 0558

❾ to make someone think about something different from what they were thinking about before — d i s t r a c t — 0581

❾ the large size of a person or object — b u l k — 0561

❾ to show a likeness of someone or something using images or words — p o r t r a y — 0522

❾ a way of thinking that is shared by all the people in a group — c o n s e n s u s — 0503

❿ a long trip that is made over water or through space — v o y a g e — 0527

Stage 7

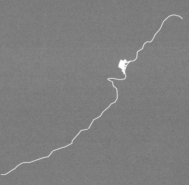

Where there's a will, there's a way.
志あるところに道あり。

☐☐☐ 0601

insult / 動 ɪnsʌ́lt 名 ínsʌlt /

動 to do or say something that is not nice to someone

〈人〉を侮辱する

≒ curse, ridicule

⇔ compliment, flatter, praise

🔑〈in-（上に）+sult（跳ぶ）〉

例 The group was so **insulted** by the actions of the prime minister that they never came back.

その団体は総理大臣の振る舞いにひどく侮辱されたため、二度と戻ってこなかった。

名 something rude that is said to hurt someone or make them angry

侮辱

⇔ compliment

例 The brothers got into a fight over a meaningless **insult**.

兄弟はつまらない侮辱の言葉を巡ってけんかを始めた。

☐☐☐ 0602

glow / glóʊ /

動 to shine with a light that is low and steady

蛍光を発する

≒ glimmer

ⓘ grow（育つ）と混同しないように注意。

例 The cave is filled with worms that **glow** in the dark.

洞窟には暗闇の中で蛍光を発する虫がいっぱいいる。

☐☐☐ 0603

celebrity / səlébrəti /

名 a famous person

有名人

≒ star

⇔ nobody

ⓘ カタカナ語の「セレブ」はcelebrityの略語。

例 A large number of American **celebrities** live in California.

多くのアメリカの有名人がカリフォルニアに住んでいる。

□□□ 0604

imitate

/ ímətèɪt /

名 imitation まね；模造品
形 imitative 模倣の

🔵 to copy someone or something else

～をまねる、模倣する

≒ mirror, mimic, replicate

🔑 〈imit(模倣する)+-ate(動詞)〉

例 Her son can **imitate** 10 different bird calls.

彼女の息子は10種類の鳥の鳴き声をまねできる。

□□□ 0605

revive

/ rɪváɪv /

名 revival 復活、再生

🔵 to make someone or something return to a strong, healthy, or active condition

～を復活させる、よみがえらせる

≒ rejuvenate, revitalize

🔑 〈re- (再び) +vive (生きる)〉

0607 語

例 The rain **revived** the flowers that had been wilting in the garden.

雨は庭でしおれていた花をよみがえらせた。

□□□ 0606

deed

/ díːd /

🔵 an action of some kind

行為、行い

≒ act

例 Robin Hood is known for the good **deeds** he did to help the poor.

ロビン・フッドは貧しい人たちを助けるためにした善行で知られている。

□□□ 0607

worthwhile

/ wɔ́ːrθwáɪl /

🔵 good, important, or valuable enough to spend time and energy doing

時間 [労力] を費やす価値がある

≒ beneficial

⇔ worthless

ⓘ 〈It is worthwhile *do*ing/to *do*〉(～することは価値がある) の形も押さえておこう。

例 The trip to Europe had been **worthwhile**, even though she didn't find her birth parents.

彼女は生みの親を見つけられなかったが、ヨーロッパ旅行はする価値があった。

□□□ 0608

primitive
/ prímətɪv /

形 ① **belonging to or looking like something that is from a very long time ago**

原始時代の、太古の

≒ primeval, archaic

⇔ modern, current

🔑 〈prim (第一の) +-itive (形容詞)〉

例 Even over 1 million years ago, **primitive** man was eating meat.

100万年以上前でも原始人は肉を食べていた。

② **done or made in a way that is basic or involves little skill**

原始的な

例 Archaeologists continue to discover **primitive** tools from ancient people every year.

考古学者たちは毎年、古代人の原始的な道具を発見し続けている。

□□□ 0609

infinite
/ ínfənət /

名 infinity 無限

形 without limit

無限の、果てしない

≒ endless, eternal　　⇔ limited

🔑 〈in- (否定) +finite (有限の)〉

ⓘ アクセントは in の位置。

例 There is not an **infinite** supply of oil, so humans must learn to use other resources.

石油の供給量は無限ではないので、人間は別の資源を使えるようになる必要がある。

□□□ 0610

ethical
/ éθɪkl /

名 ethics 道徳、規範

形 (relating to questions of what behavior is) right or good

倫理の、倫理的な

⇔ immoral, corrupt

ⓘ 「環境や社会に配慮した」商品や消費活動を形容する「エシカル」というカタカナ語にもなっている。

例 **Ethical** treatment of animals has become important in the past 30 years.

動物を倫理的に正しく扱うことが、ここ30年で重要になっている。

□□□ 0611

dignity

/ dígnəti /

動 dignify ～に威厳をつける

名 a way of acting that shows seriousness and self-control

威厳

≒ grace

🔑 〈dign (価値) +-ity (名詞)〉

例 She showed great **dignity** in her loss and didn't shed a single tear.

彼女は負けても素晴らしい威厳を示し、涙一つこぼさなかった。

□□□ 0612

rotate

/ róuteɪt /

名 rotation 回転、自転；交替

動 to move or turn in a circle

回転する

≒ spin, revolve

🔑 〈rot (車輪) +-ate (動詞)〉

例 One day is 24 hours because of the speed at which the Earth **rotates**.

1日が24時間なのは地球の自転する速度による。

□□□ 0613

grief

/ gríːf /

動 grieve 嘆き悲しむ

名 a deep sadness, especially one caused by someone's death

悲しみ

≒ mourning, sorrow

⇔ happiness, delight

例 The counselor helped her to deal with her **grief** over the loss of her mother.

カウンセラーは、母を失った悲しみを彼女が乗り越える手助けをした。

□□□ 0614

formulate

/ fɔ́ːrmjəlèɪt /

名 formulation 公式化
名 formula 公式

動 to create something new using careful thought and effort

〈案・計画など〉を考え出す

≒ come up with, devise

例 New drugs to fight cancer are always being **formulated**.

新しい抗がん剤が常に考え出されている。

0614語

261

☐☐☐ **0615**

fierce
/ fíərs / 副 fiercely 激しく

形 ① showing strong or intense emotion

〈行為・感情などが〉
激しい

≒ aggressive ⇔ calm, quiet

例 The two sisters have had a **fierce** rivalry since they were little girls.

その2人の姉妹は幼い頃から激しく競い合っている。

② very powerful or strong

〈風雨などが〉強烈な、
激しい

≒ brutal

⇔ calm, gentle, mild

例 A **fierce** storm caused many trees in the neighborhood to fall down.

猛烈な嵐で界隈の多くの木が倒れた。

☐☐☐ **0616**

competent
/ ká:mpətənt / 名 competence 能力

形 having the skills that are needed to do something

有能な

≒ able, capable, skilled

⇔ incompetent, incapable

例 The woman is a **competent** teacher in all subjects, but her best subject is math.

その女性はすべての教科において有能な先生だが、最も得意な教科は数学だ。

☐☐☐ **0617**

migrate
/ máigreit /
名 migration 移住
形 migratory 〈動物が〉移動性の

動 to move from one (distant) place to another to live there or at different times of the year

移住する、〈鳥などが〉
渡る

≒ emigrate, immigrate

⇔ stay, remain

💡〈migr (移る) +-ate (動詞)〉

例 Salmon **migrate** back to the river where they were born to lay their eggs.

サケは産卵のために自分が生まれた川に戻ってくる。

□□□ 0618

humble

/ hʌ́mbl /　　图 humility 謙遜

形 ① thinking of yourself as not being better than others

謙虚な

≒ modest

⇔ arrogant, proud

例 The girl was very **humble** and never acted like she was better than anyone else.

その女の子はとても謙虚で、ほかの誰より自分の方が優れているといった振る舞いは決してしなかった。

② low in rank or status

(身分の)低い、卑しい

0620語

≒ base

例 Those with a **humble** background were not allowed to talk to the queen directly.

下層階級の者は女王と直接話すことが許されなかった。

□□□ 0619

hatred

/ héɪtrɪd /　　動 hate ～を嫌悪する

名 a very strong feeling of dislike for someone or something

強い嫌悪

≒ disgust

⇔ admiration, respect

例 The man had an unreasonable **hatred** of ham.

その男性はハムをわけもなく嫌っていた。

□□□ 0620

gradual

/ grǽdʒuəl /　　图 grade 段階
　　　　　　　　　副 gradually 徐々に

形 moving or changing slowly (over a long period of time)

少しずつの、段階的な

⇔ abrupt, sudden

例 The snow eventually melts from the **gradual** increase in temperature.

雪は気温が徐々に上がることで最終的に溶けてしまう。

□□□ **0621**

preliminary
/ prɪlímənèri /

形 being done or starting before the main part of something

予備の、準備の

(i) 「予備の」は「備蓄した」の意味ではないので注意。

例 **Preliminary** research has shown that the drug helps patients sleep better.

予備調査は、その薬が患者の睡眠を助けることを示している。

名 something that comes before the main part of something to introduce it

下準備、予備段階

例 All of the usual **preliminaries** were finished before the start of the wedding ceremony.

結婚式が始まる前に、通常の下準備はすべて終わった。

□□□ **0622**

grind
/ gráind /

動 to crush something into small pieces by pushing it against a rough thing or using a machine

〈穀物など〉をひく

(i) grind-ground-groundと活用する。grindstoneは「砥石」。

例 Coffee tastes best when it is **ground** right before brewing it.

いれる直前にひいたコーヒーが一番おいしい。

□□□ **0623**

rage
/ réɪʤ /

名 a strong feeling of anger that is hard to control

激怒

≒ fury, indignation

⇔ calmness, indifference

例 The man shook with **rage** as he watched his daughter break all of his vases.

その男性は、娘が自分の花瓶をすべて割るのを見て、怒りに震えた。

□□□ 0624

prescribe

/ prɪskráɪb /

名 prescription 処方（箋）

動 to officially tell someone to do or use something (e.g. medicine) that will help them

～を処方する

🔑 〈pre-(前もって)+scribe(書く)〉

例 The doctor **prescribed** her three different medications for her sore throat.

医者は彼女ののどの痛みのために、3種類の薬を処方してやった。

□□□ 0625

persist

/ pərsíst /

形 persistent 粘り強い
名 persistence 粘り強さ

動 to continue doing something even though it is hard or others want you to stop

固執する

0626語

≒ persevere, insist

⇔ give up, cease

🔑 〈per-(通して)+sist(立つ)〉

例 The woman told him that she didn't want to go on a date, but he **persisted** and asked her every day.

その女性は彼にデートしたくないと言ったが、彼は粘って、毎日彼女を誘った。

□□□ 0626

chill

/ tʃíl /

形 chilling 身も凍る
形 chilly 冷え冷えする

動 to make someone or something cooler in temperature

～を冷やす、冷却する

≒ cool down, refrigerate

⇔ warm up, heat

例 Beer should be **chilled** in the refrigerator before you drink it.

ビールは飲む前に冷蔵庫で冷やす方がよい。

名 a cold feeling, usually unpleasant

冷たさ、冷気

⇔ warmth

例 Even in the summer, there is a **chill** in the night air in some places.

夏でも場所によっては夜気が冷たく感じられる。

□□□ **0627**

hospitality

/ hà:spətǽləti /

形 hospitable 温かく迎える

名 friendly treatment of guests and people visiting

もてなし、接待

≒ friendliness

ⓘ hospit は「客」を意味する語根で hospital（病院）も同語源語。

例 Japanese **hospitality** is praised all over the world.

日本のおもてなしは世界中で称賛されている。

□□□ **0628**

literacy

/ lítərəsi /

形 literate 読み書きができる

名 the ability to read and write

読み書きの能力

⇔ illiteracy

ⓘ computer literacy（コンピュータリテラシー）のように、抽象的な「（特定分野に関する）技能、能力」の意味でも使われる。

例 **Literacy** rates in Japan are some of the highest in the world.

日本の識字率は世界でトップクラスだ。

□□□ **0629**

penetrate

/ pénətrèɪt /

名 penetration 貫通

動 to go into something or go through it

～に入り込む、～を貫通する

≒ enter, pierce

例 Bullets cannot **penetrate** the doors of the president's car easily.

銃弾を撃っても、大統領の車のドアは簡単には貫通できない。

□□□ **0630**

viewpoint

/ vjúːpɔ̀ɪnt /

名 a way of looking at or thinking about something

観点

≒ angle, perspective

🔑 〈view（見る）+point（点）〉

例 *Anne of Green Gables* is told from the **viewpoint** of a young orphan girl.

『赤毛のアン』は年若い孤児の女の子の視点で語られている。

□□□ **0631**

diminish
/ dımínıʃ /

名 diminution 減少
形 diminutive 非常に小さい

動 to (make something) become smaller in size, strength, etc.

減少する；〜を減少させる

≒ reduce, lower, decrease

⇔ expand, raise, increase

例 The doctor promised his patient that the drug's side effects would **diminish** with time.

その医者は患者に、時間がたてば薬の副作用は弱まるだろうと保証した。

□□□ **0632**

prejudice
/ prédʒədəs /

名 a feeling (of dislike) for someone or something that is not fair, reasonable, etc.

偏見、先入観

0633語

≒ discrimination

🔑 〈pre-(前に)+judice(判断)〉

例 The group fights to get rid of **prejudices** against African-Americans in the United States.

そのグループは、アメリカでのアフリカ系アメリカ人への偏見をなくそうと闘っている。

□□□ **0633**

endeavor
/ ındévər /

名 a serious attempt or effort to do something

努力、試み

ⓘ イギリス英語では endeavour とつづる。

例 All her artistic **endeavors** have failed, and now she has no money.

彼女の芸術活動はすべて失敗し、今、彼女にはお金がない。

動 to try to do something with continued effort

努力する、試みる

≒ strive

ⓘ 〈endeavor to *do*〉(〜しようと努力する) の形で押さえておこう。

例 This school program **endeavors** to make sure that no child comes to school hungry.

この学校の制度では、おなかをすかせて登校する子どもが確実にいなくなるような試みがなされている。

☐☐☐ 0634

linguistic

/ lɪŋgwístɪk /

名 linguistics 言語学
名 linguist 言語学者

形 **relating to (the study of) language(s)**

言語の、言語学の

例 His research looks at the **linguistic** differences between the people of Hokkaido and Okinawa.

彼の研究は、北海道と沖縄の人々の言語の違いを調べるものだ。

☐☐☐ 0635

revenge

/ rɪvénʤ /

名 **an act that is done to hurt another because of something they did to you**

復讐、報復

🔑 〈re-(激しく)+venge(仕返す)〉

例 She promised she would get **revenge** on all the people who had bullied her.

彼女は自分をいじめたすべての人に復讐すると誓った。

☐☐☐ 0636

supervise

/ súːpərvàɪz /

名 supervision 監督、管理
名 supervisor 指導者、監督者

動 **to be in charge of someone or something and make sure things are done right**

〜を監督する

≒ watch, oversee

🔑 〈super(上から)+vise(見る)〉

例 Each teacher was assigned to **supervise** 10 students on the field trip.

遠足では各先生が10人の生徒の監督に割り当てられた。

☐☐☐ 0637

means

/ míːnz /

名 **a way of doing or achieving something**

方法、手段

≒ ability

ⓘ 単複同形。by means of (〜によって)、by any means (何が何でも)、by no means (決して〜ない) という表現も覚えておこう。

例 Compared to trains and buses, taxis are an expensive **means** of transportation.

電車やバスと比べると、タクシーはお金のかかる交通手段だ。

□□□ 0638

alternate
/ 動 ɔ́:ltərnèit 形 ɔ́:ltərnət /

副 **alternately** 代わる代わる
名 **alternation** 変更

動 to happen in a repeated series

交替で行われる

例 The door had been designed by **alternating** between two different colors of wood.

そのドアは異なる2色の木材を交互に組み合わせたデザインになっていた。

形 happening in a repeated series

交互に起こる

例 **Alternate** colors of glass made up the window.

その窓は色ガラスを交互に並べてできていた。

□□□ 0639

0640語

dumb
/ dʌ́m /

形 not showing or having intelligence

頭の悪い

≒ stupid, unintelligent

⇔ smart, clever

ⓘ bは発音しない。

例 The child pretended she was **dumb** so that she didn't have to try hard.

その子は頑張らなくてもいいように、頭の悪いふりをした。

□□□ 0640

forbid
/ fərbíd /

動 to order someone not to do something, or to say that something is not allowed

～に禁じる；～を禁じる

≒ ban, prohibit

⇔ permit

ⓘ forbid-forbad(e)-forbiddenと活用する。

例 The boy was **forbidden** from playing video games until he finished his entrance exams.

その男の子は入試が終わるまでテレビゲームで遊ぶのを禁じられた。

☐☐☐ **0641**

metropolitan

/ mètrəpáːlətən /

名 metropolis 大都会

形 relating to a large city and the cities and towns that are very close to it

大都市の

≒ urban

⇔ provincial, rural

例 The Tokyo **metropolitan** area is one of the most heavily populated areas in the world.

首都圏は世界で最も人口の密集した地域の一つだ。

☐☐☐ **0642**

optimistic

/ àːptəmístɪk /

名 optimism 楽天主義
名 optimist 楽天家

形 feeling positive about the future

楽観的な、楽天的な

⇔ pessimistic

例 The mayor of the town is **optimistic** that the economy of the town will grow again.

町長は町の経済が復活することに楽観的だ。

☐☐☐ **0643**

economical

/ èkənáːmɪkəl /

形 economic 経済の
副 economically 経済的に

形 not expensive to own or use

経済的な、安価な

≒ cheap, efficient, cost-effective

⇔ inefficient

例 Japanese cars are known for being **economical** to drive.

日本車は安く運転できることで知られている。

☐☐☐ **0644**

constraint

/ kənstréɪnt /

動 constrain ～を束縛する

名 something that limits what someone or something can do

拘束、制限

≒ limitation, restraint

例 Budget **constraints** forced them to cancel their trip to Hawaii.

予算に限りがあったので、彼らはハワイ旅行を取りやめなければならなかった。

□□□ 0645

outbreak / áʊtbrèɪk /

名 a sudden start or increase of fighting or disease

（戦争などの）勃発、
（病気などの）突発

ⓘ break out（勃発する、突発する）という表現も覚えておこう。

例 Over 700 people died during the SARS **outbreak** in 2002 and 2003.

2002年から2003年にかけてのSARSの流行中に、700人以上の人が亡くなった。

□□□ 0646

postpone / poʊstpóʊn / 名 postponement 延期

動 to decide that something will be done at a later time instead

～を延期する

≒ put off, delay, suspend

🔑 〈post-（後に）+pone（置く）〉

例 Many sporting events across the city were **postponed** because of the weather.

天気のせいで、市のあちこちで多くのスポーツイベントが延期された。

□□□ 0647

adhere / ædhíər / 名 adhesion 粘着
名 adhesive 接着剤

動 ① to act in the way that a rule or something else says to

（規則・約束などに）
忠実に従う

≒ follow, comply, observe

🔑 〈ad-（～に）+here（付着する）〉

⇔ disregard, ignore, disobey

例 If they don't agree to **adhere** to the contract conditions, the project cannot continue.

彼らが契約条件に従うことに同意しないなら、プロジェクトは続けられない。

② to stick to another thing

くっつく、付着する

≒ attach

⇔ detach, come off

例 The stamp failed to **adhere** to the envelope, so he had to use glue.

切手が封筒につかなかったので、彼はのりを使わなければならなかった。

☐☐☐ **0648**

compliment / 名 ká:pləmənt 動 ká:pləmènt /

形 **complimentary** 称賛の；
優待の

名 a comment that says a good thing about someone or something

賛辞

≒ praise, commendation, admiration

⇔ criticism, condemnation

ⓘ complement（補完物；〜を補う）と同音。

🔑 〈com-(共に)+pli(満たす)+
-ment (名詞)〉

例 He got a **compliment** from his teacher yesterday.

彼は昨日、先生から褒めても
らった。

動 to say something nice about someone or something

〜を褒める、称賛する

≒ praise, commend

⇔ criticize, condemn

例 She was often **complimented** on her good fashion sense.

彼女はファッションセンスがい
いことをよく褒められた。

☐☐☐ **0649**

inhabit / ɪnhǽbət /

名 **inhabitant** 住民

動 to live in a place

〜に住んでいる、居住
する

≒ reside, populate

ⓘ 他動詞である点に注意。

🔑 〈in-(中に)+habit(保つ)〉

例 Hundreds of unusual animals **inhabit** the island.

その島には何百匹もの珍獣が
生息している。

☐☐☐ **0650**

spacious / spéɪʃəs /

名 **space** 空間

形 having a lot of space

広々とした

≒ vast

⇔ cramped

例 The family needed a backyard **spacious** enough for their two dogs to play in.

その一家は2匹の犬が遊べる
だけの広い裏庭を必要として
いた。

□□□ 0651

ignorant / ígnərənt /

動 ignore ～を無視する
名 ignorance 無知

形 lacking knowledge or information

知らない、無学の

≒ naive

⇔ educated

ⓘ アクセントは i の位置。be ignorant of [about]（～について知らない）の形で押さえておこう。

例 Many people are still **ignorant** of the dangers of drinking alcohol.

多くの人はいまだに飲酒の危険性を知らない。

□□□ 0652

due / d(j)úː /

形 ① having reached the time by which something must be paid

（支払い）期限が来て

例 Rent payments are **due** on the first of each month.

家賃は毎月1日が支払い日だ。

② expected or required to happen or arrive

～する予定で、締め切りで

ⓘ 「生まれる予定で」という意味もある。例：Her baby was due in July, but he was born at the end of June.（彼女の赤ん坊は7月に生まれる予定だったが、6月末に生まれた。）

例 Remember that the report is **due** this Friday, so you only have three days left to finish it.

ほら、レポートの締め切りは今度の金曜日だから、終わらせるのにあと3日しか残ってないよ。

③《due to》because of something

～のために、～が原因で

≒ owing to

例 His success was **due to** his hard work, not luck.

彼の成功は運ではなく、勤勉によるものだった。

☐☐☐ 0653

wicked

/ wíkɪd /

形 morally bad

不道徳な、邪悪な

≒ evil, immoral

⇔ good, righteous, virtuous

ⓘ edの発音に注意。

例 The **wicked** stepmother in *Cinderella* tries to trick the prince.

『シンデレラ』に出てくる邪悪な義母は、王子をだまそうとする。

☐☐☐ 0654

token

/ tóʊkən /

名 something that is used to show your feelings

印、証拠

≒ expression, symbol

例 The man gave the police officer a small gift as a **token** of his gratitude.

その男性は警察官に感謝の印として、ちょっとした贈り物をあげた。

☐☐☐ 0655

accelerate

/ əksélərèɪt /

名 acceleration 加速（度）、促進

動 ① to go faster

加速する

≒ quicken, hasten, speed up ⇔ slow down

ⓘ 「アクセル」はacceleratorを略した和製英語。

例 The plane must **accelerate** quickly so that it can take off before the end of the runway.

飛行機は滑走路の先端に行きつく前に離陸できるよう、急速に加速しなければならない。

② to make something happen sooner or more quickly

〜を加速させる

≒ hurry ⇔ delay, slow

例 The government claimed that the tax increase would **accelerate** economic growth for the country.

政府は、増税によって国の経済成長が加速すると主張した。

274

□□□ **0656**

rational / ræʃənəl /

形 based on facts and not emotions

合理的な

≒ logical, reasonable

🔑 〈ratio(n)(計算)+-al(形容詞)〉

⇔ irrational, illogical, unreasonable

ⓘ rationaleは「論拠、理由づけ」。

例 Doctors need to be able to make **rational** decisions even in highly tense situations.

医師は非常に緊迫した状況においても理性的な判断を下せる必要がある。

□□□ **0657**

furnish / fə́ːrnɪʃ /

形 furnished 家具つきの
名 furniture 家具

0658語

動 to put furniture in a room or building

〈部屋・家など〉に
家具などを備えつける

≒ equip, provide, supply

ⓘ 〈furnish A with B〉(AにBを備えつける)の形も覚えておこう。

例 They had to **furnish** their new home on a small budget.

彼らは少ない予算で新居に家具を備えつけなければならなかった。

□□□ **0658**

prevail / prɪvéɪl /

形 prevalent 普及している
名 prevalence 普及

動 ① to be common or popular

普及する

🔑 〈pre-(〜より) +vail (強い)〉

例 That house was built in a style that **prevailed** in the 1960's.

その家は1960年代に普及した様式で建てられた。

② to defeat someone, especially after a long or difficult contest

勝つ、勝る

≒ triumph, beat

ⓘ prevail over [against] (〜に勝つ)の形で押さえておこう。

例 Viewers were shocked when the young boxer **prevailed** over the famous champion.

その若いボクサーが有名なチャンピオンに勝つのを見て、視聴者は衝撃を受けた。

□□□ **0659**

erase

/ ɪréɪs /

名 eraser 消しゴム

動 to delete something

〜を消す、削除する

≒ remove, eliminate

⇔ add

🔑〈e- (外に) +rase (こする)〉

例 The secretary **erased** many important files from the computer by mistake.

秘書は多くの重要なファイルを誤ってコンピュータから削除してしまった。

□□□ **0660**

aesthetic

/ esθétɪk /

名 aesthetics 美学

形 relating to art or being beautiful

美の、美的な

≒ artistic

ⓘ ae の発音に注意。

例 There are both **aesthetic** and practical reasons to plant flowers.

花を植えることには美的かつ実用的理由がある。

□□□ **0661**

sigh

/ sáɪ /

動 to let out a long breath in a way that shows feelings of relief or unhappiness

ため息をつく

≒ exhale ⇔ inhale

ⓘ gh は発音しない。

例 The mother **sighed** in relief when she saw her son's name wasn't on the list of injured people.

息子の名前が負傷者リストにないことがわかって、母親は安堵のため息をついた。

名 the act of letting out a long breath to show relief or unhappiness

ため息

≒ exhalation ⇔ inhalation

例 He gave a long **sigh** and turned on his computer to start working again.

彼は長々とため息をついて、再び仕事を始めるためにコンピュータの電源を入れた。

276

□□□ 0662

gratitude

/ grǽtət(j)ùːd /

名 a feeling of being thankful

感謝（の気持ち）

例 The journalist felt **gratitude** toward everyone who had helped her write her story.

そのジャーナリストは、記事を書くのに協力してくれた全員に感謝の思いを抱いた。

□□□ 0663

verbal

/ və́ːrbəl /

副 verbally 口頭で

形 spoken and not written

口頭の

≒ oral

🔑 〈verb（言葉）+-al（形容詞）〉

0664語

ⓘ nonverbal（言葉を使わない）という語も覚えておこう。

例 Students often do well on the written part of the exam and then fail the **verbal** part because they are shy.

生徒たちは恥ずかしがり屋なので、試験の筆記問題はよくできるが、口頭問題になると落第することがよくある。

□□□ 0664

rally

/ rǽli /

動 to get people to join together in public to support or go against something or someone

〈人〉を集める、結集する

≒ gather, organize

🔑 〈r(e)-（再び）+ally（集まる）〉

例 The organization is trying to **rally** people together to vote in the next election.

その組織は次の選挙で投票する人々を一堂に集めようとしている。

名 a meeting done in a public place to support or go against someone or something

（大規模な）集会

≒ gathering

ⓘ テニス、バドミントンなどの「ラリー」もこのrally。

例 There are sometimes **rallies** in front of Tokyo Station to support women's rights.

東京駅の前でときどき、女性の権利を擁護するための集会がある。

☐☐☐ 0665

pedestrian / pədéstriən /

名 a person who is walking along a road or on a sidewalk

歩行者

ⓘ ped-は「足」を意味する語根で、pedal（ペダル）、expedition（遠足）などにも含まれる。

例 Drivers need to be careful of **pedestrians**, especially at crosswalks.

ドライバーは、特に横断歩道では、歩行者に注意する必要がある。

☐☐☐ 0666

plead / plíːd / 名 plea 嘆願

動 to ask for something in an emotional way

嘆願する

≒ beg

ⓘ plead-pleaded/pled-pleaded/pledと活用する。

例 She **pleaded** with her grandfather to be allowed to go to the concert, but he said no.

彼女はコンサートに行かせてくれるよう祖父に嘆願したが、彼はだめだと言った。

☐☐☐ 0667

tense / téns / 名 tension 緊張

形 not able to relax

緊張した、張り詰めた

≒ anxious, agitated ⇔ calm

ⓘ tend/tens/tentは「引っ張って伸ばす」を意味する語根で、extend（～を広げる）、tent（テント）なども同語源語。

例 It is natural to feel **tense** before a large test but important to try to relax.

大きなテストの前に緊張するのは当然だが、リラックスするよう心がけることが大事だ。

☐☐☐ 0668

frighten / fráɪtn / 名 fright 恐怖
形 frightened おびえた

動 to scare someone

〈人〉を怖がらせる

≒ terrify

⇔ soothe

🔑 〈fright（恐れ）+-en（動詞）〉

例 Many people are really **frightened** by clowns.

多くの人はピエロが本当に怖い。

278

☐☐☐ **0669**

commute

/ kəmjúːt / 图 commuter 通勤者

動 to travel from one place to another regularly, especially between home and work or school

通勤する

例 She has to **commute** over an hour into the city to get to work every day.

彼女は毎日出勤するために、町まで1時間以上かけて通勤しなければならない。

图 the trip that is made from one place to another regularly, usually from your home to work or school

通勤

0671語

例 His **commute** takes him two hours, and he has to ride three different trains.

彼は通勤に2時間かかり、3種類の電車に乗らなければならない。

☐☐☐ **0670**

thereby

/ ðèərbáɪ /

副 by means of something

それによって

≒ thus

例 He signed a contract, **thereby** giving away his rights to the script.

彼は契約書にサインし、それによって原稿の著作権を譲渡した。

☐☐☐ **0671**

feast

/ fíːst /

图 a special meal that has large amounts of food and drink

ごちそう

≒ dinner, banquet

ⓘ fe(a)stは「祝祭」を意味する語根でfestival（祭り）なども同語源語。

例 The family gathers together each year to have a large Christmas **feast**.

その一家はクリスマスのごちそうをたっぷりと食べるために、毎年集合する。

☐☐☐ **0672**

erect
/ ɪrékt /

名 erection 建築（物）

動 to build something, especially something large

〜を建てる、建設する

≒ put up, construct

⇔ take down, demolish

🔑 〈e-(外に)+rect(真っすぐな)〉

例 The villagers **erected** a wall around their village to protect it.

村人たちは村を守るためにその周囲に壁を建てた。

形 in a straight position

直立した

≒ upright

例 The soldiers stood **erect**, waiting for their orders.

兵士たちは直立して命令を待った。

☐☐☐ **0673**

confine
/ kənfáɪn /

動 to make someone or something stay within a certain area, limit, etc.

〜を制限する

≒ constrain, detain

🔑 〈con-(共に)+fine(限界)〉

⇔ let go, let out

例 The tumor was **confined** to a single area, so the doctors were able to remove it safely.

腫瘍は1か所に留まっていたので、医師たちは安全に除去することができた。

☐☐☐ **0674**

terrific
/ tərífɪk /

形 very good

素晴らしい

≒ fantastic, wonderful

⇔ awful, terrible

ⓘ terror（恐怖）などと同語源語だが、現在はふつういい意味で使う。

例 Everyone had a **terrific** time at the party and left very happy.

みんながそのパーティーで素晴らしい時を過ごし、とても満足して帰った。

280

□□□ 0675

gaze / géɪz /

動 to look at someone or something for a long time

見つめる

≒ stare

例 She **gazed** out the window at the falling snow, deep in thought.

彼女は物思いにふけって、降る雪を窓から見つめた。

□□□ 0676

manuscript / mǽnjəskrìpt /

名 the original copy of something written before being printed or published

原稿

ⓘ 原義は「手で書かれたもの」だが、今はタイプしたものも指す。

🔑 〈manu (手) +script (書く)〉

例 She sent the **manuscript** of her novel to 10 publishing companies before one of them accepted it.

彼女は自分の小説の原稿を10の出版社に送り、そのうちの1社が受け入れてくれた。

0678語

□□□ 0677

affection / əfékʃən /

形 affectionate 愛情のこもった

名 a feeling of liking for someone or something

愛情、好意

≒ care, love　⇔ hatred

例 After living in England for 20 years, she had developed a deep **affection** for the country.

イギリスに20年住んで、彼女はその国がとても好きになっていた。

□□□ 0678

minimal / mínəməl /

副 minimally 最小限に

形 very small in size or amount

最小限の、最低限の

≒ minimum

⇔ large, maximum

例 Everyone was lucky that the storm caused **minimal** damage.

嵐が引き起こした損害は最小限で、みんな運がよかった。

□□□ **0679**

fluent
/ flúːənt /

副 **fluently** 流ちょうに
名 **fluency** 流ちょうさ

形 **able to speak a language very well**

流ちょうな

〈flu（流れる）+-ent（形容詞）〉

例 His wife is **fluent** in four languages.

彼の妻は4か国語に堪能だ。

□□□ **0680**

hypothesis
/ haɪpáːθəsɪs /

動 **hypothesize** ～と仮定する
形 **hypothetical** 仮説の

名 **an unproven idea that leads to more study or discussion**

仮説

ⓘ 複数形はhypotheses[haɪpáːθəsìːz]。

〈hypo（下に）+thesis（置く）〉

例 The results of the chemist's experiment proved his **hypothesis** was right.

その化学者の実験結果は、彼の仮説が正しいことを証明した。

□□□ **0681**

eternal
/ ɪtə́ːrnl /

副 **eternally** 永遠に
名 **eternity** 永遠

形 **continuing forever**

永遠の、永久の

≒ ceaseless, never-ending

⇔ finite, temporary, transient

例 The woman prayed that she would have **eternal** youth.

その女性は永遠に若いままでいられますようにと祈った。

□□□ **0682**

doctrine
/ dáːktrən /

名 **a group of ideas that are believed to be true**

（宗教の）教義、（学術の）学説

≒ dogma

ⓘ docは「教える」を意味する語根で、doctor（医師、博士）やdocument（文書）などと同語源語。

例 Teaching religious **doctrine** in schools is not allowed.

学校で宗教の教義を教えることは許されていない。

☐☐☐ **0683**

fascinate
/ fǽsənèɪt /

名 fascination 魅せられること；魅力
形 fascinating 魅力的な

動 **to make someone become deeply interested in something or someone**

～を魅了する

≒ charm ⇔ bore

例 The paintings of Van Gogh **fascinate** people worldwide.

ヴァン・ゴッホの絵は世界中の人々を魅了している。

☐☐☐ **0684**

omit
/ oʊmít /

名 omission 省略

0685 語

動 **to not include someone or something in something**

～を抜かす、省略する

≒ leave out, skip

⇔ add

💡〈o-（反対に）+mit（送る）〉

例 The newspaper confessed that they had **omitted** important details to make the story sound more exciting.

その新聞は、記事をより刺激的な感じにするために、重要な詳細を省略したことを認めた。

☐☐☐ **0685**

rigid
/ rídʒɪd /

名 rigidity 固いこと；厳格

形 ① **not able to change easily**

〈規則などが〉厳しい、厳格な

≒ fixed, definite

⇔ loose, flexible

例 The rules for entering the country to work are very **rigid**.

働くためにその国に入国するルールはとても厳しい。

② **not able to be bent easily**

曲がらない、堅い

≒ stiff, hard

⇔ malleable, flexible, pliable

例 A **rigid** steel pole was used to support the tree during the storm.

嵐の間その木を支えるために、頑丈な鋼鉄の支柱が使われた。

☐☐☐ 0686

brutal

/ brúːtl / 名 brute 冷酷な人；獣
名 brutality 残酷な行為

形 very cruel or harsh

厳しい、過酷な

≒ hard, tough, severe

例 The **brutal** winter weather caused many animals to freeze to death.

過酷な冬の天候のために多くの動物が凍死した。

☐☐☐ 0687

enrich

/ ɪnrítʃ / 名 enrichment 豊かにすること

動 to make someone richer or make something better

〜を豊かにする、質的に向上させる

≒ improve, enhance

⇔ worsen

🔑 〈en-(〜にする)+rich(豊かな)〉

例 The research done by the university has **enriched** the world's understanding of the sickness.

その大学が行った研究により、世界の人々はその病気について より深く理解できるようになった。

☐☐☐ 0688

exotic

/ ɪgzáːtɪk / 名 exoticism 異国趣味

形 ① from a different part of the world

外国産の、外来種の

≒ foreign

⇔ native

ⓘ アクセントは o の位置。

例 The zoo has many **exotic** birds to show their guests.

その動物園には来園者に見せる外来種の鳥がたくさんいる。

② very different from what you know, especially because it is from another country

異国風の、エキゾチックな

例 The dancers wore **exotic** costumes for their performance.

ダンサーたちは公演用のエキゾチックな衣装を着ていた。

]□□ 0689

devise

/ dıváız / 名 device 装置、考案品

動 to create or plan something that is difficult　　〜を考案する

≒ invent, formulate

🔑 〈de- (離れて) +vise (見る)〉

例 The farmers **devised** a new way to keep insects away from their crops.

農民たちは虫を作物に寄せつけない新しい方法を考案した。

]□□ 0690

inferior

/ ınfíəriər / 名 inferiority 劣等

形 of low quality or rank　　下級の

⇔ superior, higher

ⓘ inferior to (〜より劣った) の形で押さえておこう。

例 The woman had felt **inferior** to her older sister since she was a child.

その女性は子どもの頃から自分の姉に劣等感を抱いていた。

]□□ 0691

merchandise

/ mɔ́ːrtʃəndàız / 名 merchandising 販売戦略
名 merchant 商人

名 objects that are bought and sold　　商品

≒ goods, products, items

ⓘ 不可算名詞。集合的に「商品」を表す。

例 New **merchandise** was shipped to the store every afternoon.

毎日午後になると、新たな商品がその店に発送された。

□□□ 0692

subscribe

/ səbskráıb / 名 subscription 定期購読
名 subscriber 定期購読者

動 to pay money for an ongoing service or publication　　(定期) 購読する

≒ sign up, register

🔑 〈sub- (下に) +scribe (書く)〉

例 Less people **subscribe** to the newspaper every year.

その新聞の購読者は毎年減っている。

0692語

□□□ **0693**

herd
/ hə́ːrd /

名 a group of animals that live or are kept together

（家畜の）群れ

≒ flock

ⓘ heard（hear の過去形・過去分詞）と同音。

例 The **herd** of cows ate happily in the field.

牛の群れは原っぱで気持ちよさそうに草を食んだ。

□□□ **0694**

likelihood
/ láɪklihòd /

形 likely 可能性のある

名 the chance of something happening

可能性、見込み

≒ possibility, probability, prospect

例 The **likelihood** that the book will become popular is small.

その本が人気を集める可能性は低い。

□□□ **0695**

acquaintance
/ əkwéɪntəns /

動 acquaint ～を知らせる

名 someone that you know but is not a close friend

知り合い

≒ associate, contact

例 He ran into an old **acquaintance** while he was at the mall.

彼はショッピングセンターに行ったときに昔の知り合いに出くわした。

□□□ **0696**

flourish
/ flə́ːrɪʃ /

動 to grow well or be successful

成長する、繁栄する

≒ blossom, bloom

⇔ wither

🔑 〈flour（花）+-ish（動詞）〉

ⓘ our の発音に注意。

例 The flowers **flourished** after they were moved to the window.

その花々は窓の方に移された後によく成長した。

□□□ 0697

perfume

/ pə́ːrfjuːm /

名 a liquid that you put on your body to make yourself smell nice

香水

≒ fragrance

🔑 〈per- (完全に) +fume (煙)〉

例 Many people are sensitive to the smell of **perfume** and cough when they are near it.

多くの人は香水のにおいに敏感で、香水に近づくと咳をする。

□□□ 0698

heap

/ híːp /

0700語

名 a large and unorganized pile of something

(乱雑に積み重ねられた) 山

≒ mound

例 The teenager left her clothes in a **heap** on the floor.

そのティーンエージャーは服を床に山積みにしていた。

□□□ 0699

tease

/ tíːz /

動 to make fun of someone, either playfully or in a way that is cruel and unkind

～をからかう、いじめる

≒ ridicule　⇔ praise, flatter

例 The girl was **teased** so badly about her hair color that she changed schools.

その女の子は髪の色のことでひどくいじめられて転校した。

□□□ 0700

textile

/ tékstàɪl /

名 a woven or knit fabric

織物、布地

≒ cloth

(i) textは「織られたもの」が原義で、texture (手触り) も同語源語。

例 Many clothes are produced in Bangladesh, which relies on its **textile** industry.

多くの衣服がバングラデシュで製造されており、同国は繊維工業に依存している。

章末ボキャブラリーチェック

次の語義が表す英単語を答えてください。

語義	解答	連番
❶ a way of acting that shows seriousness and self-control	d i g n i t y	0611
❷ to make fun of someone, either playfully or in a way that is cruel and unkind	t e a s e	0699
❸ to (make something) become smaller in size, strength, etc.	d i m i n i s h	0631
❹ a comment that says a good thing about someone or something	c o m p l i m e n t	0648
❺ thinking of yourself as not being better than others	h u m b l e	0618
❻ a liquid that you put on your body to make yourself smell nice	p e r f u m e	0697
❼ to continue doing something even though it is hard or others want you to stop	p e r s i s t	0625
❽ an act that is done to hurt another because of something they did to you	r e v e n g e	0635
❾ to move or turn in a circle	r o t a t e	0612
❿ to do or say something that is not nice to someone	i n s u l t	0601
⓫ to move from one (distant) place to another to live there or at different times of the year	m i g r a t e	0617
⓬ very cruel or harsh	b r u t a l	0686
⓭ something that is used to show your feelings	t o k e n	0654
⓮ a deep sadness, especially one caused by someone's death	g r i e f	0613
⓯ spoken and not written	v e r b a l	0663
⓰ to shine with a light that is low and steady	g l o w	0602
⓱ relating to a large city and the cities and towns that are very close to it	m e t r o p o l i t a n	0641
⓲ to ask for something in an emotional way	p l e a d	0666
⓳ an unproven idea that leads to more study or discussion	h y p o t h e s i s	0680

語義	解答	連番
❷⓿ a group of animals that live or are kept together	h e r d	0693
❷❶ to get people to join together in public to support or go against something or someone	r a l l y	0664
❷❷ to delete something	e r a s e	0659
❷❸ to pay money for an ongoing service or publication	s u b s c r i b e	0692
❷❹ very small in size or amount	m i n i m a l	0678
❷❺ not able to change easily	r i g i d	0685
❷❻ to build something, especially something large	e r e c t	0672
❷❼ to go into something or go through it	p e n e t r a t e	0629
❷❽ to order someone not to do something, or to say that something is not allowed	f o r b i d	0640
❷❾ relating to art or being beautiful	a e s t h e t i c	0660
❸⓿ to create or plan something that is difficult	d e v i s e	0689
❸❶ a feeling of liking for someone or something	a f f e c t i o n	0677
❸❷ being done or starting before the main part of something	p r e l i m i n a r y	0621
❸❸ a feeling of being thankful	g r a t i t u d e	0662
❸❹ to go faster	a c c e l e r a t e	0655
❸❺ to let out a long breath in a way that shows feelings of relief or unhappiness	s i g h	0661
❸❻ to create something new using careful thought and effort	f o r m u l a t e	0614
❸❼ able to speak a language very well	f l u e n t	0679
❸❽ to live in a place	i n h a b i t	0649
❸❾ to be in charge of someone or something and make sure things are done right	s u p e r v i s e	0636
❹⓿ not expensive to own or use	e c o n o m i c a l	0643
❹❶ a strong feeling of anger that is hard to control	r a g e	0623
❹❷ to copy someone or something else	i m i t a t e	0604
❹❸ without limit	i n f i n i t e	0609

語義	解答	連番
❹ not able to relax	t e n s e	0667
❺ a large and unorganized pile of something	h e a p	0698
❻ to make someone richer or make something better	e n r i c h	0687
❼ of low quality or rank	i n f e r i o r	0690
❽ not showing or having intelligence	d u m b	0639
❾ to be common or popular	p r e v a i l	0658
❺⓿ to make someone or something return to a strong, healthy, or active condition	r e v i v e	0605
❺❶ belonging to or looking like something that is from a very long time ago	p r i m i t i v e	0608
❺❷ an action of some kind	d e e d	0606
❺❸ to travel from one place to another regularly, especially between home and work or school	c o m m u t e	0669
❺❹ very good	t e r r i f i c	0674
❺❺ friendly treatment of guests and people visiting	h o s p i t a l i t y	0627
❺❻ lacking knowledge or information	i g n o r a n t	0651
❺❼ based on facts and not emotions	r a t i o n a l	0656
❺❽ to grow well or be successful	f l o u r i s h	0696
❺❾ continuing forever	e t e r n a l	0681
❻⓿ a special meal that has large amounts of food and drink	f e a s t	0671
❻❶ feeling positive about the future	o p t i m i s t i c	0642
❻❷ by means of something	t h e r e b y	0670
❻❸ from a different part of the world	e x o t i c	0688
❻❹ to act in the way that a rule or something else says to	a d h e r e	0647
❻❺ to scare someone	f r i g h t e n	0668
❻❻ moving or changing slowly (over a long period of time)	g r a d u a l	0620
❻❼ to crush something into small pieces by pushing it against a rough thing or using a machine	g r i n d	0622

語義	解答	連番
❻ a group of ideas that are believed to be true	d o c t r i n e	0682
❻ (relating to questions of what behavior is) right or good	e t h i c a l	0610
❼ to look at someone or something for a long time	g a z e	0675
❼ the ability to read and write	l i t e r a c y	0628
❼ to happen in a repeated series	a l t e r n a t e	0638
❼ morally bad	w i c k e d	0653
❼ a woven or knit fabric	t e x t i l e	0700
❼ to make someone or something cooler in temperature	c h i l l	0626
❼ good, important, or valuable enough to spend time and energy doing	w o r t h w h i l e	0607
❼ a sudden start or increase of fighting or disease	o u t b r e a k	0645
❼ objects that are bought and sold	m e r c h a n d i s e	0691
❼ having a lot of space	s p a c i o u s	0650
❽ to put furniture in a room or building	f u r n i s h	0657
❽ the original copy of something written before being printed or published	m a n u s c r i p t	0676
❽ the chance of something happening	l i k e l i h o o d	0694
❽ to officially tell someone to do or use something (e.g. medicine) that will help them	p r e s c r i b e	0624
❽ to make someone become deeply interested in something or someone	f a s c i n a t e	0683
❽ a famous person	c e l e b r i t y	0603
❽ to decide that something will be done at a later time instead	p o s t p o n e	0646
❽ a serious attempt or effort to do something	e n d e a v o r	0633
❽ showing strong or intense emotion	f i e r c e	0615
❽ having the skills that are needed to do something	c o m p e t e n t	0616
❾ a feeling (of dislike) for someone or something that is not fair, reasonable, etc.	p r e j u d i c e	0632

語義	解答	連番
❾❶ to not include someone or something in something	<u>o</u> <u>m</u> <u>i</u> <u>t</u>	0684
❾❷ a way of looking at or thinking about something	<u>v</u> <u>i</u> <u>e</u> <u>w</u> <u>p</u> <u>o</u> <u>i</u> <u>n</u> <u>t</u>	0630
❾❸ a very strong feeling of dislike for someone or something	<u>h</u> <u>a</u> <u>t</u> <u>r</u> <u>e</u> <u>d</u>	0619
❾❹ relating to (the study of) language(s)	<u>l</u> <u>i</u> <u>n</u> <u>g</u> <u>u</u> <u>i</u> <u>s</u> <u>t</u> <u>i</u> <u>c</u>	0634
❾❺ a way of doing or achieving something	<u>m</u> <u>e</u> <u>a</u> <u>n</u> <u>s</u>	0637
❾❻ having reached the time by which something must be paid	<u>d</u> <u>u</u> <u>e</u>	0652
❾❼ to make someone or something stay within a certain area, limit, etc.	<u>c</u> <u>o</u> <u>n</u> <u>f</u> <u>i</u> <u>n</u> <u>e</u>	0673
❾❽ something that limits what someone or something can do	<u>c</u> <u>o</u> <u>n</u> <u>s</u> <u>t</u> <u>r</u> <u>a</u> <u>i</u> <u>n</u> <u>t</u>	0644
❾❾ someone that you know but is not a close friend	<u>a</u> <u>c</u> <u>q</u> <u>u</u> <u>a</u> <u>i</u> <u>n</u> <u>t</u> <u>a</u> <u>n</u> <u>c</u> <u>e</u>	0695
❿ a person who is walking along a road or on a sidewalk	<u>p</u> <u>e</u> <u>d</u> <u>e</u> <u>s</u> <u>t</u> <u>r</u> <u>i</u> <u>a</u> <u>n</u>	0665

Stage 8

Rome wasn't built in a day.
ローマは一日にして成らず。

□□□ 0701

fragile
/ frǽdʒəl / 图 fragility 壊れやすさ

形 ① easily broken or damaged
壊れやすい

≒ delicate, feeble, frail

⇔ durable, tough

🔑 〈frag (壊す) +-ile (形容詞)〉

ⓘ「割れもの注意」はFragileと書く。

例 Bones become more **fragile** with age.
骨は年齢とともにもろくなる。

② not strong
脆弱な、はかない

≒ delicate

⇔ solid, stable

例 The peace agreement between the two countries is still very **fragile**.
その2国間の和平合意はまだ非常におぼつかないものだ。

□□□ 0702

summon
/ sÁmən / 图 summons 呼び出し、召喚

動 to tell someone they have to come to a place
～を呼び出す、召喚する

≒ call (on)

⇔ send away, dismiss

例 The princess **summoned** her servants to her room to help wash her hair.
王女は洗髪を手伝ってもらうために召し使いを自室に呼んだ。

□□□ 0703

corrupt
/ kərÁpt / 图 corruption 堕落

形 not honest, moral, or good
堕落した

≒ unethical

⇔ ethical, trustworthy, respectable

🔑 〈cor-(完全に)+rupt (壊れた)〉

例 Indifference to politics will lead to a **corrupt** society.
政治への無関心は堕落した社会をもたらす。

MP3 0704-0706

□□□ 0704

utter
/ ˈʌtər / 　名 utterance 発声、発言

動 to make a sound or say something using your voice

〈声・言葉〉を発する、〈考え〉を述べる

≒ mention, express

例 He can hardly **utter** a word without saying something wrong.

彼は何か言葉を発すると必ず間違ったことを言う。

形 (used to emphasize that something is) complete and total

まったくの

0706語

例 The product was an **utter** failure, and the company lost millions of dollars.

その製品は完全な失敗に終わり、その会社は何百万ドルもの損失を出した。

□□□ 0705

souvenir
/ sùːvəníər /

名 something that you keep to remind you of a place visited or an event attended

(旅などの) 記念品

≒ memento, reminder

① アクセントはnirの位置。ほかの人のために買う「お土産」は present、gift などと言う。

例 The only **souvenir** she bought on her trip to New York was a small key chain.

彼女がニューヨーク旅行で買った唯一の記念品は小さなキーホルダーだった。

□□□ 0706

emit
/ ɪmít / 　名 emission 放出、排出

動 to send out something, such as light or energy

〈光・エネルギーなど〉を発する

≒ radiate, give off

🔑 〈e- (外に) +mit (送る)〉

① LEDは light-emitting diode の略。「光を発するダイオード」=「発光ダイオード」。

例 Many flowers sold in flower shops don't **emit** a strong smell.

花屋で売られている多くの花は強いにおいがしない。

☐☐☐ 0707

precaution

/ prɪkɔ́:ʃən /

形 precautionary 予防的な

名 **something done to keep people safe or stop problems from happening in the future**

用心、予防措置

≒ preparation

🔑 〈pre-（前もって）+caution（注意）〉

例 People living in Japan need to take **precautions** against earthquakes.

日本に住んでいる人は地震に備える必要がある。

☐☐☐ 0708

straightforward

/ strèɪtfɔ́:rwərd /

形 **not complicated or hard to understand**

明快な、わかりやすい

≒ simple

⇔ complex

例 Making an egg salad sandwich is very **straightforward**.

卵サラダサンドを作るのはとても簡単だ。

☐☐☐ 0709

raid

/ réɪd /

動 **to suddenly enter a place by force to look for someone or something**

〜を襲撃する

≒ invade

例 Police **raided** the store and found a lot of drugs in the basement.

警察はその店を強制捜査し、地下で大量の麻薬を見つけた。

名 **a surprise attack organized by soldiers and other military groups**

襲撃

≒ assault

例 The bombing **raids** during World War II destroyed much of Tokyo.

第二次世界大戦中の爆撃で東京の大部分が破壊された。

□□□ 0710

condemn / kəndém /

名 condemnation（激しい）非難

動 to say strongly that someone or something is bad

～を責める、非難する

≒ criticize, denounce

⇔ praise, compliment

❢〈con-（完全に）+demn（害を加える）〉

ⓘ mnのnは発音しない。

例 The woman was **condemned** as a liar by everyone around her.

その女性は周囲の皆からうそつきだと非難された。

0712語

□□□ 0711

faint / féɪnt /

形 not easy to see, taste, hear, or feel

かすかな、ほのかな

≒ weak, slight

⇔ powerful, potent

ⓘ 同音語のfeint（見せかけ、フェイント）と混同しないように注意。

例 There was a **faint** smell of roses coming in through the window.

かすかなバラの香りが窓を通って漂ってきた。

□□□ 0712

warrant / wɔ́ːrənt /

名 warranty 保証

動 ① to need or deserve something

～を要する、～に値する

例 The ideas presented by the students **warrant** further study.

その生徒たちが示した考えはさらに研究する価値がある。

② to promise something about a product

〈商品など〉を保証する

≒ guarantee

例 The seller **warranted** that the car had no problems, but it broke down after one week.

販売員はその車に何の問題もないことを保証したが、車は1週間後に故障した。

☐☐☐ **0713**

conceal
/ kənsíːl /

名 concealment 隠すこと

動 to hide someone or something so that they cannot be seen

〜を隠す、隠ぺいする

≒ cover, mask

⇔ reveal, uncover

〈con-（完全に）+ceal（隠す）〉

例 The entrance to the club is **concealed** behind a large tree.

そのクラブの入り口は大木の後ろに隠されている。

☐☐☐ **0714**

altitude
/ ǽltət(j)ùːd /

名 the height of something above sea level

高さ、海抜

≒ elevation

〈alt（高い）+-itude（名詞）〉

例 People who live in areas of high **altitude** need less oxygen.

海抜の高いところに住む人は、必要とする酸素の量が少ない。

☐☐☐ **0715**

glimpse
/ glímps /

名 a brief view of or look at someone or something

ちらりと見えること、ひと目

≒ glance

例 The students caught a **glimpse** of their new teacher through the window.

生徒たちは窓越しに新任の先生がちらっと見えた。

動 to look at or see someone or something for only a very short time

〜をちらっと見る

≒ glance

例 They **glimpsed** the dog through the door as they walked past the house.

彼らはその家を通り過ぎるとき、ドア越しにその犬がちらっと見えた。

□□□ 0716

tidy / táɪdi /

形 clean and organized

整然とした、小ぎれいな

≒ orderly, neat

⇔ untidy, messy

ⓘ 原義は「tide（時）に合った」。

例 The teacher always kept her desk **tidy** so that she could find things easily.

その先生はものを簡単に見つけられるように机を常にきれいにしておいた。

0718語

動 to make something clean and organized

～をきちんとする

例 Her father **tidied** the house before the guests arrived.

彼女の父親は来客が到着する前に家を片づけた。

□□□ 0717

damp / dǽmp / 動 dampen ～を湿らせる

形 slightly wet

湿っぽい、じめじめした

≒ moist

⇔ dry

例 Her mother wiped the juice off the table with a **damp** cloth.

彼女の母親はぬれぶきんでテーブルからジュースをふき取った。

□□□ 0718

cooperate / koʊɑ́:pərèɪt / 名 cooperation 協力
形 cooperative 協力的な

動 to work together with others to do something

協力する

≒ collaborate, coordinate

🔑 〈co-（共に）+oper（働く）+ -ate（動詞）〉

例 The team members will have to **cooperate** with each other to defeat their rival.

チームのメンバーはライバルを負かすために互いに協力しなければならない。

☐☐☐ **0719**

outgoing / áʊtgòʊiŋ /

形 ① (friendly and) liking to meet and be around others

社交的な

≒ extroverted, sociable, talkative

⇔ introverted, shy

例 People with **outgoing** personalities are usually more popular at school.

社交的な性格の人の方がたいてい学校で人気がある。

② leaving a particular place rather than arriving

(ある場所から)出ていく

≒ departing, outbound

⇔ incoming, inbound

例 All **outgoing** flights were canceled because of the hurricane.

ハリケーンのため全出発便が欠航になった。

☐☐☐ **0720**

predecessor / prédəsèsər /

名 a person who was in a position before someone else

前任者

⇔ successor

例 The new company president was grateful for all the progress his **predecessor** had made.

新社長は前任者が果たしたあらゆる発展に感謝していた。

☐☐☐ **0721**

abolish / əbáːlɪʃ / 名 abolition 廃止

動 to officially get rid of something (e.g. a law)

～を廃止する

≒ nullify

⇔ pass, validate

例 Slavery was **abolished** in the United States in 1865.

奴隷制度はアメリカでは1865年に廃止された。

□□□ 0722

biography

/ baɪɑ́:grəfi /

形 biographical 伝記の

名 **a story of a real person's life that is written by someone else**

伝記

ⓘ 「自分」を意味する接頭辞 auto- のついた autobiography は「自伝」という意味。

例 A new **biography** of the president will be released next year.

大統領の新しい伝記が来年発売される。

□□□ 0723

pity

/ píti /

形 pitiful 痛ましい
形 pitiless 無慈悲な

名 **a feeling of sadness or sympathy for someone or something**

哀れみ、同情

≒ compassion　⇔ indifference

例 Their life has been easy, so they don't deserve your **pity**.

彼らは気ままに暮らしているのだから、あなたが同情する必要はない。

□□□ 0724

census

/ sénsəs /

名 **the official process of gathering information about the number of people living somewhere**

国勢調査

例 The most recent **census** was done five years ago.

直近の国勢調査は5年前に行われた。

□□□ 0725

correspondence

/ kɔ̀:rəspɑ́:ndəns /

動 correspond 連絡する；一致する

名 **(the activity of sending) e-mails, letters, or other written messages**

書簡（による通信）

🔑〈cor-（共に）+respond（応答する）+-ence（名詞）〉

例 The court required her to share all **correspondence** between her and the suspect.

裁判所は容疑者とのやりとりをすべて明かすよう彼女に求めた。

□□□ **0726**

peculiar / pɪkjúːljər /

副 **peculiarly** 特に
名 **peculiarity** 特性

形 ① not usual or normal

風変わりな、変わった

≒ strange, odd, weird, abnormal

⇔ typical, common

例 The cat's **peculiar** behavior worried its owners.

その猫の変わった行動は飼い主を心配させた。

② relating to a specific place, situation, or person

独特の、固有の

≒ unique

例 Each house has its own **peculiar** smell.

家にはそれぞれ独特のにおいがある。

□□□ **0727**

surrender / səréndər /

動《surrender *oneself*》to agree to stop resisting, fighting, or hiding because you know you cannot succeed

降伏する、自首する

≒ give up, submit, concede

🔑〈sur-(上に)+render(与える)〉

例 The thief **surrendered himself** to the police after three days in hiding.

その泥棒は3日間の潜伏後、警察に自首した。

□□□ **0728**

selfish / sélfɪʃ /

形 only thinking about yourself and not caring about the needs of others

利己的な、自分勝手な

≒ self-centered

🔑〈self(自己)+-ish(的な)〉

⇔ selfless, unselfish, altruistic

例 That singer is only interested in meeting her own **selfish** needs.

あの歌手は自分の利己的な欲求を満たすことにしか興味がない。

□□□ 0729

despair / dɪspéər /

名 the feeling someone has when all hope is lost

絶望、失望

ⓘ spair/sperは「希望」を意味する語根で、desperate（必死の）やprosperous（繁栄した）なども同語源語。

例 The parents were filled with **despair** when they couldn't find their children.

親たちはわが子を見つけられず、絶望に包まれた。

0731語

動 to have no hope left that things will get better

絶望する、失望する

例 Even when he ran out of food, the boy did not **despair**; he knew he would find his way out of the woods eventually.

食べ物が尽きても少年は希望を失わなかった。彼はいつかは森から抜け出す方法を見つけられるとわかっていた。

□□□ 0730

ripe / ráɪp /

動 ripen 実る、熟す

形 ready or suitable to be eaten or used, often refers to fully developed fruits and vegetables

熟した、実った

≒ mature

⇔ unripe

例 The apples are nearly **ripe** and will be ready to be harvested soon.

リンゴはほとんど熟していて、すぐに収穫できる状態になるだろう。

□□□ 0731

ornament / ɔ́ːrnəmənt /

形 ornamental 装飾の

名 a small item that is used to decorate another object or room

装飾品

≒ decoration, accessory

例 The entire family hung **ornaments** on the Christmas tree together every year.

その家族は毎年みんなでクリスマスツリーに飾りをつるした。

□□□ 0732

illuminate

/ ɪlú:mənèɪt /

名 illumination 照明

動 ① to give something light or shine light on something

〜を照らす、明るくする

≒ brighten, light up

⇔ darken

🔑 〈il-（上に）+lumin（光）+-ate（動詞）〉

例 They used candles to **illuminate** the room for the haunted house.

彼らはお化け屋敷の部屋を照らすのにろうそくを使った。

② to make an idea or problem easier to understand

〈問題など〉を解き明かす

≒ clarify, illustrate

例 This book does a great job of **illuminating** the history of early Christianity.

この本は初期キリスト教の歴史を見事に解き明かしている。

□□□ 0733

splendid

/ splÉndɪd /

名 splendor 壮麗さ

形 very impressive and nice to look at

〈景色・建物などが〉華麗な、壮麗な

≒ beautiful, dazzling, marvelous

⇔ ugly

例 They had a **splendid** view of Manhattan from their hotel room.

彼らのホテルの部屋からは、マンハッタンの素晴らしい景色が見えた。

□□□ 0734

ample

/ æmpl /

副 amply 十分に

形 having or giving (more than) enough of something that is needed

十分な、豊富な

≒ abundant, sufficient, plentiful

⇔ lacking, inadequate

例 The police found **ample** evidence of a fight in the living room.

警察は居間で争いがあった十分な証拠を発見した。

□□□ 0735

inflict
/ ɪnflíkt /

图 inflliction（打撃・損害などを）
与えること

**動 to make someone experience something
unpleasant or dangerous**

〈苦痛・損害など〉を
与える

≒ wreak

💡〈in-（上に）+flict（打つ）〉

例 Hornets are able to **inflict** strong pain on people that
get in their way.

スズメバチは行く手をさえぎる
人間に強い痛みを与えること
ができる。

□□□ 0736

0737語

clash
/ klǽʃ /

**图 a short fight or disagreement between
people**

衝突、対立

≒ confrontation

ⓘ「衝突する」という動詞の意味もある。擬音語からできた語で、
音の近いcrashも「衝突（する）」を意味する。

例 Some protesters were hurt in recent **clashes** with the
police.

最近の警察との衝突で、抗議
者が何人かけがをした。

□□□ 0737

queue
/ kjúː /

**图 a line of people or cars that are waiting
for something**

列、行列

ⓘ 発音に注意。主にイギリス英語。米語ではlineを使う。

例 The **queue** to enter the new store went all the way
out into the street.

新しい店に入るための列は通
りまでずっと伸びていた。

動 to make or wait in a line

列を作る

≒ line up

例 The young people **queued** outside the concert hall
and waited for the doors to open.

若者たちはコンサートホールの
外に並んで開場を待った。

☐☐☐ **0738**

refuge

/ réfjuːʤ /

名 a place where someone can be protected from danger or trouble

名 refugee 難民

避難(所)、保護

≒ sanctuary, haven, shelter

🔑 〈re-(後ろに)+fuge(逃げる)〉

例 The dog took **refuge** under the bridge to keep dry in the rain.

その犬は雨に濡れないように橋の下に避難した。

☐☐☐ **0739**

informative

/ ɪnfɔ́ːrmətɪv /

動 inform 〜に知らせる
名 information 情報
形 informational 情報に関する

形 giving information

情報を提供する、有益な

≒ educational, explanatory

⇔ uninformative

例 The documentary on the tsunami was very **informative**.

その津波に関するドキュメンタリーはとても有益だった。

☐☐☐ **0740**

vacant

/ véɪkənt /

名 vacancy 空き、欠員
動 vacate 〜をからにする

形 ① not used, filled, or lived in

空いている、使われていない

≒ empty, free, available

🔑 〈vac(からの)+-ant(形容詞)〉

⇔ taken, unavailable

例 The grass has started to grow in the **vacant** land next to the hospital.

病院の隣の空き地で草が伸び始めた。

② not occupied by someone, usually referring to a job

欠員の

≒ open, unfilled

⇔ filled

例 The position has remained **vacant** since the old secretary quit last year.

高齢の秘書が去年やめてから、そのポストは空いたままになっている。

□□□ **0741**

speculate
/ spékjəlèɪt /

名 speculation 推測、憶測
形 speculative 推測の

動 **to think about something and make guesses about it**

（…だと）推測する

≒ hypothesize

🔑 〈spec（見る）+-ulate（動詞）〉

例 Since nobody knows what really happened there, we can only **speculate**.

そこで実際に何が起きたのか誰も知らないので、私たちは推測することしかできない。

0743 語

□□□ **0742**

imaginary
/ ɪmǽʤənèri /

名 imagination 想像力
形 imaginative 想像力に富む

形 **unreal and existing only in your mind**

想像上の、架空の

≒ made-up, fictional

⇔ factual, real, proven

例 Many people play with an **imaginary** friend when they are young.

多くの人は小さいときに架空の友達と遊ぶ。

□□□ **0743**

pledge
/ pléʤ /

動 **to promise formally that something will be given or done**

〜を誓う、約束する

≒ guarantee, vow

例 The mayor **pledged** to cut taxes in the city.

市長は市税を軽減すると約束した。

名 **a serious promise about something you will or will not do**

誓約、誓い

≒ guarantee, vow, oath

例 My father made a **pledge** to never smoke again.

父は二度とタバコを吸わないと誓った。

□□□ **0744**

abnormal

/ æbnɔ́ːrməl /

图 abnormality 異常

囮 different from what is normal

異常な、ふつうでない

≒ odd, weird, strange, unusual

⇔ normal, typical, common

🔑 〈ab-(離れて)+normal(正常な)〉

例 There was an **abnormal** green light coming from the bathroom.

トイレから異常な緑色の光が出ていた。

□□□ **0745**

stroll

/ stróul /

囫 to walk slowly in a relaxed way

ぶらぶら歩く

ⓘ stroller(ストローラー（折りたたみ式ベビーカー））はカタカナ語にもなっている。

例 The couple **strolled** along the river and looked at the flowers.

そのカップルは川沿いをぶらぶらと歩き、花を眺めた。

□□□ **0746**

litter

/ lítər /

囫 to throw or leave garbage on the ground in a public place

ごみを散らかす

≒ discard, throw away

⇔ pick up, collect

例 It is illegal to **litter** in many cities, but people still leave their garbage everywhere.

多くの都市でごみのポイ捨ては違法だが、人々はそれでも至るところにごみを置いていく。

图 things that have been thrown away and are left lying on the ground in a public place

散らかったもの、ごみ

≒ trash, garbage, junk

例 There are volunteer groups that go to parks to clean up **litter** every weekend.

毎週末、公園に行ってごみを拾うボランティアグループがいる。

308

□□□ 0747

fasten / fǽsn /

⑩ to put something in a position or place from which it will not move

～を締める

≒ tie

⇔ undo, unfasten

ⓘ tは発音しない。「～するもの」を意味する-erがついたのが fastener（留め具、ファスナー）。

例 The highway bus didn't move until everyone had **fastened** their seat belts.

ハイウェイバスは全員がシートベルトを締めるまで動かなかった。

□□□ 0748

reassure / rìəʃúər / 图 reassurance 安心

⑩ to help someone feel less upset

～を安心させる

≒ comfort, console, cheer up

⇔ bring down

🔑 〈re-（再び）+assure（安心させる）〉

例 The prime minister's office continued to **reassure** the public that everything was under control.

首相官邸はすべてのことが管理下にあると言って国民を安心させ続けた。

□□□ 0749

fetch / féʧ /

⑩ ① to go and get something and bring it back (for someone)

～を行って取ってくる

≒ collect, grab, retrieve

例 The dog will **fetch** the Frisbee after it is thrown.

その犬は、フリスビーを投げると行って取ってくる。

② to be sold for a certain amount of money

〈値段〉で売れる

≒ earn, bring in

例 The antique vase **fetched** a high price at the auction.

そのアンティークの花びんはオークションで高値で売れた。

0750

pastime / pǽstàɪm /

图 an activity that you like to do when you have free time

娯楽、気晴らし

≒ distraction, recreation

🔑 〈pas(t)(過ぎる)+time(時間)〉

例 His favorite **pastime** is sewing.

彼のお気に入りの気晴らしは縫い物だ。

0751

deceive / dɪsíːv /

图 deceit 欺くこと
形 deceitful 詐欺の

動 to tell someone a lie and make them believe it is true

〜をだます、欺く

≒ trick, betray

🔑 〈de-(〜から)+ceive(取る)〉

例 Her parents took away her cell phone after she tried to **deceive** them about the party she went to.

彼女は自分が行ったパーティーについて両親をだまそうとしたため、両親は彼女の携帯電話を取り上げた。

0752

reckon / rékən /

動 to think something

…と思う

≒ consider, suppose

ⓘ 進行形では使わない。

例 I **reckon** that the festival will be canceled if it starts to snow.

雪が降り始めたらフェスティバルは中止になると思う。

0753

inquire / ɪnkwáɪər /

图 inquiry 質問

動 to ask for information

尋ねる、問い合わせる

🔑 〈in-(中に)+quire(求める)〉

例 She **inquired** at the information desk about where she could rent a bicycle.

彼女は案内所で自転車をレンタルできる場所を聞いた。

310

☐☐☐ 0754

reign / réɪn /

名 the period of time that someone is the ruler of a country

治世、統治期間

≒ dynasty

ⓘ gは発音しない。rain（雨）、rein（手綱）と同音。

例 Emperor Meiji's **reign** lasted 45 years.

明治天皇の治世は45年続いた。

0756語

動 to rule a country as its royal leader

君臨する

≒ command, govern

⇔ abdicate

例 Queen Victoria **reigned** over Britain for over 60 years.

ヴィクトリア女王は60年以上イギリスに君臨した。

☐☐☐ 0755

vain / véɪn /

形 not being successful or producing a desired result

無駄な、無益な

≒ futile, pointless

ⓘ in vain（無駄に）の形で押さえておこう。

例 The man tried in **vain** to get tickets to the concert.

男性はそのコンサートのチケットを入手しようとしたが、無駄だった。

☐☐☐ 0756

subsidy / sʌ́bsədi /

動 subsidize ～に助成金[補助金]を与える

名 money that a government or organization pays to keep the price of certain products or services lower to make sure they are successful

助成金、補助金

≒ aid, grant

例 Farming **subsidies** protect local farmers from the international market.

農業助成金は地元の農家を国際市場から守る。

☐☐☐ **0757**

testify

/ téstəfàɪ /

名 testimony 証言
名 testimonial 証明書、保証書

動 to talk about something or answer questions about it, usually in court, while promising that you are telling the truth

〜を証言する

≒ declare, swear, attest

例 The man agreed to **testify** against his drug dealer but only if he wouldn't go to prison.

その男は、投獄されないという条件で麻薬密売人に不利な証言をすることに同意した。

☐☐☐ **0758**

console

/ kənsóʊl /

名 consolation 慰め
形 consolatory 慰めの

動 to try to help someone feel better when they are sad or disappointed

〜を慰める

≒ comfort, reassure, cheer up

⇔ bring down, upset

例 It took many days to **console** her daughter after their pet turtle died.

ペットのカメの死後、彼女の娘を慰めるのに何日も要した。

☐☐☐ **0759**

creep

/ kríːp /

動 ① to move slowly with your body close to the ground

はう

≒ crawl

ⓘ creep-crept-creptと活用する。

例 She watched in fear as a large spider **crept** across the kitchen floor.

彼女は大きなクモがキッチンの床をはって横切るのをびくびくしながら見ていた。

② to move slowly and quietly, usually to avoid being noticed

忍び寄る

例 The cat **crept** up behind the dog and then jumped on his back.

猫は犬の背後に忍び寄り、それから犬の背中に飛び乗った。

□□□ 0760

liable

/ láɪəbl / 图 liability 法的責任；債務

形 ① legally responsible for something

法的責任がある

≒ accountable

例 The car maker could be **liable** if a person is injured because of a problem with one of its cars.

自社の車の故障で人がけがをしたら、その自動車メーカーに責任が生じるかもしれない。

0762語

② having a high chance of doing something

（〜する）傾向がある

≒ prone

ⓘ 〈be liable to *do*〉（〜する傾向がある）の形で押さえておこう。

例 That man is **liable** to say anything to get what he wants.

あの男は欲しいものを手に入れるためにどんなことでも言いがちだ。

□□□ 0761

riot

/ ráɪət / 图 rioter 暴徒

图 a situation that involves a large group of people who are acting violently and out of control

暴動

≒ uprising

ⓘ 発音に注意。

例 Many shop windows were broken and cars lit on fire in **riots** in Toronto in 2010.

2010年のトロントの暴動では、多くの店の窓が割られ、車には火がつけられた。

□□□ 0762

pest

/ pést /

图 an animal or insect that causes problems for people, such as by damaging their crops

害虫、有害な動物

例 Chemicals are used to protect crops from **pests**.

作物を害虫から守るために化学物質が使われる。

□□□ **0763**

transplant
/ trǽnsplænt /

動 ① to perform a procedure in which an organ is taken from one person's body and put into another person's body

〈臓器〉を移植する

ⓘ He got a liver transplant. (彼は肝臓の移植を受けた) のように名詞としても使う。名詞の発音は [trǽnsplænt]。

🔑 〈trans- (向こうに) +plant (植える)〉

例 A person who receives a **transplanted** organ has to take medicine to make sure their body accepts it.

臓器を移植された人は、体がその臓器を確実に受け入れるように、薬を飲まなければならない。

② to take a plant from the ground or its pot and move it somewhere else

〈植物〉を移植する

例 He carefully **transplants** the young tomato plants to the outside garden every spring.

彼は毎年春になるとトマトの苗を外の庭に注意深く植え替える。

□□□ **0764**

hierarchy
/ háɪərɑ̀ːrki /

形 hierarchical 階層性の

名 a system that divides people or things into different groups based on their rank in society

階級制度、ヒエラルキー

例 The group of gorillas has a strict social **hierarchy**.

ゴリラのグループには厳格な社会的階級制度がある。

□□□ **0765**

cuisine
/ kwɪzíːn /

名 a style of cooking

料理 (法)

≒ food, dishes

ⓘ フランス語から。発音に注意。

例 Korean **cuisine** has become very popular globally because of K-POP.

K ポップのおかげで韓国料理は世界中で大人気になっている。

314

□□□ 0766

restrain
/ rɪstréɪn /

名 restraint 抑制

動 to stop a person or animal from doing something

～を抑える、抑制する

≒ limit, confine, subdue, suppress

🔑〈re-（後ろに）+strain（縛る）〉

⇔ allow, permit

例 The man had to **restrain** his dog from attacking the cat in their backyard.

その男性は自分の犬が裏庭でその猫を攻撃するのを制止しなければならなかった。

□□□ 0767

furious
/ fjúəriəs /

名 fury 激怒

形 very angry

激怒した

≒ enraged

例 The boy's mother was **furious** when she found out he had skipped school.

その男の子の母親は、息子が学校をサボったことを知ると、激怒した。

□□□ 0768

irritate
/ írətèɪt /

名 irritation いら立ち
形 irritant 刺激性の

動 ① to make someone feel angry or annoyed about something

～をいらいらさせる

≒ bother, provoke

⇔ please, delight

例 All the passengers on the bus were **irritated** by the man talking on his phone.

バスの乗客は皆、携帯で話している男性にいらいらしていた。

② to cause a part of your body to feel pain or be damaged

～に炎症を起こさせる

例 Frequent hand washing can **irritate** the skin and make it red.

頻繁に手を洗うと肌に炎症が起きて赤くなることがある。

□□□ **0769**

indulge

/ ɪndʌ́lʤ /

名 **indulgence** ふけること
形 **indulgent** (子どもなどに) 甘い

動《indulge *oneself*》to let yourself have or do something special to make yourself happy

(快楽・趣味などに) ふける

≒ spoil, pamper

例 On payday, the woman always **indulges herself** and buys an expensive chocolate bar.

その女性は給料日にはいつもぜいたくをして高価な板チョコを買う。

□□□ **0770**

pressing

/ présɪŋ /

形 **needing to be dealt with quickly**

急を要する

≒ urgent

例 There is a **pressing** need for change in the country's healthcare system.

その国の医療制度はすぐにでも改革する必要がある。

□□□ **0771**

conserve

/ kənsə́ːrv /

名 **conservation** 保存、保護
形 **conservative** 保守的な

動 **to save something or use it carefully to stop damage from happening**

～を節約する、保存する

≒ preserve

例 Volunteer groups are working to **conserve** the world's remaining natural forests.

複数のボランティアグループが世界に残っている自然林を保存する活動をしている。

□□□ **0772**

absurd

/ əbsə́ːrd /

副 **absurdly** 無茶に
名 **absurdity** ばからしさ

形 **very silly or unreasonable**

ばかげた

≒ ridiculous, crazy

⇔ wise, realistic

例 That man always puts an **absurd** amount of pepper on his pasta.

あの男はいつもパスタにとんでもない量のこしょうをかける。

□□□ 0773

haunt
/ hɔ́ːnt /

囮 **haunted** 幽霊の出る、
とりつかれた

動 ① **to visit somewhere often**

～に出没する、頻繁に
現れる

≒ frequent

(i) 他動詞である点に注意。

例 The woman spends her days off **haunting** all the local bookstores.

その女性は地元のすべての本
屋に入り浸って休日を過ごす。

② **to continually come back to the mind of someone and make them sad or upset**

（記憶・考えなどが）
～にとりつく

例 The soldier was **haunted** by his memories of the war and couldn't sleep.

その兵士は戦争の記憶にとり
つかれて眠れなかった。

□□□ 0774

apparatus
/ æ̀pərǽtəs /

名 **a tool that is used to do specific things**

器具

≒ device, gear

(i) アクセントはraの位置。

例 The firefighter had to use a breathing **apparatus** so he could enter the house to save the kittens.

消防士は子猫を助けに家に入
れるように、呼吸器を使わなけ
ればならなかった。

□□□ 0775

deprive
/ dɪpráɪv /

動 **to take something away or not let someone or something have something**

～から（…を）奪う

≒ remove, strip

🔑 〈de-（完全に）+prive（奪う）〉

⇔ give, grant

(i) 〈deprive A of B〉（AからBを奪う）の形で押さえておこう。

例 Children in many countries are being **deprived** of a good education.

多くの国の子どもが十分な教
育を受けられずにいる。

□□□ **0776**

lessen

/ lésn / 形 less より少ない

動 ① to reduce something and make it smaller

〜を少なくする、減らす

≒ decrease, curtail

⇔ increase, expand, extend

ⓘ lesson（レッスン、授業）と同音。

🔑 〈less（より少ない）+-en（〜にする）〉

例 To **lessen** the burden on his wife, Mr. Jones decided to stop doing overtime.

妻の負担を減らすため、ジョーンズさんは残業をやめることにした。

② to become smaller in amount

減少する

≒ decrease, reduce, lower

⇔ increase, rise

例 The pain of the injury will **lessen** with time.

そのけがの痛みは時間がたてば和らぐだろう。

□□□ **0777**

rubbish

/ rʌ́bɪʃ /

名 things that have been thrown away because they are not needed or useful

ごみ

≒ garbage, trash, litter

ⓘ 主にイギリスで使われる。

例 The students picked all the **rubbish** up off the ground.

生徒たちは地面からすべてのごみを拾った。

□□□ **0778**

amend

/ əménd / 名 amendment（法律・規則などの）改正

動 to change a part of something, usually in a document or a law

〈法律・規則など〉を修正する

≒ alter, revise

🔑 〈a-（離れて）+mend（欠点）〉

例 The law was **amended** to allow American women to vote in 1920.

1920年にアメリカの女性が投票できるように法律が改正された。

318

□□□ 0779

generalization
/ ʤènərələzéɪʃən /

形 **general** 一般的な
動 **generalize** 一般的に述べる

名 **a statement that is based on only a few things and is very basic**

一般化、概括

ⓘ イギリス英語ではgeneralisationともつづる。

例 The politician made several **generalizations** about women and many people complained.

その政治家が女性を一般化する発言を何度かすると、多くの人が抗議した。

0781語

□□□ 0780

supposedly
/ səpóʊzɪdli /

形 **supposed** 推定される
名 **supposition** 推測

副 **according to what someone else has said or is thought to be true**

たぶん、おそらく

≒ apparently

ⓘ edの発音に注意。

例 This dish soap is **supposedly** better for the environment than the other brand.

この食器洗剤はもう一つのブランドより環境にいいと思われている。

□□□ 0781

bully
/ búli /

動 **to do mean things to a person who is normally smaller or weaker than you**

～をいじめる

≒ oppress, intimidate

ⓘ 「いじめ」は bullying と言う。

例 She **bullied** other kids as a child, and she felt very bad about it when she got older.

彼女は子どもの頃ほかの子たちをいじめ、大人になってそのことをとても後悔した。

名 **someone who does mean things to people who are smaller or weaker**

いじめっ子

例 Everyone ran away when they saw the neighborhood **bully** coming on his bicycle.

近所のいじめっ子が自転車に乗ってやって来るのを見ると、みんな逃げた。

□□□ **0782**

invaluable / ɪnvǽljuəbl /

形 **having high value or being very useful**

非常に貴重な

≒ priceless

⇔ worthless, cheap

🔑 〈in-（否定）+valuable（評価できる）〉

例 Studying abroad is an **invaluable** experience.

留学は非常に貴重な経験だ。

□□□ **0783**

pierce / píərs /

動 **to create a hole in or through something**

～を突き通す

≒ prick, penetrate

ⓘ stabは突き刺すだけで貫通を含意しない。

例 The girl **pierced** her own ears with a needle.

その女の子は針で自分の耳にピアスの穴を開けた。

□□□ **0784**

successive / səksésɪv /

副 successively 連続して
名 succession 連続
名 successor 後継者

形 **coming one after the other**

連続する、相次ぐ

≒ consecutive, subsequent

例 The basketball team won their fourth **successive** victory at the tournament.

そのバスケットボールチームはトーナメントで4連覇した。

□□□ **0785**

deliberate / dɪlíbərət /

副 deliberately 故意に；慎重に
名 deliberation 熟考

形 **done or said intentionally or after careful thought**

故意の；熟慮された

≒ intentional, planned

⇔ unintentional, unplanned, accidental

ⓘ アクセントはliの位置。

🔑 〈de-（強意）+liberate（天秤にかける）〉

例 The TV show was aired in a **deliberate** attempt to embarrass the actress.

そのテレビ番組は、その女優に恥をかかせることを故意に狙って放送された。

□□□ 0786

coincide / kòuɪnsáɪd /

形 coincidental 偶然の
名 coincidence (偶然の) 同時発生

動 ① to happen at the same time as another thing

同時に起きる

≒ correspond, accompany

♀ ⟨co-(共に)+incide(起こる)⟩

ⓘ アクセントは cide の位置。

0788語

例 The concert was scheduled to **coincide** with the anniversary of Freddie Mercury's death.

そのコンサートはフレディー・マーキュリーの命日と重なるように計画された。

② to agree completely with something or be the same as something

一致する

≒ concur, match, synchronize

⇔ oppose, clash

例 Moving abroad **coincided** well with the woman's career goals.

海外移住はその女性の仕事の目標とぴったりと一致した。

□□□ 0787

starve / stɑ́ːrv /

名 starvation 飢餓

動 to suffer or die from not eating enough

飢える、餓死する

例 There are many organizations that raise money to help children who are **starving**.

飢えている子どもたちを救うために募金をしている組織は多い。

□□□ 0788

anecdote / ǽnɪkdòʊt /

形 anecdotal 逸話の (ような)

名 a funny or interesting short story about a real person or event

逸話

ⓘ アクセントは a の位置。

例 One trick to make a speech more enjoyable is to start with an interesting **anecdote**.

スピーチをより楽しいものにする一つの秘訣は、面白い逸話で始めることだ。

□□□ 0789

irony / áɪrəni /

形 ironic 皮肉な
副 ironically 皮肉なことに

名 ① **words that mean the opposite of what is true or thought, often used to be funny**

皮肉、あてこすり

≒ sarcasm

例 The minister talked about her experience abroad with great **irony**.

その大臣は海外での経験を大変な皮肉を込めて話した。

② **a situation in which things happen in a way that seems to be the opposite of what was expected**

皮肉な状況

例 The **irony** is that he damaged his teeth by brushing them too much.

皮肉にも彼は歯を磨きすぎて傷めてしまった。

□□□ 0790

forthcoming / fɔːrθkʌ́mɪŋ /

形 **coming or happening soon**

来たるべき、今度の

≒ impending, upcoming, approaching

例 The author read a page from her **forthcoming** novel at the event.

その作家はイベントで、発売間近の小説のあるページを読んだ。

□□□ 0791

cling / klíŋ /

動 **to hold strongly onto something or someone**

くっつく、しがみつく

≒ stick

⇔ let go, release

ⓘ cling-clung-clungと活用する。cling to（〜にしがみつく、固執する）の形で押さえておこう。

例 The koala **clung** to the tree in fear as the fire surrounded it.

そのコアラは炎に取り囲まれて恐怖で木にしがみついた。

□□□ 0792

comprehend

/ kà:mprɪhénd /

图 comprehension 理解

動 to understand an idea or concept

～を理解する

≒ perceive, discern

⇔ misunderstand, misinterpret, mistake

例 As a firefighter, you must be able to quickly **comprehend** any situation.

❓〈con- (共に) +prehend (つかむ)〉

消防士として、きみはどのような状況もすぐに把握できなければいけない。

0794語

□□□ 0793

multitude

/ mʌ́ltət(j)ùːd /

图 a large number of things or people

多数

≒ myriad

⇔ handful, few

ⓘ〈a multitude of ＋複数名詞〉(多数の～) の形で押さえておこう。

例 There are a **multitude** of reasons why climbing Mt. Fuji in the winter is a bad idea.

冬に富士山に登るのがまずいことである理由はたくさんある。

□□□ 0794

temper

/ témpər /

图 a person's tendency to become angry

怒りっぽい性格

ⓘ「気分、機嫌」の意味もあるが、その意味では mood を使う方がふつう。

例 As a boy, he had quite a **temper**, and he often got into fights over small things.

少年の頃、彼は非常に短気で、よくささいなことでけんかになった。

....

動 to make something less extreme

～を和らげる、抑制する

≒ alleviate, assuage, mitigate, curb

⇔ incite, agitate, aggravate

例 The hot sunny weather was **tempered** by a gentle breeze.

暑いカンカン照りはそよ風で和らいだ。

☐☐☐ **0795**

curse / kə́ːrs /

名 ① **a rude word that people say when they are upset**

悪態、ののしり

≒ swearword

例 The woman muttered a **curse** when she realized she had forgotten her wallet.

その女は財布を忘れたことに気づいて、ののしりの言葉をつぶやいた。

② **something that causes bad luck**

災い（の元）

≒ jinx

⇔ blessing, fortune

例 The child's intelligence was not only a blessing but also a **curse** because she couldn't make friends with other kids.

その子の高い知能は恵みであるばかりでなく災いでもあった。彼女はほかの子どもと友達になれなかったのだ。

☐☐☐ **0796**

prolong / prəlɔ́ːŋ / 形 prolonged 長引く

動 to make something continue or last for a longer time

～を引き延ばす、長引かせる

≒ lengthen, delay, drag out

⇔ shorten

🔑 〈pro-（前に）+long（長い）〉

例 Salt can be used to **prolong** the shelf life of food.

食品の日持ちを延ばすのに塩が使われることがある。

☐☐☐ **0797**

concise / kənsáɪs / 副 concisely 簡潔に

形 using only the amount of words needed

簡潔な

≒ short, compact

⇔ lengthy, wordy

🔑 〈con-（完全に）+cise（切る）〉

ⓘ アクセントは cise の位置。

例 The doctor gave a short and **concise** explanation of the surgery to the patient and his family.

医師は患者とその家族に手術について短く簡潔に説明した。

□□□ **0798**

reap

/ ríːp /

動 ① **to get something in return for something you have done**

〈恩恵・報酬など〉を得る

≒ receive, gain, obtain

(i) leap（跳ぶ）と混同しないように注意。

0800語

例 The couple **reaped** large benefits from their investments.

その夫婦は投資で大きな利益を得た。

② **to cut and collect a crop, plant, etc.**

〜を刈り取る

≒ harvest, pick, gather

例 Everyone was out in the field **reaping** crops.

みんなが畑に出て作物を刈り取っていた。

□□□ **0799**

complement

/ káːmpləmènt /

形 complementary 補足的な

動 to make something complete or better

〜を補う、補完する

≒ supplement

⇔ detract

(i) 「補完物」という名詞の意味もある。compliment（〜を褒める）と同音。

例 Those blue earrings **complement** her clothes well.

あの青いイアリングは彼女の服をよく引き立てている。

□□□ **0800**

trivial

/ tríviəl /

名 trivia ささいなこと

形 not important

ささいな、つまらない

≒ unimportant, minor, negligible

⇔ essential, major, meaningful

例 Compared to the problems her sister was having, hers seemed **trivial**.

彼女の姉が抱えている問題に比べれば、彼女自身の問題はささいなことに思われた。

章末ボキャブラリーチェック

次の語義が表す英単語を答えてください。

語義	解答	連番
❶ to happen at the same time as another thing	c o i n c i d e	0786
❷ to tell someone they have to come to a place	s u m m o n	0702
❸ (friendly and) liking to meet and be around others	o u t g o i n g	0719
❹ an animal or insect that causes problems for people, such as by damaging their crops	p e s t	0762
❺ not easy to see, taste, hear, or feel	f a i n t	0711
❻ a system that divides people or things into different groups based on their rank in society	h i e r a r c h y	0764
❼ a situation that involves a large group of people who are acting violently and out of control	r i o t	0761
❽ to put something in a position or place from which it will not move	f a s t e n	0747
❾ (the activity of sending) e-mails, letters, or other written messages	c o r r e s p o n d e n c e	0725
❿ different from what is normal	a b n o r m a l	0744
⓫ to hold strongly onto something or someone	c l i n g	0791
⓬ to create a hole in or through something	p i e r c e	0783
⓭ to walk slowly in a relaxed way	s t r o l l	0745
⓮ a large number of things or people	m u l t i t u d e	0793
⓯ a small item that is used to decorate another object or room	o r n a m e n t	0731
⓰ to help someone feel less upset	r e a s s u r e	0748
⓱ a short fight or disagreement between people	c l a s h	0736
⓲ to try to help someone feel better when they are sad or disappointed	c o n s o l e	0758
⓳ to think about something and make guesses about it	s p e c u l a t e	0741
⓴ not honest, moral, or good	c o r r u p t	0703

語義	解答	連番
㉑ to get something in return for something you have done	<u>r e a p</u>	0798
㉒ a brief view of or look at someone or something	<u>g l i m p s e</u>	0715
㉓ to perform a procedure in which an organ is taken from one person's body and put into another person's body	<u>t r a n s p l a n t</u>	0763
㉔ to work together with others to do something	<u>c o o p e r a t e</u>	0718
㉕ a feeling of sadness or sympathy for someone or something	<u>p i t y</u>	0723
㉖ a story of a real person's life that is written by someone else	<u>b i o g r a p h y</u>	0722
㉗ not being successful or producing a desired result	<u>v a i n</u>	0755
㉘ to take something away or not let someone or something have something	<u>d e p r i v e</u>	0775
㉙ to save something or use it carefully to stop damage from happening	<u>c o n s e r v e</u>	0771
㉚ money that a government or organization pays to keep the price of certain products or services lower to make sure they are successful	<u>s u b s i d y</u>	0756
㉛ a line of people or cars that are waiting for something	<u>q u e u e</u>	0737
㉜ to do mean things to a person who is normally smaller or weaker than you	<u>b u l l y</u>	0781
㉝ words that mean the opposite of what is true or thought, often used to be funny	<u>i r o n y</u>	0789
㉞ to think something	<u>r e c k o n</u>	0752
㉟ done or said intentionally or after careful thought	<u>d e l i b e r a t e</u>	0785
㊱ ready or suitable to be eaten or used, often refers to fully developed fruits and vegetables	<u>r i p e</u>	0730
㊲ an activity that you like to do when you have free time	<u>p a s t i m e</u>	0750
㊳ a funny or interesting short story about a real person or event	<u>a n e c d o t e</u>	0788
㊴ using only the amount of words needed	<u>c o n c i s e</u>	0797
㊵ the feeling someone has when all hope is lost	<u>d e s p a i r</u>	0729

語義	解答	連番

41 to send out something, such as light or energy — e m i t — 0706

42 needing to be dealt with quickly — p r e s s i n g — 0770

43 very silly or unreasonable — a b s u r d — 0772

44 something done to keep people safe or stop problems from happening in the future — p r e c a u t i o n — 0707

45 to go and get something and bring it back (for someone) — f e t c h — 0749

46 not usual or normal — p e c u l i a r — 0726

47 a person's tendency to become angry — t e m p e r — 0794

48 legally responsible for something — l i a b l e — 0760

49 《------- oneself》 to let yourself have or do something special to make yourself happy — i n d u l g e — 0769

50 the height of something above sea level — a l t i t u d e — 0714

51 to throw or leave garbage on the ground in a public place — l i t t e r — 0746

52 clean and organized — t i d y — 0716

53 to say strongly that someone or something is bad — c o n d e m n — 0710

54 not important — t r i v i a l — 0800

55 unreal and existing only in your mind — i m a g i n a r y — 0742

56 having high value or being very useful — i n v a l u a b l e — 0782

57 to make something continue or last for a longer time — p r o l o n g — 0796

58 to make a sound or say something using your voice — u t t e r — 0704

59 to suddenly enter a place by force to look for someone or something — r a i d — 0709

60 to make someone feel angry or annoyed about something — i r r i t a t e — 0768

61 to make someone experience something unpleasant or dangerous — i n f l i c t — 0735

62 to reduce something and make it smaller — l e s s e n — 0776

63 slightly wet — d a m p — 0717

語義	解答	連番
❻❹ a place where someone can be protected from danger or trouble	r e f u g e	0738
❻❺ to make something complete or better	c o m p l e m e n t	0799
❻❻ to promise formally that something will be given or done	p l e d g e	0743
❻❼ a statement that is based on only a few things and is very basic	g e n e r a l i z a t i o n	0779
❻❽ easily broken or damaged	f r a g i l e	0701
❻❾ a tool that is used to do specific things	a p p a r a t u s	0774
❼⓪ to tell someone a lie and make them believe it is true	d e c e i v e	0751
❼❶ things that have been thrown away because they are not needed or useful	r u b b i s h	0777
❼❷ to visit somewhere often	h a u n t	0773
❼❸ a style of cooking	c u i s i n e	0765
❼❹ a rude word that people say when they are upset	c u r s e	0795
❼❺ only thinking about yourself and not caring about the needs of others	s e l f i s h	0728
❼❻ to change a part of something, usually in a document or a law	a m e n d	0778
❼❼ coming one after the other	s u c c e s s i v e	0784
❼❽ the period of time that someone is the ruler of a country	r e i g n	0754
❼❾ not used, filled, or lived in	v a c a n t	0740
❽⓪ something that you keep to remind you of a place visited or an event attended	s o u v e n i r	0705
❽❶ very angry	f u r i o u s	0767
❽❷ the official process of gathering information about the number of people living somewhere	c e n s u s	0724
❽❸ to stop a person or animal from doing something	r e s t r a i n	0766
❽❹ to officially get rid of something (e.g. a law)	a b o l i s h	0721
❽❺ not complicated or hard to understand	s t r a i g h t f o r w a r d	0708

329

86 to suffer or die from not eating enough — s t a r v e — 0787

87 《--------- *oneself*》 to agree to stop resisting, fighting, or hiding because you know you cannot succeed — s u r r e n d e r — 0727

88 coming or happening soon — f o r t h c o m i n g — 0790

89 having or giving (more than) enough of something that is needed — a m p l e — 0734

90 a person who was in a position before someone else — p r e d e c e s s o r — 0720

91 to talk about something or answer questions about it, usually in court, while promising that you are telling the truth — t e s t i f y — 0757

92 to ask for information — i n q u i r e — 0753

93 to give something light or shine light on something — i l l u m i n a t e — 0732

94 giving information — i n f o r m a t i v e — 0739

95 to hide someone or something so that they cannot be seen — c o n c e a l — 0713

96 to move slowly with your body close to the ground — c r e e p — 0759

97 according to what someone else has said or is thought to be true — s u p p o s e d l y — 0780

98 to understand an idea or concept — c o m p r e h e n d — 0792

99 to need or deserve something — w a r r a n t — 0712

100 very impressive and nice to look at — s p l e n d i d — 0733

Stage 9

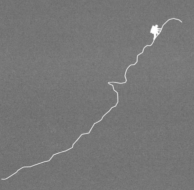

Put your best foot forward.
ベストを尽くせ。

☐☐☐ 0801

dwell
/ dwél /

動 to live somewhere

≒ inhabit, reside

ⓘ dwell-dwelt/dwelled-dwelt/dwelledと活用する。

例 The family had **dwelled** in the same town for generations.

名 dweller 居住者
名 dwelling 住居

住む、居住する

その一族は何世代にもわたって同じ町に住んでいた。

☐☐☐ 0802

embarrass
/ ɪmbérəs /

動 to make someone feel bad or silly in front of others

≒ shame

例 His mother always **embarrassed** him in front of his friends.

名 embarrassment 恥ずかしさ、困惑

～に恥ずかしい思いをさせる

彼の母親はいつも彼の友達の前で彼に恥ずかしい思いをさせた。

☐☐☐ 0803

defective
/ dɪféktɪv /

形 having a flaw

≒ faulty

ⓘ 傷などの外面的な欠陥はflawと言う。

例 The car has a **defective** steering wheel that has to be fixed.

名 defect 欠点、欠陥

欠陥のある

その車のハンドルには、修理の必要な欠陥がある。

☐☐☐ 0804

wrinkle
/ ríŋkl /

名 a small fold that forms on your skin when you get older, or a small fold in a material

しわ

ⓘ wは発音しない。

例 There are many beauty products made to help make **wrinkles** smaller.

しわを目立たなくするために作られた美容製品はたくさんある。

□□□ 0805

disguise

/ dɪsɡáɪz /

🔳 **to change something or someone so that people cannot recognize it**

〜を偽装する、偽る

≒ hide, mask

⇔ expose

例 The spy **disguised** himself using a wig and some makeup.

そのスパイはかつらと化粧で変装した。

0807語

🔳 **the act of changing how you look so people will not recognize you**

偽装、変装

≒ camouflage, concealment

例 That spy was known as a master of **disguise** when he worked for the government.

そのスパイは政府のために活動していた頃は変装の達人として知られていた。

□□□ 0806

contradict

/ kàntrədíkt /

形 contradictory 矛盾した
名 contradiction 矛盾

🔳 **to be different from something in a way that suggests that it is false, wrong, etc.**

〜と矛盾する

⇔ agree, support

🔑 〈contra-（反対）+dict（言う）〉

例 The information in the book **contradicts** what the news article says.

その本の情報はニュース記事に書かれていることと矛盾している。

□□□ 0807

pave

/ péɪv /

名 pavement 舗装

🔳 **to cover the ground with something that makes it level and easy to walk or drive on**

〜を舗装する

ⓘ pave the way for で「〜に道を開く」という比喩的な意味でも用いられる。

例 In the countryside, there are some mountain roads that aren't **paved**.

田舎には舗装されていない山道がある。

□□□ **0808**

slap
/ slǽp /

動 to hit someone or something with the front or the back of a flat hand

〜をピシャリとたたく

例 The woman **slapped** the table in anger.

その女性は怒ってテーブルをピシャッとたたいた。

□□□ **0809**

mourn
/ mɔ́ːrn /

名 mourning 悲嘆；服喪
形 mournful とても悲しい

動 to have a strong feeling of sadness because someone has died or something has been lost

〈死・不幸など〉を悲しむ

≒ lament

例 The child **mourned** the death of her grandmother for many weeks.

その子は何週間も祖母の死を悲しんだ。

□□□ **0810**

cram
/ krǽm /

動 to fill something until there is no room for anything else

〜に詰め込む

≒ stuff, pack

ⓘ cram schoolは、詰め込み教育をする「学習塾」という意味。

例 The little boy **crammed** his pockets with candy before going to meet his friends.

その小さな男の子は友達に会いに行く前にキャンディをポケットに詰め込んだ。

□□□ **0811**

invalid
/ ɪnvǽlɪd /

動 invalidate 〜を無効にする
名 invalidity 無効

形 being ineffective

無効の、効力のない

≒ null, void

🔑 〈in- (否定) +valid (有効な)〉

⇔ valid

例 The man was arrested for driving with an **invalid** license.

その男は無効な免許証で運転して逮捕された。

□□□ 0812

betray

/ bɪtréɪ /　名 betrayal 裏切り

動 ① to hurt someone who trusted you by doing something that makes them feel bad

〜を裏切る

≒ deceive

⇔ aid, assist

💡〈be-(強意)+tray(引き渡す)〉 0814語

例 The boy **betrayed** his friend by supporting another student in the election for class president.

その男の子は学級委員長選挙で別の生徒を支持することによって友達を裏切った。

② to tell or show someone something that is supposed to be a secret

〈秘密など〉を漏らす

≒ spill

例 She would never **betray** the secrets of a friend.

彼女は友達の秘密を決して漏らさないだろう。

□□□ 0813

sanction

/ sǽŋkʃən /

名 an action done to make a country follow international laws

制裁措置

≒ embargo, ban

例 The United Nations put trade **sanctions** on the country for helping terrorists.

国際連合はテロリストを支援しているとしてその国に貿易制裁を科した。

□□□ 0814

terrify

/ térəfàɪ /　名 terror 恐怖

動 to make someone feel very afraid

〜をひどく怖がらせる

≒ scare, frighten

⇔ comfort, reassure

💡〈terr(驚かす)+-ify(〜にする)〉

例 The sight of the snake **terrified** him.

彼はヘビを見てひどく怖がった。

☐☐☐ **0815**

vow
/ váʊ /

動 to make a serious promise to do something or act in a specific way

～を誓う

≒ pledge, swear

ⓘ 〈vow to *do*/(that)...〉（～する／…だと誓う）の形で押さえておこう。

例 The knight **vowed** to protect the princess with his life.

騎士は命をかけて王女を守ると誓った。

名 a serious promise to do something or act in a specific way

誓い

≒ oath, pledge

例 The couple exchanged their wedding **vows** at the church.

2人は教会で結婚の誓いを交わした。

☐☐☐ **0816**

dim
/ dím /

形 not having much light or being hard to see

薄暗い

≒ gloomy

⇔ clear, bright

例 The **dim** light in the room made it impossible to read.

その部屋は明かりが暗かったので、本を読めなかった。

☐☐☐ **0817**

adore
/ ədɔ́ːr /

名 adoration 熱愛

動 to love someone or something very much

～が大好きである

≒ cherish, treasure

⇔ hate, detest

🔑 〈ad-(～に)+ore(嘆願する)〉

例 The girl has **adored** her little brother since the day he was born.

その女の子は弟が生まれた日からずっと弟が大好きだ。

□□□ 0818

esteem /ɪstíːm/

動 to have a high opinion of someone or something

～を尊ぶ、(高く)評価する

≒ respect, revere

⇔ scorn, look down on

0820語

例 The professor is highly **esteemed** for her work helping homeless children.

その教授はホームレスの子どもたちを救済する活動で高く評価されている。

名 respect felt for someone or something

尊敬、尊重

≒ admiration

⇔ contempt, scorn

例 The man has won **esteem** from many for his work in AIDS research.

その男性はエイズ研究における活動で多くの人から尊敬を集めている。

□□□ 0819

stubborn /stʌ́bərn/

形 not willing to change your ideas or stop doing something

頑固な

≒ obstinate, persistent

⇔ submissive, yielding

例 The young man is too **stubborn** to admit that he is wrong.

その若者は非常に頑固で、自分が間違っていると認めることができない。

□□□ 0820

famine /fǽmɪn/

名 a situation in which many people do not have enough food to eat

飢饉

例 The potato **famine** in Ireland in 1845 made many people move to North America.

1845年のアイルランドのジャガイモ飢饉で多くの人が北米に渡った。

☐☐☐ 0821

doom

/ dúːm /

形 doomed 破滅する運命の

動 to make sure that someone or something will fail, die, suffer, etc.

～を（悪く）運命づける

ⓘ be doomed to で「～の運命にある」という意味。

例 Many species are **doomed** to extinction because of rising ocean temperatures.

多くの種が海水温の上昇のために絶滅する運命にある。

名 very bad events or situations that are not able to be avoided

運命、破滅

≒ catastrophe, disaster

例 Everyone had a sense of **doom** as they watched the tsunami approach the shore.

津波が岸に迫るのを見て、誰もがもうだめだと感じた。

☐☐☐ 0822

oblige

/ əbláɪdʒ /

名 obligation 義務
動 obligate ～を義務づける
形 obligatory 義務的な

動 to make someone or something do something because there is a need or rule

～を義務づける

≒ compel, force

⇔ release, allow, let off

🔑 〈ob-(～に)+lige(結びつける)〉

例 The law **obliges** TV shows to get permission to show people's faces.

その法律はテレビ番組に人の顔を映す許可を取ることを義務づけている。

☐☐☐ 0823

contempt

/ kəntémpt /

形 contemptuous 軽蔑的な

名 a feeling that other things or people do not deserve respect

軽蔑、軽視

≒ scorn

例 People look at her with **contempt** because she doesn't share any of her wealth.

自分の富を人に分け与えないので、人々は彼女を軽蔑の目で見ている。

□□□ 0824

tame / téim /

形 not wild; trained to listen to orders

飼い慣らされた

≒ docile

⇔ aggressive

例 The deer that live in Nara like to eat crackers from people, but they are not **tame**.

奈良に生息している鹿は人々からせんべいをもらって食べるのが好きだが、飼い慣らされてはいない。

動 to train an animal to listen to orders

〜を飼い慣らす

≒ domesticate

例 It took a whole summer to **tame** the horse enough so that it could be ridden.

人を乗せられるようになるまでその馬を飼い慣らすのに、ひと夏かかった。

□□□ 0825

weep / wíːp /

動 to cry because of a strong emotion, usually sadness

(悲しみのために) 泣く

≒ sob, shed tears ⇔ smile, laugh

ⓘ weep-wept-weptと活用する。

例 The man **wept** when he heard about the death of his wife.

その男性は妻が亡くなったことを聞いて泣いた。

□□□ 0826

reunion / rìːjúːnjən /

名 an event where people get together again after being apart for a while

同窓会、再会の集い

⚷ 〈re- (再び) +union (結合)〉

例 They have a family **reunion** every year on December 26.

彼らは毎年12月26日に家族で集まる。

0826語

☐☐☐ 0827

selective / səléktɪv /

動 select 〜を(慎重に)選ぶ
名 selection 選択

形 careful to choose only what is best

入念に選択する

≒ choosy, picky

例 The man is very **selective** of what meat he buys at the supermarket.

その男性はスーパーでどの肉を買うかとても入念に選ぶ。

☐☐☐ 0828

fertile / fə́ːrtl /

名 fertility 肥沃
名 fertilizer 肥料

形 able to support plants and make them grow well

肥沃な

≒ rich, productive

⇔ infertile

例 Their crops always grew well because the land was very **fertile**.

土地が非常に肥沃だったので、彼らの作物は常によく育った。

☐☐☐ 0829

imaginative / ɪmǽdʒənətɪv /

名 imagination 想像力
形 imaginary 想像上の

形 having the skill of thinking of new and interesting ideas

想像力に富んだ

⇔ unimaginative

例 For his homework, the boy wrote an **imaginative** story about living on Mars with turtles.

その男の子は宿題で、カメと一緒に火星で暮らすという想像力に富んだ話を書いた。

☐☐☐ 0830

utmost / ʌ́tmòust /

形 highest in degree or amount

最大の、最高の

≒ ultimate

ⓘ 名詞の前で使う。

例 It is of the **utmost** importance to wash your hands a lot when you work at a restaurant.

レストランで働くときは何度も手を洗うことが最も重要だ。

340

□□□ 0831

overtake
/ òʊvərtéɪk /

動 ① to go past someone or something by going faster than they are

～を追い抜く

⇔ fall behind

🗝 〈over-(超えて)+take(取る)〉   0833語→

(i) overtake-overtook-overtakenと活用する。

例 The girl started to cry when her brother **overtook** her in the race.

その女の子は競走で弟に追い抜かれると泣き出した。

② to become higher in amount or importance than something else

～を上回る、しのぐ

≒ exceed, surpass

例 The company worked hard so that it wouldn't be **overtaken** by its competitors.

その会社は商売がたきに負けないように頑張った。

□□□ 0832

bathe
/ béɪð /   名 bath 入浴

動 to wash a person or animal in a bath

～を入浴させる

(i) aとtheの発音に注意。

例 The couple always **bathe** their baby after eating dinner.

その夫婦は夕食を取った後に必ず赤ちゃんを入浴させる。

□□□ 0833

compel
/ kəmpél /

形 compulsory 必須の
形 compulsive 衝動的な
名 compulsion 無理強い

動 to make someone do something

～に無理に(…)させる

≒ force, oblige

🗝 〈com-(共に)+pel(押す)〉

⇔ dissuade, discourage

(i) 〈compel A to do〉(Aに無理に～させる)の形で押さえておこう。形容詞compellingは「強制的な」のほか、「感動的な、説得力のある」という意味でも使われる。

例 Sickness **compelled** the woman to stay in bed for two weeks.

その女性は病気のため2週間寝ていなければならなかった。

☐☐☐ 0834

worsen

/ wə́ːrsn /

動 to (make someone or something) get worse

悪化する；～を悪化させる

≒ deteriorate

⇔ improve, enhance, upgrade

例 The police encouraged people to go home before the weather conditions **worsened** any further.

警察は人々に、天候がそれ以上悪化しないうちに帰宅するよう促した。

☐☐☐ 0835

underline

/ ʌ́ndərlàin /

動 to show that something is important

～を強調する

≒ highlight, stress

ⓘ 文字通り「下線（を引く）」の意味もある。

例 The report **underlines** the importance of eating breakfast before school.

そのリポートは登校前に朝食を取る重要性を強調している。

☐☐☐ 0836

analogy

/ ənǽlədʒi /　形 analogous 類似した

名 a comparison of two things based on something that they have in common

類似、類比

例 The poet tried to draw an **analogy** between spring and youth in his poetry.

詩人は自分の詩の中で春と若さの類似を示そうとした。

☐☐☐ 0837

chore

/ tʃɔ́ːr /

名 a small job that is done on a regular basis

（日常的な）家事、雑用

ⓘ ch の発音に注意。

例 The children were given money for finishing their weekly **chores**.

その子どもたちは毎週の雑用を終えるとお金をもらった。

342

□□□ 0838

subtract
/ səbtrǽkt /

图 subtraction 引き算

動 to take away an amount from another amount

～を引く、減じる

≒ remove, deduct, take off

0841語

⇔ add, increase

🔑 〈sub- (下に) +tract (引く)〉

例 **Subtracting** 10 from 36 gives you 26.

36から10を引くと26になる。

□□□ 0839

refrain
/ rɪfréɪn /

動 to stop yourself from doing something

控える

≒ hold back

ⓘ 〈refrain from doing〉(～することを控える) の形で押さえておこう。

例 Guests at the party were asked to **refrain** from smoking inside.

パーティーの客たちは室内での喫煙を控えるよう求められた。

□□□ 0840

discriminate
/ dɪskrímənèɪt /

图 discrimination 差別

動 to treat someone or a group of people unfairly because something about them is different

差別する

例 We should not **discriminate** against people because of their sex or race.

私たちは性別や人種で人々を差別するべきではない。

□□□ 0841

ascend
/ əsénd /

图 ascension 上昇
形 ascendant 上昇する

動 to rise or go up (something)

(～を) 登る、上がる

≒ climb

🔑 〈a- (～に) +scend (登る)〉

⇔ descend

例 They **ascended** the mountain just in time to see the sunrise.

彼らはその山に登り、日の出を見るのにちょうど間に合った。

☐☐☐ **0842**

prestige / prestíːʒ /

形 **prestigious** 有名な、名誉ある

名 respect that someone or something gets because they are important or successful

名声、威信

≒ reputation

例 His achievements in medicine have brought him a lot of **prestige**.

医療における業績で彼は大いなる名声を得ている。

☐☐☐ **0843**

flatter / flǽtər /

名 **flattery** お世辞

動 to (try to) make someone feel pleased, often by saying nice things about them and for reasons that are hidden

お世辞を言う

≒ compliment

⇔ insult, condemn

例 The man **flattered** the waitress with compliments about her beautiful eyes.

その男性はウエイトレスに目がきれいだねとお世辞を言った。

☐☐☐ **0844**

envy / énvi /

形 **envious** うらやんで

名 the feeling of wanting something that another person has

ねたみ、嫉妬

≒ jealousy

🔑 〈en- (上に) +vy (見る)〉

例 The hairdresser looked at her hair with **envy**.

美容師は彼女の髪をうらやましそうに見た。

動 to want something that someone else has

～をねたむ

≒ covet

例 He was **envied** by all for his success in business.

彼は事業に成功したことで皆にねたまれた。

344

□□□ 0845

contaminate / kəntǽmənèit /

名 contamination 汚染
名 contaminant 汚染物質

動 to make something dirty by adding something dangerous or unclean to it

～を汚染する

0848語

≒ pollute

⇔ clean, cleanse

例 The bay has been **contaminated** by the oil spill that happened a few years ago.

その湾は数年前に起きた原油流出によって汚染されている。

□□□ 0846

unify / júːnəfàɪ /

名 unification 統一、統合

動 to get people or things to join together

～を統一する

≒ bring together, combine

⇔ divide, separate

🔑 〈uni (1つ) +-fy (～にする)〉

例 China was first **unified** in 221 B.C. after a long period of war.

中国は長期にわたる戦争を経て紀元前221年に初めて統一された。

□□□ 0847

nuisance / n(j)úːsəns /

名 something or someone that is annoying or causes problems

迷惑、厄介なもの［人］

≒ annoyance, bother

ⓘ iは発音しない。

例 Her allergies were a **nuisance** and stopped her from working well.

彼女のアレルギーは厄介で、そのおかげで彼女はしっかりと仕事をすることができなかった。

□□□ 0848

earnest / ə́ːrnɪst /

副 earnestly 真面目に

形 serious and not playful

真面目な、真剣な

≒ sincere ⇔ insincere

例 The young journalist was praised for being an **earnest** worker.

その若いジャーナリストは真面目な働きぶりを褒められた。

□□□ 0849

congratulate

/ kəngrǽtʃəlèɪt /

名 congratulation お祝い
形 congratulatory お祝いの

動 **to say that you are happy for someone because of their success or good luck**

〈人〉を祝う

ⓘ 〈congratulate A on B〉（BのことでAを祝福する）の形で押さえておこう。

🔑 〈con- (共に) +grat (喜び) + -ulate (動詞)〉

例 The teacher **congratulated** her students on their win at the debate.

先生は生徒たちが討論で勝ったことを祝福した。

□□□ 0850

exile

/ éɡzaɪl /

名 **a person who has been made to leave the place they are from and cannot return**

追放者、亡命者

≒ refugee

ⓘ 「追放、亡命」の意味もある。

例 The children of many Cuban **exiles** live in the United States.

多くのキューバからの亡命者の子どもたちがアメリカに住んでいる。

□□□ 0851

mock

/ máːk /

名 mockery あざけり

動 **to make fun of someone or something that they do by copying them**

～を(まねして)からかう

例 In school, her accent was often **mocked** by the other children.

学校で彼女はよくほかの子どもたちになまりをまねされ、からかわれた。

形 **done or made in a way to make it look real**

偽の、模擬の

≒ pretend, fake

⇔ real, authentic, genuine

例 The class decided to do a **mock** battle for their history presentation.

そのクラスは歴史の発表で模擬戦を演じることにした。

□□□ 0852

perish
/ périʃ /

形 perishable 壊れやすい；
腐りやすい

0854語

動 to die or be killed

死ぬ、滅びる

≒ pass away

⇔ flourish

例 Thousands of animals have **perished** in the forest fires.

その森林火災で何千匹もの動物が死んだ。

□□□ 0853

aspire
/ əspáɪər /

名 aspiration 熱望

動 to want to successfully do something

目指す、熱望する

≒ desire, endeavor

💡〈a-(〜に)+spire(息をする)〉

ⓘ〈aspire to A/to do〉(A／〜することを切望する) の形で押さえ
ておこう。

例 He **aspires** to become a game programmer when he
graduates from university.

彼は大学卒業後にゲームプログラマーになることを目指している。

□□□ 0854

disgust
/ dɪsɡʌ́st /

形 disgusting 非常に不快な

**動 to make someone feel a strong dislike by
being unpleasant in some way**

〈人〉に嫌悪感を起こ
させる

例 The thought of eating raw eggs **disgusts** many
Americans.

生卵を食べるという考えは多くのアメリカ人に嫌悪感を抱かせる。

**名 a strong feeling of dislike for someone or
something because something about
them is unpleasant**

嫌悪感

≒ revulsion, distaste

⇔ love, adoration, approval

例 She felt nothing but **disgust** when she looked at the
garbage next to the river.

川辺のごみを見て、彼女は嫌悪感しか抱かなかった。

□□□ 0855

roar / rɔ́ːr /

動 to make a sound that is long and loud　　轟音を立てる、どよめく

≒ growl

例 The baseball fans **roared** when the player hit a home run.

その選手がホームランを打つと、野球ファンたちは大歓声を上げた。

名 a sound that is loud and does not stop for a long time　　轟音

例 The **roar** of the airplane engines made it hard to hear anything.

飛行機のエンジンの轟音で何もかも聞きづらかった。

□□□ 0856

inclination / ìnklənéɪʃən /　　形 inclined 傾向がある

名 a feeling of wanting to or preferring to do something instead of another thing　　好み、愛好

≒ leaning, preference

⇔ aversion

例 Her natural **inclination** is to read books when she is stressed.

彼女は生来、ストレスがあると本を読みたくなる。

□□□ 0857

persecute / pə́ːrsəkjùːt /　　名 persecution 迫害

動 to treat someone badly, especially because of their race or religion　　～を迫害する

≒ oppress

⇔ protect, defend, safeguard

🔑 〈per-(完全に)+secute(追う)〉

ⓘ アクセントは per の位置。

例 They were **persecuted** by the public because of their religion.

彼らは信じる宗教のために人々に迫害された。

☐☐☐ 0858

marvelous

/ máːrvələs / 動 marvel 驚く

形 very good or enjoyable

驚くべき、素晴らしい

≒ wonderful, fantastic   ⇔ terrible

ⓘ イギリス英語では marvellous とつづる。

例 That young man is a **marvelous** poet.

その若者は素晴らしい詩人だ。

☐☐☐ 0859

applaud

/ əplɔ́ːd / 名 applause 称賛

動 to show approval or support for someone or something

～を称賛する

≒ praise

⇔ denounce, condemn

🔑 〈ap-(～に)+plaud(拍手する)〉

例 The city's efforts to clean up the neighborhood were **applauded** by everyone.

その地区をきれいにしようとする市の努力を誰もが称賛した。

☐☐☐ 0860

prosper

/ prάːspər / 名 prosperity 繁栄
形 prosperous 繁栄した

動 to become successful

繁栄する

≒ thrive

🔑 〈pro-(前に)+sper(希望)〉

例 The economy **prospered** under the direction of the new prime minister.

新首相の指揮のもと、経済は繁栄した。

☐☐☐ 0861

amuse

/ əmjúːz / 形 amusing 面白い
名 amusement 娯楽

動 to make someone laugh, smile, or feel happy

～を面白がらせる、楽しませる

≒ delight

⇔ depress, disappoint

🔑 〈a-(～に)+muse(思案する)〉

例 That comedian never fails to **amuse** me.

あのコメディアンは必ず私を楽しませてくれる。

□□□ **0862**

disregard

/ dìsrɪgάːrd /

動 to ignore something or act like it is not important

（故意に）〜に注意を払わない、〜を無視する

≒ dismiss

例 The doctor **disregarded** her worries about the pain in her arm until it was too late.

その医師は手遅れになるまで、腕の痛みについての彼女の心配を無視した。

□□□ **0863**

addict

/ ǽdɪkt /

名 addiction 中毒
形 addictive 中毒性の
形 addicted 中毒になって

名 a person who cannot stop doing something even though it may be harming them (e.g. taking drugs)

中毒者、依存症の人

例 More programs to support **addicts** are needed to help them quit drugs.

中毒者が麻薬をやめるのを助けるために、もっと多くの支援プログラムが必要だ。

□□□ **0864**

naive

/ nɑːíːv /

形 lacking experience and knowledge

未熟な、世間知らずの

≒ inexperienced, ignorant

⇔ experienced, knowledgeable

ⓘ ai の発音に注意。否定的な意味合いの語で、「繊細な」を表すには delicate、sensitive などを使う。

例 People that have never traveled are sometimes **naive** about other people and cultures.

旅行をしたことがない人は時にほかの人々や文化に対する見識が浅い。

□□□ **0865**

witty

/ wíti /

名 wit 機知

形 funny and smart

機知のある、気の利いた

≒ clever

例 That boy is always making **witty** jokes in class to make his friends laugh.

その男の子は友達を笑わせようと、クラスでいつも気の利いた冗談を言っている。

☐☐☐ 0866

greed
/ gríːd / 形 greedy 貪欲な

名 a selfish desire to have more of something than you need

貪欲

⇔ generosity

例 The CEO of the company was known for his **greed** and unkindness.

その会社のCEOは貪欲で非情なことで知られていた。

0869語

☐☐☐ 0867

tremble
/ trémbl /

動 to shake slightly because you are afraid, nervous, excited, etc.

震える

ⓘ tremは「震える」を意味する語根で、tremor（身震い）、tremolo（(音楽用語の)トレモロ）なども同語源語。

例 Her hands **trembled** in excitement as she opened her university acceptance letter.

大学の合格通知を開くとき、彼女の手は興奮で震えた。

☐☐☐ 0868

fuss
/ fʌs / 形 fussy うるさい

名 unusual and often unnecessary activity or excitement

（くだらないことでの）
大騒ぎ

ⓘ make a fuss（騒ぎ立てる）という表現も覚えておこう。

例 The artist's new painting has caused a lot of **fuss** in the art world.

その画家の新しい絵は美術界に大騒ぎを引き起こしている。

☐☐☐ 0869

proficient
/ prəfíʃənt / 名 proficiency 上達、熟練

形 able to do something well

熟達した、技量のある

≒ adept, competent, capable

⇔ incompetent, incapable

例 Her teacher is **proficient** in three different languages.

彼女の先生は3か国語に熟達している。

□□□ **0870**

mortal
/ mɔ́ːrtl /

名 mortality 死ぬべき運命
副 mortally 致命的に

形 ① (possibly) causing or related to death

致命的な、命にかかわる

≒ fatal, deadly

🔑 〈mort (死) +-al (形容詞)〉

例 The soldier suffered a **mortal** injury during the fight.

その兵士は戦闘中に致命傷を負った。

② unable to live forever

死を免れない

⇔ immortal

例 All humans are **mortal**, and we must accept that we cannot live forever.

人間は皆、死を免れない。私たちは永遠に生きられないということを受け入れなければならない。

□□□ **0871**

exclaim
/ ɪkskléɪm /

名 exclamation 叫び；感嘆

動 to cry out or say something suddenly and loudly, especially because of a strong emotion or feeling

叫ぶ

≒ shout, yell
⇔ whisper, mutter

🔑 〈ex- (外に) +claim (大声で呼ぶ)〉

ⓘ 「!」(エクスクラメーションマーク) は名詞形の exclamation から。

例 The boys **exclaimed** happily when they saw the Christmas tree for the first time.

少年たちはクリスマスツリーを初めて見て喜びの声を上げた。

□□□ **0872**

stereotype
/ stériətàɪp /

形 stereotypical 典型的な

名 a belief that many people have about a specific group of people or things, especially one that is not true or fair

固定観念、既成概念

ⓘ 「ステレオタイプ」はカタカナ語にもなっている。

例 Racial **stereotypes** are harmful and can be very dangerous.

人種についての固定観念は、有害で非常に危険な場合がある。

352

0876語

□□□ **0873**

stern

/ stə́ːrn /

膨 very serious, usually in an unfriendly way

厳格な、厳しい

≒ harsh, strict, rigid

⇔ relaxed, easy-going, gentle

例 The manager gave a **stern** warning to his workers about keeping their desks clean.

部長は部下に、机をきれいにしておくよう厳しく注意した。

□□□ **0874**

prudent

/ prúːdənt /

图 prudence 慎重さ

膨 having or showing the ability to make good, careful decisions

慎重な、用心深い

≒ cautious

⇔ careless, reckless

例 She is a **prudent** investor, so she almost never loses money.

彼女は慎重に投資するので、損をすることはほぼない。

□□□ **0875**

orphan

/ ɔ́ːrfən /

图 orphanage 孤児院

图 a child who has no parents, usually because they are dead

孤児

例 After her parents died in a plane accident, she was left an **orphan**.

両親が航空機事故で死に、残された彼女は孤児になった。

□□□ **0876**

devastating

/ dévəstèitiŋ /

働 devastate 〜を完全に破壊する

膨 causing a lot of damage or harm

破壊的な、致命的な

≒ disastrous, destructive

⇔ mild

例 A **devastating** flood hit the region and destroyed everything.

怒とうの洪水がその地域を襲い、すべてを破壊した。

□□□ **0877**

despise / dɪspáɪz /

🔲 **to dislike someone or something a lot**

⇔ love, adore, cherish

例 Her grandfather **despises** rock music.

～をひどく嫌う、軽蔑
する

🍴 〈de-（下を）+spise（見る）〉

彼女の祖父はロック音楽をひど
く嫌っている。

□□□ **0878**

compulsory / kəmpʌ́lsəri /

🔲 **required according to a law or rule**

≒ mandatory, obligatory
⇔ optional, voluntary

例 Attending class is **compulsory** in order to finish this
course.

名 compulsion 無理強い
形 compulsive 衝動的な

必須の

🍴 〈com-（共に）+puls（駆り立
てる）+-ory（形容詞）〉

このコースを修了するために
は授業への出席が必須だ。

□□□ **0879**

blink / blíŋk /

🔲 **to close and then open your eyes very
quickly**

≒ wink
ⓘ 明かりの明滅にも使う。

例 He couldn't stop himself from **blinking** when the light
flashed.

まばたきをする

ライトが光ったとき、彼はまば
たきを止められなかった。

□□□ **0880**

nourish / nə́ːrɪʃ /

🔲 **to give someone or something the food
and other things they need to live and be
healthy**

ⓘ ourの発音に注意。

例 Honey is added to some shampoo to help **nourish**
hair.

名 nourishment 栄養物

～を育てる、養う

髪に栄養を与えるのを補助す
るためにハチミツが加えられて
いるシャンプーもある。

□□□ 0881

uneasy / ʌníːzi /

形 worried about something

不安な、心配な

≒ anxious, nervous

🔑 ⟨un-(否定)+easy(気楽な)⟩

⇔ calm, relaxed

例 Her daughter is **uneasy** about changing schools halfway through the school year.

彼女の娘は年度途中で転校するのが不安だ。

□□□ 0882

intellect / íntəlèkt /

形 intellectual 知的な

名 the ability to think about things in a way that is logical

知性

≒ intelligence

例 The teacher made her students read a new book every week to develop their **intellects**.

先生は生徒たちの知能を伸ばすために、毎週新しい本を1冊読ませた。

□□□ 0883

bankrupt / bǽŋkrʌpt /

名 bankruptcy 破産、倒産

形 unable to pay back borrowed money

破産した、倒産した

ⓘ go bankrupt(破産する)の形を覚えておこう。

🔑 ⟨bank(銀行)+rupt(破れた)⟩

例 The company went **bankrupt** when the economy crashed.

経済が破綻すると、その会社は倒産した。

□□□ 0884

pollute / pəlúːt /

名 pollution 汚染

動 to make something (e.g. water, air, etc.) dirty, unsafe, or unusable

～を汚染する

≒ contaminate, infect, taint

⇔ purify, sterilize, clean

例 The ocean has been **polluted** by all the plastic humans use.

海は人間が使うあらゆるプラスチックで汚染されている。

□□□ 0885

infamous / ínfəməs /

形 known by a lot of people as being bad

悪名高い

≒ notorious

ⓘ fa の発音に注意。アクセントは in の位置。

例 That city is **infamous** for its high crime rate.

その都市は高い犯罪率で悪名高い。

□□□ 0886

secondhand / sékəndhǽnd /

形 having been owned before

中古の

≒ used

ⓘ「2つ目の手に移った」が原義。

例 To save money, he only buys **secondhand** clothes.

節約のため、彼は古着しか買わない。

□□□ 0887

poke / póuk /

動 to push your finger or another thin thing into someone or something

（指・ひじ・棒などで）～をつつく

例 Her grandfather always **pokes** her in the cheeks when he sees her.

彼女のおじいちゃんは彼女に会うと必ず頬をつつく。

□□□ 0888

precedent / présədənt / 動 precede ～に先立つ

名 something done or said that can be used in the future as an example of what to do

前例、慣例

≒ model, standard

ⓘ unprecedented は「前例のない、空前の」。

🔑〈pre-（前に）+ced（行く）+ -ent（形容詞）〉

例 The judge set a dangerous **precedent** when he allowed the thief to go free without charges.

その裁判官は窃盗犯を無罪放免にして、危険な前例を作った。

□□□ **0889**

reconstruct / rì:kənstrʌ́kt / 图 reconstruction 再建

動 to build something again after it has been damaged or destroyed

〜を再建する

≒ rebuild, restore

🔑〈re-（再び）+construct（建設する）〉

例 After the earthquake, whole communities needed to be **reconstructed**.

その地震の後、地域社会全体を再建する必要があった。

□□□ **0890**

sovereign / sá:vərən / 图 sovereignty 主権、統治権

形 having power or authority that is not limited

主権を有する

ⓘ 発音に注意。gは発音しない。

例 The **sovereign** power of a king cannot be questioned by anyone.

国王の主権は何人も疑うことができない。

□□□ **0891**

underlie / ʌ̀ndərláɪ /

動 to form the basis of an idea, process, etc.

〈思想・行動など〉の根底にある

ⓘ underlie-underlay-underlainと活用する。他動詞である点に注意。

🔑〈under-（下に）+lie（ある）〉

例 Love is the theme that **underlies** most of his films.

愛は彼のほとんどの映画の根底にあるテーマだ。

□□□ **0892**

restless / réstləs /

形 feeling nervous or not calm, and usually moving around a lot because of it

落ち着きのない、そわそわした

🔑〈rest（休息）+-less（ない）〉

例 The crowd became more and more **restless** the longer they waited for the store to open.

群衆は店が開くのを待てば待つほど、どんどん落ち着きがなくなってきた。

□□□ 0893

shrug / ʃrʌ́g /

動 to raise (and lower) your shoulders to show that you do not know or care about something

〈肩〉をすくめる

ⓘ 「肩をすくめる」という自動詞の意味もある。

例 The woman just **shrugged** her shoulders when the man asked her what she wanted for lunch.

男性がランチに食べたいものを聞くと、女性はただ肩をすくめた。

□□□ 0894

frown / fráʊn /

動 to move your eyebrows down to show anger, confusion, sadness, or concentration

眉をひそめる

ⓘ ow の発音に注意。

例 Her boyfriend was **frowning** when she got home, so she knew that he had had a bad day.

彼女が帰宅すると、ボーイフレンドは眉をひそめていたので、その日彼はついていなかったことが彼女にはわかった。

□□□ 0895

dread / dréd / 形 dreadful ひどい

動 to feel worry or fear about something that will or might happen

～をとても心配する、恐れる

⇔ look forward to, welcome

例 She **dreads** the day she'll have to present her final thesis.

彼女は最終論文を提出しなければならない日を恐れている。

□□□ 0896

diplomacy / dɪplóʊməsi / 名 diplomat 外交官
形 diplomatic 外交の

名 the things done to keep relationships between different governments positive

外交

例 The country was able to avoid going to war through good **diplomacy**.

その国は優れた外交によって開戦を避けることができた。

0897

magnify
/ mǽgnəfàɪ /

动 to make something look bigger

≒ amplify, enlarge

⇔ reduce, lessen

例 The **magnified** view of the image allowed the doctors to find the tumor and save her life.

名 magnification 拡大
名 magnifier 拡大鏡、虫眼鏡

〈レンズなどが〉～を拡大する

💡〈magn (大きな) +-ify (～にする)〉

画像を拡大して見ることで医師たちは腫瘍を発見し、彼女の命を救うことができた。

0900語

0898

intelligible
/ ɪntélɪʤəbl /

形 able to be understood

≒ understandable

⇔ unintelligible, ambiguous, obscure, vague

例 The two-year-old girl talked a lot, but her speech was only **intelligible** to her family.

理解できる、わかりやすい

その2歳の女の子はたくさんおしゃべりしたが、その話は家族にしか理解できなかった。

0899

tumble
/ tʌ́mbl /

动 to fall down quickly and without warning

例 The man wasn't looking where he was walking and **tumbled** into a hole.

転ぶ

その男性は自分が歩いている場所を見ておらず、穴に転げ落ちた。

0900

liberate
/ líbərèɪt /

动 to free someone or something from the control of another person or thing

≒ release

⇔ confine, restrain

例 Americans fought to **liberate** themselves from the British during the American Revolution.

形 liberal 自由な
名 liberation 解放

～を自由にする、解放する

独立戦争中、アメリカ人はイギリス人から自由になるために戦った。

章末ボキャブラリーチェック

次の語義が表す英単語を答えてください。

語義	解答	連番
❶ a selfish desire to have more of something than you need	g r e e d	0866
❷ careful to choose only what is best	s e l e c t i v e	0827
❸ having the skill of thinking of new and interesting ideas	i m a g i n a t i v e	0829
❹ to dislike someone or something a lot	d e s p i s e	0877
❺ to show approval or support for someone or something	a p p l a u d	0859
❻ to have a strong feeling of sadness because someone has died or something has been lost	m o u r n	0809
❼ lacking experience and knowledge	n a i v e	0864
❽ to treat someone or a group of people unfairly because something about them is different	d i s c r i m i n a t e	0840
❾ causing a lot of damage or harm	d e v a s t a t i n g	0876
❿ unable to pay back borrowed money	b a n k r u p t	0883
⓫ able to do something well	p r o f i c i e n t	0869
⓬ to (make someone or something) get worse	w o r s e n	0834
⓭ having a flaw	d e f e c t i v e	0803
⓮ to (try to) make someone feel pleased, often by saying nice things about them and for reasons that are hidden	f l a t t e r	0843
⓯ to have a high opinion of someone or something	e s t e e m	0818
⓰ to make a sound that is long and loud	r o a r	0855
⓱ to shake slightly because you are afraid, nervous, excited, etc.	t r e m b l e	0867
⓲ unusual and often unnecessary activity or excitement	f u s s	0868
⓳ respect that someone or something gets because they are important or successful	p r e s t i g e	0842

語義	解答	連番
⑳ having or showing the ability to make good, careful decisions	p r u d e n t	0874
㉑ to free someone or something from the control of another person or thing	l i b e r a t e	0900
㉒ to cry because of a strong emotion, usually sadness	w e e p	0825
㉓ to make someone feel very afraid	t e r r i f y	0814
㉔ worried about something	u n e a s y	0881
㉕ to cover the ground with something that makes it level and easy to walk or drive on	p a v e	0807
㉖ to form the basis of an idea, process, etc.	u n d e r l i e	0891
㉗ to show that something is important	u n d e r l i n e	0835
㉘ to treat someone badly, especially because of their race or religion	p e r s e c u t e	0857
㉙ to want to successfully do something	a s p i r e	0853
㉚ to take away an amount from another amount	s u b t r a c t	0838
㉛ to make something dirty by adding something dangerous or unclean to it	c o n t a m i n a t e	0845
㉜ to make a serious promise to do something or act in a specific way	v o w	0815
㉝ being ineffective	i n v a l i d	0811
㉞ to say that you are happy for someone because of their success or good luck	c o n g r a t u l a t e	0849
㉟ to fall down quickly and without warning	t u m b l e	0899
㊱ a situation in which many people do not have enough food to eat	f a m i n e	0820
㊲ a child who has no parents, usually because they are dead	o r p h a n	0875
㊳ to make someone do something	c o m p e l	0833
㊴ a small job that is done on a regular basis	c h o r e	0837
㊵ serious and not playful	e a r n e s t	0848
㊶ to ignore something or act like it is not important	d i s r e g a r d	0862
㊷ to die or be killed	p e r i s h	0852

語義	解答	連番
❸ an action done to make a country follow international laws	<u>s a n c t i o n</u>	0813
❹ very good or enjoyable	<u>m a r v e l o u s</u>	0858
❺ a small fold that forms on your skin when you get older, or a small fold in a material	<u>w r i n k l e</u>	0804
❻ to make someone laugh, smile, or feel happy	<u>a m u s e</u>	0861
❼ to get people or things to join together	<u>u n i f y</u>	0846
❽ the ability to think about things in a way that is logical	<u>i n t e l l e c t</u>	0882
❾ to move your eyebrows down to show anger, confusion, sadness, or concentration	<u>f r o w n</u>	0894
❺⓿ to make something look bigger	<u>m a g n i f y</u>	0897
❺❶ to make sure that someone or something will fail, die, suffer, etc.	<u>d o o m</u>	0821
❺❷ to make fun of someone or something that they do by copying them	<u>m o c k</u>	0851
❺❸ to fill something until there is no room for anything else	<u>c r a m</u>	0810
❺❹ not having much light or being hard to see	<u>d i m</u>	0816
❺❺ having been owned before	<u>s e c o n d h a n d</u>	0886
❺❻ feeling nervous or not calm, and usually moving around a lot because of it	<u>r e s t l e s s</u>	0892
❺❼ to cry out or say something suddenly and loudly, especially because of a strong emotion or feeling	<u>e x c l a i m</u>	0871
❺❽ a belief that many people have about a specific group of people or things, especially one that is not true or fair	<u>s t e r e o t y p e</u>	0872
❺❾ to close and then open your eyes very quickly	<u>b l i n k</u>	0879
❻⓿ to feel worry or fear about something that will or might happen	<u>d r e a d</u>	0895
❻❶ a person who has been made to leave the place they are from and cannot return	<u>e x i l e</u>	0850
❻❷ to stop yourself from doing something	<u>r e f r a i n</u>	0839
❻❸ able to support plants and make them grow well	<u>f e r t i l e</u>	0828

語義	解答	連番
❻ to change something or someone so that people cannot recognize it	d i s g u i s e	0805
❻ to wash a person or animal in a bath	b a t h e	0832
❻ to love someone or something very much	a d o r e	0817
❻ required according to a law or rule	c o m p u l s o r y	0878
❻ funny and smart	w i t t y	0865
❻ the things done to keep relationships between different governments positive	d i p l o m a c y	0896
❼ to make something (e.g. water, air, etc.) dirty, unsafe, or unusable	p o l l u t e	0884
❼ the feeling of wanting something that another person has	e n v y	0844
❼ able to be understood	i n t e l l i g i b l e	0898
❼ to be different from something in a way that suggests that it is false, wrong, etc.	c o n t r a d i c t	0806
❼ a feeling that other things or people do not deserve respect	c o n t e m p t	0823
❼ to build something again after it has been damaged or destroyed	r e c o n s t r u c t	0889
❼ to hurt someone who trusted you by doing something that makes them feel bad	b e t r a y	0812
❼ to go past someone or something by going faster than they are	o v e r t a k e	0831
❼ to make someone feel bad or silly in front of others	e m b a r r a s s	0802
❼ to give someone or something the food and other things they need to live and be healthy	n o u r i s h	0880
❽ to make someone or something do something because there is a need or rule	o b l i g e	0822
❽ a feeling of wanting to or preferring to do something instead of another thing	i n c l i n a t i o n	0856
❽ highest in degree or amount	u t m o s t	0830
❽ very serious, usually in an unfriendly way	s t e r n	0873
❽ to live somewhere	d w e l l	0801

語義	解答	連番
㉟ not wild; trained to listen to orders	t a m e	0824
㊱ not willing to change your ideas or stop doing something	s t u b b o r n	0819
㊲ a comparison of two things based on something that they have in common	a n a l o g y	0836
㊳ (possibly) causing or related to death	m o r t a l	0870
㊴ to rise or go up (something)	a s c e n d	0841
㊵ to hit someone or something with the front or the back of a flat hand	s l a p	0808
㊶ something or someone that is annoying or causes problems	n u i s a n c e	0847
㊷ to make someone feel a strong dislike by being unpleasant in some way	d i s g u s t	0854
㊸ to raise (and lower) your shoulders to show that you do not know or care about something	s h r u g	0893
㊹ to become successful	p r o s p e r	0860
㊺ to push your finger or another thin thing into someone or something	p o k e	0887
㊻ something done or said that can be used in the future as an example of what to do	p r e c e d e n t	0888
㊼ an event where people get together again after being apart for a while	r e u n i o n	0826
㊽ a person who cannot stop doing something even though it may be harming them (e.g. taking drugs)	a d d i c t	0863
㊾ known by a lot of people as being bad	i n f a m o u s	0885
㊿ having power or authority that is not limited	s o v e r e i g n	0890

Stage 10

The best view comes after the hardest climb.
最高の景色は最も辛い登りの先にひらける。

□□□ **0901**

sober

/ sóʊbər /

图 sobriety 真面目；しらふ

形 ① **plain in color and design**

〈色などが〉地味な

≒ subdued

⇔ loud, gaudy

例 The woman was known for always wearing a **sober** gray suit.

その女性はいつも地味なグレーのスーツを着ていることで知られていた。

② **not drunk**

酔っていない、しらふの

例 One friend agreed to stay **sober** and drive his friends home from the party.

友人の一人が酒を飲まずに友人たちをパーティーから家へ車で送ることを引き受けてくれた。

□□□ **0902**

accustomed

/ əkʌ́stəmd /

動 accustom ～を慣らす

形 **used to something in a way that makes it feel normal**

慣れている

⇔ unaccustomed

ⓘ 〈be accustomed to A/doing〉(A／～することに慣れている)の形で押さえておこう。

🔑 〈ac-(～に)+custom (習慣)+-ed〉

例 The man is **accustomed** to loud children because he works in a kindergarten.

その男性は幼稚園で働いているので、うるさい子どもたちに慣れている。

□□□ **0903**

roam

/ róʊm /

動 **to go to places randomly without a plan or purpose**

(～を)歩き回る

≒ wander

ⓘ Rome (ローマ) と同音。

例 Chickens that can **roam** freely are happier than caged chickens.

自由に歩き回れるニワトリの方が、かごに閉じ込められたニワトリより幸せだ。

□□□ 0904

quarrel / kwɔ́ːrəl /

名 an angry argument or disagreement, especially about something personal

口論、口げんか

ⓘ have a quarrel (with) ((〜と) 口論する) の形で押さえておこう。

例 She had a **quarrel** with her boyfriend about money.

彼女はお金のことでボーイフレンドと口げんかをした。

動 to argue or disagree about something

口論する、けんかする

≒ squabble

例 The children **quarreled** a lot when they were growing up.

その子どもたちは成長していく中でよくけんかした。

□□□ 0905

sentimental / sèntəméntl /

名 sentiment 感情；感傷

形 based on feelings and not reason or thought

心情的な、感情による

≒ emotional

例 She cannot sell her wedding dress because of **sentimental** reasons.

彼女は自分のウェディングドレスを心情的な理由で売れない。

□□□ 0906

amenity / əménəti /

名 something that makes life easier or more pleasant

生活を快適にするもの、施設

≒ comfort, convenience

ⓘ 「アメニティーグッズ」は和製英語。amenity が指すものは石鹸や歯ブラシなどの備品よりもずっと広い。

例 From its large fitness center to its luxury spa, this hotel has every **amenity** you might need.

広いフィットネスセンターから高級スパに至るまで、このホテルには客が必要とするかもしれないあらゆる設備がある。

☐☐☐ 0907

temperate

/ témpərət /

形 emotionally calm and in control

節度のある、穏やかな

≒ controlled, restrained

⇔ uncontrolled

ⓘ temperature（気温、体温）の原義は「適度に混ぜられた状態」。

🔑〈temper（調整する）+-ate（形容詞）〉

例 He is a **temperate** man and is well known for keeping calm during disagreements.

彼は穏やかな男性で、もめている最中でも冷静でいることでよく知られている。

☐☐☐ 0908

hardship

/ há:rdʃɪp /

名 difficulties in life

苦難

≒ suffering ⇔ blessing

ⓘ -ship は「状態、地位、能力」などを意味する接尾辞。
例：championship（選手権）、citizenship（市民権）、craftsmanship（職人技）

例 The family experienced great **hardship** after they lost their house in the flood.

その一家は洪水で家を失った後大変な苦難を経験した。

☐☐☐ 0909

glare

/ gléər /

形 glaring まぶしい；けばけばしい

動 ① to shine with a harsh, bright light

ぎらぎら光る、目立つ

≒ blaze

例 The August sun **glared** down on the marathon runners.

8月の太陽が、マラソンランナーたちにぎらぎらと照りつけた。

② to look at someone using an angry expression

にらみつける

例 His wife **glared** at him when he accidentally told their friend her secret.

彼がうっかり共通の友人に妻の秘密を口にすると、彼女は彼をにらみつけた。

□□□ 0910

soothe / súːð /

形 soothing 落ち着かせる；和らげる

動 **to help someone feel calmer and relax**

〜をなだめる、落ち着かせる

≒ pacify

⇔ provoke, aggravate, agitate

例 She **soothed** the crying baby by rubbing its back.

彼女は泣いている赤ん坊の背中をさすってなだめた。

□□□ 0911

diligent / díliʤənt /

副 diligently 勤勉に
名 diligence 勤勉

形 **working with care or continued effort**

勤勉な、熱心な

≒ hardworking, industrious

⇔ lazy

例 She is a **diligent** worker who always meets deadlines.

彼女は締め切りを必ず守る勤勉な社員だ。

□□□ 0912

solitude / sáːlət(j)ùːd /

名 **a situation in which you are alone, often by choice**

孤独

≒ isolation

ⓘ solは「単独の」を意味する語根で、solo（独奏）、solitary（単独の；孤独な）なども同語源語。

例 She liked the **solitude** of walking through the forest by herself.

彼女は一人で森の中を歩く孤独を好んだ。

□□□ 0913

eccentric / ɪkséntrɪk /

名 eccentricity 奇妙さ

形 **tending to act in ways that are unusual**

風変わりな、変な

≒ odd, weird

⇔ conventional, normal, typical

🔑 〈ec-（外に）+centr（中心）+ -ic（形容詞）〉

例 People think his aunt is rather **eccentric**.

彼のおばはちょっと風変わりだと思われている。

0913語

☐☐☐ 0914

savage / sǽvɪʤ /

形 ① not under the control of humans

野生の、獰猛な

≒ wild

⇔ tame

ⓘ 対応するフランス語 sauvage（野生の）はカタカナ語「ソバージュ」になっている。

例 Many **savage** beasts live in the world's large forests.

世界の大きな森には多くの野生の獣が生息している。

② very violent, cruel, or aggressive

残忍な、残虐な

≒ brutal

例 The **savage** criminal has attacked three people, and one of them is still in the hospital.

その暴漢は3人を襲い、そのうちの1人はまだ入院している。

☐☐☐ 0915

devour / dɪváuər /

動 to quickly eat all of something

～をむさぼり食う

ⓘ our の発音に注意。

例 The boy **devoured** his lunch after he got home from soccer practice.

その男の子はサッカーの練習から帰宅すると、昼食をがつがつと食べた。

☐☐☐ 0916

endangered / ɪndéɪnʤərd /

動 endanger ～を危険にさらす

形 《of a plant or animal》 very rare and in danger of disappearing completely

（絶滅の）危機に瀕した

≒ threatened, at risk

ⓘ endangered language（絶滅の危機に瀕した言語）のように生き物以外にも使う。

🔑〈en-（～にする）+danger（危機）〉

例 Many animals are **endangered** because they were hunted by humans.

多くの動物が人間に狩られたために絶滅の危機に瀕している。

☐☐☐ 0917

detach

/ dɪtǽtʃ / 图 detachment 分離

動 to separate something from another thing

〜を取り外す、分離する

≒ disconnect

⇔ attach, connect

🔑〈de-(離れて) +tach (触る)〉

例 You can **detach** the hood from this coat.

このコートのフードは取り外すことができる。

☐☐☐ 0918

clumsy

/ klʌ́mzi /

形 awkwardly made or done

不器用な、ぎこちない

⇔ graceful, coordinated

例 She made a **clumsy** attempt to cross the log bridge but tripped and fell in the water.

彼女はぎこちなく丸太橋を渡ろうとしたが、足を踏み外して川に落ちた。

☐☐☐ 0919

sane

/ séin / 图 sanity 正常さ

形 having a healthy mind that can think normally

正気の、正常な

≒ rational

⇔ insane, crazy

例 No **sane** person would try to drive their car in a snowstorm like this.

正気の人なら、こんな吹雪の中で車を運転しようとはしないだろう。

☐☐☐ 0920

paralyze

/ pérəlàɪz / 图 paralysis まひ

動 to cause something or someone to be unable to move, function, etc.

〜をまひさせる

≒ disable

ⓘ イギリス英語では paralyse ともつづる。

例 The train network was **paralyzed** by the storm.

鉄道網は嵐でまひした。

☐☐☐ 0921

startle

/ stάːrtl /

形 startling 驚くような

動 to surprise someone in a way that is not serious

〜をびっくりさせる

≒ shock, frighten

例 The dog was **startled** by the sound of the vacuum cleaner.

その犬は掃除機の音に驚いた。

☐☐☐ 0922

indifferent

/ ɪndífərənt /

副 indifferently 無関心に
名 indifference 無関心

形 not concerned about or interested in something

無関心な

≒ apathetic, detached

⇔ curious

ⓘ be indifferent to（〜に無関心な）の形で押さえておこう。

例 The boy was **indifferent** to his father's anger about his test results.

その男の子は自分のテスト結果に父親が怒っていることに無関心だった。

☐☐☐ 0923

conspicuous

/ kənspíkjuəs /

形 getting attention by being impressive

人目を引く、顕著な

≒ outstanding, noteworthy

⇔ inconspicuous

🔑〈con-（完全に）+spicuous（見える）〉

例 The Nobel Prize is given to people who have **conspicuous** achievements.

ノーベル賞は顕著な功績を残した人々に与えられる。

☐☐☐ 0924

rot

/ rάːt /

形 rotten 腐った

動 to (make something) decay over time

腐る；〜を腐らせる

≒ decompose

例 The meat was left out in the sun for too long, and it **rotted**.

その肉は非常に長い間日光にさらされて腐った。

□□□ 0925

gloomy

/ glúːmi / 图 gloom 憂うつ

形 ① feeling sad or depressed

憂うつな、ふさぎ込んだ

⇔ cheerful, lively

例 Her father had never seen her look so **gloomy** before.

彼女の父親はそれほどふさぎ込んだ彼女の表情をそれまで見たことがなかった。

② without much hope or promise

悲観的な、希望のない

≒ dismal, bleak

⇔ promising, hopeful, encouraging

例 The economic forecasts show a **gloomy** picture of the future.

経済予測は今後の悲観的な展望を示している。

□□□ 0926

affluent

/ ǽfluənt / 图 affluence 富、裕福

形 having a lot of money and expensive things

裕福な、富裕な

≒ rich, wealthy

⇔ poor, impoverished

🔑 〈af- (〜に) +flu (流れる) + -ent (形容詞)〉

例 They live in an **affluent** neighborhood where every house has its own security guard.

彼らは、どの家も独自に警備員を置いている裕福な地区に住んでいる。

□□□ 0927

foresee

/ fɔːrsíː / 形 foreseeable 予測可能な

動 to see or guess something that has not happened yet

〜を予感する、見越す

≒ predict, foretell

🔑 〈fore-(前もって)+see(見る)〉

ⓘ foresee-foresaw-foreseenと活用する。

例 The investors **foresaw** the potential of the company and invested in it quickly.

投資家たちはその会社の将来性を見越して、すぐにその会社に投資した。

☐☐☐ 0928

cynical

/ sínɪkl /

名 cynicism 皮肉 (な言葉)

形 **believing that people are mostly selfish and not honest**

皮肉な、冷笑的な

≒ skeptical, suspicious

ⓘ 「シニカル」はカタカナ語にもなっている。

例 **Cynical** people usually say there is no such thing as true love.

皮肉屋はたいてい真の愛などというものはないと言う。

☐☐☐ 0929

resent

/ rɪzént /

形 resentful 憤慨している
名 resentment 憤慨

動 **to be upset about someone or something that you think is not fair**

～に憤慨する

ⓘ 他動詞である点に注意。

💡 〈re- (再び) +sent (感じる)〉

例 She has always **resented** being told what to do by her brother.

彼女は兄にああしろこうしろと言われることにずっと憤慨している。

☐☐☐ 0930

ruthless

/ rúːθləs /

副 ruthlessly 無情にも

形 **having or showing no pity or mercy**

無慈悲な、無情な

≒ brutal

⇔ compassionate, merciful

例 The media was **ruthless** in their criticism of the president.

メディアは容赦なく大統領を批判した。

☐☐☐ 0931

meditate

/ médətèɪt /

名 meditation 瞑想
形 meditative 瞑想にふける

動 **to spend time thinking quietly to relax or for religious needs**

瞑想する

例 The monks in that temple **meditate** every morning and evening.

その寺の僧侶たちは毎朝毎晩瞑想している。

0935語

□□□ 0932

irresistible

/ ìrɪzístəbl /

副 irresistibly 思わず

形 impossible to resist

抵抗できない、非常に魅力的な

≒ alluring, tempting, seductive

🔑〈ir-(否定)+resist(抵抗する)+ -ible(できる)〉

例 Ice cream is an **irresistible** treat in the summer.

アイスクリームは夏にはたまらないごちそうだ。

□□□ 0933

menace

/ ménəs /

形 menacing 脅すような
副 menacingly 脅すように

名 someone or something that is dangerous and might hurt you

脅威、危険な人[もの]

≒ threat, risk, hazard

例 The government has created new programs to fight the **menace** of drug addiction.

政府は麻薬中毒の脅威と闘う新制度を創設した。

□□□ 0934

recede

/ rɪsíːd /

名 recession (景気)後退

動 to move away little by little

遠ざかる

≒ retreat

🔑〈re-(後ろに)+cede(行く)〉

例 The floodwaters slowly **receded** after the rain stopped.

雨がやむと、洪水はゆっくりと引いた。

□□□ 0935

audible

/ ɔ́ːdəbl /

副 audibly 聞こえるように

形 able to be heard

聞こえる、聞き取れる

⇔ inaudible, silent

🔑〈aud(聞く)+-ible(できる)〉

ⓘ audは「聞く」を意味する語根で、audience(聴衆)、auditorium (講堂)なども同語源語。

例 Her voice was barely **audible** over the sound of the radio.

彼女の声はラジオの音でほとんど聞き取れなかった。

□□□ **0936**

subordinate

/ səbɔ́ːrdənət /

名 **subordination** 下位 (に置くこと)；従属

形 in a position that has less power than someone else

下位の、位が低い

≒ inferior ⇔ commanding

ⓘ subordinate to（〜より下位の）という表現も覚えておこう。

🔑 〈sub-(下に)+ordin(命令)+ -ate(動詞)〉

例 All **subordinate** officers had to report to the police chief at the end of their shift.

下級警察官は皆、交代勤務終了時に署長に報告しなければならなかった。

名 a person in a position that has less power than someone else

部下、下位の人

例 He speaks very politely to everyone, even his **subordinates**.

彼はたとえ部下に対してであれ、すべての人にとても丁寧に話しかける。

□□□ **0937**

mischief

/ mísʧɪf /

形 **mischievous** いたずらな

名 a behavior or action that is annoying but not meant to cause serious harm or damage

いたずら、悪さ

≒ joke

ⓘ アクセントは mi の位置。

例 The neighborhood children are always getting into **mischief** after school.

近所の子どもたちは放課後にいつもいたずらをしている。

□□□ **0938**

arouse

/ əráʊz /

動 to cause an emotion or thought

〈感情など〉を呼び起こす、刺激する

≒ provoke, rouse, stir

ⓘ ou の発音に注意。

例 The company's new product **aroused** a lot of interest in the public.

その会社の新製品は世間で多くの関心を呼んだ。

□□□ 0939

solemn

/ sá:ləm / 　名 solemnity 厳粛さ

0942語

形 very serious in behavior or expression

厳粛な

≒ sober, stern　　⇔ cheerful, excited, joyful

ⓘ nは発音しない。

例 The doctor exited the operating room with a very **solemn** look on his face.

医師はとてもいかめしい顔つきで手術室を出た。

□□□ 0940

barren

/ bérən /

形 not having many plants or being bad for plants

〈土地が〉不毛の

≒ infertile, desolate　　⇔ fertile

例 There are few animals that can do well in such a **barren** land.

そのような不毛の地で問題なく暮らせる動物はほとんどいない。

□□□ 0941

coward

/ káʊərd / 　形 cowardly 臆病な

名 a person who is too afraid to do what is right or expected of them

臆病者

≒ chicken

ⓘ owの発音に注意。形容詞形は -ly で終わる。

例 The soldier was called a **coward** after he ran away from battle.

その兵士は戦場から逃亡して臆病者と呼ばれた。

□□□ 0942

ingenious

/ ɪndʒí:njəs / 　名 ingenuity 巧妙さ、創意

形 very smart, or using clever ideas

工夫に富む、利口な

≒ creative, inventive

例 The movie has an **ingenious** plot that everyone will enjoy.

その映画は、誰もが楽しめる工夫をこらした筋立てになっている。

□□□ **0943**

obedient

/ oʊbíːdiənt /

形 **willing to do whatever someone or something tells you to do**

≒ compliant ⇔ disobedient

例 After months of training, the dog became **obedient** to its master.

名 obedience 従順さ
動 obey ～に従う

従順な、素直な

何か月も訓練を受けて、その 犬は主人に従順になった。

□□□ **0944**

shiver

/ ʃívər /

動 **to shake slightly because you are cold or afraid**

≒ tremor

例 The girl **shivered** when her brother put an ice cube in her shirt.

（寒さ・恐怖などで） 震える

その女の子は、弟が彼女のシャ ツの中に氷を1個入れたとき、 震えた。

□□□ **0945**

sob

/ sάːb /

動 **to cry noisily while taking in short, sudden breaths**

≒ weep

例 They found their daughter **sobbing** in front of her broken toy.

すすり泣く

彼らは娘が壊れたおもちゃの 前ですすり泣いているのを見 つけた。

□□□ **0946**

pessimistic

/ pèsəmístɪk /

形 **always expecting that something bad will happen**

≒ negative ⇔ optimistic, positive

例 Many scientists have a **pessimistic** view of the future of the environment.

名 pessimism 悲観主義
名 pessimist 厭世家

悲観的な、厭世的な

多くの科学者は、自然環境の 未来に悲観的な見解を持って いる。

□□□ 0947

dismay / dɪsméɪ / 形 dismal 陰気な

名 a strong feeling of worry or disappointment

狼狽、落胆

ⓘ sの発音は濁らない。

🔑 〈dis (無い) +may (力)〉

例 The family watched in **dismay** as their home burned.

その一家は、自分たちの家が燃えるのをうろたえながら見つめた。

動 to make someone feel very worried or upset

～を落胆させる、狼狽させる

⇔ assure

例 Her university choice **dismayed** her parents.

彼女が選んだ大学は両親を落胆させた。

□□□ 0948

traitor / tréɪtər /

名 a person who betrays a group or country by helping their enemies

反逆者、裏切り者

⇔ loyalist, patriot

🔑 〈trait (引き渡す) +-or (人)〉

例 The **traitor** told all of his company's secrets to their rivals.

その裏切り者は自分の会社のあらゆる秘密をライバル会社に教えた。

□□□ 0949

eminent / émənənt / 名 eminence 名声

形 having more respect or success than a normal person

著名な

≒ distinguished, renowned
⇔ unknown, ordinary

🔑 〈e-(外に)+min (突き出る)+-ent (形容詞)〉

例 The university employs many **eminent** scientists to teach its students.

その大学は学生を教育するために多くの著名な科学者を雇っている。

☐☐☐ **0950**

imaginable

/ ɪmǽʤənəbl /

形 **possible to imagine**

≒ conceivable, plausible, comprehensible

⇔ unimaginable

例 You can buy any camera **imaginable** in Tokyo.

形 imaginary 想像上の
形 imaginative 想像力に富む

想像できる、考えられる

🔑 〈imagin (想像する) +-able
(できる)〉

東京なら考えられる限りのどん
なカメラでも買うことができる。

☐☐☐ **0951**

horrify

/ hɔ́ːrəfàɪ /

動 **to make someone feel very shocked or upset**

≒ alarm, appall

⇔ relieve

例 His parents were **horrified** to find out that he had quit school to be a musician.

形 horrible 恐ろしい
名 horror 恐怖

〈人〉をぞっとさせる

彼がミュージシャンになるため
に学校をやめたと知って、両親
はショックを受けた。

☐☐☐ **0952**

vocation

/ voʊkéɪʃən /

名 **a job that suits someone very well**

≒ profession, calling

例 For him, teaching wasn't just a job; it was a **vocation**.

形 vocational 職業の

天職、使命

彼にとって教えることは単なる
仕事ではなかった。それは天
職だった。

☐☐☐ **0953**

extinguish

/ ɪkstíŋgwɪʃ /

動 **to make something stop burning**

≒ put out

⇔ light, ignite

ⓘ extinguisher (消火器) という語も覚えておこう。

例 The firefighters were able to **extinguish** the flames easily.

〈火など〉を消す

消防士たちは簡単に火を消す
ことができた。

380

□□□ 0954

zeal

/ zíːl /

形 zealous 熱心な

名 a strong feeling of interest or excitement that motivates someone to do something

熱意、熱心さ

≒ passion

⇔ disinterest, apathy, indifference

例 That politician is known in the community for his **zeal** for reform.

その政治家は地域社会では改革への熱意で知られている。

□□□ 0955

astonish

/ əstáːnɪʃ /

形 astonishing 驚くべき
名 astonishment 驚き

動 to surprise someone or make them feel great wonder

〈人〉を（非常に）驚かせる

≒ amaze, astound

💡〈as-（〜に）+ton（雷）+-ish（動詞）〉

例 The Taj Mahal **astonishes** anyone who sees it.

タージ・マハルは見る人誰をも驚嘆させる。

□□□ 0956

superstition

/ sùːpərstíʃən /

形 superstitious 迷信深い

名 a belief that some objects or actions bring good or bad luck

迷信

例 It is a common **superstition** that breaking a mirror will give you seven years of bad luck.

鏡を割ると7年不運が続くというのはよくある迷信だ。

□□□ 0957

hereditary

/ hərédətèri /

名 heredity 遺伝

形 passed from parent to child by blood before birth

遺伝性の、遺伝的な

≒ genetic, inherited

⇔ acquired

例 Her green eyes are **hereditary**.

彼女の緑の目は遺伝だ。

☐☐☐ 0958

murmur
/ mə́ːrmər /

動 to say something quietly

ぶつぶつ言う、つぶやく

≒ mutter, mumble, whisper ⇔ shout, scream

例 She **murmured** something about needing to go buy milk.

彼女は牛乳を買いに行かなくちゃ、というようなことをつぶやいた。

名 speech or a way of speaking that is quiet

ささやき、つぶやき

≒ mutter, mumble, whisper

⇔ shout, scream

例 There were **murmurs** in the crowd when the president forgot what he was going to say.

大統領が言おうとしたことを忘れると、群衆の中にひそひそ声が起こった。

☐☐☐ 0959

enchant
/ ɪntʃǽnt / 名 enchantment 魅力

動 to get someone to pay attention by being interesting or pretty

〈人〉を魅惑する、うっとりさせる

≒ charm, fascinate, captivate

⇔ bore, disturb

🔑 〈en-（中に）+chant（歌う）〉

例 The man was **enchanted** by the woman's beauty.

その男性はその女性の美しさに魅了された。

☐☐☐ 0960

epoch
/ épək /

名 a point in time that was important to history

（重要な出来事などで特徴づけられる）時代、時期

≒ age, era

ⓘ epoch-making（画期的な、新時代を画する）という語も覚えておこう。

例 The invention and spread of the Internet marked an important **epoch** in world history.

インターネットの発明とその広がりは、世界史における重要な時代の幕開けとなった。

□□□ 0961

bribe

/ bráɪb /

名 bribery 贈収賄

0964語

名 something valuable, usually money, that is given to make someone do something

賄賂

≒ kickback

例 The politicians were caught accepting **bribes**.

その政治家たちは賄賂を受け取っているところを目撃された。

□□□ 0962

slender

/ sléndər /

形 thin in a way that is seen as looking good

細長い、すらりとした

≒ slim, lean

⇔ fat, obese

ⓘ 「スレンダー」はカタカナ語にもなっている。

例 Deer have **slender** legs that help them jump easily.

鹿の脚はすらりとしていて、そのおかげで軽々と跳躍できる。

□□□ 0963

aptitude

/ ǽptət(j)ùːd /

形 apt 適した；傾向がある

名 a natural ability or skill to do or learn something

適性、素質

≒ talent

ⓘ aptitude test（適性検査）という表現も覚えておこう。

例 She has a real **aptitude** for learning new languages.

彼女には新しい言語を習得する真の適性がある。

□□□ 0964

habitual

/ həbítʃuəl /

名 habit 習慣
動 habituate〈人〉を慣らす

形 done regularly

常習的な、習慣的な

≒ routine, repeated

ⓘ アクセントはbiの位置。

🔑〈habit（習慣）+-ual（形容詞）〉

例 The woman was fired because of her **habitual** lateness.

その女性は常習的な遅刻で解雇された。

☐☐☐ 0965

timid

/ tímɪd /

名 timidity 臆病、小心

形 **feeling or showing a lack of confidence or courage**

臆病な、小心な

≒ shy　⇔ confident

例 Her daughter has always been **timid** around strangers.

彼女の娘は知らない人がいるといつも臆病だ。

☐☐☐ 0966

oppress

/ əprés /

形 oppressive 圧制的な
名 oppression 圧制、圧迫

動 **to treat a person or group of people badly or restrict their freedom**

〜を虐げる、圧迫する

≒ persecute

🔑 〈op-(上から)+press(押す)〉

例 The people of that country are being **oppressed** by a dictator.

その国の人々は独裁者に虐げられている。

☐☐☐ 0967

assimilate

/ əsíməlèɪt /

名 assimilation 同化

動 ① **(to cause a person or group) to become part of a different country, community, etc. and no longer be separate**

(〜を) 同化する

≒ adapt, blend in
⇔ reject

🔑 〈as-(〜に)+simil(似た)+ -ate(動詞)〉

例 Children of immigrants can **assimilate** more easily by going to school.

移民の子どもは学校に通うことによって、より簡単に同化することができる。

② **to learn something in a way that you completely understand it**

〈知識・思想など〉を消化する

≒ comprehend, grasp, take in

例 The new teachers had a lot of new information to **assimilate** before they were ready to teach a class.

新任教師たちには、クラスを教える準備が整うまでに消化すべき多くの新しい情報があった。

□□□ 0968

hasty / héɪsti /

名 haste 急ぐこと
副 hastily 急いで
動 hasten ～を急がせる

0970語

形 ① acting too fast

軽率な

≒ impulsive, reckless

⇔ considered, cautious, careful

例 The woman realized later that her decision to break up with her boyfriend had been too **hasty**.

その女性は、ボーイフレンドと別れようと決めたのはあまりにも性急だったと、後になって気づいた。

② done or made in a fast way

急な、迅速な

≒ quick, swift

例 The girl wrote a **hasty** note to her mother before going to school.

その女の子は登校する前に母親に急ぎのメモを書いた。

□□□ 0969

sanitation / sæ̀nətéɪʃən /

動 sanitize ～を清潔にする
形 sanitary 衛生的な

名 the act and process of keeping things and places clean, especially to prevent disease, infection, etc.

公衆衛生

≒ hygiene, cleanliness

例 Proper **sanitation** is needed in hospitals to keep both doctors and patients safe.

医者と患者の両方の安全を守るために病院内の衛生を適切に保つ必要がある。

□□□ 0970

innumerable / ɪn(j)úːmərəbl /

形 more than can be counted

無数の、数え切れない

≒ countless

⇔ countable

🔑 〈in-（否定）+numer（数）+ -able（できる）〉

例 There are **innumerable** ways to become friends with someone.

人と友達になる方法は無数にある。

□□□ 0971

spectacle

/ spéktəkl /

形 spectacular 壮観な

名 a very impressive show

（大仕掛けの）見せ物

🔑 〈spect(a)(見る)+-cle(指小辞)〉

例 The Broadway show was an amazing **spectacle** to see.

ブロードウェイのショーは驚くべき見せ物だった。

□□□ 0972

scrutinize

/ skrú:tənàɪz /

名 scrutiny 綿密な検査

動 to look and think about something in a careful and critical way

〜を綿密に調べる

≒ analyze

ⓘ イギリス英語では scrutinise ともつづる。

例 The boxer watched hours of videos of his opponent, **scrutinizing** his fighting style.

そのボクサーは何時間も対戦相手のビデオを見て、その戦い方を徹底的に調べた。

□□□ 0973

mumble

/ mʌ́mbl /

動 to say something so quietly or unclearly that it is hard for people to understand what was said

（〜を）もごもご言う

≒ mutter, whisper, murmur

例 He could never understand his boss because he always **mumbled**.

彼の上司はいつもぼそぼそと話すので、彼は上司の言うことをまったく理解できなかった。

□□□ 0974

eloquent

/ éləkwənt /

名 eloquence 雄弁

形 having or showing the ability to use language in a very skilled way

雄弁な、説得力のある

≒ articulate, well-spoken

🔑 〈e-（外に）+loqu（話す）+-ent（形容詞）〉

例 Barack Obama is a very **eloquent** speaker.

バラク・オバマはとても雄弁に演説をする。

□□□ 0975

0977語

cosmopolitan

/ kà:zməpá:lətən /

形 ① **having people who come from many different parts of the world**

国際的な

≒ multicultural

🔑〈cosmo(世界)+politan(市民)〉

例 New York is one of the most **cosmopolitan** cities in the world.

ニューヨークは世界で最も国際的な都市の一つだ。

② **showing that you have an interest in different cultures or ideas**

国際感覚のある

≒ cultured, worldly, sophisticated

例 Young people have a more **cosmopolitan** attitude than many of their parents.

若者は親たちの多くよりも国際感覚に富んだ考え方をする。

□□□ 0976

renounce

/ rɪnáʊns /

名 renunciation 放棄、断念

動 to give up something in a formal way

～を放棄する、断念する

≒ disown

⇔ embrace, claim

例 The king **renounced** the throne so that he could marry someone outside the royal family.

その王は王族でない人と結婚できるよう王位を放棄した。

□□□ 0977

humiliate

/ hjuːmílièɪt /

名 humiliation 屈辱

動 to make someone feel silly or embarrassed about something

～に恥をかかせる

≒ shame ⇔ flatter

ⓘ 他動詞である点に注意。

例 The woman felt **humiliated** when she realized her boyfriend had been lying to her.

その女性はボーイフレンドが自分にうそをついていたことに気づいて屈辱を感じた。

□□□ 0978

scorn

/ skɔ́ːrn / 形 scornful 軽蔑した

動 to show that you think someone or something does not deserve respect

～を軽蔑する、ばかにする

≒ mock

例 She **scorns** anyone who makes less money than her.

彼女は自分より稼ぎが少ない人は誰であろうとばかにする。

名 a feeling that someone or something does not deserve to be respected

軽蔑

≒ mockery, ridicule, disdain

⇔ approval

例 They feel nothing but **scorn** for people that hurt animals.

彼らは動物を傷つける人に軽蔑しか感じない。

□□□ 0979

considerate

/ kənsídərət /

動 consider ～を考慮する
名 consideration 考慮；思いやり

形 thinking about the feelings and rights of others and being kind to them

思いやりのある

≒ thoughtful, attentive, compassionate

⇔ inconsiderate

例 The little boy is always **considerate** of other people's feelings.

その小さな男の子はいつもほかの人の気持ちを思いやる。

□□□ 0980

censor

/ sénsər /

名 censorship 検閲

動 to examine things such as books and movies and remove anything that you think should not be shown to people

～を検閲する

ⓘ カタカナ語の「センサー」は sensor（感知装置）なので注意。

例 Letters from soldiers were heavily **censored** during the war.

戦時中は兵士からの手紙は厳しく検閲された。

388

0984語

□□□ 0981

wither / wíðər /

動 to dry up and become weak

〈花・植物が〉しおれる、枯れる

≒ decay, deteriorate ⇔ thrive

例 The flowers will all **wither** if they are not given any water.

その花々は、水をまったくやらなければすべて枯れてしまうだろう。

□□□ 0982

immigrate / ímɪɡrèɪt /

名 immigration 移住
名 immigrant 移民

動 to move to a different country to live there (permanently)

移住する

≒ emigrate, migrate, relocate

🔑 〈im-(中に)+migr(移る)+-ate(動詞)〉

例 Many Europeans **immigrated** to the Americas in the 18th and 19th centuries.

18世紀から19世紀にかけて多くのヨーロッパ人が南北アメリカに移住した。

□□□ 0983

perilous / pérələs /

名 peril 危険

形 very dangerous

危険な

≒ hazardous, precarious, treacherous
⇔ safe, secure, stable

例 The dogs had to make a **perilous** journey through a snowstorm to bring medicine to the children.

その犬たちは子どもたちに薬を届けるために、吹雪の中、危険な旅をしなければならなかった。

□□□ 0984

scant / skænt /

形 very small in size or amount

ごくわずかな、不十分な

≒ insufficient
⇔ plentiful, ample, abundant

例 Food was in **scant** supply during the Great Depression.

大恐慌の間、食物の供給は不十分だった。

□□□ 0985

incomprehensible

/ ɪnkὰ:mprɪhénsəbl /

名 incomprehension 無理解

形 not possible to understand

理解できない、不可解な

≒ confusing, perplexing

⇔ comprehensible, understandable

例 From her parents' point of view, her decision to quit such a high-paying job was **incomprehensible**.

親からすると、そんな高給の仕事を辞めるという彼女の決断は不可解だった。

□□□ 0986

intrude

/ ɪntrúːd /

名 intrusion 侵入
形 intrusive 押しつけるような

動 to enter a place where you are not wanted

（他人の領域などに）立ち入る

≒ invade, infringe

ⓘ intrude (up)on（～に侵入する）の形で押さえておこう。

例 The drone **intruded** on the country's airspace and was shot down.

そのドローンはその国の領空に侵入して撃墜された。

□□□ 0987

trifle

/ tráɪfl /

形 trifling ささいな

名 something that does not matter very much

ささいなこと

例 There is no point in worrying about such **trifles**.

そんなささいなことを気にしても仕方がない。

□□□ 0988

insistent

/ ɪnsístənt /

動 insist ～を主張する
名 insistence こだわり、主張

形 demanding something and refusing to accept anything else

強く主張する、固執する

≒ adamant, persistent

⇔ flexible

例 They offered to give her the food for free, but she was **insistent** about paying.

彼らは彼女に食べ物を無償で提供しようと言ったが、彼女は払うと言って聞かなかった。

0989

punctual / pʌ́ŋktʃuəl /

副 **punctually** 時間厳守で
名 **punctuality** 時間厳守

形 arriving or doing something at the decided time

時間厳守の

⇔ irregular, late, unreliable

例 Tourists think that the trains in Tokyo are always **punctual**.

観光客は、東京の電車はいつも定刻通りだと思っている。

0990

stray / stréɪ /

動 to move away from a group or where you should be

はぐれる、道からそれる

≒ wander, diverge

ⓘ 「はぐれた」という形容詞の意味もある。

例 The little girl **strayed** away from her class and got lost in the museum.

その小さな女の子はクラスの子たちとはぐれて美術館の中で迷子になった。

0991

recollect / rèkəlékt /

名 **recollection** 回想

動 to remember something

～を思い出す、回想する

≒ recall

⇔ forget

〈re-(再び)+collect(集める)〉

例 He couldn't **recollect** who had told him about the restaurant.

彼は誰がそのレストランのことを教えてくれたのか思い出せなかった。

0992

monotonous / mənɑ́:tənəs /

名 **monotony** 単調さ

形 boring because it never changes

単調な、変化のない

≒ tedious

ⓘ アクセントはnoの位置。

〈mono(一つの)+ton(調子)+-ous(満ちた)〉

例 Students at the school started to complain that their classes were **monotonous**.

その学校の生徒たちは授業が単調だと不満をもらし始めた。

☐☐☐ 0993

industrialize / ɪndʌ́striəlàɪz /

形 industrial 産業の
名 industrialization 産業化

動 to build and run factories and businesses all in one area

～を産業化する、工業化する

ⓘ イギリス英語では industrialise ともつづる。

例 Much of the country became **industrialized** after the war.

その国の大部分は戦後に工業化した。

☐☐☐ 0994

deserve / dɪzɔ́ːrv /

動 to behave in such a way that a particular reward, punishment, etc. should be given to you

～に値する

≒ merit, be worthy of

🔑 〈de-(完全に)+serve(役立つ)〉

例 The girl **deserves** a second chance after all her hard work.

その女の子はとても頑張ったのだから、やり直す機会が与えられるべきだ。

☐☐☐ 0995

obsess / əbsés /

名 obsession 執着、妄想
形 obsessive 頭から離れない

動 to be the only person or thing on someone's mind

～にとりつく

例 He has always been **obsessed** with getting good grades at school.

彼は学校でいい成績を取るという考えに、常にとりつかれている。

☐☐☐ 0996

odds / ɑ́ːdz /

名 the chance of one thing happening instead of another thing

見込み、公算

≒ probability, likelihood

ⓘ at odds（争って）という表現も覚えておこう。

例 The man bought many lottery tickets to increase his **odds** of winning.

男性は当たる確率を上げるために宝くじをたくさん買った。

☐☐☐ 0997

outdated / àʊtdéɪtɪd /

形 not useful or acceptable to use anymore

時代遅れの

≒ out-of-date, obsolete, archaic

⇔ up-to-date, modern, innovative

例 There are a lot of words that are **outdated** and shouldn't be used anymore.

時代遅れで、もはや使われる べきでない言葉はたくさんある。

☐☐☐ 0998

resurgence / rɪsə́ːrdʒəns / 形 resurgent 復活の、再起の

名 a period of growth after having a period where there was no growth

復活、復興

≒ rebirth, comeback, renaissance

⇔ deterioration

例 There was a **resurgence** of interest in the artist's work after he died.

その画家の死後、彼の作品へ の関心が再び高まった。

☐☐☐ 0999

vulgar / vʌ́lgər / 名 vulgarity 下品、俗悪

形 showing bad manners or taste

下品な、俗悪な

≒ dirty, nasty, improper

⇔ respectful

例 **Vulgar** language is not allowed in his grandmother's house.

彼の祖母の家では下品な言葉 が許されていない。

☐☐☐ 1000

well-being / wélbíːɪŋ /

名 the state of being healthy and happy in life

幸福、健康

例 Parents have to look after the **well-being** of their children.

親は子どもが健やかに育つよ うに世話しなければならない。

章末ボキャブラリーチェック

次の語義が表す英単語を答えてください。

語義	解答	連番
❶ willing to do whatever someone or something tells you to do	o b e d i e n t	0943
❷ the chance of one thing happening instead of another thing	o d d s	0996
❸ to separate something from another thing	d e t a c h	0917
❹ a belief that some objects or actions bring good or bad luck	s u p e r s t i t i o n	0956
❺ tending to act in ways that are unusual	e c c e n t r i c	0913
❻ to make something stop burning	e x t i n g u i s h	0953
❼ the state of being healthy and happy in life	w e l l - b e i n g	1000
❽ a job that suits someone very well	v o c a t i o n	0952
❾ to cause an emotion or thought	a r o u s e	0938
❿ feeling sad or depressed	g l o o m y	0925
⓫ a point in time that was important to history	e p o c h	0960
⓬ to treat a person or group of people badly or restrict their freedom	o p p r e s s	0966
⓭ a person who betrays a group or country by helping their enemies	t r a i t o r	0948
⓮ not under the control of humans	s a v a g e	0914
⓯ to say something so quietly or unclearly that it is hard for people to understand what was said	m u m b l e	0973
⓰ in a position that has less power than someone else	s u b o r d i n a t e	0936
⓱ able to be heard	a u d i b l e	0935
⓲ to be the only person or thing on someone's mind	o b s e s s	0995
⓳ to move to a different country to live there (permanently)	i m m i g r a t e	0982
⓴ to examine things such as books and movies and remove anything that you think should not be shown to people	c e n s o r	0980

語義	解答	連番
㉑ to help someone feel calmer and relax	s o o t h e	0910
㉒ not useful or acceptable to use anymore	o u t d a t e d	0997
㉓ a strong feeling of worry or disappointment	d i s m a y	0947
㉔ impossible to resist	i r r e s i s t i b l e	0932
㉕ to see or guess something that has not happened yet	f o r e s e e	0927
㉖ to dry up and become weak	w i t h e r	0981
㉗ based on feelings and not reason or thought	s e n t i m e n t a l	0905
㉘ a behavior or action that is annoying but not meant to cause serious harm or damage	m i s c h i e f	0937
㉙ to cause something or someone to be unable to move, function, etc.	p a r a l y z e	0920
㉚ an angry argument or disagreement, especially about something personal	q u a r r e l	0904
㉛ thinking about the feelings and rights of others and being kind to them	c o n s i d e r a t e	0979
㉜ demanding something and refusing to accept anything else	i n s i s t e n t	0988
㉝ plain in color and design	s o b e r	0901
㉞ to move away little by little	r e c e d e	0934
㉟ more than can be counted	i n n u m e r a b l e	0970
㊱ having or showing the ability to use language in a very skilled way	e l o q u e n t	0974
㊲ a strong feeling of interest or excitement that motivates someone to do something	z e a l	0954
㊳ to give up something in a formal way	r e n o u n c e	0976
㊴ to (make something) decay over time	r o t	0924
㊵ to cry noisily while taking in short, sudden breaths	s o b	0945
㊶ feeling or showing a lack of confidence or courage	t i m i d	0965
㊷ to show that you think someone or something does not deserve respect	s c o r n	0978
㊸ to shake slightly because you are cold or afraid	s h i v e r	0944

語義	解答	連番
㊹ to remember something	recollect	0991
㊺ to say something quietly	murmur	0958
㊻ very smart, or using clever ideas	ingenious	0942
㊼ possible to imagine	imaginable	0950
㊽ very small in size or amount	scant	0984
㊾ a very impressive show	spectacle	0971
㊿ the act and process of keeping things and places clean, especially to prevent disease, infection, etc.	sanitation	0969
(51) to be upset about someone or something that you think is not fair	resent	0929
(52) very serious in behavior or expression	solemn	0939
(53) to behave in such a way that a particular reward, punishment, etc. should be given to you	deserve	0994
(54) acting too fast	hasty	0968
(55) a natural ability or skill to do or learn something	aptitude	0963
(56) passed from parent to child by blood before birth	hereditary	0957
(57) to quickly eat all of something	devour	0915
(58) to look and think about something in a careful and critical way	scrutinize	0972
(59) not possible to understand	incomprehensible	0985
(60) someone or something that is dangerous and might hurt you	menace	0933
(61) ((of a plant or animal)) very rare and in danger of disappearing completely	endangered	0916
(62) to make someone feel silly or embarrassed about something	humiliate	0977
(63) having people who come from many different parts of the world	cosmopolitan	0975
(64) having or showing no pity or mercy	ruthless	0930
(65) very dangerous	perilous	0983
(66) to spend time thinking quietly to relax or for religious needs	meditate	0931

語義	解答	連番

67 to build and run factories and businesses all in one area
i n d u s t r i a l i z e
0993

68 something that makes life easier or more pleasant
a m e n i t y
0906

69 difficulties in life
h a r d s h i p
0908

70 boring because it never changes
m o n o t o n o u s
0992

71 having more respect or success than a normal person
e m i n e n t
0949

72 always expecting that something bad will happen
p e s s i m i s t i c
0946

73 to go to places randomly without a plan or purpose
r o a m
0903

74 not having many plants or being bad for plants
b a r r e n
0940

75 not concerned about or interested in something
i n d i f f e r e n t
0922

76 arriving or doing something at the decided time
p u n c t u a l
0989

77 showing bad manners or taste
v u l g a r
0999

78 used to something in a way that makes it feel normal
a c c u s t o m e d
0902

79 thin in a way that is seen as looking good
s l e n d e r
0962

80 having a lot of money and expensive things
a f f l u e n t
0926

81 awkwardly made or done
c l u m s y
0918

82 to surprise someone in a way that is not serious
s t a r t l e
0921

83 (to cause a person or group) to become part of a different country, community, etc. and no longer be separate
a s s i m i l a t e
0967

84 having a healthy mind that can think normally
s a n e
0919

85 to make someone feel very shocked or upset
h o r r i f y
0951

86 a situation in which you are alone, often by choice
s o l i t u d e
0912

87 something valuable, usually money, that is given to make someone do something
b r i b e
0961

88 to surprise someone or make them feel great wonder
a s t o n i s h
0955

89 to shine with a harsh, bright light
g l a r e
0909

⑨⓪ a person who is too afraid to do what is right or expected of them — <u>c</u> <u>o</u> <u>w</u> <u>a</u> <u>r</u> <u>d</u> — 0941

⑨① working with care or continued effort — <u>d</u> <u>i</u> <u>l</u> <u>i</u> <u>g</u> <u>e</u> <u>n</u> <u>t</u> — 0911

⑨② getting attention by being impressive — <u>c</u> <u>o</u> <u>n</u> <u>s</u> <u>p</u> <u>i</u> <u>c</u> <u>u</u> <u>o</u> <u>u</u> <u>s</u> — 0923

⑨③ believing that people are mostly selfish and not honest — <u>c</u> <u>y</u> <u>n</u> <u>i</u> <u>c</u> <u>a</u> <u>l</u> — 0928

⑨④ emotionally calm and in control — <u>t</u> <u>e</u> <u>m</u> <u>p</u> <u>e</u> <u>r</u> <u>a</u> <u>t</u> <u>e</u> — 0907

⑨⑤ done regularly — <u>h</u> <u>a</u> <u>b</u> <u>i</u> <u>t</u> <u>u</u> <u>a</u> <u>l</u> — 0964

⑨⑥ to enter a place where you are not wanted — <u>i</u> <u>n</u> <u>t</u> <u>r</u> <u>u</u> <u>d</u> <u>e</u> — 0986

⑨⑦ a period of growth after having a period where there was no growth — <u>r</u> <u>e</u> <u>s</u> <u>u</u> <u>r</u> <u>g</u> <u>e</u> <u>n</u> <u>c</u> <u>e</u> — 0998

⑨⑧ to move away from a group or where you should be — <u>s</u> <u>t</u> <u>r</u> <u>a</u> <u>y</u> — 0990

⑨⑨ to get someone to pay attention by being interesting or pretty — <u>e</u> <u>n</u> <u>c</u> <u>h</u> <u>a</u> <u>n</u> <u>t</u> — 0959

⑩⓪ something that does not matter very much — <u>t</u> <u>r</u> <u>i</u> <u>f</u> <u>l</u> <u>e</u> — 0987

この索引には本書で取り上げた約3,300語句がアルファベット順に掲載されています。数字はページ番号を示しています。色の数字は見出し語として収録され、黒い数字は語句が派生語や類義語・反意語などとして収録されていることを表しています。

A

□ abandon	089, 108
□ abandoned	108
□ abandonment	108
□ abdicate	311
□ ability	268
□ able	262
□ abnormal	302, 308
□ abnormality	308
□ abolish	300
□ abolition	300
□ abound	226
□ abrupt	263
□ absolute	024, 163, 295
□ absolutely	024
□ abstract	093, 148, 196
□ abstraction	196
□ absurd	227, 316
□ absurdity	316
□ absurdly	316
□ abundance	068, 226
□ abundant	226, 304, 389
□ abundantly	226
□ abuse	080
□ abusive	080
□ accelerate	274
□ acceleration	274
□ accelerator	274
□ accentuate	075
□ accept	047, 072, 180, 231
□ access	087
□ accessible	037
□ accessory	303
□ accident	206
□ accidental	206, 320
□ accidentally	206
□ acclaim	044
□ accommodate	141
□ accommodation	141
□ accompaniment	039
□ accompany	039, 321
□ accomplish	069

□ accomplishment	069
□ accord	154, 220
□ accordingly	169
□ account	251
□ accountable	313
□ accumulate	227
□ accumulation	227
□ accumulative	227
□ accuracy	039
□ accurate	039
□ accurately	039
□ accusation	124
□ accuse	124
□ accustom	366
□ accustomed	366
□ achieve	035, 069, 224
□ achievement	228
□ aching	168
□ acknowledge	131
□ acknowledged	131
□ acknowledgement	131
□ acquaint	286
□ acquaintance	286
□ acquire	035
□ acquired	035, 144, 381
□ acquisition	035
□ act	259
□ action	062
□ active	187, 236
□ actually	107
□ acute	211
□ acutely	211
□ adamant	390
□ adapt	021, 384
□ adaptable	068
□ add	276, 283, 343
□ addict	350
□ addicted	350
□ addiction	350
□ addictive	350
□ additionally	050
□ adept	351
□ adequate	164
□ adhere	271

☐ adhere to	235
☐ adhesion	271
☐ adhesive	271
☐ adjust	077, 090
☐ administer	033, 132, 150
☐ administration	033
☐ administrative	033
☐ admirable	049
☐ admiration	049, 263, 272, 337
☐ admire	049
☐ admission	087
☐ admit	087, 131
☐ admonish	222
☐ adopt	021
☐ adoption	021
☐ adoration	336, 347
☐ adore	336, 354
☐ advance	066
☐ advancement	102
☐ advantage	071, 145, 195, 199
☐ advertising	246
☐ aesthetic	276
☐ aesthetics	276
☐ affection	281
☐ affectionate	194, 281
☐ affiliation	036
☐ affirm	026
☐ affliction	102
☐ affluence	119, 373
☐ affluent	373
☐ age	065, 382
☐ agenda	197
☐ aggravate	323, 369
☐ aggression	110
☐ aggressive	110, 262, 339
☐ agitate	323, 369
☐ agitated	278
☐ agree	072, 333
☐ agreement	024, 091
☐ agricultural	044
☐ agriculture	235
☐ aid	080, 311, 335
☐ ailment	102
☐ aim	065, 248
☐ alarm	380
☐ alert	186
☐ alertness	186
☐ alien	166
☐ alienate	208
☐ alleviate	323
☐ alliance	206
☐ allied	206
☐ allow	315, 338
☐ allowance	189
☐ alluring	375
☐ ally	206
☐ alter	052, 077, 090, 318
☐ alteration	077
☐ alternate	269
☐ alternately	269
☐ alternation	269
☐ alternative	037, 245
☐ alternatively	037
☐ although	122
☐ altitude	298
☐ altogether	110
☐ altruistic	302
☐ amaze	239, 381
☐ amazement	239
☐ amazing	040, 101, 239
☐ ambiguous	016, 359
☐ amend	318
☐ amendment	318
☐ amenity	367
☐ ample	226, 304, 389
☐ amplify	160, 359
☐ amply	304
☐ amuse	349
☐ amusement	349
☐ amusing	349
☐ analogous	342
☐ analogy	342
☐ analyze	386
☐ anarchy	209
☐ ancestor	168
☐ ancestry	168
☐ anecdotal	321
☐ anecdote	321
☐ angle	266
☐ annoy	236, 250
☐ annoyance	250, 345
☐ annoyed	250
☐ annoying	250
☐ anticipate	155, 157
☐ anticipation	157
☐ anxiety	116, 120, 247
☐ anxious	120, 278, 355
☐ apathetic	372
☐ apathy	381
☐ appall	380
☐ apparatus	317
☐ apparent	042, 188
☐ apparently	042, 146, 319
☐ appeal	162
☐ appear	051, 156, 243
☐ appetite	212

☐ applaud	349	☐ assess	073, 126
☐ applause	349	☐ assessment	126
☐ appliance	196	☐ asset	121
☐ applicant	043	☐ assign	050, 062
☐ appoint	050	☐ assignment	062
☐ appointment	050	☐ assimilate	384
☐ appreciate	030, 044, 049	☐ assimilation	384
☐ appreciation	030	☐ assist	335
☐ appreciative	060	☐ associate	036, 171, 286
☐ apprehend	029, 167	☐ associated	036
☐ approach	051	☐ association	036
☐ approaching	322	☐ assuage	323
☐ appropriate	019, 147	☐ assumption	201
☐ appropriately	019	☐ assurance	088
☐ approval	347, 388	☐ assure	088, 126, 379
☐ approve	114, 161	☐ assured	088
☐ approximate	051	☐ astonish	239, 381
☐ approximately	051	☐ astonishing	381
☐ approximation	051	☐ astonishment	381
☐ apt	383	☐ astound	239, 381
☐ aptitude	383	☐ astounding	204
☐ archaic	260, 393	☐ at a glance	146
☐ area	061	☐ at odds	392
☐ argument	024	☐ at risk	370
☐ arise	156	☐ at stake	145
☐ armor	143	☐ at the beginning	105
☐ aroma	169	☐ at the end	105
☐ around	051	☐ at the mercy of	220
☐ arouse	193, 376	☐ attach	271, 371
☐ arrange	069, 159	☐ attachment	036
☐ arrangement	048, 189	☐ attack	209
☐ arrest	028	☐ attain	069, 224
☐ arrive	105	☐ attainment	224
☐ arrogant	263	☐ attempt	041
☐ arrow	084	☐ attentive	186, 388
☐ articulate	386	☐ attest	312
☐ artificial	084	☐ attitude	171
☐ artificially	084	☐ attribute	031, 133
☐ artistic	276	☐ attribution	133
☐ as a consequence	043	☐ atypical	074
☐ as a result	199	☐ audible	375
☐ ascend	198, 343	☐ audibly	375
☐ ascendant	343	☐ audience	375
☐ ascension	343	☐ auditorium	375
☐ ashamed	230	☐ authentic	156, 241, 346
☐ aspiration	347	☐ authorization	126
☐ aspire	347	☐ authorize	142
☐ assault	296	☐ autobiography	301
☐ assemble	069, 163	☐ available	306
☐ assembly	041, 089, 163	☐ average	079
☐ assert	226	☐ aversion	348
☐ assertion	226	☐ await	155
☐ assertive	226	☐ awful	040, 101, 107, 280

☐ awfully	107
☐ awkward	211
☐ awkwardly	211

B

☐ bad	040
☐ balanced	164
☐ ban	081, 158, 269, 335
☐ bankrupt	355
☐ bankruptcy	355
☐ banquet	279
☐ bare	092, 130
☐ barely	092
☐ barren	377
☐ barrier	172
☐ base	203, 263
☐ bath	341
☐ bathe	194, 341
☐ be honest	155
☐ be similar to	127
☐ be worthy of	392
☐ bear	198
☐ beast	180
☐ beat	130, 275
☐ beautiful	304
☐ beg	278
☐ begin	204
☐ believable	069
☐ believe	040
☐ beneficial	259
☐ benefit	071, 112, 195
☐ benevolent	107
☐ besides	140
☐ best	163
☐ bet	049, 145
☐ betray	310, 335
☐ betrayal	335
☐ biased	221
☐ bind	119
☐ binder	119
☐ biographical	301
☐ biography	301
☐ bitter	225
☐ blame	111, 133
☐ blameless	147
☐ blaze	118, 368
☐ bleak	373
☐ bleed	238
☐ blend	130
☐ blend in	384

☐ blessing	324, 368
☐ blink	354
☐ block	158, 193
☐ blood	238
☐ bloom	286
☐ blossom	286
☐ board	033
☐ boast	197
☐ boastful	202
☐ bold	105
☐ bond	036
☐ boost	153
☐ border	109
☐ bore	235, 239, 283, 382
☐ boredom	235
☐ boring	169, 235
☐ bother	315, 345
☐ bounce	223
☐ boundary	109
☐ bow	084
☐ brag	197
☐ brave	105
☐ breadth	159
☐ break	191
☐ break out	271
☐ break up	122
☐ breakdown	170
☐ breed	075, 193
☐ breeder	075
☐ bribe	383
☐ bribery	383
☐ bright	040, 336
☐ brighten	304
☐ brilliant	040, 232
☐ bring down	309, 312
☐ bring in	309
☐ bring together	345
☐ bring up	083
☐ broadcast	212
☐ broaden	043
☐ browse	250
☐ browser	250
☐ brutal	262, 284, 370, 374
☐ brutality	284
☐ brute	284
☐ bulk	239
☐ bulky	239
☐ bully	319
☐ bullying	319
☐ bump	183
☐ bump into	051
☐ bumper	183
☐ bundle	203

☐ burden	**116,** 147
☐ burdensome	**147**
☐ burst	132, **140**
☐ bury	037
☐ by accident	**206**
☐ by any means	**268**
☐ by means of	**268**
☐ by no means	**268**
☐ by virtue of	**195**

C

☐ call	**142**
☐ call (on)	**294**
☐ calling	**380**
☐ calm	**126, 250, 262, 278, 355**
☐ calmness	**264**
☐ camouflage	**333**
☐ candidate	043
☐ capable	**262, 351**
☐ capital	**048**
☐ captivate	**162, 382**
☐ captive	**029, 078**
☐ capture	**028,** 029
☐ care	**281**
☐ careful	**385**
☐ careless	**248, 353**
☐ carelessness	**158**
☐ carry on	**192**
☐ carry out	**199**
☐ carrying	**146**
☐ carve	232
☐ carving	**232**
☐ cash register	**029**
☐ cast	025, **237**
☐ casual	079
☐ casually	**079**
☐ catastrophe	**045, 047, 338**
☐ catch	**028, 167**
☐ categorize	**203**
☐ cater	223
☐ cattle	150
☐ caution	**248**
☐ cautious	248, **353, 385**
☐ cautiously	**248**
☐ cease	204, **265**
☐ cease-fire	**204**
☐ ceaseless	**204, 282**
☐ celebrity	258
☐ censor	388
☐ censorship	**388**

☐ census	301
☐ certain	**126**
☐ certificate	126
☐ certification	**126**
☐ certify	**026, 088, 126**
☐ challenge	**031**
☐ championship	**368**
☐ change	**062**
☐ channel	**183**
☐ chaos	**102,** 209
☐ character	**031**
☐ characteristic	031
☐ characterize	**031**
☐ charge	**103**
☐ charm	162, **283, 382**
☐ charming	**162**
☐ chase	**041,** 052
☐ cheap	**131, 270, 320**
☐ cheat	112
☐ cheer up	**309, 312**
☐ cheerful	**247, 373, 377**
☐ cherish	**049, 336, 354**
☐ chicken	**377**
☐ chief	**100, 163**
☐ chiefly	**079**
☐ chill	265
☐ chilling	**265**
☐ chilly	**265**
☐ choosy	**340**
☐ chore	342
☐ chunk	**240**
☐ citation	**120, 166**
☐ cite	**120,** 166
☐ citizenship	**368**
☐ claim	016, **387**
☐ clarification	**229**
☐ clarify	229, **304**
☐ clarity	**229**
☐ clash	**024, 305, 321**
☐ classification	**203**
☐ classified	**203**
☐ classify	073, **203**
☐ clause	**020**
☐ clean	**345, 355**
☐ cleanliness	**385**
☐ cleanse	**345**
☐ clear	**336**
☐ clever	**040, 062, 269, 350**
☐ climb	**198, 343**
☐ cling	322
☐ close	**037**
☐ cloth	**117, 287**
☐ clothed	**130**

☐ clue	130	☐ complaint	016
☐ clump	240	☐ complement	325
☐ clumsy	211, 371	☐ complementary	325
☐ clutch	066, 238	☐ complex	077, 093, 296
☐ coincide	249, 321	☐ compliance	235
☐ coincide with	039	☐ compliant	378
☐ coincidence	321	☐ complicated	077, 093
☐ coincidental	321	☐ compliment	044, 222, 258,
☐ coincidentally	206		272, 297, 344
☐ collaborate	299	☐ complimentary	272
☐ collapse	149	☐ comply	235, 271
☐ collect	035, 063, 065, 163, 308, 309	☐ compose	122
☐ colonial	161	☐ composed	122
☐ colonize	161	☐ composition	122
☐ colony	161	☐ comprehend	238, 323, 384
☐ combine	163, 345	☐ comprehensible	380, 390
☐ come across	051	☐ comprehension	323
☐ come off	271	☐ comprehensive	080, 230
☐ come up with	261	☐ compress	165
☐ comeback	393	☐ compromise	244
☐ comfort	236, 309, 312, 335, 367	☐ compulsion	101, 341, 354
☐ comforting	207	☐ compulsive	341, 354
☐ command	023, 128, 311	☐ compulsory	341, 354
☐ commanding	376	☐ comrade	115
☐ commence	204	☐ conceal	027, 092, 298
☐ commend	222, 272	☐ concealment	298, 333
☐ commendation	272	☐ concede	084, 302
☐ comment	160	☐ conceivable	233, 380
☐ commission	033, 041	☐ conceive	233
☐ commit	033, 038, 125	☐ concept	107, 233
☐ commitment	038	☐ concise	324
☐ committee	033, 041, 089	☐ concisely	324
☐ commodity	208	☐ conclude	050
☐ common	070, 074, 163, 302, 308	☐ conclusion	050
☐ commonly	087	☐ conclusive	050
☐ commonplace	155	☐ concrete	148, 196
☐ commute	279	☐ concur	321
☐ commuter	279	☐ condemn	111, 272, 297, 344, 349
☐ compact	207, 324	☐ condemnation	113, 272, 297
☐ companion	115	☐ conference	018
☐ compare	171	☐ confess	225
☐ compassion	201, 220, 301	☐ confession	225
☐ compassionate	374, 388	☐ confidence	032
☐ compel	338, 341	☐ confident	120, 384
☐ compelling	341	☐ confine	208, 280, 315, 359
☐ compensate	248	☐ confirm	026, 030
☐ compensation	248	☐ confirmation	026
☐ compensatory	248	☐ confiscate	167
☐ compete	031	☐ conflict	024, 249
☐ competence	262	☐ conflicting	024
☐ competent	262, 351	☐ conform	072
☐ competition	031	☐ confound	074
☐ competitive	031	☐ confront	146

☐ confrontation	305	
☐ confuse	074	
☐ confusing	390	
☐ confusion	074	
☐ congratulate	346	
☐ congratulation	346	
☐ congratulatory	346	
☐ congress	089	
☐ congressional	089	
☐ connect	371	
☐ connect to	039	
☐ connected	159	
☐ connection	036	
☐ consecutive	320	
☐ consensus	220	
☐ consent	161	
☐ consequence	043, 199, 231	
☐ consequential	043	
☐ consequently	043, 199	
☐ conservation	316	
☐ conservative	152, 195, 316	
☐ conserve	032, 065, 316	
☐ consider	077, 310, 388	
☐ considerable	077, 114	
☐ considerably	077	
☐ considerate	107, 388	
☐ consideration	388	
☐ considered	385	
☐ considering	197	
☐ consistency	073	
☐ consistent	073	
☐ consistently	073	
☐ consolation	312	
☐ consolatory	312	
☐ console	309, 312	
☐ conspicuous	372	
☐ conspiracy	072	
☐ conspire	072	
☐ constituent	193	
☐ constitute	122, 193	
☐ constitution	193	
☐ constrain	270, 280	
☐ constraint	100, 270	
☐ construct	280	
☐ consume	040, 065	
☐ consumer	065	
☐ consumption	065	
☐ contact	286	
☐ contain	141	
☐ contaminant	345	
☐ contaminate	345, 355	
☐ contamination	345	
☐ contemporary	088	
☐ contempt	337, 338	
☐ contemptuous	338	
☐ contend	031	
☐ contender	043	
☐ continual	106	
☐ continue	106, 192	
☐ continuous	106	
☐ continuously	106	
☐ contract	025, 091	
☐ contradict	024, 090, 333	
☐ contradiction	333	
☐ contradictory	172, 333	
☐ contrary	172	
☐ contribute	034, 157	
☐ contribution	034	
☐ control	023, 128	
☐ controlled	368	
☐ convenience	367	
☐ convention	018, 074	
☐ conventional	074, 241, 369	
☐ conventionally	074	
☐ converge	232	
☐ conversion	052, 070	
☐ convert	052	
☐ convertible	052	
☐ convey	184, 212	
☐ conveyance	184	
☐ convict	020	
☐ conviction	032, 038	
☐ convince	038, 153	
☐ convincing	038	
☐ cool down	265	
☐ cooperate	299	
☐ cooperation	299	
☐ cooperative	299	
☐ coordinate	237, 299	
☐ coordinated	371	
☐ coordination	237	
☐ coordinator	237	
☐ correlate	249	
☐ correspond	249, 301, 321	
☐ correspondence	301	
☐ corresponding	248, 249	
☐ correspondingly	169	
☐ corrode	230	
☐ corrosion	230	
☐ corrupt	260, 294	
☐ corruption	294	
☐ cosmopolitan	387	
☐ cost	103	
☐ cost-effective	270	
☐ cough	211	
☐ council	041	

☐ countable	385
☐ counterfeit	084, 156, 241
☐ countless	385
☐ courteous	234
☐ courtesy	234
☐ cover	143, 298
☐ covet	344
☐ coward	377
☐ cowardly	105, 377
☐ craftsmanship	368
☐ cram	334
☐ cram school	334
☐ cramped	272
☐ crash	149, 305
☐ crawl	243, 312
☐ crazy	316, 371
☐ create	076
☐ creative	377
☐ credit	017, 133
☐ creep	312
☐ crisis	045
☐ critic	114
☐ critical	091, 114, 172
☐ criticism	044, 113, 114, 272
☐ criticize	114, 272, 297
☐ crucial	085, 091, 172
☐ crucially	091
☐ cruel	231
☐ cruelly	231
☐ cruelty	220, 231
☐ cruise	124
☐ crush	172
☐ cuisine	314
☐ cultivate	235
☐ cultivation	235
☐ culture	235
☐ cultured	387
☐ curable	168
☐ curb	128, 232, 323
☐ cure	204
☐ curiosity	066
☐ curious	066, 108, 372
☐ current	260
☐ curse	200, 258, 324
☐ curtail	318
☐ curve	232
☐ cut short	123
☐ cynical	374
☐ cynicism	374

D

☐ damp	299
☐ dampen	193, 299
☐ daring	105
☐ darken	304
☐ dazzling	304
☐ deadly	352
☐ deal with	198
☐ decay	230, 389
☐ deceit	310
☐ deceitful	310
☐ deceive	310, 335
☐ decency	182
☐ decent	182, 205
☐ decision	020
☐ declare	226, 312
☐ decline	047
☐ decompose	372
☐ decoration	303
☐ decrease	025, 047, 227, 267, 318
☐ dedicate	125, 173
☐ dedication	125
☐ deduct	343
☐ deed	259
☐ deep	205, 242
☐ defeat	073, 228
☐ defect	332
☐ defective	332
☐ defend	034, 113, 143, 209, 348
☐ deficiency	243
☐ deficient	243
☐ deficit	243
☐ define	026, 229
☐ defined	016
☐ definite	026, 283
☐ definition	026
☐ definitive	024
☐ defy	072
☐ delay	164, 192, 271, 274, 324
☐ delete	200
☐ deliberate	320
☐ deliberately	206, 320
☐ deliberation	320
☐ delicate	027, 294, 350
☐ delight	143, 162, 261, 315, 349
☐ delighted	143
☐ delightful	143
☐ demand	023, 087, 210
☐ demanding	210
☐ demolish	076, 280
☐ denounce	297, 349

☐ dense	207
☐ densely	207
☐ density	207
☐ deny	016, 026, 131, 149, 161, 225
☐ depart	105
☐ departing	300
☐ departure	105
☐ dependable	100, 170
☐ depict	092, 226
☐ deposit	046, 118
☐ depress	349
☐ depressed	247
☐ deprive	111, 317
☐ deregulate	150
☐ descend	198, 343
☐ descendant	168, 198
☐ descent	198
☐ desert	108
☐ deserve	023, 392
☐ designate	142, 247
☐ designation	247
☐ desirable	150
☐ desire	150, 347
☐ desolate	377
☐ despair	221, 303
☐ desperate	221, 303
☐ desperately	221
☐ despise	354
☐ destine	233
☐ destined	233
☐ destiny	048, 233
☐ destroy	052, 076, 148
☐ destructive	353
☐ detach	271, 371
☐ detached	159, 372
☐ detachment	371
☐ detail	026
☐ detailed	140
☐ detain	280
☐ deteriorate	342, 389
☐ deterioration	393
☐ determine	050
☐ detest	336
☐ detract	182, 325
☐ devastate	353
☐ devastating	353
☐ develop	052, 132
☐ developed	125
☐ device	285, 317
☐ devise	233, 261, 285
☐ devolve	132
☐ devote	125, 173
☐ devoted	170

☐ devotion	173
☐ devour	370
☐ differ	090, 249
☐ differ from	127
☐ difference	090
☐ different	090
☐ differentiate	090
☐ difficulty	147
☐ digest	239
☐ digestion	239
☐ digestive	239
☐ dignified	203
☐ dignify	261
☐ dignity	261
☐ diligence	369
☐ diligent	369
☐ diligently	369
☐ dim	336
☐ diminish	153, 227, 267
☐ diminution	267
☐ diminutive	267
☐ dinner	279
☐ diplomacy	358
☐ diplomat	358
☐ diplomatic	358
☐ direct	152
☐ dirty	393
☐ disable	371
☐ disadvantage	145, 199
☐ disadvantageous	145
☐ disagree	249
☐ disagreement	220
☐ disappear	051, 156
☐ disappoint	349
☐ disapprove	022, 161
☐ disassemble	163
☐ disaster	045, 047, 338
☐ disastrous	047, 353
☐ discard	308
☐ discern	323
☐ discipline	061
☐ disclose	027, 222
☐ disclosure	222
☐ disconnect	036, 371
☐ disconnected	159
☐ discourage	023, 038, 156, 213, 341
☐ discouragement	213
☐ discover	201
☐ discriminate	343
☐ discrimination	267, 343
☐ disdain	388
☐ disguise	333
☐ disgust	162, 263, 347

☐ disgusting	205, 347
☐ dishes	314
☐ disinterest	381
☐ disinterested	066
☐ dislike	022, 212
☐ disloyal	170
☐ dismal	373, 379
☐ dismantle	122
☐ dismay	379
☐ dismiss	050, 294, 350
☐ disobedient	378
☐ disobey	271
☐ disorder	102, 209
☐ disordered	102
☐ disorganized	112
☐ disown	387
☐ disperse	187, 232
☐ displease	162
☐ dispose of	083, 222
☐ disqualify	088
☐ disregard	158, 191, 235, 271, 350
☐ disrespect	234
☐ disruption	170
☐ dissolve	127
☐ dissuade	023, 038, 101, 153, 213, 341
☐ distant	037
☐ distaste	347
☐ distinct	093
☐ distinction	093
☐ distinctive	093
☐ distinguish	090, 093, 143
☐ distinguished	167, 379
☐ distort	026
☐ distract	246
☐ distracted	165, 246
☐ distraction	246, 310
☐ distress	247
☐ distressed	120
☐ distressful	247
☐ distribute	063
☐ distribution	063
☐ distrust	032
☐ disturb	382
☐ diverge	391
☐ divert (*someone's* attention)	246
☐ divide	345
☐ divorce	184
☐ docile	339
☐ doctor	282
☐ doctrine	282
☐ document	282
☐ dogma	282
☐ domain	210, 234

☐ domesticate	339
☐ dominant	128, 241
☐ dominate	128
☐ domination	128
☐ donate	034, 157
☐ donation	157
☐ doom	338
☐ doomed	338
☐ doubtful	078
☐ downside	145
☐ draft	077
☐ drag	063
☐ drag out	324
☐ dread	358
☐ dreadful	358
☐ drift	212
☐ drop	047, 153
☐ drown	200
☐ dry	299
☐ dub	142
☐ due	273
☐ dull	040, 169
☐ dumb	062, 269
☐ dump	108, 222
☐ durability	240
☐ durable	240, 294
☐ durably	240
☐ during	240
☐ dwell	332
☐ dweller	332
☐ dwelling	332
☐ dye	207
☐ dynasty	311

E

☐ eager	108, 191, 221, 251
☐ earn	309
☐ earnest	345
☐ earnestly	345
☐ earnings	090
☐ ease	116
☐ easy	129
☐ easy-going	110, 353
☐ eccentric	369
☐ eccentricity	369
☐ economic	270
☐ economical	270
☐ economically	270
☐ edit	069
☐ edition	069

editor	069	
editorial	069	
educate	152	
educated	273	
educational	306	
effect	043	
effective	028	
efficiency	028	
efficient	028, 270	
efficiently	028	
elastic	068	
elegant	131	
elementary	077	
elevation	298	
eliminate	083, 276	
elimination	083	
eloquence	386	
eloquent	386	
embargo	081, 335	
embarrass	332	
embarrassed	230	
embarrassment	332	
embrace	387	
emerge	051, 156	
emergency	041, 045, 047	
emergent	041	
emerging	051	
emigrate	262, 389	
eminence	379	
eminent	379	
emission	295	
emit	295	
emotional	367	
empathy	201	
emphasis	075	
emphasize	075	
emphatic	075	
employees	151	
empty	306	
enable	142	
enchant	382	
enchantment	382	
enclose	233	
enclosure	233	
encounter	051	
encourage	023, 101, 213	
encouragement	023	
encouraging	023, 373	
end	021, 180, 204	
endanger	244, 370	
endangered	370	
endeavor	104, 173, 267, 347	
endless	260	
endurance	198	
endure	198, 240	
enemy	115, 206	
engage	028, 146	
engagement	028	
enhance	284, 342	
enjoyable	225	
enlarge	025, 043, 246, 359	
enlist	154	
enormous	078, 245	
enraged	315	
enrich	284	
enrichment	284	
ensure	030	
enter	266	
enterprise	063	
enterprising	063	
enthusiasm	191	
enthusiastic	191	
enthusiastically	191	
entice	227	
enticing	150	
entire	019, 024, 128	
entirely	019, 110	
entitle	088, 142	
entitlement	142	
envious	251, 344	
envision	233	
envy	344	
episode	025	
epoch	382	
epoch-making	382	
equal	193	
equip	129, 275	
equipment	129	
era	065, 382	
erase	200, 276	
eraser	276	
erect	280	
erection	280	
erupt	132	
eruption	132	
escape	196	
escort	039	
essential	085, 091, 163, 325	
esteem	061, 337	
estimate	044, 061	
estimated	061	
estimation	061	
eternal	260, 282	
eternally	282	
eternity	282	
ethical	260, 294	

☐ ethics	260
☐ ethnic	187, 231
☐ ethnicity	187
☐ evaluate	073, 126
☐ evaluation	073
☐ even though	093
☐ evidence	188
☐ evident	188
☐ evidently	188
☐ evil	161, 274
☐ evolution	132
☐ evolutionary	132
☐ evolve	132
☐ exact	113
☐ exactly	051
☐ exaggerate	160
☐ exaggeration	160
☐ examine	018, 205
☐ exceed	092, 341
☐ except	155
☐ exception	155
☐ exceptional	064, 079, 155
☐ exceptionally	155
☐ excess	092, 147
☐ excessive	092, 147, 164
☐ excessively	092, 147
☐ excited	377
☐ exciting	169
☐ exclaim	352
☐ exclamation	352
☐ exclude	113
☐ excluding	113
☐ exclusion	113
☐ exclusive	113
☐ excuse	111
☐ exhalation	276
☐ exhale	276
☐ exhaust	189
☐ exhaustion	189, 243
☐ exhaustive	140
☐ exile	346
☐ exit	118
☐ exotic	284
☐ exoticism	284
☐ expand	025, 181, 246, 267, 318
☐ expansion	025
☐ expansive	025
☐ expansively	025
☐ expectation	074
☐ expecting	146
☐ expedition	192, 242, 278
☐ expenditure	090
☐ expense	090
☐ experienced	350
☐ explain	026
☐ explanatory	306
☐ explode	140
☐ exploration	018
☐ explore	018
☐ explosion	140
☐ explosive	140
☐ expose	333
☐ exposed	130
☐ express	295
☐ expression	274
☐ extend	043, 080, 278, 318
☐ extension	043, 080
☐ extensive	043, 080
☐ extent	080
☐ exterior	042, 060
☐ external	042, 060
☐ extinguish	380
☐ extinguisher	380
☐ extra	064, 140
☐ extraordinarily	101
☐ extraordinary	101
☐ extraterrestrial	166
☐ extravagance	119
☐ extravagant	131
☐ extreme	034, 085
☐ extremely	034
☐ extroverted	300

F

☐ fabric	117
☐ fabricate	076
☐ fabricated	241
☐ facility	016
☐ fact	229
☐ factor	061
☐ factual	068, 307
☐ fade	127
☐ fade out	127
☐ failure	228
☐ faint	297
☐ fair	068
☐ faith	032
☐ faithful	032
☐ fake	084, 155, 241, 346
☐ fall	047
☐ fall apart	149
☐ fall behind	341
☐ fall short	092

☐ fallout	043	☐ flammable	118
☐ false	039	☐ flatter	258, 287, 344, 387
☐ fame	122	☐ flattery	344
☐ famine	337	☐ flaw	332
☐ famous	122	☐ flee	190, 196
☐ fancy	131	☐ flesh	160
☐ fantastic	040, 101, 155, 280, 349	☐ flexibility	068
☐ fantasy	229	☐ flexible	068, 283, 390
☐ fare	103	☐ flexibly	068
☐ fascinate	283, 382	☐ float (away)	212
☐ fascinating	283	☐ flock	232, 286
☐ fascination	283	☐ flourish	286, 347
☐ fasten	119, 309	☐ fluency	282
☐ fastener	309	☐ fluent	282
☐ fat	383	☐ fluently	282
☐ fatal	168, 352	☐ focus	104, 246
☐ fate	048, 233	☐ focus on	158
☐ fatigue	189, 243	☐ follow	128, 191, 271
☐ fatty	116	☐ follower	192
☐ fault	071	☐ following	117
☐ faulty	332	☐ food	314
☐ favor	022	☐ foolish	062, 224
☐ favorable	022	☐ forbid	158, 269
☐ favorite	022	☐ force	338, 341
☐ fear	198	☐ forecast	044, 074, 157
☐ feast	279	☐ forefather	168
☐ feature	031	☐ foreign	166, 284
☐ fee	103	☐ foresee	373
☐ feeble	294	☐ foreseeable	373
☐ feeling	185	☐ foretell	373
☐ fertile	340, 377	☐ forged	241
☐ fertility	340	☐ forget	391
☐ fertilizer	340	☐ forgive	111
☐ festival	279	☐ formula	261
☐ fetch	309	☐ formulate	261, 285
☐ few	323	☐ formulation	261
☐ fictional	307	☐ forthcoming	322
☐ fictitious	241	☐ fortunate	048, 119
☐ field	061, 210, 234	☐ fortunately	119
☐ fierce	262	☐ fortune	048, 119, 324
☐ fiercely	262	☐ forum	018
☐ fight	084	☐ fossil	190
☐ figuratively	107	☐ foster	021, 235
☐ filled	306	☐ found	086
☐ finally	105	☐ fragile	240, 294
☐ find	037	☐ fragility	294
☐ finish	021, 180, 186	☐ fragrance	169, 287
☐ finite	282	☐ frail	294
☐ fire	021	☐ frank	224
☐ firm	068	☐ frankly	224
☐ fix	148	☐ free	029, 306
☐ fixed	283	☐ free time	129
☐ flame	118	☐ frequency	087

frequent	087, 317
frequently	087
friend	115, 206
friendliness	266
fright	126, 278
frighten	126, 278, 335, 372
frightened	278
from scratch	082
frown	358
frustrate	236
frustration	236
fulfill	199
fulfillment	199
full	024
fundamental	086
funeral	109
furious	315
furnish	275
furnished	275
furniture	275
furthermore	050, 140
fury	264, 315
fuss	351
fussy	351
futile	311

G

gain	325
gamble	049
garbage	120, 308, 318
gather	063, 127, 277, 325
gathering	277
gaudy	366
gaze	281
gear	317
gene	144
general	016, 319
generalization	319
generalize	319
generate	052
generation	052, 065
generosity	107, 351
generous	107, 114
generously	107
genetic	144, 381
genetically	144
gentle	262, 353
genuine	084, 156, 241, 346
get divorced	184
get soaking wet	194

gift	295
gifted	040
give	111, 317
give away	157
give in	030
give off	295
give up	020, 031, 035, 084, 089, 224, 265, 302
given	197
glance	146, 298
glare	141, 368
glaring	368
glimmer	258
glimpse	146, 298
gloom	373
gloomy	247, 336, 373
glorify	113
glorious	113
glory	113
gloss over	075
glow	258
go after	041, 052
go bankrupt	355
go on	066
goal	065
good	161, 274
goods	208, 285
govern	132, 311
government	132
grab	066, 167, 309
grace	261
graceful	371
grade	073, 263
gradual	263
gradually	263
grain	063
grant	019, 311, 317
grasp	066, 238, 384
grateful	060
gratitude	277
grave	142
greed	351
greedy	107, 351
greet	070
grief	242, 261
grieve	261
grim	129
grind	264
grindstone	264
grip	238
grocery	104
grocery store	104
gross	128

☐ ground(s)	201	
☐ grow	132	
☐ grow up	125	
☐ growl	348	
☐ grown-up	125	
☐ guarantee	030, 035, 226, 297, 307	
☐ guard	067	
☐ guess	044	

H

☐ habit	070, 383
☐ habitual	383
☐ habituate	383
☐ halt	066, 186, 204
☐ hand in	030
☐ handful	323
☐ handicap	145
☐ happiness	242, 261
☐ hard	085, 283, 284
☐ hardly	092
☐ hardship	147, 368
☐ hardworking	369
☐ harm	148
☐ harmony	209
☐ harsh	129, 353
☐ harvest	115, 127, 325
☐ haste	385
☐ hasten	274, 385
☐ hastily	385
☐ hasty	385
☐ hate	263, 336
☐ hatred	263, 281
☐ haunt	317
☐ haunted	317
☐ haven	306
☐ hazard	375
☐ hazardous	389
☐ headmaster	053
☐ heal	071
☐ healing	071
☐ heap	081, 287
☐ heat	265
☐ hence	221
☐ herd	232, 286
☐ hereditary	144, 381
☐ heredity	381
☐ heritage	124
☐ hesitant	164, 251
☐ hesitate	164
☐ hesitation	164

☐ hidden	167
☐ hide	092, 181, 333
☐ hierarchical	314
☐ hierarchy	314
☐ high	034
☐ higher	285
☐ highlight	075, 342
☐ hike	047
☐ hinder	149
☐ hint	106
☐ hire	154
☐ hold back	064, 343
☐ hold up	123
☐ honestly	224
☐ hopeful	043, 373
☐ horrible	380
☐ horrify	380
☐ horrifying	207
☐ horror	198, 380
☐ hospitable	266
☐ hospital	266
☐ hospitality	266
☐ housing	067
☐ however	250
☐ HR	151
☐ huge	078, 245
☐ human resources	151
☐ humble	202, 263
☐ humiliate	387
☐ humiliation	387
☐ humility	263
☐ hunt	052
☐ hurry	274
☐ hygiene	385
☐ hypothesis	282
☐ hypothesize	282, 307
☐ hypothetical	282

I

☐ identical	037
☐ identify	093, 143
☐ idle	236
☐ ignite	380
☐ ignorance	141, 273
☐ ignorant	273, 350
☐ ignore	036, 052, 075, 144, 223, 271, 273
☐ illegal	123
☐ illiteracy	266
☐ illogical	275

☐ illuminate	304
☐ illumination	304
☐ illusion	229
☐ illusory	229
☐ illustrate	026, 092, 226, 304
☐ illustration	092
☐ imaginable	380
☐ imaginary	307, 340, 380
☐ imagination	307, 340
☐ imaginative	307, 340, 380
☐ imitate	259
☐ imitation	259
☐ imitative	259
☐ immature	125
☐ immense	245
☐ immensely	245
☐ immigrant	389
☐ immigrate	262, 389
☐ immigration	389
☐ imminent	078
☐ immoral	260, 274
☐ immortal	352
☐ impede	128, 154
☐ impending	078, 322
☐ implication	106, 231
☐ implicit	106
☐ imply	106, 231
☐ impose	087
☐ imposition	087
☐ impoverished	373
☐ imprecise	113
☐ impress	239
☐ improbability	074
☐ improbable	210
☐ improper	019, 182, 205, 393
☐ improve	153, 239, 284, 342
☐ impulse	251
☐ impulsive	251, 385
☐ in deed	259
☐ inaccessible	037
☐ inaccurate	039
☐ inactive	236
☐ inadequate	304
☐ inappropriate	019, 182
☐ inattentive	248
☐ inaudible	375
☐ inbound	300
☐ incapable	262, 351
☐ incidence	025
☐ incident	025
☐ incidental	025
☐ incite	130, 323
☐ inclination	348

☐ inclined	348
☐ include	113
☐ income	090
☐ incoming	300
☐ incompetent	262, 351
☐ incomplete	024, 140, 170
☐ incomprehensible	390
☐ incomprehension	390
☐ inconsiderable	114
☐ inconsiderate	388
☐ inconsistent	073
☐ inconspicuous	372
☐ increase	025, 047, 127, 181, 267, 318, 343
☐ incredible	069
☐ incredibly	069
☐ incurable	168
☐ indecent	205
☐ indefinite	148
☐ independent	224
☐ indifference	212, 264, 301, 372, 381
☐ indifferent	066, 108, 191, 372
☐ indifferently	372
☐ indignation	264
☐ indulge	316
☐ indulgence	119, 316
☐ indulgent	316
☐ industrial	392
☐ industrialization	392
☐ industrialize	392
☐ industrious	369
☐ inefficient	028, 270
☐ inessential	085, 086, 091
☐ inevitability	233
☐ inevitable	078
☐ inevitably	078
☐ inexperienced	350
☐ infamous	356
☐ infect	245, 355
☐ infection	245
☐ infectious	245
☐ inferior	114, 163, 171, 285, 376
☐ inferiority	285
☐ infertile	340, 377
☐ infinite	260
☐ infinity	260
☐ inflate	160
☐ inflict	305
☐ infliction	305
☐ influence	153, 194
☐ influential	194
☐ inform	306

☐ informal	079	☐ instruct	152
☐ information	306	☐ instruction	152
☐ informational	306	☐ instructive	152
☐ informative	306	☐ instructor	152
☐ infrequently	052, 087	☐ insufficiency	243
☐ infringe	390	☐ insufficient	226, 389
☐ ingenious	377	☐ insult	258, 344
☐ ingenuity	377	☐ insurance	226
☐ ingest	040, 065	☐ insure	226
☐ ingredient	061	☐ integral	086
☐ inhabit	272, 332	☐ intellect	355
☐ inhabitant	272	☐ intellectual	355
☐ inhalation	276	☐ intelligence	355
☐ inhale	276	☐ intelligible	359
☐ inherit	191	☐ intend	065
☐ inheritance	191	☐ intense	085
☐ inherited	381	☐ intensify	085, 230
☐ initial	105	☐ intensity	085, 230
☐ initially	105	☐ intensive	085, 230
☐ initiate	105	☐ intensively	230
☐ initiation	105	☐ intent	165
☐ initiative	109	☐ intention	065, 165
☐ inject	151	☐ intentional	065, 320
☐ injustice	031	☐ intentionally	206
☐ inner	042, 060	☐ interact	188
☐ innocence	147	☐ interaction	188
☐ innocent	147	☐ interactive	188
☐ innovate	102	☐ interest	235
☐ innovation	102	☐ interested	066
☐ innovative	102, 393	☐ interfere	154
☐ innumerable	385	☐ interference	154
☐ inquire	310	☐ interior	042, 060
☐ inquiry	310	☐ intermediate	237
☐ inquisitive	066	☐ intermittent	106
☐ insane	371	☐ internal	042
☐ insert	151, 233	☐ interpret	091
☐ insertion	151	☐ interpretation	091
☐ insight	141	☐ interpreter	091
☐ insightful	141	☐ interrupt	123
☐ insignificant	077, 086, 142, 194	☐ interruption	123, 170
☐ insincere	345	☐ interval	203
☐ insist	016, 265, 390	☐ intimidate	028, 126, 319
☐ insistence	390	☐ introduce	021, 053
☐ insistent	390	☐ introverted	300
☐ inspect	205	☐ intrude	154, 390
☐ inspection	205	☐ intrusion	390
☐ inspire	023, 156	☐ intrusive	390
☐ inspiring	169	☐ intuition	141
☐ instinct	194	☐ invade	190, 209, 296, 390
☐ instinctive	194	☐ invader	209
☐ institute	053	☐ invalid	123, 334
☐ institution	053	☐ invalidate	334
☐ institutional	053	☐ invalidity	334

☐ invaluable	320
☐ invasion	209
☐ invent	285
☐ inventive	377
☐ invest	039
☐ investigate	036
☐ investigation	036
☐ investment	039
☐ involuntary	224
☐ ironic	322
☐ ironically	322
☐ irony	322
☐ irrational	224, 275
☐ irregular	074, 391
☐ irregularly	087
☐ irrelevant	076
☐ irresistible	375
☐ irresistibly	375
☐ irritant	315
☐ irritate	208, 250, 315
☐ irritation	315
☐ isolate	208
☐ isolated	037, 208
☐ isolation	208, 369
☐ item	208
☐ items	285

J

☐ jealous	251
☐ jealousy	251, 344
☐ jinx	324
☐ join	029
☐ joke	376
☐ journey	228
☐ joy	143, 242
☐ joyful	247, 377
☐ judge	114, 126
☐ junk	308
☐ just	031
☐ justice	031
☐ justification	113
☐ justified	113
☐ justify	031, 113

K

☐ keen	108, 211
☐ keenly	108
☐ keep	050, 077
☐ keep going	192
☐ key	130
☐ kickback	383
☐ kind	231
☐ kingdom	234
☐ knowledgeable	350

L

☐ lack	243
☐ lacking	226, 304
☐ lament	117, 334
☐ landscape	022, 162
☐ large	281
☐ late	391
☐ latter	117
☐ laugh	339
☐ launch	021
☐ lawful	123
☐ lazy	369
☐ lead	128
☐ leak	181
☐ leakage	181
☐ leaky	181
☐ lean	116, 383
☐ lean on	116
☐ leaning	348
☐ leap	204
☐ lease	202
☐ leave	029, 052, 077
☐ leave out	283
☐ legacy	124
☐ legal	123
☐ legalize	081
☐ legislate	111
☐ legislation	111
☐ legislative	111
☐ legislature	111
☐ legitimate	123, 156
☐ leisure	129
☐ lengthen	324
☐ lengthy	324
☐ less	318
☐ lessen	153, 318, 359
☐ let go	028, 050, 066, 165, 167, 238, 280, 322
☐ let off	338
☐ let out	183, 280
☐ liability	121, 313
☐ liable	313

☐ liberal	152, 359
☐ liberate	152, 359
☐ liberation	359
☐ liberty	152
☐ lift	153
☐ light	380
☐ light up	304
☐ likelihood	286, 392
☐ likely	210, 286
☐ likewise	207
☐ limit	100, 158, 315
☐ limitation	100, 270
☐ limited	080, 152, 170, 260
☐ line	305
☐ line of work	067
☐ line up	305
☐ lingual	164
☐ linguist	268
☐ linguistic	268
☐ linguistics	268
☐ link	036
☐ literacy	266
☐ literal	107
☐ literally	107
☐ literary	182
☐ literate	266
☐ literature	182
☐ litter	308, 318
☐ little	114
☐ liveliness	243
☐ lively	169, 373
☐ livestock	150
☐ log in	029
☐ log out	029
☐ logic	083
☐ logical	083, 275
☐ lone	185
☐ look down on	337
☐ look forward to	155, 358
☐ look through	250
☐ loose	283
☐ lose	020, 035, 050, 227
☐ loss	073, 228
☐ loud	366
☐ love	281, 347, 354
☐ lovely	107
☐ low	034, 203
☐ lower	153, 267, 318
☐ lowest	114, 163
☐ loyal	170
☐ loyalist	379
☐ loyally	170
☐ loyalty	170

☐ lucky	119
☐ lump	240
☐ luxurious	119
☐ luxury	119

M

☐ made-up	307
☐ magnification	359
☐ magnificence	232
☐ magnificent	232
☐ magnifier	359
☐ magnify	232, 359
☐ main	053
☐ mainly	079
☐ mainstream	241
☐ maintain	086, 149
☐ major	325
☐ make a fuss	351
☐ make up	122
☐ malicious	161
☐ malleable	283
☐ management	033
☐ mandatory	354
☐ maneuver	213
☐ manners	234
☐ manufacture	076
☐ manufactured	084
☐ manufacturer	076
☐ manufacturing	076
☐ manuscript	281
☐ many	060
☐ margin	121
☐ marginal	121
☐ marvel	349
☐ marvelous	304, 349
☐ mask	298, 333
☐ mass	081
☐ massive	078
☐ master	078
☐ match	321
☐ mate	075, 193
☐ materialize	051
☐ mature	125, 303
☐ maturity	125
☐ maximum	281
☐ mean	107, 231
☐ meander	123
☐ meaningful	325
☐ means	268
☐ meditate	374

☐ meditation	374
☐ meditative	374
☐ memento	295
☐ memorial	109
☐ menace	375
☐ menacing	375
☐ menacingly	375
☐ mention	160, 166, 295
☐ merchandise	285
☐ merchandising	285
☐ merchant	285
☐ merciful	220, 374
☐ merciless	220
☐ mercy	220
☐ mere	142
☐ merely	142
☐ merit	071, 392
☐ mess	114
☐ messy	112, 114, 299
☐ metaphorically	107
☐ metropolis	270
☐ metropolitan	270
☐ microscope	159
☐ migrate	262, 389
☐ migration	262
☐ migratory	262
☐ mild	034, 262, 353
☐ mimic	193, 259
☐ minimal	281
☐ minimally	281
☐ minimum	281
☐ minor	053, 091, 142, 163, 211, 325
☐ mirror	259
☐ mischief	376
☐ mischievous	376
☐ misconception	229
☐ miserable	247
☐ misery	247
☐ misinterpret	091, 238, 323
☐ miss	143, 144
☐ mistake	074, 323
☐ mistreat	080
☐ mistreatment	080
☐ misunderstand	091, 238, 323
☐ misuse	080
☐ mitigate	323
☐ mock	346, 388
☐ mockery	346, 388
☐ model	237, 356
☐ moderate	085, 147, 164
☐ moderation	164
☐ moderato	164
☐ modern	088, 260, 393

☐ modest	202, 263
☐ modesty	202
☐ modification	090
☐ modify	077, 090
☐ moist	299
☐ mold	237
☐ monotonous	391
☐ monotony	391
☐ monster	180
☐ monument	157
☐ monumental	157
☐ mood	323
☐ mop	110
☐ moreover	050, 140
☐ mortal	352
☐ mortality	352
☐ mortally	352
☐ motivate	130, 156, 248
☐ motivation	156, 248
☐ motive	156, 248
☐ mound	081, 287
☐ mourn	334
☐ mournful	334
☐ mourning	261, 334
☐ multicultural	387
☐ multitude	323
☐ mumble	382, 386
☐ murmur	229, 382, 386
☐ mutter	162, 352, 382, 386
☐ mutual	159
☐ mutuality	159
☐ mutually	159
☐ myriad	323

N

☐ naive	273, 350
☐ naked	130
☐ namely	180
☐ narrate	251
☐ narration	251
☐ narrative	072, 105, 251
☐ narrow	152
☐ nasty	107, 129, 205, 393
☐ native	166
☐ navigate	213
☐ navigation	213
☐ navigator	213
☐ near	037
☐ neat	112, 299
☐ neatly	112

☐ negative	378
☐ neglect	032, 144, 158, 223
☐ negligence	158
☐ negligent	158
☐ negligible	325
☐ negotiation	091
☐ nervous	355
☐ net	128
☐ neutral	221
☐ neutrality	221
☐ neutralize	221
☐ never-ending	282
☐ nevertheless	093, 250
☐ newcomer	154
☐ nightmare	228
☐ nobility	203
☐ noble	203
☐ nobody	258
☐ nod	149
☐ nominate	247
☐ nonetheless	093, 250
☐ nonverbal	277
☐ normal	070, 155, 163, 308, 369
☐ noteworthy	079, 155, 372
☐ notion	107
☐ notorious	356
☐ nourish	235, 354
☐ nourishment	354
☐ nude	130
☐ nuisance	345
☐ null	334
☐ nullify	300
☐ number	060
☐ numeral	060
☐ numerous	060

O

☐ oath	307, 336
☐ obedience	378
☐ obedient	378
☐ obese	383
☐ obey	128, 132, 191, 235, 378
☐ object	068
☐ objective	065, 068
☐ objectively	068
☐ obligate	338
☐ obligation	338
☐ obligatory	338, 354
☐ oblige	338, 341
☐ obscure	026, 092, 167, 188, 359

☐ observe	271
☐ obsess	392
☐ obsession	392
☐ obsessive	392
☐ obsolete	393
☐ obstacle	172
☐ obstinate	337
☐ obstruction	172
☐ obtain	224, 325
☐ obvious	167, 188
☐ occasionally	052
☐ occupation	067, 151
☐ occupational	151
☐ occurrence	025
☐ odd	069, 302, 308, 369
☐ odds	392
☐ offend	208
☐ offense	208
☐ offensive	208
☐ offer	111
☐ often	087
☐ omission	283
☐ omit	283
☐ on purpose	206
☐ on the contrary	172
☐ open	152, 306
☐ operate	213
☐ operation	063
☐ opportunity	109
☐ oppose	321
☐ opposite to	172
☐ oppress	319, 348, 384
☐ oppression	384
☐ oppressive	384
☐ optimism	270
☐ optimist	270
☐ optimistic	270, 378
☐ optional	091, 354
☐ opulence	119
☐ oral	164, 277
☐ order	102, 209
☐ orderly	299
☐ ordinary	101, 379
☐ organize	237, 277
☐ organized	112
☐ origin	180
☐ original	180
☐ originally	105
☐ originate	180
☐ ornament	303
☐ ornamental	303
☐ orphan	353
☐ orphanage	353

☐ outbound	300
☐ outbreak	271
☐ outcome	045
☐ outdated	393
☐ outer	042, 060
☐ outfit	129
☐ outgoing	300
☐ outlaw	081
☐ outlet	161, 183
☐ outline	093
☐ outlook	171
☐ out-of-date	393
☐ output	027
☐ outrage	208
☐ outrageous	227
☐ outstanding	064, 079, 167, 372
☐ overcome	020
☐ overlook	143, 144, 158
☐ oversee	268
☐ overtake	341
☐ overturn	086
☐ overuse	080
☐ overwhelm	204
☐ overwhelming	204
☐ owing to	273

P

☐ pacify	369
☐ pack	334
☐ packed	207
☐ pair	171
☐ pamper	148, 316
☐ panel	041
☐ panorama	022
☐ paragraph	020
☐ paralysis	371
☐ paralyze	371
☐ pardon	111, 124
☐ part	042, 170
☐ partial	024, 170
☐ partially	019, 170
☐ particular	016
☐ partly	079, 110
☐ partner	115
☐ pass	300
☐ pass away	347
☐ pass on	191
☐ pass over	144
☐ passion	381
☐ passive	187

☐ pastime	310
☐ patriot	379
☐ pave	333
☐ pave the way	333
☐ pavement	333
☐ pay attention to	158
☐ peace	024
☐ peculiar	069, 302
☐ peculiarity	302
☐ peculiarly	302
☐ pedal	278
☐ pedestrian	278
☐ pedigree	075
☐ peek	146
☐ peer	171
☐ penetrate	266, 320
☐ penetration	266
☐ perceive	143, 323
☐ percentage	087
☐ perceptible	143
☐ perception	143
☐ perfume	287
☐ peril	389
☐ perilous	389
☐ periodically	052
☐ perish	347
☐ perishable	347
☐ permission	161
☐ permit	158, 161, 231, 269, 315
☐ perplex	074
☐ perplexing	390
☐ persecute	348, 384
☐ persecution	348
☐ persevere	265
☐ persist	198, 265
☐ persistence	265
☐ persistent	265, 337, 390
☐ personnel	151
☐ perspective	171, 266
☐ persuade	038, 101, 153, 227
☐ persuasion	153
☐ persuasive	153
☐ pessimism	378
☐ pessimist	378
☐ pessimistic	270, 378
☐ pest	313
☐ phase	078
☐ phrase	020
☐ pick	127, 325
☐ pick up	035, 308
☐ picky	340
☐ piece	061
☐ piece together	209

☐ pierce	**266**, 320
☐ pile	081
☐ pile up	**227**
☐ pinch	**165**
☐ pioneer	192
☐ pitiful	**301**
☐ pitiless	**301**
☐ pity	301
☐ pivotal	**091**
☐ plan	**197**
☐ planned	**320**
☐ plausible	**069**, 380
☐ play down	**160**
☐ plea	**278**
☐ plead	278
☐ pleasant	**129**, **225**
☐ please	**208**, **315**
☐ pledge	307, **336**
☐ plentiful	**060**, **304**, **389**
☐ pliable	**068**, **283**
☐ plot	072, **105**, **251**
☐ pointless	**311**
☐ poke	356
☐ policy	**048**
☐ politeness	**234**
☐ pollutant	**355**
☐ pollute	**345**, 355
☐ pollution	**355**
☐ poor	**064**, **068**, **373**
☐ populate	**272**
☐ portion	042, **220**
☐ portrait	**226**
☐ portray	226
☐ portrayal	**226**
☐ pose	045
☐ positive	**378**
☐ possess	050
☐ possession	**050**
☐ possibility	**286**
☐ possible	**210**
☐ postpone	**192**, 271
☐ postponement	**271**
☐ potent	**297**
☐ poverty	068, **119**
☐ powerful	**085**, **297**
☐ praise	**017**, 044, **114**, **222**, **258**, **272**, **287**, **297**, **349**
☐ precarious	**389**
☐ precaution	296
☐ precautionary	**296**
☐ precede	**356**
☐ precedent	356
☐ preceding	**117**

☐ precise	113
☐ precisely	**051**, **113**
☐ precision	**113**
☐ predecessor	300
☐ predict	044, **061**, **157**, **373**
☐ predictable	**044**
☐ prediction	**044**
☐ prefer	**022**
☐ preference	**348**
☐ pregnancy	**146**
☐ pregnant	146
☐ prejudice	267
☐ prejudiced	**068**
☐ preliminary	264
☐ premature	**125**
☐ premise	201
☐ preparation	**189**, **296**
☐ prescribe	265
☐ prescription	**265**
☐ present	**088**, **295**
☐ preservation	**032**
☐ preserve	032, **149**, **316**
☐ pressing	**172**, 316
☐ pressure	**116**
☐ prestige	**113**, 344
☐ prestigious	**344**
☐ presumption	**201**
☐ pretend	155, **346**
☐ pretender	**155**
☐ pretense	**155**
☐ prevail	275
☐ prevalence	**275**
☐ prevalent	**275**
☐ prevent	**081**
☐ previous	**117**
☐ price	**103**
☐ priceless	**320**
☐ prick	**320**
☐ primarily	079
☐ primary	**079**
☐ prime	100
☐ primeval	**260**
☐ primitive	260
☐ principal	053
☐ principally	**053**
☐ prior	117
☐ priority	**117**
☐ privilege	**199**
☐ privileged	**199**
☐ probability	**074**, **210**, **286**, **392**
☐ probable	210
☐ probably	**210**
☐ probe	**036**

☐ problem	071
☐ procedure	109
☐ proceed	066
☐ process	066
☐ procession	066
☐ produce	052, 076
☐ product	208
☐ production	027, 076
☐ productive	340
☐ products	285
☐ profess	225
☐ profession	067, 151, 380
☐ professional	067
☐ proficiency	351
☐ proficient	351
☐ profit	184
☐ profitable	184
☐ profound	242
☐ profoundly	242
☐ program	063, 109
☐ progress	195
☐ progression	070
☐ progressive	152, 195
☐ prohibit	081, 158, 269
☐ prohibition	081, 158
☐ prohibitive	158
☐ project	044
☐ prolong	186, 324
☐ prolonged	324
☐ prominence	046, 167
☐ prominent	053, 167
☐ promise	088
☐ promising	373
☐ prompt	130
☐ prone	313
☐ proper	182
☐ proportion	087, 165
☐ proportional	087
☐ prospect	074, 171, 286
☐ prospective	074
☐ prosper	349
☐ prosperity	349
☐ prosperous	303, 349
☐ protect	032, 348
☐ protection	143
☐ proud	263
☐ proven	307
☐ provide	189, 275
☐ provincial	044, 270
☐ provision	189
☐ provoke	315, 369, 376
☐ prudence	353
☐ prudent	353

☐ publicity	246
☐ publicize	246
☐ pull back	118
☐ punctual	391
☐ punctuality	391
☐ punctually	391
☐ pure	024
☐ purify	355
☐ purpose	248
☐ pursue	041, 052
☐ pursuit	041
☐ put in	151
☐ put off	271
☐ put out	380
☐ put up	280
☐ puzzle	074

Q

☐ qualification	088, 126
☐ qualified	088
☐ qualify	088
☐ quarrel	367
☐ quest	192, 242
☐ question	192
☐ queue	305
☐ quick	385
☐ quicken	274
☐ quiet	262
☐ quit	089, 108, 249
☐ quotation	120
☐ quote	120, 166

R

☐ race	231
☐ racial	231
☐ racism	231
☐ radiate	091, 295
☐ radical	163, 195
☐ radicalism	163
☐ radically	163
☐ radioactive	091
☐ rage	264
☐ raid	296
☐ raise	083, 153, 267
☐ rally	277
☐ rare	070
☐ rating	017

☐ ratio	087, 165		☐ regret	117
☐ rational	275, 371		☐ regretful	117
☐ rationale	083, 275		☐ regrettable	117
☐ rationalize	113		☐ regular	074, 155
☐ ray	091		☐ regulate	150, 237
☐ reach	069		☐ regulation	150
☐ reaction	043		☐ reign	311
☐ real	148, 307, 346		☐ reimburse	248
☐ realistic	316		☐ reject	019, 026, 043, 047,
☐ reality	229			131, 231, 384
☐ realize	199		☐ rejuvenate	259
☐ really	107		☐ relate	036
☐ realm	234		☐ relaxation	116, 129
☐ reap	325		☐ relaxed	079, 110, 120, 353, 355
☐ rear	083		☐ release	028, 029, 066, 165,
☐ reasonable	069, 123, 224, 275			238, 322, 338, 359
☐ reassurance	309		☐ relevance	076
☐ reassure	088, 309, 312, 335		☐ relevant	076
☐ rebirth	393		☐ reliable	100
☐ rebound	223		☐ reliance	100
☐ rebuild	357		☐ relief	116
☐ recall	391		☐ relieve	380
☐ recede	375		☐ relocate	389
☐ receive	063, 212, 325		☐ reluctance	251
☐ recession	375		☐ reluctant	251
☐ reciprocal	159		☐ reluctantly	251
☐ reckless	248, 353, 385		☐ rely	100
☐ reckon	310		☐ remain	118, 262
☐ recollect	391		☐ remark	079, 160
☐ recollection	391		☐ remarkable	064, 079, 101, 155, 160
☐ recommend	101		☐ remarkably	079, 160
☐ reconstruct	357		☐ remedial	204
☐ reconstruction	357		☐ remedy	204
☐ recover	071		☐ reminder	295
☐ recreation	129, 310		☐ remodel	062
☐ recruit	154		☐ remote	037
☐ recruiter	154		☐ remove	083, 111, 151, 276, 317, 343
☐ recruitment	154		☐ renaissance	393
☐ reduce	267, 318, 359		☐ render	234
☐ refer to	166		☐ renew	186
☐ refine	239		☐ renewable energy	186
☐ refined	189, 239		☐ renewal	186
☐ refinement	239		☐ renewed	186
☐ reform	062		☐ renounce	387
☐ refrain	072, 343		☐ renovate	062
☐ refrain from	064		☐ renown	122
☐ refrigerate	265		☐ renowned	167, 379
☐ refuge	067, 306		☐ rent	202
☐ refugee	306, 346		☐ renunciation	387
☐ refuse	019, 072, 180		☐ repair	148
☐ regardless	093		☐ repeated	383
☐ register	029, 285		☐ repel	153
☐ registration	029		☐ replicate	193, 259

☐ reprimand	222	
☐ reproduce	075, 193	
☐ reproduction	193	
☐ reproductive	193	
☐ repulsive	150	
☐ reputable	046	
☐ reputation	046, 344	
☐ request	192	
☐ rescue	089	
☐ research	018	
☐ resemblance	127	
☐ resemble	127	
☐ resent	374	
☐ resentful	374	
☐ resentment	374	
☐ reserve	032, 064	
☐ reside	272, 332	
☐ resign	249	
☐ resignation	249	
☐ resilient	240	
☐ resist	072	
☐ resistance	072	
☐ resistant	072	
☐ resort	131	
☐ resource	017, 121	
☐ resourceful	017	
☐ respect	263, 337	
☐ respectable	205, 294	
☐ respectful	393	
☐ respective	248	
☐ respectively	248	
☐ restless	357	
☐ restoration	042	
☐ restore	042, 357	
☐ restrain	315, 359	
☐ restrained	368	
☐ restraint	270, 315	
☐ restrict	128	
☐ restriction	100, 128	
☐ resurgence	393	
☐ resurgent	393	
☐ retain	050, 085	
☐ retire	249	
☐ retreat	118, 190, 209, 375	
☐ retrieve	309	
☐ reunion	339	
☐ reveal	027, 201, 222, 225, 298	
☐ revelation	027	
☐ revenge	268	
☐ revenue	090	
☐ revere	240, 337	
☐ reversal	086	
☐ reverse	086	
☐ revert	086	
☐ revise	062, 318	
☐ revitalize	259	
☐ revival	259	
☐ revive	259	
☐ revolutionary	163	
☐ revolve	261	
☐ revulsion	347	
☐ rich	340, 373	
☐ ridicule	227, 258, 287, 388	
☐ ridiculous	121, 227, 316	
☐ right	039	
☐ righteous	161, 274	
☐ rigid	068, 283, 353	
☐ rigidity	283	
☐ riot	313	
☐ rioter	313	
☐ ripe	303	
☐ ripen	303	
☐ rise	047, 127, 318	
☐ risk	375	
☐ ritual	223	
☐ ritualistic	223	
☐ rival	171	
☐ rivalry	024	
☐ roam	366	
☐ roar	348	
☐ rob	169	
☐ robber	169	
☐ robbery	169	
☐ rookie	154	
☐ rot	230, 372	
☐ rotate	261	
☐ rotation	261	
☐ rotten	372	
☐ rough	194	
☐ roughly	051	
☐ rouse	376	
☐ routine	070, 383	
☐ routinely	070	
☐ rub	103	
☐ rubber	103	
☐ rubbish	120, 318	
☐ rudimentary	077	
☐ ruin	225	
☐ rule	128, 132	
☐ ruling	020	
☐ rupture	132	
☐ rural	044, 270	
☐ ruthless	374	
☐ ruthlessly	374	

S

- [ ] sacred — 164
- [ ] sacrifice — 173
- [ ] safe — 389
- [ ] safeguard — 348
- [ ] sail — 124, 213
- [ ] saint — 195
- [ ] same — 037
- [ ] sanction — 335
- [ ] sanctuary — 032, 067, 306
- [ ] sane — 371
- [ ] sanitary — 385
- [ ] sanitation — 385
- [ ] sanitize — 385
- [ ] sanity — 371
- [ ] sarcasm — 322
- [ ] savage — 370
- [ ] save — 065
- [ ] scan — 250
- [ ] scant — 389
- [ ] scarcely — 092
- [ ] scare — 028, 126, 207, 335
- [ ] scary — 126, 207
- [ ] scatter — 187, 232
- [ ] scattered — 207
- [ ] scene — 162
- [ ] scenery — 162
- [ ] scenic — 162
- [ ] scent — 169
- [ ] schedule — 197
- [ ] scheme — 048, 072
- [ ] scold — 222
- [ ] scope — 159
- [ ] scorn — 337, 338, 388
- [ ] scornful — 388
- [ ] scrape — 082
- [ ] scratch — 082
- [ ] scream — 162, 382
- [ ] script — 105
- [ ] scrutinize — 114, 386
- [ ] scrutiny — 386
- [ ] sculpt — 232
- [ ] search — 036, 250
- [ ] secondarily — 079
- [ ] secondary — 100
- [ ] secondhand — 356
- [ ] section — 042, 220
- [ ] secure — 034, 389
- [ ] securely — 034
- [ ] security — 034
- [ ] seductive — 375
- [ ] seek — 041
- [ ] seeming — 146
- [ ] seemingly — 042, 146
- [ ] segment — 220
- [ ] segmentation — 220
- [ ] seize — 029, 167
- [ ] seizure — 167
- [ ] select — 340
- [ ] selection — 340
- [ ] selective — 340
- [ ] self-centered — 302
- [ ] selfish — 302
- [ ] selfless — 302
- [ ] semester — 249
- [ ] send away — 294
- [ ] sensation — 185
- [ ] sensational — 185
- [ ] sense — 083
- [ ] sensibility — 224
- [ ] sensible — 224
- [ ] sensibly — 224
- [ ] sensitive — 027, 350
- [ ] sensitively — 027
- [ ] sensitivity — 027
- [ ] sensor — 388
- [ ] sentence — 020
- [ ] sentiment — 367
- [ ] sentimental — 367
- [ ] separate — 036, 093, 208, 345
- [ ] separation — 184
- [ ] sequence — 159
- [ ] sequential — 159
- [ ] series — 159
- [ ] serious — 079
- [ ] servant — 078
- [ ] serve — 132
- [ ] severe — 211, 284
- [ ] sew — 188
- [ ] shake — 130
- [ ] shake one's head — 149
- [ ] shallow — 205
- [ ] shame — 230, 332, 387
- [ ] shameful — 230
- [ ] share — 063, 064, 184
- [ ] shed — 202
- [ ] shed tears — 339
- [ ] sheer — 295
- [ ] shelter — 067, 306
- [ ] shield — 067, 143
- [ ] shiver — 378
- [ ] shock — 372
- [ ] short — 140, 324
- [ ] shortage — 140

☐ shortcoming	071, 090	
☐ shorten	324	
☐ shortfall	140	
☐ shout	162, 352, 382	
☐ show	092	
☐ show off	197	
☐ shrewd	108	
☐ shrink	181, 227, 246	
☐ shrug	358	
☐ shy	300, 384	
☐ side with	022	
☐ sigh	276	
☐ sign up	029, 285	
☐ significant	077, 114	
☐ silent	375	
☐ silly	121	
☐ simple	062, 093, 296	
☐ sin	121	
☐ sincere	345	
☐ sinful	121	
☐ single	185	
☐ skeptical	374	
☐ skilled	262	
☐ skip	283	
☐ slap	334	
☐ slave	078	
☐ slavery	078	
☐ slender	383	
☐ slight	297	
☐ slim	383	
☐ slip	181	
☐ slow	274	
☐ slow down	274	
☐ small	078, 245	
☐ smart	062, 269	
☐ smash	172	
☐ smile	339	
☐ snatch	066	
☐ soak	194	
☐ sob	339, 378	
☐ sober	366, 377	
☐ sobriety	366	
☐ sociable	300	
☐ sole	185	
☐ solely	185	
☐ solemn	377	
☐ solemnity	377	
☐ solid	148, 294	
☐ solitary	369	
☐ solitude	369	
☐ solo	369	
☐ soothe	126, 250, 278, 369	
☐ soothing	369	
☐ sophisticate	189	
☐ sophisticated	189, 387	
☐ sophistication	189	
☐ sore	168, 242	
☐ sorrow	143, 242, 261	
☐ sorrowful	242	
☐ sorry	242	
☐ sour	225	
☐ source	045	
☐ souvenir	295	
☐ sovereign	357	
☐ sovereignty	357	
☐ space	272	
☐ spacious	272	
☐ span	203	
☐ spare	064	
☐ sparse	207	
☐ special	104	
☐ specialization	104	
☐ specialize	104	
☐ specialty	061, 104	
☐ specific	016, 113, 196	
☐ specifically	016	
☐ specify	016	
☐ spectacle	386	
☐ spectacular	386	
☐ speculate	307	
☐ speculation	307	
☐ speculative	307	
☐ speed up	274	
☐ sphere	159	
☐ spill	147, 181, 335	
☐ spin	261	
☐ splendid	232, 304	
☐ splendor	304	
☐ spoil	148, 225, 316	
☐ sponsor	082	
☐ sponsorship	082	
☐ spread	187	
☐ squabble	367	
☐ squeeze	165	
☐ stab	320	
☐ stable	294, 389	
☐ stack	081	
☐ staff	151	
☐ stage	078	
☐ stagger	244	
☐ staggering	204	
☐ stain	236	
☐ stake	049, 145	
☐ stand out	064	
☐ standard	356	
☐ star	258	

☐ stare	141, 281	
☐ start	108	
☐ startle	372	
☐ startling	372	
☐ starvation	321	
☐ starve	321	
☐ state	222	
☐ stay	118, 262	
☐ steady	073, 100, 106	
☐ steep	156	
☐ step down	249	
☐ stereotype	352	
☐ stereotypical	352	
☐ sterilize	355	
☐ stern	353, 377	
☐ stick	322	
☐ stiff	068, 283	
☐ stimulate	193	
☐ stimulation	193	
☐ stimulus	193	
☐ stir	130, 376	
☐ stitch	188	
☐ stop	021, 066, 149	
☐ storage	103	
☐ store	103	
☐ story	105	
☐ straightforward	296	
☐ strain	116	
☐ strange	302, 308	
☐ stranger	115	
☐ stray	391	
☐ stress	075, 226, 342	
☐ stretch	043	
☐ strict	353	
☐ string	018	
☐ stringent	210	
☐ strip	111, 317	
☐ strive	173, 267	
☐ strive for	041	
☐ stroll	308	
☐ stroller	308	
☐ strong	034, 085	
☐ struggle	084	
☐ stubborn	337	
☐ stuff	334	
☐ stumble	244	
☐ stupid	040, 062, 269	
☐ subdue	315	
☐ subdued	366	
☐ subjective	068	
☐ submerge	194	
☐ submission	030	
☐ submissive	337	
☐ submit	030, 302	
☐ subordinate	376	
☐ subordinate to	376	
☐ subordination	376	
☐ subscribe	285	
☐ subscriber	285	
☐ subscription	285	
☐ subsequent	320	
☐ subsidize	311	
☐ subsidy	311	
☐ substance	060	
☐ substantial	077, 114	
☐ substantially	114	
☐ substitute	037, 245	
☐ substitution	245	
☐ subtract	343	
☐ subtraction	343	
☐ suburb	132	
☐ suburban	044, 132	
☐ success	073	
☐ succession	320	
☐ successive	320	
☐ successively	320	
☐ successor	300, 320	
☐ sudden	263	
☐ sue	190	
☐ suffering	247, 368	
☐ sufficient	226, 304	
☐ suggest	045, 106	
☐ suitable	019, 182	
☐ summarize	093	
☐ summary	093	
☐ summon	294	
☐ summons	294	
☐ superficial	242	
☐ superfluous	147	
☐ superior	171, 285	
☐ supermarket	104	
☐ superstition	381	
☐ superstitious	381	
☐ supervise	268	
☐ supervision	268	
☐ supervisor	268	
☐ supplement	182, 325	
☐ supplementary	182	
☐ supply	111, 149, 275	
☐ support	022, 113, 333	
☐ supporter	206	
☐ suppose	310	
☐ supposed	319	
☐ supposedly	042, 319	
☐ supposition	319	
☐ suppress	315	

□ supremacy	163
□ supreme	114, 163
□ surf	250
□ surmount	020
□ surpass	092, 341
□ surplus	068, 140, 243
□ surrender	031, 050, 084, 089, 302
□ survivable	168
□ suspend	192, 271
□ suspense	192
□ suspension	192
□ suspicious	374
□ sustain	149
□ sustainable	149
□ sustenance	149
□ swallow	040
□ swear	200, 312, 336
□ swearword	324
□ sweep	110
□ sweeping	110
□ sweet	194
□ swell	181, 246
□ swift	385
□ symbol	274
□ sympathetic	201, 231
□ sympathize	201
□ sympathy	201, 220
□ synchronize	321

T

□ tackle	146
□ tailor	188
□ taint	355
□ take apart	163
□ take care of	080
□ take down	280
□ take in	021, 384
□ take off	343
□ take up	108, 180
□ taken	306
□ talent	383
□ talkative	300
□ tame	339, 370
□ tarnish	236
□ tease	287
□ tedious	391
□ telescope	159
□ tell the truth	155
□ temper	323
□ temperate	368

□ temperature	368
□ temporary	282
□ tempt	227
□ temptation	227
□ tempting	150, 227, 375
□ tender	194
□ tenderly	194
□ tenderness	194
□ tense	278
□ tension	116, 278
□ tent	278
□ term	203, 249
□ terminal	168
□ terminate	168
□ terrible	040, 101, 107, 198, 280, 349
□ terrific	280
□ terrify	126, 198, 278, 335
□ terrifying	207
□ territory	210, 234
□ terror	126, 198, 280, 335
□ terrorism	198
□ terrorist	198
□ testify	312
□ testimonial	312
□ testimony	312
□ textile	117, 287
□ texture	287
□ thankful	060
□ that is (to say)	180
□ thereby	279
□ thorough	140
□ thoroughly	140
□ thoughtful	388
□ thread	018
□ threat	028, 375
□ threaten	028
□ threatened	370
□ thrive	349, 389
□ throw away	308
□ throw up	040
□ thus	221, 279
□ tidy	112, 299
□ tie	309
□ tilt	116
□ timid	105, 384
□ timidity	384
□ tiny	078, 245
□ tip	130
□ tire	189, 239
□ tiredness	243
□ token	274
□ tolerance	231
□ tolerant	231

☐ tolerate	198, 231
☐ tomb	142
☐ torment	247
☐ total	128, 170
☐ totally	019
☐ tough	284, 294
☐ townscape	022
☐ trace	106
☐ traceability	106
☐ traceable	106
☐ track	106
☐ train	152
☐ traitor	379
☐ transact	091
☐ transaction	091
☐ transform	052, 085
☐ transformation	070, 085
☐ transient	282
☐ transition	070
☐ transitional	070
☐ transmission	212
☐ transmit	184, 212
☐ transmitter	212
☐ transplant	314
☐ transport	184
☐ trash	120, 308, 318
☐ treacherous	389
☐ treasure	049, 336
☐ treat	071
☐ treaty	154
☐ trek	242
☐ tremble	351
☐ tremolo	351
☐ tremor	351, 378
☐ trick	310
☐ trifle	390
☐ trifling	390
☐ trip	244
☐ triumph	073, 228, 275
☐ triumphant	228
☐ trivia	325
☐ trivial	091, 194, 325
☐ true	039
☐ trustworthy	100, 294
☐ truth	229
☐ truthfully	107
☐ tumble	359
☐ turn around	086
☐ turn down	047
☐ turn to	131
☐ typical	069, 070, 074, 079, 163, 302, 308, 369
☐ typically	087

U

☐ ugly	304
☐ ultimate	114, 340
☐ ultimately	114
☐ unacceptable	123
☐ unaccustomed	366
☐ unappreciative	060
☐ unashamed	230
☐ unavailable	306
☐ unbelievable	069
☐ unbiased	068, 221
☐ uncertain	078
☐ uncharacteristic	031
☐ unclear	016
☐ uncommon	070, 074
☐ uncontrolled	368
☐ unconventional	241
☐ uncover	037, 201, 298
☐ undependable	170
☐ underlie	357
☐ underline	342
☐ understandable	359, 390
☐ understate	075
☐ undertake	180
☐ undesirable	150
☐ undeveloped	125
☐ undo	086, 309
☐ unearth	201
☐ uneasy	120, 355
☐ unethical	294
☐ unexceptional	079
☐ unexciting	169
☐ unfairness	031
☐ unfasten	309
☐ unfilled	306
☐ unfinished	140
☐ unfortunate	119
☐ ungrateful	060
☐ unification	345
☐ unify	345
☐ unimaginable	380
☐ unimaginative	340
☐ unimportant	077, 085, 172, 325
☐ uninformative	306
☐ unintelligent	062, 269
☐ unintelligible	359
☐ unintentional	320
☐ uninterrupted	106
☐ unique	302
☐ unknown	379
☐ unlikelihood	074

☐ unlikely	210
☐ unnecessary	086
☐ unplanned	320
☐ unpleasant	205, 225
☐ unprecedented	356
☐ unprofitable	184
☐ unreasonable	224, 227, 275
☐ unrefined	189
☐ unreliable	073, 100, 391
☐ unremarkable	064, 155
☐ unripe	303
☐ unsafe	034
☐ unsecure	034
☐ unselfish	302
☐ unsophisticated	189
☐ unsteady	106
☐ unsubstantial	077
☐ untidy	299
☐ untie	119
☐ untrustworthy	100, 170
☐ unused	236
☐ unusual	069, 074, 101, 241, 308
☐ unveil	027
☐ unwittingly	206
☐ upcoming	322
☐ upgrade	342
☐ upright	280
☐ uprising	313
☐ upset	312
☐ upside	145
☐ up-to-date	393
☐ urban	044, 270
☐ urge	101
☐ urgency	101, 172
☐ urgent	101, 172, 316
☐ urgently	172
☐ used	356
☐ utmost	340
☐ utter	295
☐ utterance	295

V

☐ vacancy	306
☐ vacant	306
☐ vacate	306
☐ vague	016, 113, 188, 196, 241, 359
☐ vain	311
☐ valid	123, 334
☐ validate	123, 300
☐ validity	123

☐ valuable	076
☐ value	071
☐ vanish	051, 127, 156, 243
☐ vast	272
☐ venerate	240
☐ veneration	240
☐ venture	104
☐ verbal	277
☐ verbally	277
☐ verdict	020
☐ verify	026
☐ veteran	154
☐ vice	090, 195
☐ victory	073
☐ viewpoint	171, 266
☐ vigor	243
☐ violate	191, 235
☐ violation	191
☐ violent	194
☐ virtue	195
☐ virtuous	274
☐ vital	085, 091
☐ vitality	085
☐ vitally	085
☐ vivid	241
☐ vocal	164
☐ vocation	067, 380
☐ vocational	380
☐ void	334
☐ voluntarily	224
☐ voluntary	224, 354
☐ vomit	040
☐ vow	200, 307, 336
☐ voyage	228
☐ vulgar	205, 393
☐ vulgarity	393

W

☐ wander	123, 366, 391
☐ warm up	265
☐ warmth	265
☐ warrant	297
☐ warranty	035, 297
☐ watch	268
☐ watchful	248
☐ waver	164
☐ weak	034, 085, 240, 297
☐ weakness	090
☐ wealth	048, 068
☐ wealthy	373

☐ wear out	189
☐ weave	209
☐ weep	339, 378
☐ weird	069, 302, 308, 369
☐ welcome	047, 358
☐ welfare	112
☐ well-being	112, 393
☐ well-spoken	386
☐ whereas	122
☐ while	122
☐ whisper	162, 229, 352, 382, 386
☐ wicked	274
☐ wild	370
☐ willing	224, 251
☐ win	020
☐ wink	354
☐ wise	316
☐ wit	350
☐ with abandon	108
☐ withdraw	089, 111, 118, 151, 190, 209
☐ withdrawal	118
☐ wither	286, 389
☐ witty	350
☐ wonderful	040, 101, 107, 280, 349
☐ wordy	324
☐ work	151
☐ work toward	041
☐ worldly	189, 387
☐ worsen	071, 284, 342
☐ worship	240
☐ worth	071
☐ worthless	259, 320
☐ worthwhile	259
☐ wreak	305
☐ wrinkle	332

Y

☐ yell	162, 352
☐ yield	020, 027, 084, 115
☐ yielding	337

Z

☐ zeal	381
☐ zealous	191, 381

［編者紹介］

ロゴポート

語学書を中心に企画・制作を行っている編集者ネットワーク。編集者、翻訳者、ネイティブスピーカーなどから成る。おもな編著に『英語を英語で理解する 英英英単語® 初級編／上級編／超上級編』、『最短合格! 英検®1級／準1級 英作文問題完全制覇』、『最短合格! 英検®2級英作文&面接 完全制覇』、『出る順で最短合格! 英検®1級／準1級 語彙問題完全制覇［改訂版］』、『出る順で最短合格! 英検®1級〜3級単熟語EX 第2版』(ジャパンタイムズ出版)、『TEAP単熟語Grip1500』(アスク出版)、『分野別 IELTS英単語』(オープンゲート) などがある。

本書のご感想をお寄せください。
https://jtpublishing.co.jp/contact/comment/

英語を英語で理解する
英英英単語® 中級編

2020年 9 月20日　初版発行
2024年12月20日　第7刷発行

編　者　ジャパンタイムズ出版 英語出版編集部＆ロゴポート
　　　　©The Japan Times Publishing, Ltd. & Logoport, 2020

発行者　伊藤秀樹

発行所　株式会社 ジャパンタイムズ出版

　　　　〒102-0082 東京都千代田区一番町2-2
　　　　　　　　　　一番町第二TGビル 2F
　　　　ウェブサイト　https://jtpublishing.co.jp/

印刷所　株式会社 光邦

本書の内容に関するお問い合わせは、上記ウェブサイトまたは郵便でお受けいたします。
定価はカバーに表示してあります。
万一、乱丁落丁のある場合は、送料当社負担でお取り替えいたします。(株)ジャパンタイムズ出版・出版営業部あてにお送りください。
Printed in Japan　ISBN 978-4-7890-1756-5